'Mustapha's magisterial analysis of Musl
Nigeria remains the unrivalled origir
collection. Ideal for teaching yet require

C000082004

– Paul M. Lubeck, Acti
Jo

'will surely come to be regarded as a reference book for dealing with those Sufi, Islamist, Salafist, and terrorist movements developing in multi-ethnic and multireligious societies in Africa and elsewhere. Mustapha's multi-dimensional and multifaceted approach offers a credible and intelligible analysis of the relevant historical, political, socio-economic, and socio-cultural issues which led to the current situation in Northern Nigeria.'

– Heinrich Bergstresser, *Africa Spectrum*

'Mustapha's volume is an important corrective in the discourse about Boko Haram specifically and Islamic violence – indeed, all religious violence – generally, and it should be read by anyone who claims the authority to pronounce on any of these matters.'

– Jack David Eller, *Anthropology Review Database*

'Abdul Raufu Mustapha's edited volume *Sects & Social Disorder* is most welcome, considering the escalation of conflict in Northern Nigeria in recent years and the fact that a plethora of crises has triggered a tsunami of analysis of variegated quality … Overcoming many of the shortcomings of the current literature, it fills a major gap in research and analysis.'

– Roman Loimeier, Institute for Social and Cultural
Anthropology, University of Göttingen, *Africa*

Sects
& Social
Disorder
MUSLIM IDENTITIES
& CONFLICT IN
NORTHERN NIGERIA

Edited by Abdul Raufu Mustapha

JC JAMES CURREY

James Currey
is an imprint of
Boydell & Brewer Ltd
PO Box 9, Woodbridge
Suffolk IP12 3DF (GB)
www.jamescurrey.com
and of
Boydell & Brewer Inc.
668 Mt Hope Avenue
Rochester, NY 14620-2731 (US)
www.boydellandbrewer.com

First published in hardback 2014
Published in paperback 2015 (Africa-only) and 2017

British Library Cataloguing in Publication Data
A catalogue record for this book is available on request from the British Library

ISBN 978-1-84701-107-7 (James Currey cloth)
ISBN 978-1-84701-159-6 (James Currey paperback)
ISBN 978-1-84701-116-9 (Africa-only paperback)

The publisher has no responsibility for the continued existence or accuracy of URLs for
external or third-party internet websites referred to in this book, and does not guarantee
that any content on such websites is, or will remain, accurate or appropriate.

Typeset in 11/13 Bembo with Albertus MT display
by Avocet Typeset, Somerton, Somerset TA11 6RT

for Grannie and Malam – with gratitude

Contents

List of Maps, Figures & Tables

MAPS

FIGURES

TABLES

Notes on Contributors

ABDUL RAUFU MUSTAPHA is an Associate Professor in African Politics at the Oxford Department of International Development (ODID), University of Oxford, and the Kirk-Greene Fellow at St. Antony's College. He studied Political Science at Ahmadu Bello University, Zaria and St Peter's College, University of Oxford. He is the Principal Researcher in the Nigeria Research Network and a member of the editorial advisory boards of the *Review of African Political Economy*, Sheffield, and the *Premium Times*, Abuja. He is the chair of the Board of Trustees of the Development Research and Projects Centre (dRPC), Kano. Dr Mustapha held previous academic positions at Bayero University, Kano, and Ahmadu Bello University, Zaria. His areas of research interest are religion and politics in Nigeria, the politics of rural societies, the politics of democratization, and identity politics in Africa. His recent publications include the following edited volumes: *Gulliver's Troubles: Nigeria's Foreign Policy After the Cold War*; *Turning Points in African Democratization*; and *Conflicts & Security Governance in West Africa*.

MUKHTAR UMAR BUNZA is a Professor of Social History at the Usmanu Danfodiyo University, Sokoto, Nigeria. He obtained his B.A., M.A. and Ph.D. in History from the same institution. He was a laureate of the Centre for Research and Documentation (CRD), Kano (1999), Fellow of Leventis Postdoctoral Research, SOAS, University of London (2001), ISITA Fellow, Northwestern University, Evanston, USA (2002) and SACRI Fellow for Summer School at the Babes Bolyai University, Cluj, Romania (2004). He was Acting Dean and Deputy Dean Postgraduate School (2002–6), as well as Head of Department of History, Usmanu Danfodiyo University, Sokoto, Nigeria (2012–14). Bunza is a member of many professional and academic associations in Nigeria and internationally. His main areas of research interest are the Sokoto Caliphate, the Middle East and Religious Movements in Nigeria.

YAHAYA HASHIM holds a Masters Degree (1987) and Ph.D. (1994) in Development Studies from the Institute of Social Studies, University of Erasmus, The Netherlands. He holds a second Masters in Business Management from Ahmadu Bello University, Zaria, Nigeria, 1979. He is the founding Director of the development Research and Projects Centre (dRPC) and served as the Chief of Party of the USAID-funded Leadership Development for Reproductive Health for Traditional and Religious Leaders 2009–13. He has served as an adviser to several international development partners on working with traditional and religious leaders in northern Nigeria. He is the Project Director SLaB Grand Challenges funded project.

HANNAH HOECHNER is a Wiener Anspach Postdoctoral Researcher at the Laboratoire d'Anthropologie des Mondes Contemporains at the Université Libre de Bruxelles, Belgium, and a Research Associate at the Oxford Department of International Development, United Kingdom. She holds a doctorate in Development Studies from the University of Oxford from where she previously earned an M.Phil in Development Studies. She also holds a B.A. in International Relations from the University of Dresden, Germany. Her research focuses on the experiences of young people growing up in poverty and on the role education plays in their lives.

MURRAY LAST is Professor Emeritus in the Department of Anthropology, University College London. His Ph.D. in 1964 was the first to be awarded by a Nigerian university (University College Ibadan); his previous degrees were from Cambridge (1959) and Yale (1961). He specializes in both the pre-colonial history of Muslim northern Nigeria and the ethnography of illness and healing. He has been working in or on northern Nigeria since 1961, researching a wide variety of subjects especially with colleagues in Bayero University, Kano (where he was Professor of History 1978–80); he visits Nigeria every year for a month at least. He has been both a 'traditional' Muslim student in Birnin Zaria and a guest for two years in a Maguzawa (non-Muslim Hausa) farmstead. In 1967 he published *The Sokoto Caliphate* (London: Longmans Green, now published also in Hausa as *Daular Sakkwato*) and in 1986 he edited (with G.L. Chavunduka) *The Professionalisation of African Medicine* (Manchester: Manchester University Press for the International African Institute). In addition he has over a hundred publications on African history and anthropology. He was sole editor of the International African Institute's journal *AFRICA* for 15 years (1986–2001).

JUDITH-ANN WALKER holds a Masters Degree (1989) and Ph.D. (1995) in Development Studies from the Institute of Social Studies, University of Erasmus, The Netherlands. She is a specialist in Gender and Development Effectiveness. She is a founding member of the development Research and Projects Centre (dRPC) and the Strategic Director of Knowledge Management. Judith-Ann is an Ashoka Innovators Fellow who specialized in providing technical assistance to interventional development partners on public health programming in northern Nigeria. She has been on the full-time staff of the dRPC since its formation in 1994 where she has coordinated the Institute of International Education, USAID Nigeria and Ford Foundation projects.

Foreword

I am pleased to introduce this volume of richly documented and insight-fully amazing case-studies of Islamic movements and their historical background, social origins, religious beliefs and practices, and their emergence in the economic and political context of Nigeria. The valuable contributions of the individual chapters and the volume as a whole are better appreciated in light of the older literature on Islamic movements in Nigeria, and the more recent literature on violent conflicts, security studies and inter-group relations among Nigeria's ethno-religious communities, especially in the context of what one of the authors in this volume terms 'fractious politics', since Nigeria's return to democracy in 1999. In contrast to the disciplinary orientation in much of the literature on these themes, the present volume stands apart by its sustained and thorough engagement with the different disciplinary orientations, thereby enriching its contri-butions and enhancing the analytical bases for its policy recommenda-tions.

Broadly, Islamic movements in Nigeria have been studied in waves that can be traced to the early colonial era, or even the travelogues of European explorers in the eighteenth and nineteenth centuries. Social scientists have often focused on the political and sociological dimensions of Islamic movements, without any sophisticated appreciations of the importance of the religious dimensions, often treated as an epiphenomenon that can be safely discounted. Similarly, humanities scholars, particularly historians and specialists of Islamic and Arabic studies, are only slightly better in their engagement with the religious dimensions. More than the social scien-tists, scholars of the humanities have been more attentive to the relevance of the longstanding traditions of Islamic movements dating back to the jihad of Shaikh 'Uthman dan Fodio at the beginning of the nineteenth century, and then going forward all the way to the *Maitatsine* uprisings in the 1980s and 1990s, and the rise of *Boko Haram* insurgency at the turn of the twenty-first century. Although laudable, some of the historical tracings have not captured discontinuities and novel developments in the *longue durée* of the evolution of Islamic movements in Nigeria.

Over the last two decades, inter-group relations among the numerous ethno-religious communities in Nigeria have become more and more characterized by violent conflicts. In the light of the frequency and intensity of these conflagrations, a burgeoning body of research and publications has been accumulating, seeking to illuminate the backgrounds and contexts, factors and actors, as well as forces and conditions that are relevant for tracing the origins, analysing the evolution, and articulating policy implications of the conflicts and designing strategies of intervention. Seasoned scholars and many self-designated 'experts' from various disciplines, including security, peace and conflict studies, have published essays and volumes of variable quality and insight. But in general, the treatments of Islamic movements in the newly emerging literature leave much to be desired, particularly because of the conspicuous lack of solid empirical research, or even adequate familiarity with the older literature on Islamic movements. Factual errors, shallow analyses, and unsupported contentions and sweeping generalization are all too common in the many publications that have been clearly rushed to print, apparently without the benefit of rigorous research or academic peer-review. These lapses are particularly discernible in the growing publications on the *Boko Haram* insurgency, as amply documented in the annotated and continuously updating bibliography prepared by Stuart Elden.[1] The present volume is a bold and successful attempt to overcome the shortcomings in the current literature.

First and foremost, all the chapters in this volume are based upon solid empirical research and thorough documentation of the data supporting the contentions of the authors. For example, in a refreshing departure from the conventional wisdom and opinionated pronouncements that disciples in the traditional Qur'anic schools, the *almajirai,* provide a readily available pool for recruitment into violent movements, Hannah Hoechner's chapter on the *almajirai* is based on multiple sources of data collected in the course of 13 months of field research that she conducted between 2009 and 2011, with extended field observations in selected Qur'anic schools. She reveals the complexity in the world of the *almajirai,* convincingly supported with the empirical data from 'fieldwork observations, as well as semi-structured interviews, group conversations and casual interactions with *almajirai*, their parents, caregivers and teachers as well as some former *almajirai*'. Similarly, the meticulous approach in the chapter by Yahaya Hashim and Judith-Ann Walker allows them to clearly identify the large universe of voluntary associations and ethnic minority

---

[1] See: http://progressivegeographies.com/2013/02/14/boko-haram-an-annotated-bibliography.

Muslim organizations registered in Kano, from which they identified 23 associations relevant for their chapter, and verified the existence of 17 associations to study, using 'in-depth interviews for individuals and group interviews for executives of the Muslim minorities associations'. I believe the reader will be impressed by the admirable diligence with which all the authors support their contentions with empirical data, rather than conveniently repackaging popular stereotypes with the opinionated comments that saturate the journalistic accounts and Internet materials on which most authors have come to rely.

A second major strength of this volume is its combination of the historical and the contemporary perspectives in its examination of the evolution of Islamic movements. Murray Last, the doyen of historical and anthropological research on northern Nigeria, provides the richly nuanced historical tracing of dissent and dissidence in the region over the *longue durée,* plus insightful examination of their various sites and forms in both urban and rural settings. As a venerable veteran, Last draws from decades of his research and his insightful analysis of how the religious and political dimensions have historically coalesced, and thereby reveals the important insight: 'Extreme piety remains both the language of discontent and the logic for political resistance as a moral act.' Equally important attention to the religious dimensions is discernible in the chapter by Mustapha and Bunza, focusing on the historical developments of Islamic movements for most of the twentieth century, by not only combining the social scientific and humanistic disciplinary perspectives, but also by highlighting the intricate symbiosis between religious beliefs and ritual practices on the one hand, and social tension and political cleavages on the other hand. Merging insights from different disciplines has been a rare feature in the older literature, and virtually absent in the more recent publications by scholars of security studies and inter-group relations and conflict; hence this is a major contribution, yielding another wholesome feature in the present volume.

A very nuanced and sophisticated conceptualization is visibly present in the profound analysis of the multiple dimensions and factors, linkages and ruptures, and ideological shifts and continuous changes in strategy and tactics that bring the complexities of Islamic movements into bold relief. Rather than the facile invocation of economic deprivation, governance deficit, political incompetence, religious intolerance and security failures that are commonly cited in the literature, this volume takes the refreshing conceptual approach of avoiding single-factor causation by methodically and insightfully dissecting the various channels and trajectories through which all of these factors come into play. In both the introductory and concluding chapters, as well as in the other chapters, we find not just the routine claim that radicalization of Islamic movements is the consequence of poverty or even economic deprivation more generally, but also the more important identification of the mechanisms and conditions that connect the radicalization of Islamic movements with economic factors more broadly. For the first time, I find my longstanding scepticism against the explanatory power of economic deprivation significantly but happily diminished, if not totally eliminated.

By deftly presenting the various conspiracy theories about the radicalization of Islamic movements, especially *Boko Haram*, the reader is presented with the convincing argument that despite their absurdity, these conspiracy theories are very important for explaining key political dimensions in Nigeria. Chapter 6 demonstrates how conspiracy theories seem to inform President Goodluck Jonathan's virtual denial of the *Boko Haram* insurgency, thereby shedding significant light on the Jonathan administration's terribly incoherent response to the massive deaths and destruction resulting from the insurgency.

I hope I have sufficiently whetted the appetite of readers by highlighting some of the many strengths of this volume. I am very confident that it will educate even the die-hard conspiracy theorists; they may even be persuaded to rethink their deeply cherished but preposterous views. Strong empirical data, rich documentation of sources, nuanced historical analysis, multidisciplinary approach and sophisticated conceptualization do together provide not only valuable contributions to knowledge, but equally important solid bases for crafting effective strategies of intervention. Policy makers must read this volume if they seriously want to tackle the daunting challenges facing northern Nigeria. It is imperative that journalists and pundits keep it constantly within reach for quick reference if they truly want to enlighten the public. The general reader will easily find explanations for some of the many puzzles which have come to characterize Nigerian society and politics. Researchers will tremendously benefit by taking cue and inspiration. Instructors and lecturers at colleges and universities will help their students well by assigning this volume in their courses. By offering something to so many constituencies, this volume is bound to become an enduring landmark.

Muhammad Sani Umar (Ph.D.)
Professor, Department of History, Ahmadu Bello University,
Zaria, Nigeria.

Acknowledgements

This book started life as a research project of the Nigeria Research Network, a loose network of scholars across three continents, anchored at the Oxford Department of International Development and the Development Research and Projects Centre in Kano, Nigeria. I am grateful to all members and affiliates of the network who have over the years contributed to its research programmes. In particular, the late Professor Nur Alkali deserves special mention. Along with Professor Murray Last, he provided an impressive historical depth for our concerns with more contemporary challenges. The network won a research bid to work on the Islam Research Project, Abuja, supported by the Ministry of Foreign Affairs of The Netherlands. I am grateful to the latter for its support of our research programme and for putting our researchers in touch with other researchers in various countries with substantial Muslim populations. I am particularly grateful to Ambassador Bert Ronhaar, Annemieke van Soelen and Maurice Paulusen, all of whom went beyond the call of duty to facilitate the work of our network. Needless to say, none of the views expressed in this volume reflects the position of the Ministry or any of its past or present officials.

The network also benefitted from our team of academic advisers: Professor Auwalu Yadudu, Bishop Mathew Hassan Kukah, Hajia Bilkisu Yusuf, Dr Jibrin Ibrahim, Professor Gerrie ter Haar and Dr Eric Morier-Genoud. I am grateful to them for their selfless contributions. Elizabeth Donnelly and the Africa Section of Chatham House, London, Abubakar Kawu Monguno and Malam Garba Sambo of the University of Maiduguri, Ailsa Allen of the Geography Department University of Oxford, the African Studies Program and Cartographic Laboratory of the University of Wisconsin-Madison, and Professor Marc-Antoine Pérouse de Montclos and the Institut Français de Géopolitique generously provided various maps. The Pew Foundation and Gallup kindly gave permission to use some of their survey materials on Nigeria. I am grateful to them all.

Professor Sabina Alkire and Dr Adriana Conconi of the Oxford Poverty and Human Development Initiative, Queen Elizabeth House, University of Oxford, gladly took on the task of doing all calculations and maps concerning poverty and inequality in Nigeria. I am greatly indebted to them for this invaluable service. Margaret Meagher and Asma'u Mustapha gave technical assistance with graphs, while Seyi Mustapha was my computer trouble-shooter. In their various ways, they made my task easier. Jaqueline Mitchell and Lynn Taylor at James Currey were firm but sympathetic task masters, and gave me many valuable suggestions. Finally, I would like to thank Kate Meagher for always being there with words of support and encouragement.

Abdul Raufu Mustapha
1 October 2014
Oxford

Glossary

A'jami	Hausa language – and similar African languages such as Swahili – written in the Arabic script
Ahl al-dhimma	'people of protection', non–Muslim inhabitants in the Islamic state
Ahl al-sunna	the People of the Sunna, who model their lives on the Holy Qur'an, on what the Prophet said (*hadith*) and on what He did (*sira*) – the three components of the *sunna*
Almajiri (pl. *almajirai*)	from *al-muhajiroun*, 'emigrants'; young Muslim scholar, usually male, who leaves home in search of Islamic knowledge under the guidance of a teacher or *Malam* (pl. *Malamai*)
Al-salaf al-salih	pious predecessors, the first generations of Muslims after the death of the Prophet, considered as the gold standard of Islamic conduct and morality. Salafists harken back to this early community
Al-Umma (*umma,* *ummah*)	pan-Islamic concept denoting the global common wealth of all Islamic peoples. It can also be used to designate each people within that commonwealth.
Amir al-mu'minin	leader of all the Faithful; title of the Sultan of Sokoto as head of the Muslim community
Ansar	helper of Islam, drawing from the history of the Prophet's migration to Medina. In the context of the Sokoto jihad, it connotes volunteers prepared to fight for the jihad
Assalatu	'prayers', is a combination of sermons, lectures and actual prayers, usually performed by ethnic Yoruba Muslim groups, especially the Women's wings, on a set day of the week when the members congregate

Bante (Hausa)	loin cloth
Baraka	beneficent force from God which can be manifested as grace or charisma in a saint who can also transmit the flow of this beneficence to others
Bi'da	harmful innovation in Islam
Bilad al-siba	twentieth-century Morocco was believed to be divided into two zones: the Bilad al-Makhzan (the 'government's place') along the coast under direct government control and inhabited by Arabic speakers; and Bildad al-Siba in the interior mountains and the desert, where central control was contested, and inhabited by Berbers
Dar al-Islam	literally *house of Islam,* usually used by Muslims to refer to countries under the rule of Islam.
Dhikr (zikr)	repeated recital of short phrases or prayers, silently or aloud, individually or in group, in praise of God or in supplication to Him. Usually accompanied with the counting of rosaries
Dhimmi	non-Muslim resident of an Islamic state. In return for a special tax, *jizyah,* they enjoy some rights under the law, but also faced some restrictions. However, they are also excused from some specific duties assigned to Muslims
Gandu (Hausa)	family farms that are farmed collectively, though the members may also have their individual plots of land.
Hijra	the migration of Prophet Muhammad and his followers from Mecca to the city of Medina in 622 CE
Hisba (hisbah)	'verification', is an Islamic doctrine of keeping within the laws of Allah, based on the Qur'anic injunction of enjoining what is good and forbidding what is wrong
Ikhwan	Islamic 'Brotherhood' or 'Brethren'
Jama'a	community of the Muslim faithful
Kalam	cosmological arguments for the existence of God as the cause of the universe
Khalwa	a Sufi practice of solitary retreat, usually for 40 days during which a disciple does spiritual exercises under the direction of a Shaikh
Kuffar (kaffir, kafir, kuffir, kufr)	non-Muslims, especially those who are not of the 'People of the Book' (Christians and Jews)
Maguzawa	non-Muslim Hausa
Malam (pl. *Malamai*)	traditional Muslim scholar and cleric; Arabic: *Mu-alim* and *'ulema/'ulama* respectively)

Maulid	the birthday of the Prophet or of leading Sufi saints.
Mujaddid	a reformer who appears at the turn of every century of the Islamic calendar to revive the faith and restore it to its pristine purity
Mujahid (pl. *mujahidun*, commonly used in south Asia as *mujahideen*)	one who exerts himself in a jihad to promote the faith of Islam
Nasara	the followers of the New Testament or Christians (Nazarenes)
Salla (Hausa)	the two major Islamic festivals of Eid el–Fitr and Eid el-Kabir
Takfir	the practice of declaring another Muslim as a *kafir*
Taqiyya	dissimulation; a school of thought in Islam argues that Muslims in danger of their lives can dissimulate, pretending to accept situations which, deep down, they remain opposed to
Tariqa (pl. *turuq*; Hausa, *Darika*)	'the path'; refers to an order or brotherhood within Sufism
Tsangaya (Hausa)	learning centre, of pre-colonial origins, where Qur'anic education is imparted
'Ulama	(see *Malam*)
Umma	Islamic scholars (see *al-ummah* above)

1

Introduction
Interpreting Islam
Sufis, Salafists, Shi'ites & Islamists in northern Nigeria

ABDUL RAUFU MUSTAPHA

Introduction

Since the 1980s, but especially since 1999, northern Nigeria has been racked by repeated episodes of religious and ethno-religious violence involving the loss of thousands of lives, the displacement of hundreds of thousands of people and the destruction of vast quantities of property. This orgy of violence has become worse since 2009 with the transformation of the Salafist *Yusufiyya* sect into the jihadist *Jama'atu Ahlul Sunnah li Da'awati wal Jihad* (People Committed to the Propagation of the Prophet's Teachings and Jihad) or *Boko Haram*. Religion simultaneously constrains and enables action by its adherents, but does so in a way heavy with social memory and the institutional residue of the past. Along with providing a critique of, or justification for, the status quo, it also promises personal salvation and collective redemption. In these many guises, religion is frequently the idiom through which the warring communities in northern Nigeria are mobilized and it is also an important lens through which wider social and political processes, not directly related to the divine, play themselves out in societies like Nigeria, where the people are regarded in one global survey 'as the most religious people worldwide' (Ben Amara 2011, 9). This book is about the social and political effects of religion; specifically, it is about the impact on northern Nigerian society of changing Islamic identities.[1]

Islam was introduced into the territory now known as northern Nigeria through trade across the Sahara desert from North Africa, reaching the Kanem-Borno Empire, in the north-east zone, as early as the ninth

---

[1] According to Ali A. Mazrui (2011, xi) Nigeria has the largest concentration of Muslims on the African continent and 'the part of Nigeria which is Muslim is larger than the number of Muslims in any single Arab country, including Egypt'.

century AD (Alkali 1993; Kyari 1992; Usman 1983). The religion made headway and developed rapidly because of the interplay of factors such as the expansion of trade, respect for scholarship, the record-keeping needs of indigenous administrations and the subsequent conversion of local rulers to the new faith. Islam started gaining political relevance in Hausaland by the mid-fifteenth century. During the reign of Muhammad Rumfa in Kano (1463–1499), Sharia as a legal system was introduced, and the *shura* (advisory council), consisting of learned scholars, was institutionalized to guide the governance of the state. The system was adopted and implemented in accordance with the advice of Muhammad al-Maghili (c. 1425–1504), a North African scholar (from Tlemcen in modern-day Algeria) who visited several cities in Sub-Saharan Africa including Kano and Katsina, in the late fifteenth century. At the request of Muhammad Rumfa, al-Maghili wrote a treatise on government, the *Taj al-Din fi ma Yajib ala al-Muluk* (The Crown of Religion Concerning the Obligation of Princes), as a guide to Muslim rulers.

The arrival, from Senegambia and Mali, of migrant Muslim scholars like the Wangarawa, Fulani and Kunta, contributed a second stream of the spread of Islam among the various peoples of pre-colonial northern Nigeria.[2] Musa Jakollo, a Toronkawa Fulani, arrived around 1450; many generations later, in 1755, his family of scholars and teachers produced Shaikh 'Uthman dan Fodio, who led the jihad of 1804 that established the Sokoto Caliphate, a theocracy composed of 30 emirates and sub-emirates, stretching from present-day Burkina Faso in West Africa, to Cameroon in Central Africa (Kane 2003, 33). The jihad rose out of an Islamic revivalist movement founded by Shaikh dan Fodio to promote his *tajdeed* (reform) principles. He championed the revival of the *Sunna* of the Prophet and the stricter implementation of Qur'anic legal principles. His call for reform of governance ultimately pitted him against the erstwhile rulers who were seen as nominally Muslim. Despite the victory of the jihad and efforts to consolidate its ideological hegemony, the death of Shaikh dan Fodio in 1817 saw the gradual restoration of many pre-jihad practices and titles. This erosion formed the basis for subsequent calls for reform and revivalism, especially after the imposition of colonial rule and the formal transfer of power to Christian aliens. Therefore, from the mid-nineteenth century, dissent became a defining feature of emirate society. Within this context, many in northern Nigeria continue to look for inspiration to the history of the 1804 jihad and the Caliphate. However, this constant struggle to promote revivalism and reformism has also fuelled the further fragmentation of the Muslim community into competing sects and engendered a climate of hostility between some of them.

---

[2]   A third stream of Islam into the Nigeria region, this time into Lagos in the south-west, came with the return of Muslim ex-slaves from Brazil.

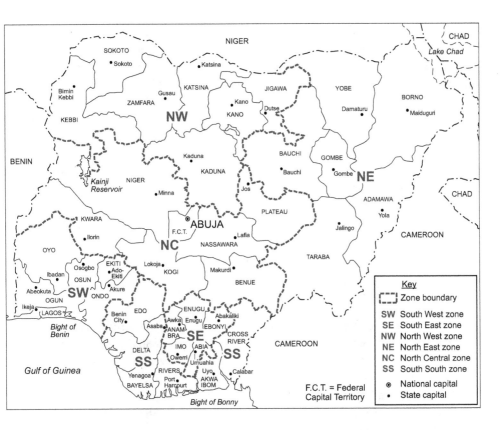

Map 1.1 Nigeria Zones
(courtesy of Chatham House, The Royal Institute of International Affairs, London)

There are different approaches to studying the hostilities which have characterized *intra*-Muslim relations in northern Nigeria, especially since the 1970s. Some analysts see the hostilities as the result of an intrusion of foreign radical Wahhabi ideology and Saudi money onto a pacifist African Sufi canvas (Alexiev 2005; McCormack 2005; Hill 2010). This perspective emphasizes global Islamism's continued expansion, the secondary agency of African Muslims, and is coloured primarily by Western security concerns. An alternative approach (Clarke & Linden 1984; Otayek & Soares 2007) reverses the emphasis and starts its investigations from the internal dynamics and historicity of African Muslim societies. Clarke & Linden (1984, 8) note that while the 1960s and 1970s were a period of optimistic nationalism in Africa, the 1980s, characterized by 'African disappointment and dismay', marked the re-emergence of Muslim and Christian religious revivalism.

Throughout the decades of the late twentieth century, Muslims in northern Nigeria have endured an unprecedented degree of social change and dislocation which have led to the erosion of older communities and

ways of being and unleashed a process of cultural and institutional differentiation. These rapid changes in the material conditions of Muslim
societies called into question the nationalist-cum-technological visions of
the 1960s and ushered in the relevance of religious beliefs which seem to
address the vagaries of everyday realities (Clarke & Linden 1984, 92–3).
In the context of rapid changes, heightened uncertainty and widespread
challenges, religion provided some measure of certainty and orientation.
The interaction between material utility and ideal utility becomes 'central
to the rationality of religious behavior' (Bano 2012, 12). It is this sociology
of Muslim societies, rooted in their agency, ideals, history, challenges and
material conditions, that forms the approach of this volume whose central
concern is the political and social consequences of sectarian fragmenta-
tions within northern Nigerian Islam.

Individualization & religious fragmentation

By the time of the Sokoto jihad in 1804, the overwhelming majority of
the leadership of the jihad, following the example of Shaikh 'Uthman dan
Fodio, the spiritual and political leader of the movement, were members
of the Qadiriyya *tariqa* (Brotherhood) within the wider Sunni Islam. So
prevalent was membership of this *tariqa* that the jihadists were known
locally as 'qadirawa', or followers of the Qadiriyya. Shaikh dan Fodio was
even reported to have said: 'I belong to the Qadiriyya and everyone who
follows me belongs to it' (Loimeier 1997, 21). The victory of the jihad
and the establishment of the Sokoto Caliphate consolidated Qadiriyya
dominance in the region. But this dominance was gradually undermined,
first by the rise of the Tijaniyya *tariqa* in the 1830s, and then by 'the rise
of Mahdist expectations and the agitation of "fanatics"' by the time of
the colonial occupation in 1903 (Chafe 1994, 99). It is indicative of the
erosion of Qadiriyya hegemony that of the 12 Emirs imprisoned by the
British in Lokoja in 1903, six were affiliated to the Tijaniyya, one to the
Qadiriyya, another one to the Mahdiyya, and four were not affiliated to
any religious order (Loimeier 1997, 27).

Today in northern Nigeria, different sects of Islam are to be found:
from the Sufis of the Qadiriyya and Tijaniyya in the dominant Sunni
core of the Muslim population; to reformist Salafists who vehemently
reject all Sufi ideas; to Shi'ites inspired by the Islamic Republic of Iran;
to 'heretical' sects like the *Maitatsine* and *Boko Haram* who have developed
their own home-grown idiosyncratic versions of Islam; and finally to a
large body of 'neutral' Muslims who, wary of the turmoil unleashed by
sectarianism, shun any sectarian affiliation. According to the Pew Forum,
a sample survey conducted in 2009 showed that, nationally, 38 per cent

of Muslims identified themselves as Sunni, 12 per cent as Shi'a, 3 per cent as Ahmadiyya but 44 per cent as 'just Muslim' (Pew Forum, 2010). This diversification of religious affiliation reflects the emergence of new sites of interpretation and contestation within the Muslim community.

The post-jihad political and administrative consolidation of the Caliphate, the jockeying for dynastic privileges, pressure from the gradual encroachment by the British from the south, and general economic change all contributed to the divergence of interests and of religious affiliation within the Caliphate. These developments altered the original balance between the individual and the Qadiriyya jihadi community and there was the consequent reshaping of the frameworks of sociability. The changes in the social matrices which determined affiliation, thought and actions led to an unprecedented focus on the individual and away from the erstwhile 'qadirawa' communal bonds. In short, there was a disembedding of some Muslims from the original Qadiriyya template as the social matrices of that template weakened. The focus on the individual was accompanied by the rise of the ethical self as the guide to religious conduct.

However, associated with this process of disembedding were other equally important factors promoting the development of sectarianism. At the doctrinal level, some scholars cite the Qur'an (2: 159) for justification: 'Those that hide the clear proofs and guidance We have revealed after We had proclaimed them in the Scriptures shall be cursed by God.' Some read this as a duty to pursue differing interpretations of previously agreed texts. Similarly, others argued that the Prophet had himself noted that after his death, the *umma* would split into 73 sects, out of which only one would see salvation (Loimeier 1997, 286–7; Casey 2008, 68). Many saw their self-chosen sect as *the* sect that would be saved. But the resulting disputes between sects often went beyond spiritual matters. They were also driven by competition for followership within the *'ulama* (Islamic scholars) and the *umma*. Such a followership was critical for the prestige of the individual Muslim ruler, or the economic and political influence of the individual cleric within the 'prayer economy'.[3] Conversely, the Shaikh's hold on his followers may be enhanced by his access to political and economic elites within the society. In this way, sacred and mundane motives were frequently interwoven into personal quests which resulted in networks of religious scholars in constant flux. These networks are instruments of clerical collective action, shaped by their responses to the structural strains within society, their interpretation of Islamic texts in the context of these strains and their mobilization strategies for establishing a followership.

[3] The 'prayer economy' is 'an economy of religious practice in which substantial gifts are exchanged for blessings, prayers, and intercession with God' (Soares 2005, 11). For the key features of Religious Market Theory/Religious Economy see Ben Amara (2011, 60–61).

For much of the nineteenth century, this dynamic process of sectarian fragmentation involved only a relatively small circle of scholars and aristocratic elites. From the 1940s the process accelerated in pace, increasingly from the 1970s, and included many more people than hitherto. Rapid social and political changes in these periods eroded older communities, triggered institutional and cultural differentiation and further undermined communal values and authority structures. As a result, more

> people are now 'role performers' in isolation so that their moral beliefs and values have had to be privately contrived and constructed. The arbitrary quality of behaviour that results from this privatisation of morals and values is profoundly disturbing, and is worsened by the pressured and frenetic character of urban life, corruption and near social breakdown in large cities. (Clarke & Linden 1984, 92)

Within the context of this rapid social change – especially during the years of oil boom and bust of the 1970s and 1980s, the droughts of the 1970s and highly disruptive structural adjustment economic policies of the 1980s – many Muslim are confronted with awkward questions to which they have had to find individual answers: What does it mean to be a Muslim in these circumscribed circumstances? How does one reconcile the religion with modernity? It is these concerns, rather than the global Islamist 'symbolic confrontation' with Western modernity (Otayek & Soares 2007, 18) which is driving much of the sectarianism and fundamentalism described and analysed in this book. As Eickelman and Anderson (1999, 7) note, the 'increasingly vocal debates on what it means to be a Muslim and to live a Muslim life frequently translate in highly divergent ways'.

Texts, contexts & takfir

The conflict over how to be a good Muslim frequently split the Muslim *umma* into sectarian factions which often resorted to violence against each other. As Murray Last noted about the jihad of 1804, it was primarily a movement for 'reforming lax Muslims, not converting pagans' (Last 1979, 237). Many of the sectarian differences revolved around the interpretation of key religious texts and ritual practices. For example, when the Salafist Shaikh Abubakar Gumi translated the Qur'an into Hausa, his version was rejected by the Sufi Shaikh Nasiru Kabara who then proceeded to produce his own counter version (Loimeier 1997, 59). Within these Muslim communities, as elsewhere, there is a constant struggle over the literal or allegorical interpretation and translation of texts. While some seek an abstract definition of religious texts as part of 'a pure religion beyond time and space' (Roy 2004, 11), others insist on 'in-context' interpretation and translation:

> [W]hen translation becomes not a translation but a way of seeking the Truth of God, then it becomes different every day ... for it is impossible to put a limit on the limitless and to say this is the exact meaning of any word, verse or chapter. (Ibrahim Abu Nab, cited in Lawrence 2006, 197)

Some argue that in reconciling reason with revelation, a broad selection of texts is necessary for deciding which aspects of the Qur'an applies to a given situation: where, when and to whom. Scholars must necessarily select broadly amongst themes, issues and emphasis (Lawrence 2006, 13–14). Texts must therefore be interpreted in the context of their historical specificity and contemporary relevance. On the other hand, others see the meaning of texts as immutably fixed, without regard to the historical, political and economic contexts. Such an approach assumes a singularity and continuity of Islam quite removed from its actual history. For example there are multiple schools of law within Islam, and around the time of the scholar at-Tabari (913 CE) there were 14 different ways of reading and reciting the Qur'an (Lawrence 2006, 84). Devoid of context, Islamic texts stand the danger of becoming an ahistorical force rather than part of a lived reality. Indeed, contrary to the Khawarij doctrine of the undesirability of 'any human mediation of God's Word' (Lawrence 2006, 15), Eickelman and Piscatori (1990, 20) suggest the impossibility of eternal religious truths that

> like other beliefs, are perceived, understood and transmitted by persons historically situated in 'imagined' communities, who knowingly or inadvertently contribute to the reconfiguration or interpretation of those verities, even as their fixed and unchanging natures are affirmed.

In the past, debates over doctrinal interpretation amounted to different ideological positions with important social ramifications. These debates often went hand-in-hand with differences in ritual practices – for example, whether one prayed with the hands across the chest as in the *kablu* style of the Tijaniyya, or down at one's sides as in the *sadlu* style of the Qadiriyya. These ideational and ritual differences delineated religious networks and constituencies from each other. Sartorial and fashion styles involving beards, turbans, gowns and similar accoutrements and signifiers were further used to highlight group boundaries. While the craving for unity is a defining characteristic of Muslims in northern Nigeria (Adeleye 1971, 7) the reality is more one of continuous sectarian fragmentation. These sectarian tendencies also 'afforded a welcome basis for *takfir*, the "accusation of unbelief"" (Loimeier 1997, 174). Given our interest in this volume with the interactions between Muslim sectarian identities and social disorder, it is pertinent to reflect on two of the most conflict-inducing doctrines that have accompanied sectarianism: *takfir*, and the duty to command right and forbid wrong.[4]

Takfir or 'the imputation of *kufr* (unbelief)' (Hodgkin 1976, 112) has been basically a process by which some Muslims adjudged other 'nominal' or 'lax' Muslims to be unbelievers on account of their beliefs, behaviour or ritual practices. Though this was often regarded as an extreme measure only taken as a last resort, it was reportedly 'more prevalent in Northern Nigeria than elsewhere' (Kane 2003, 125) given the dynamics of sectarianism in the region. Because of the complexity of the religion and its ritualistic demands, believers may be expected to make some mistakes in good faith. This is justified under the concept of *husn an-niya* (acting in good faith). Only when the Muslim deviates from the prescriptions of the religion repeatedly, and defends these deviations, might such a person be regarded as an unbeliever. However, many scholars are quick to point out the important difference between mistakes and sins on the one hand, and unbelief on the other. In the 1450s for example, al-Maghili argued: 'None of the people of the *qiblah* may be adjudged an unbeliever on account of sin' (Hodgkin 1976, 112).

In northern Nigeria in more recent times, Shaikh Qaribullah Kabara, leader of the Qadiriyya argued that declaring Muslims as 'non-believers' is based on incorrect interpretations of the Qur'an and the Sunna, and went on to list Islamic authorities including Ibn Ḥanbal, Imam al-Ghazālī, and even Ibn 'Abd al-Wahhāb to back up his position (Ben Amara 2011, 235). In northern Nigeria, however, the important distinctions between mistakes, sin and unbelief were frequently blurred by sectarian recklessness and *takfir* are freely deployed to impugn the religious integrity of opponents and justify attacks against them. In an insightful paper, Hodgkin (1976) traces some of the probable deep historical roots of this intolerance in northern Nigerian Islam.[5] Undoubtedly, there is some truth in the argument that

---

[4] 'Let there be one community of you, calling to good, and commanding right and forbidding wrong; those are the prosperers' (Qur'an 3: 104). The injunction appears in seven further Qur'anic verses (Cook 2004, 13)

[5] Hodgkin draws attention to three possible sources.
i. From the Ibadi rulers of Fezzan who brought Islam to Kanem-Borno in the tenth century, and were reported to have had some Khawarij influences. Kharijism held the doctrine that 'grave sin, *ma 'asin*, can make a man a kafir' (1976, 106).
ii. A second source might be the Almoravids who swept into Sub-Saharan Africa about 1072. The Almoravids had a puritanical, egalitarian, ascetic and highly legalistic interpretation of Islam and may have contributed 'to the implantation of a particular form of Islam – with its emphasis on Sunni orthodoxy' (107–9).
iii. The final possible source was the traveller, scholar and teacher, al-Maghili, who was very intolerant of Jews in his native North Africa, and emphasized the struggle against 'venal scholars' and the importance of the *al-mujaddid* (renewer), who will come and purify the religion of all wrongful accretions (110–12).

proclaiming 'other Muslims infidels is the worst innovation threatening peace and unity among Muslims' (cited in Kane 2003, 133, fn. 24).

The second doctrine, the duty to command right and forbid wrong, has been another aggravating factor in sectarian intolerance in northern Nigeria. According to Cook (2004, 9–10) this duty has very radical implications in the sense that in principle, the 'executive power of the law of God is vested in each and every Muslim'. The average believer has a duty to issue orders in pursuance of the implementation of God's laws, and these orders can even be issued to one's social superiors. However, these principles are context-specific, and their specific meaning can vary 'with time and place, sect to sect, from school to school, and from scholar to scholar'. Given the frequent recourse to violence in sectarian disputes in Nigeria, Cook gives an apposite and interesting example from early Islamic history, when Abu Hanifa, founder of the Hanafi *fiqh*[6] was asked about his views on the general application of this doctrine:

> Abu Hanifa is confronted with the question: 'How do you regard someone who commands right and forbids wrong, acquires a following on this basis, and rebels against the community (*jama'a*)? Do you approve of this? He answers that he does not. But why, when God and His Prophet have imposed on us the duty of forbidding wrong? He concedes that this is true enough, but counters that in the event the good such rebels can achieve will be outweighed by the evil they bring about. (Cook 2004, 8)

Clearly from Abu Hanifa's perspective, this injunction must be implemented in a context-specific manner, and not in an abstract ahistorical one. Such a contextualization will recognize the possible dangers of subversion on the one hand, and invasion of privacy on the other, since both 'represent significant ways in which the virtuous performance of the duty can degenerate into vice' (Cook 2004, 12). In the context of rigid interpretation of texts by some sects in northern Nigeria, most of the nuances surrounding this injunction are lost in translation, resulting in the perpetration of subversive violence or the invasion of individual privacy in the course of allegedly doing 'God's work'.

---

[6] Imam Abu Hanifa was the first person to undertake the task of codifying Islamic law. He established the first school of *fiqh* (Islamic jurisprudence), the Hanafi school, which is the largest and most influential among the four schools (*madhabs*) of *fiqh*. He believed that a code of laws cannot stay static for too long without running the risk of losing relevance and no longer meeting the needs of the people. Thus he advocated interpreting the sources of Islamic law (*usul al-fiqh*) in response to the needs of the people at any given time. This dynamic form of legalism used the Qur'an and Sunna to derive laws that addressed the issues that people dealt with in their immediate lives. 'The Life of Imam Abu Hanifa', http://lostislamichistory.com/the-life-of-imam-abu-hanifa.

Changing attitudes to the state

An important matter in our investigations is the orientation of these sects towards the state. There is a mistaken tendency to see the Sufi sects as 'peaceful' and the Wahhabi or Salafists as prone to violence (Anon. 2012, 140). In reality, Sufis and Salafists sometimes make common cause in making demands on the state (Sanusi 2007, 184). It also presents the wrong suggestion that *all* Salafists are prone to violence against the state. Worse still, as Western security analysts prosecute their 'war on terror', this perspective is likely to lead to dangerous policies of trying to use the Sufi orders against the Salafists (Hill 2010). Such a 'pragmatic' policy approach from the West can only aggravate the crisis already facing Muslim societies in places like northern Nigeria. Against the background of this important caution, this section explores the changing and complex attitudes of Muslim groups to the Nigerian state.

By the 1960s the template of the Nigerian state was already set along the lines imposed by the erstwhile colonial administration. The symbols of the state, the structure of the working week and the style of governance were all based on an essentially secular Western model which many Muslims resented as 'Christian' (Clarke & Linden 1984, 60). Yet, most Muslims were prepared to live-and-let-live under this state. As discussed in Mustapha and Bunza in this volume, for the Tijani adept, as an example, Sharia is an important part of Islam and consisted of five parts: *l'itiqa-adaat* (sets of core beliefs about the Prophet, the Holy Books, the Day of Judgement and the Hereafter); *Ibadat* (worship rituals performed in glorification of Allah including salat, zakat, fasting, haj and jihad); *muamalat* (contractual obligations between the faithful and all of Allah's creatures – including marriage contracts, settlement of disputes, contractual terms for trade and loans); *kaffarat* (expiation of sins against God and his creatures); and *uqubaat* (grave sins requiring capital punishment).[7] For many Tijani, if the Nigerian state made it possible for them to achieve the first four elements of Sharia without hindrance, then there would be no practical need for the fifth element, *uqubaat*.[8] Most Muslims could therefore grudgingly accept the model of the state inherited from colonialism, provided it met this minimalist function.

By the 1970s, however, this benign attitude began to change. For many Muslims, the growing moral, political and economic crisis of the state, was identified 'as the failure of an "imported" western legal system ... they felt that this legal system purveyed a "spirit" that was alien to

---

[7] Interview with Shaikh Mukhtar Adam Abdallah, Jos, 18th April 2014.
[8] Interview with Professor Abdullahi El-Okene, Zaria, 10th April 2014.

Nigeria' (Clarke & Linden 1984, 92). Increasingly, while some Muslim – reformists – demanded the reform of the religion and society, others – Islamists – wanted to Islamize the state by capturing political power and establishing the rule of God. The Islamists 'believed that the rule of God must be established first' before the reforms (Kane 2003, 7–8). As continued crisis aggravated the anxiety of many in the 1970s and 1980s, many Muslim groups – Salafists and Shi'ites in particular – turned towards 'political Islam' or Islamism and made demands for an Islamic State (Clarke & Linden 1984; Loimeier 1997; Kane 2003). Some Sufis can equally be found amongst the Islamists (see Kane 2003, 77).

However, many Salafists were reformers and only a sub-set of them were Islamists. For example, the main Salafist movement, *Izala*, explicitly supports the Nigerian constitution, especially Article 25 which forbids the state from adopting a state religion and guarantees the freedom of belief, conscience and worship, individually or collectively. The *Izala* Salafists are not opposed to the Nigerian state; they want to embed more Islamic sensibilities and interests within it, especially their own. Significantly, Sharia law is mentioned only once in the constitution of *Izala* and, according to one astute scholar of the movement, the 'major enemies of the '*Yan Izala* are not the Christians but the "Muslim sects"' (Loimeier 1997, 231–2). In short, *Izala* is mainly about countering 'nominal Muslims'. Similarly, the study of Kano *'ulama* by Wakili (2009) shows that Islamists can turn around and become reformers. The return to democratic politics in 1999 opened up a space for electoral contestation that the Kano clerics were willing to embrace to promote their vision of Islamic reforms. They argued that Islam was compatible with democratic politics, and that it was the duty of every Muslim to take part in the electoral system to resist fraud. They believed that the involvement of Muslims in politics could help 'sanitize' the state and in 'a shift from the period prior to 1999, when a popular view was that they should reject – and overthrow if possible – the secular state', the clerics urged Muslims

> to vote for the most credible candidates regardless of political affiliation and perhaps even religious disposition. Political and religious affiliations, and even the implementation of Sharia, were secondary, while the emphasis was placed on the candidates' character and personality. (Wakili 2009, 1)

As Wakili shows for Kano, this political engagement with the state proved problematic as the Shekarau-led State Government tended, from the point of view of its own political interests, to include some sects, while excluding others. This tactic of selective incorporation by state governments in power exacerbated the tensions between the different sects. In Kano, while the Qadiriyya and the Tijaniyya rejected Shekarau for preferring Salafists, some Salafists rejected him as well, for discriminating against their own tendency within the Salafist movement. It was a similar problematic engagement with the Ali Modu Sheriff-led State Government in Borno State which precipitated the transformation of the Salafist *Yusufiyya* sect into the jihadi *Boko Haram*. All the while, millenarian movements like the *Maitatsine* continue to see the state as an evil that must be avoided through the removal of the sect from society, or confronted by force. We must therefore avoid a mechanical reading of the political orientation of the sects we are studying as we seek to make sense of the social and political consequences of sectarianism within northern Nigerian Islam.

Outline of contents

This volume seeks to explain the contemporary religious challenges facing northern Nigerian Muslim communities in the context of the long religious and socio-political history of the region. Appropriately, therefore, it starts in Chapter 2 with a re-interpretation of the Sokoto jihad of 1804 not as a conflict to establish the Islamic Caliphate, but as a conflict *within* the Muslim community, between reformist Muslims and 'nominal' Muslims. Murray Last points out the dissent against the jihad by some established Muslim authorities of the day. He even notes some dissent against the jihad within the jihadi *jama'a* or movement. He notes that dissent revolved around differences in the interpretation of doctrines, pointing out the importance of beliefs, rituals and spiritual ecstasy in the development of dissenting groups. He argues that dissent and protests are tied up with politics, dynastic ambitions, the pious life and human passions. Holiness can become addictive, and so can collective violence. He explores the brutality that is often visited on dissidents, on doctrinal and political grounds. However, he argues that dissent need not be expressed only in violence or some dramatic acts. He outlines the strategies and sites of non-violent dissent in everyday life, highlighting the importance of establishing a following for the eventual success of the dissent movement.

In Chapter 3, Mustapha and Bunza seek to root this historical dynamic within the contemporary situation by analysing the dynamics of sectarian fragmentation within northern Nigerian Muslim communities today. They identify all the major sects and groups, up to and including *Boko Haram*, and establish their historical trajectory. Special emphasis is placed on: (1) their historical background; (2) their doctrinal beliefs; (3) their ritual practices; and (4) their social composition and connections with the wider society. This enables the reader to clearly identify the major actors in the religious politics of the Muslim communities today against the background of the region's past. The chapter suggests that *Boko Haram* is only taking doctrinal disagreements to new heights with 'the ease with which they label other Muslims as unbelievers, the lack of distinction between sin and unbelief, the quarrelsomeness and predisposition to easily kill for even minor infractions' (K. Mohammed 2014, 18). The emphasis in this chapter is on understanding the world as seen through the lens of the different sects.

In Chapter 4, Hannah Hoechner looks at the alleged role of *almajirai* as the storm-troopers of religious violence in northern Nigeria. *Almajirai* are boys and young men enrolled in 'traditional' Qur'anic schools rather than formal education. As Hoechner documents in her contribution, in national discussions of religious violence in northern Nigeria, the *almajirai* are assumed to be the key players in the enactment of violence. Some even see their informal schools as jihad factories nurturing potential *Boko Haram* members. For example, according to Frank Nweke Jr, former Minister of Information and current Director General of the Nigerian Economic Summit Group:

> As a child, I watched as the seeds of Boko Haram were sown in Maiduguri, where I grew up. As we were taken to school every day, we saw the kids sitting under trees being indoctrinated. As we returned from school in the afternoon, we saw the same children at the round-abouts, begging for alms and as we went to catechism in the evening, we found them back under the trees receiving their own religious studies. Majority of them did not attend any formal school. Today, they have become the cause of insurgency to the nation; a nation that failed them. (Isine 2014)

Hoechner argues that we need to take a critical look at the *almajiri* system in order to ascertain what is actually happening in the schools. Nothing in the limited curriculum of the schools is suggestive of a process of systematic radicalization and these are clearly not the 'madrassas from hell' that Western security analysts warn about in places like Pakistan (Bano 2012) and Saudi Arabia. Focusing on the alleged indoctrination of the young Qur'anic students, without even analysing the content of what they are taught deflects attention from the real issues – the serious structural constraints that reproduce poor educational outcomes in much of northern Nigeria and incentivize poor rural families to choose the *almajiri* system over a costly and ineffective Western education system whose outcomes are, to say the least, doubtful. The problem with the *almajirai* is not what they are taught, but the abysmal conditions of marginality and adverse incorporation under which they grow up.

Critics of the *almajiri* system make unsubstantiated claims about the radicalizing *content* of the education they receive, while totally ignoring the *context* of the educational system – one which has a high possibility of frustrating and alienating the students and thereby pushing them in the direction of anti-social youth gangs like the *'Yan daba*. Finally, Hoechner notes that the *almajirai* are often victims of sectarianism themselves. Followers of the reformist *Izala* frequently refuse begging *almajirai* food on doctrinal grounds, and may even beat them. Furthermore, while the students and teachers of the *almajiri* system are unlikely to embrace reformist ideas, they are not necessarily members of the Sufi Brotherhoods either, though stickers with the bust of Tijaniyya Shaikh Ibrahim Niass decorate many *almajirai*'s phones and begging bowls. Which *tariqa* (brotherhood) one identifies with is not a divisive issue amongst the *almajirai*, some of whom do not even share their teacher's *tariqa* affiliation. All of these arguments suggest that we cannot assume that the *almajirai* are being radicalized by their educational process. If some of them gravitate towards religious violence, we should start by examining the alienating context of their everyday lives – a context not much different from those of the real street fighters, the areligious *'Yan daba*. Finally, Hoechner's contribution draws our attention to the class divisions, inequalities and poverty plaguing the Muslim communities in northern Nigeria.

If Hoechner draws our attention to the influences of economic inequality within the Muslim communities, in Chapter 5, Hashim and Walker address the equally contentious issue of ethnic cleavage within the communities. In their study of non-Hausa Muslim minorities in the Hausa city of Kano, they highlight a tendency for the Hausa Muslim majority to look down on the Muslims from other ethnicities. They highlight the structural vulnerability of these non-Hausa Muslims, caught as they are between their Hausa co-religionists on the one hand and their Christian co-ethnics and neighbours on the other. They highlight a series of 11 ethno-religious riots in Kano between 1953 and 2011, with the non-Hausa Muslims increasingly attacked by both sides – by one side for not being Hausa, and by the other for being Muslim. The authors note that the failure of the state to provide security in cities like Kano is forcing residents to resort to self-help para-military outfits for their own protection.

In Chapter 6 I address the cobweb of misunderstanding, even misinformation, that has shrouded the phenomenon of *Boko Haram* insurgency. For example, former Governor Ali Modu Sheriff under whom the insurgency developed in Borno State, and who was accused by some of complicity in the emergence of the sect, has explained away the insurgency by claiming that Mohammed Yusuf 'the late sect leader was insane' (Bello 2009). Which then begs the question: how did an insane person manage to organize such a highly organized and motivated sect? The chapter highlights the various conspiracy theories that have dominated public discourse of the issue in the Nigerian public sphere, as well as the political agendas they seek to serve. Finally, an empirically based multi-dimensional approach is proposed through which the many causations of the insurgency can be identified and integrated into a more realistic explanation. The relevant strands in the analysis include: (1) religious doctrines; (2) poverty and inequality; (3) the political context of post-1999 electoral competition; (4) the personal agency of the youth directly involved in *Boko Haram*; and (5) the geographical and international context of the insurgency.

In the concluding chapter, I draw the discussion to a close by returning to the theme of violence and social disorder caused by sectarian extremism. I argue that, as a consequence of the religious and political dynamics of sectarianism in northern Nigeria, the region has witnessed four overlapping patterns of violent conflict since the 1940s. The first pattern, from the late 1940s, but especially from the 1970s, is driven by doctrinal differences within Islam. The second pattern, seen largely from the 1950s, had an ethnic and regional logic at its core, but with strong religious undertones. The third pattern, discernible from 1980, was characterized by millenarian uprisings against the state and society by sects composed of socially marginalized and economically disgruntled Muslims, while the fourth, starting in 2009, is characterized by the emergence of Islamist insurgencies. The chapter concludes by making the important point that bad governance created a fertile ground for doctrinal intolerance to germinate into violence, and goes on to examine three key areas in which better governance can improve the counter-insurgency against *Boko Haram*.

Bibliography

Adeleye, R.A., 1971, *Power and Diplomacy in Northern Nigeria, 1804–1906*, Humanities Press, New York.
Alexiev, A., 2005, 'From the Editor's Desk', editorial comment on D. McCormack, 'An African Vortex: Islamism in Sub-Saharan Africa', Occasional Papers Series 4, The Center for Security Policy, Washington, January.
Alkali, N.M. (ed.), 1993, 'Islam in the Central Sudan and the Emergence of Kanem', in his *Islam in Africa*, Nigeria; Spectrum.
Anon., 2012, 'The Popular Discourses of Salafi Radicalism and Salafi Counter-radicalism in Nigeria: A Case Study of Boko Haram', *Journal of Religion in Africa*, 42 (2), 118–44
Bano, Masooda, 2012, *The Rational Believer: Choices and Decisions in the Madrasas of Pakistan*, Ithaca NY and London: Cornell University Press.
Bello, Emma, 2009, 'Boko Haram crisis: crisis was not religious – Gov Modu Sheriff', *Leadership*, 8 August 2009, http://leadership.ng, accessed on 8 August 2009.
Ben Amara, Ramzi, 2011, 'The Izala Movement in Nigeria: Its Split, Relationship to

Sufis and Perception of Sharī'a Re-Implementation', D.Phil. Dissertation, Bayreuth International Graduate School of African Studies, BIGSAS, Universitat Bayreuth, Germany.

Casey, C., 2008, '"Marginal Muslims": Politics and the Perceptual Bounds of Islamic Authenticity in Northern Nigeria', *Africa Today*, 54 (3), 67–92.

Chafe, K.S., 1994, 'Challenges to the hegemony of the Sokoto Caliphate: a preliminary examination', *Paideuma: Mitteilungen zur Kulturkunde Paideuma*, Frobenius-Institut, Bd. 40, 99–109.

Clarke, Ian and Peter Linden, 1984, *Islam in modern Nigeria: A Study of a Muslim Community in a Post-Independence State (1960–80)*, Mainz: Gruenewald.

Cook, M., 2004, *Commanding Right and Forbidding Wrong in Islamic Thought*, Cambridge University Press, Cambridge.

Eickelman, D.F. and J. Piscatori, 1990, 'Social Theory in the Study of Muslim Societies', in D. Eickelman and J. Piscatori (eds), *Muslim Travelers: Pilgrimage, Migration, and the Religious Imagination*, Berkeley CA: University of California Press.

Eickelman, D.F. and J.W. Anderson (eds), 1999, *New Media in the Muslim World: The Emerging Public Sphere*, Bloomington IN: Indiana University Press.

Hill, Jonathan, 2010, 'Sufism in Northern Nigeria: Force for Counter-Radicalization?' Strategic Studies Institute, U.S. Army War College, Carlisle, PA, www.Strategic-StudiesInstitute.army.mil, accessed on 1 June 2010.

Hodgkin, T., 1976, 'The Radical Tradition in Muslim West Africa', in D.P. Little (ed.), *Essays on Islamic Civilization: Presented to Niyazi Berkes*, Leiden: Brill.

Isine, Ibanga, 2014, 'How the seed of Boko Haram was sown when I was a kid – Ex-Minister Nweke', 1 May 2014, *Premium Times*, www.premiumtimesng.com, accessed on 1 May 2014.

Kane, Ousmane, 2003, *Muslim Modernity in Postcolonial Nigeria: A Study of the Society for the Removal of Innovation and Reinstatement of Tradition*. Leiden: Brill.

Kyari, M., 1992, 'History of Imamship of Borno under Elkanemi Dynasty' M.A. dissertation, Bayero University Kano.

Last, M., 1979, 'Some Economic Aspects of Conversion in Hausaland (Nigeria)', in Levtzion, N. (ed.) *Conversion to Islam*. London: Holmes & Meier.

Lawrence, B., 2006, *The Qur'an: A Biography*, Atlantic Books, London.

Loimeier, R., 1997, *Islamic Reform and Political Change in Northern Nigeria*, Northwestern University Press, Evanston, Illinois.

Mazrui, A.A., 2011, 'The Politics of the Sharia in Nigeria: A Foreword in Comparative Perspective', Foreword to R.R. Larémont, 2011, *Islamic Law and Politics in Northern Nigeria*, Trenton NJ: Africa World Press.

McCormack, D., 2005, 'An African Vortex: Islamism in Sub-Saharan Africa', Occasional Papers Series 4, Washington DC: Center for Security Policy.

Mohammed, Kyari, 2014, 'The message and methods of Boko Haram', in Marc-Antoine Pérouse de Montclos (ed.), *Boko Haram: Islamism, Politics, Security and the State in Nigeria*, West African Politics and Society Series, Vol. 2, Leiden and Ibadan: African Studies Centre and Institut Français de Recherche en Afrique.

Mu'azzam, Ibrahim and Jibrin Ibrahim, 2000, 'Religious Identity in the Context of Structural Adjustment in Nigeria', in A. Jega, (ed.), *Identity Transformation and Identity Politics Under Structural Adjustment in Nigeria*, Uppsala: Nordiska Afrikainstitutet.

Otayek, R. and B.F. Soares, 2007, 'Introduction: Islam and Muslim Politics in Africa', in B.F. Soares and R. Otayek (eds), 2007, *Islam and Muslim Politics in Africa*, Basingstoke: Palgrave MacMillan.

Pew Forum on Religion and Public Life (2010) 'Tolerance and Tension: Islam and Christianity in Sub-Saharan Africa', Washington DC: Pew Research Center.

Roy, Olivier, 2004, *Globalized Islam: The Search for a New Ummah*, New York: Columbia University Press.

Sanusi, L.S., 2007, 'Politics and Sharia in Northern Nigeria', in B.F. Soares and R. Otayek (eds), 2007, *Islam and Muslim Politics in Africa*, Basingstoke: Palgrave Macmillan.

Soares, B.F., 2005, *Islam and the Prayer Economy: History and Authority in a Malian Town*, Edinburgh: Edinburgh University Press.

Usman, Y.B., 1983, 'A Reflection of the History of Relations between Borno and Hausaland before 1804', in Usman, B. and Alkali, N. (eds), *Studies in the History of Pre-Colonial Borno*, Zaria: Northern Nigerian Publishing.

Wakili, H., 2009, 'Islam and the Political Arena in Nigeria: The Ulama and the 2007 Elections', Institute for the Study of Islamic Thought in Africa (ISITA), Working Paper 09-004, Evanston IL: Buffet Center, Northwestern University.

2

From dissent to dissidence
The genesis & development of reformist Islamic groups in northern Nigeria

MURRAY LAST

Introduction: The ubiquity of dissent

In this chapter I wish to show that the Muslim *umma* in northern Nigeria
has never been without religious dissidence. There is a *process* to the development of separatist Muslim communities which needs to be studied if
Government is to formulate both successful policies of containment and
a *programme* that leads the Government to self-reform: for these 'extreme'
movements of protest (even *Boko Haram*) may articulate real concerns,
even ideals, at the grass-roots level that it is unwise to ignore. This was
true in the past; it is still true today – hence I will briefly re-analyse as
an early example the most successful of all northern Nigeria's religious
protest movements, the jihad of the Shaikh 'Uthman dan Fodio (referred
to hereafter as 'the Shehu') that lasted four years (April 1804 – December
1808), and led to the establishment of the Sokoto Caliphate, a confed-
eration of emirates that stretched from today's Burkina Faso in the west
to deep into Cameroon in the east; from the edge of the Sahel in the
north to the start of the forests six hundred miles to the south. But I will
also survey movements that failed, and try to explore the dynamics that
underlie violence in the name of religion. In seeking to understand the
Muslim opposition to jihad I may be offering readers an unusual, certainly
a controversial perspective. I personally think the jihad, and the Caliphate
that arose out of it, was one of the most remarkable achievements in the
history of Nigeria, if not of Africa. The start of the Sokoto Caliphate in
1804 has not been marked by any Nigerian event of any kind – whether
to celebrate the political acumen that made it possible or to analyse and
assess the considerable human costs involved on all sides of the violence.
This chapter, then, hopes both to provoke the reader and to open eyes
onto data that may have been overlooked.

I will start by taking a rather unusual perspective on it by examining the Shehu's dissident movement through the eyes of the established Muslim authorities. As ultimate losers in the jihad, these authorities (with one significant exception – Shaikh Muhammad al-Amin al-Kanemi in Borno) have left little contemporary record of the range of opinions of all those who opposed the jihad.[1] After this I will move on to the dissent and then dissidence that developed among those *within* the jihadi *jama'a* – the disillusion that led in its turn to splits, first within the *jama'a,* then within the Caliphate that emerged from the successful jihad. In focusing on dissent I am not saying that the dissenters were always 'right' to dissent, to split off or militarily oppose the Muslims then in office: I am, instead, suggesting we need to try and recognize both the rationales and the emotions that underlie the refusals to accept the existing political regime (even when it is 'reformist'). My argument is that today's dissidents, such as the notorious *Boko Haram,* are part of a tradition of dissidence; and that neither are they a new phenomenon nor will they be the last of their kind. More important, perhaps, is the suggestion that the flame of dissent should be left with air to burn (preferably away from a city centre) rather than be extinguished by military force. Whatever the case, we need to recognize that ordinary Muslims will always be willing to at least tolerate (if not support) such dissidents in some way or other. For ordinary Muslims, 'pleasing Allah' is a serious, practical strategy to have both for daily life and for the governance of the community in which one lives, prays and raises a family.

The legitimate conditions for dissent

At its root, dissent in Islamic communities depends on what is considered *bid'a,* innovation. Ideally, individuals (and the community or *jama'a* as a whole) should in their daily lives re-enact the lifestyle of the Prophet and his Companions – in short, they should behave exactly as did the earliest Muslims (*al-salaf*), not just in ritual but, say some, in mundane details too. We know the details of this lifestyle from the Holy Qur'an, and from both what the Prophet said (*hadith*) and what He did (*sira*) – these together constitute the Sunna, which is the 'way' Muslims should follow without any deviation throughout their lives. This injunction is taken literally. Exact, literal details of the Sunna, however, are not all agreed

---

[1] In the letters exchanged between the Imam in Sokoto, 'Uthman dan Fodio and his son Muhammad Bello, and the Shaikh Muhammad al-Amin al-Kanemi in Borno, the propriety of the *mujahidun* sacking the capital of the ancient Caliphate of Borno was strongly disputed: the correspondence (in Arabic) is reproduced in Muhammad Bello, *Infaq al-maisur* (1812). See also Brenner 1992, for a more Borno-based perspective.

upon; interpretations vary, and some traditions are regarded as unsound – even for the Sharia there are four distinct schools of law. Nonetheless there is consensus (*ijma'*), and it is agreed which compilations of *hadith* are the most sound. Yet within these constraints there is still room for idiosyncratic interpretations and preferences that individuals may pick on as being what is for them the 'true' Sunna. Furthermore, there is for some a category of 'good innovations' (as well as one of seriously 'evil' ones) – but this too can be disputed.[2]

Inevitably over the centuries, as circumstances changed, some Islamic governments have permitted practices and technologies that were simply not available at the time of the Prophet – the most acceptable (and very early) innovation being of course the compilation of the Qur'an into a single book; others include the *tarawih* prayers in Ramadan. But many old-established religious practices, involving for example visiting tombs, the celebration of the Prophet's birthday (*maulid*) or Sufi techniques, remain controversial; ritual procedures are areas that are especially problematic. More mundane aspects of life – such as the use of gadgets like watches or the teaching of modern scientific data (especially where such data are at variance with the knowledge that is given in the Qur'an) – have been regarded by some as wholly unacceptable to any individual or community seriously seeking to replicate in their own lives the lifestyle of the Prophet.

These communities refer to themselves as *ahl al-sunna wa'l-jama'a*; in rejecting some key dimensions of contemporary life – whether technologies or ideas – these *ahl al-sunna* groups are seeking a purity that contemporary society does not have; they therefore shut themselves off from contemporary society and exclude influences or people from outside. For them, modern governments are themselves *bid'a*, and so should be removed from having any power over Muslims – for the Holy Qur'an explicitly and succinctly forbids *bid'a*. Thus, for *ahl al-sunna*, living strictly according to the Sunna becomes an end in itself – it is the sole purpose for being in this world, it is the meaning of their existence: to outsiders, it may look like an obsession, almost a drug, so intense, so addictive is the commitment to holiness, but to those living such a pure life, the Sunna trumps all possible arguments. This is not a phenomenon confined to Muslims: it is well known among the Christian ultra-'pious' as well as, say, Buddhist monks or Hindu ascetics. Their concern is not how to cope with modernity, live with other cultures or manage the diversity found within Muslim society – any compromise is a denial of the Sunna.

---

[2] See the discussion by Dr Abdullah bin Bayyah at www.SuhaibWebb.com. The Sokoto Caliphate followed Maliki law, but was ready by the jihad's end to take into account the rulings of the three other schools of law (cf. the Shehu's *Najm al-ikhwan*).

Dissent against governmental *bid'a* is therefore, from this Salafi perspective, not an option but a requirement for the good Muslim. Compromise is out of the question. Nonetheless there are let-out clauses, most notably the recommendation that Muslims in danger of their lives can dissimulate (*taqiyya*): they can collude in governmental *bid'a* while in their hearts rejecting it – but only in exceptional circumstances, not in everyday life.[3] There is thus a righteousness in any properly consti- tuted *ahl al-sunna* taking up arms to kill all those, even Muslims, who are opposed to the *ahl al-sunna*. In response, of course, governments use their security forces to eliminate any *ahl al-sunna* that resorts to violence[4], and that counter-violence then only escalates the confrontation: govern- ments become *kuffar* in the eyes of Salafi Muslims and any of their agents 'deserve' to be killed. Such a stance does not require elaborate ideological justification: the argument is basic – *dar al-Islam* needs to be established, say the reformers, and kept free of *bid'a*. It takes much more sophisti- cated argumentation to 'prove' Islamically that an *ahl al-sunna* is wrong. Its position may be 'impractical', 'out-dated', even 'stupid' etc.; the 'consensus' of *'ulama* may be against it (as indeed it is) but does not power tend to pervert even the *'ulama*?

It is easy thus to interpret dissent *politically*, but that is only one dimension of a religious commitment that may be as much emotional as coolly pragmatic. I suggest that in eighteenth-century Hausaland there was a widespread surge in the quest for spiritual experience, mainly through *dhikr* and *khalwa* (in caves, for example, or underground rooms), that was not available through traditional religion (not even *bori*). The Sufi *turuq* (brotherhoods), especially the Qadiriyya, were the main vehicles for such experiences, but Muslims' quest was not limited to them. There were Shaikhs living like hermits in the countryside who could offer the training and guidance needed for young Muslims; as hermits they may have been isolated and remote, yet they had networks along which they (and their students) moved. In this sense, there was a rural religiosity of an intensity and a variety that perhaps the more controlled urban-Muslim world lacked.[5] 'Uthman dan Fodio started life in this rural milieu but as he grew more authoritative and influential as a Shaikh, he sought to 'tidy' up this religious scene, reasserting the primacy of Sunna and condemning both all the *bid'a* and the contentiousness to be found among enthusiastic

---

[3]   There was considerable debate in Sokoto and Gwandu over *taqiyya* once the Christian British (*Nasara*) took over Sokoto in 1903: see Adeleye (1968) citing Muhammad Bukhari (1903) and Ahmad b. Sa'd (1903); and Omar Bello (n.d.), who is translating al-qadi 'Abdullah, who favoured *hijra* over *taqiyya*.

[4]   There is also a loyalist strand in the Salafi view that opposes the rejectionist argument. See Wagemakers 2012.

[5]   My main source for the historicity of these hermit-style scholars and their idiosyncratic Sufism is the late Alhaji Garba Sa'id. I talked to some in deep-rural Adamawa when recording old Fulfulde poetry.

new Muslims (such as the *mutakallimun* who pestered less learned Muslims with trick questions on *kalam*).[6] What was the underlying cause for this upsurge in spiritual questing is not known: socio-economic conditions can be tritely offered as can, say, political collapse brought about by defeat in war (as in Zamfara, where the Shehu started his preaching) but it could be some more idiosyncratic factor which made 'trance' or spiritual ecstasy a new, illuminating experience for hard-worked, wifeless youth. Nor do we know, for example, what shamanic or other kinds of use people might have made of tobacco, then (in the eighteenth century) a relatively new import into Hausaland; its effects were strongly debated and rejected by *'ulama* as it clearly altered its users' minds.[7] 'Holiness' we know can become addictive, but so too can collective violence if it is successful: the emotional 'buzz' of both should not, I suggest, be left to one side when analysing dissent; protest may be political, it may be pious too, but it also permits passions to flame.

The eighteenth century (pre-jihad) climate for dissent

In all five of the major emirates in Hausaland – Gobir, Kebbi, Katsina, Kano, Zaria – not only was the ruling elite patently Muslim but there were powerful reform-minded Muslim factions among them who managed at the end of the century to have their reform candidate elected Emir.[8] Furthermore, the dominant scholar-merchant elite who advised the Emir on matters Islamic (and no doubt on other matters too) were often long-established Muslim Wangarawa people who came out of the Timbuktu/Songhai world of trade and Islamic scholarship; their partners in trade were Arabic-speaking North Africans and Berbers. In Katsina

[6] The Shehu wrote his *Ihya' al-sunna wa'l-ikhmad al-bid'a* in 1794 as a guide to what a reformist Muslim must and must not do, in everyday life as well as Sufi practice; once the jihad was going, apparently a copy was given to each *amir* given a flag. On the Shehu and Sufism, see Brenner 1987. On the popularity of *kalam*, see El-Masri 1978, 20.

[7] Tobacco was permitted by Ahmad Baba in 1607 but subsequently scholars like Muhammad al-Wali (writing later in the eighteenth century in what is now Chad – I owe this reference to Dorrit van Dalen) rejected smoking it. For the whole debate, see Batran 2003. In South America, where tobacco originates, it is widely used for shamanic rituals, and visiting Europeans trying it for the first time in the sixteenth century found it had psychotropic effects (Wilbert 1987, ch. 2). Tobacco can vary in strength; we do not know how West Africans in the eighteenth century experienced, let alone experimented with, various ways of using tobacco – smoked, chewed or turned into a concentrated juice. But whatever they did, it caused such real concern to some contemporary *'ulama* that it must have been having some effects on its users. However neither Shaikh 'Uthman nor his brother 'Abdullahi (who mentioned it) banned chewing tobacco. It is the smell (*wari*) of tobacco smoke that offends today's radicals, not the taste or its effects, apparently; but perhaps in the eighteenth century, smoking (like alcohol) offered experiences that 'blew' the mind and called down on it the wrath of the *'ulama*?

[8] Kano: the ruler was called *al-Wali* (*Kano Chronicle*, tr. Palmer, 127). Katsina: Usman 1981, 69 (on Gozo).

the scholars had colleagues who had emigrated and gained recognition for their teaching and writing in Cairo and elsewhere.[9] In short, theirs was a cosmopolitan Muslim society – on the edges perhaps, but still part of, the wider Islamic world. Later they were to be known (and disparaged?) by the jihadi victors as *Haben birni*.[10] Outside these Muslim cities were hinterlands that supplied the townsmen with food and with labour – both as caravan-men and as soldiers; some of these villages and farmsteads will have been practising non-Islamic rituals, and the people doing so were condoned as *ahl al-dhimma,* and given appropriate *dhimmi* labels derived from Middle-Eastern history – such as Maguzawa, Samodawa, Rumawa, Jalutawa and many others (Last 1980). Not all of these *dhimmi* groups were Hausa-speakers; some were Fulbe (such as the Rahazawa), others had Beriberi or Songhai connections (such as the Sullebawa, Lekawa or Ngudawa). The jihad was *not* against them.

Within this wider, Muslim-controlled world there were also, in the countryside, more radical Muslim groups doing Sufi practices. Some were part of wider *tariqa* (brotherhood) networks – like the Shehu 'Uthman with his Qadiri affiliation linked to the Kunta of Timbuktu; but there were others, for example in upper Zamfara (near Birnin Gada), apparently without any well-known *tariqa* affiliation – like hermits, they had spiritual experiences which were widely spoken of. Muslim and pagan could live side by side and be on good terms, able to banter with each other. Shehu 'Uthman, even as a young man, was free to travel round, especially in Zamfara, preaching and drawing large crowds; he travelled to read or borrow books – often to the capital of Gobir, Alkalawa, with his son; even as far as Tafadek in the Sahara north of Agades. On these trips he met, or learned of the teachings of, other itinerant scholars (like Jibril b. 'Umar al-Aqdasi, who was an extreme 'dissenter' in the Tuareg context), and could debate with them.

In this reformist milieu in which new institutions like the Qadiriyya were attracting great interest, the ruling Emirs in Hausa cities instituted

[9] Muhammad al-Kashnawi is the most notable, with his best-selling text in Cairo on magic; he came from Kurmin Dan Ranko, a Wangarawa trading town in southern Katsina on the Gonja kola route. For an early Wangara text from Kano, see M.A. Al-Hajj (1968). Merchants, whether North African or local men from the ancient Borno Caliphate were also regular residents trading in these Hausa cities, and acted as advisers and teachers. Fulbe scholars (such as Galadima Doshero in Alkalawa) were also residents there, sometimes participating in government. The cities were truly cosmopolitan. Both Kano and Katsina are noted for the tombs of several famous scholars and for people's pious visits to them as saints (*waliyyai*); in some cases, cemeteries have grown up around them. Note that, in books written pre-jihad, the Shehu had not declared these Hausa rulers to be *kuffar*: that came later.

[10] The late President of Nigeria, Umar Yar'aduwa, came from one of these old scholarly families who opposed the jihad. As an 'outgroup' they still tend to have allies and aides from the Niger Republic. To speak of any of these Hausa Emirs as *Habe*, a term of contempt used by Fulbe for 'blacks', unbelievers or autochthons, is literally to denigrate them as not real Muslims and to adopt the attitudes and language of their victorious opponents.

reforms themselves such as cancelling the 'fetishization' of the palace's Holy Qur'an (in Katsina and Kano). The Holy Qur'an had been kept as part of the 'secret' potency (*asiri*) that sustained the palace system, and this was now unacceptable. One of the Emirs (in Gobir) did *khalwa* as part of his Sufi initiation; the palace there hired Shehu 'Uthman to teach the princes. I think we have to recognize that these reforms were instigated by the reform-minded Muslim faction in each city; opposed to them were the less scholarly, more military-minded elite on whom the defence (and territorial growth) of each emirate depended – it was they who, for example in south-eastern Kano, relocated huge numbers of captives and settled them in newly-built towns which, interestingly, are oriented exactly towards Mecca, 15 degrees north of east (Last 1983a). The *asiri* of military men – *jarumai* – can involve non-Islamic aspects; soldiery were not into Sharia (and they grew their hair long, unlike shaven-headed Muslims who wore turbans if they could). In this milieu, the Shehu's students had started to multiply and become a distinct *jama'a*.

Shaikh 'Uthman's dissenting movement

PHASE ONE: CREATING AN *AHL AL-SUNNA* C. 1794–1804

This pre-jihad decade was the period when the Shehu's followers started to wear turbans as a mark of their piety (or distinctiveness), whatever 'class', background or age group they originally came from. Once the Shehu, at the significantly mature age of 40, had stopped touring and travelling, he settled, not in Zamfara, but with his students and followers well away from any major emirate city. His community was based at Degel, a new camp-hamlet (*qarya*) in the bush to the west away from the major river (and route) yet accessible from there; but they were in effect out in an area between Kebbi and Gobir. There young scholars on the rise came to be taught by him, but there was also a mixture of older scholars, some poets, others mystics, living nearby. The Shehu not only taught but wrote in 1794 his first book *Ihya' al-sunna,* in which no mention is made of jihad or turning to violence but instead focuses on *bid'a* in everyday life; his other works include much Fulfulde poetry (or songs) in which the proper practice of Islam is spelt out, or he is criticizing improperly Muslim customs he sees happening (like scanty clothing on young women).[11]

---

[11] The whole corpus of the Shehu's Fulfulde poetry has yet to be translated. I read a draft translation into Hausa of some 50 poems made at Gaskiya and the Jama'atu Nasril Islam c. 1965 but it has now been lost. For a list of poems copied and kept now in Ahmadu Bello University's Northern History Research Scheme, see Last (1967a: 43–6).

Associated with the year 1794 is a widely – if naively – quoted text (e.g. Hiskett 1973) that describes a vision by the Shehu where he is given the sword of truth (*saif al-haq*) by his Shaikh 'Abd al-Qadir as instructed by the Prophet Himself. The trouble with this text is that it is unlike any of the Shehu's own well-authenticated writings: there is no proper title, no date to it, in some texts there is no author specified, no other contemporary author mentions it, and its provenance is unknown – it came to prominence in the 1950s. Though the Shehu is recorded as having had other visions, this one is suspiciously opportune, perhaps even 'new'.[12]

Whatever the authenticity of this text, it seems likely that actual fighting was not on the Shehu's agenda yet – not least because many in his *jama'a* might die even if they did not lose the war; but also because Shaikhs of his calibre simply did not engage in fighting, at least not with weapons of war, or indeed ride on stallions (scholars go on donkeys or mules or, failing that, a mare: but *no-one* takes a mare into a town).[13] Islamic students were allowed to carry only sticks for self-defence (against animals if not people); there was, it seems, an awareness that sword-carrying young men, even if still *almajirai* (young Muslim scholars), could pose a threat. In general, weapons were not allowed into marketplaces either. No doubt not many *almajirai* either had horses or were adept at fighting on them. In short, risking on the battlefield the lives of those in the *jama'a* who knew the Holy Qur'an by heart was unwise: their loss, as martyrs, could jeopardize the whole knowledge-base of the Muslim community. I may be wrong, but my understanding is that war and scholarship were at this time conceived of as two wholly separate enterprises.

Finally, for Muslims to kill Muslims was simply wrong: the Shehu knew the Gobirawa were Muslims (at least their elite were; so too were their co-residents in Alkalawa), so there was a very real risk he would be killing fellow Muslims or enslaving them, acts that were both strictly forbidden (and about which he was apparently very worried indeed at the end of his life – such was his honesty).[14] In this phase, then, there was no reason or enthusiasm for conflict – yet his new *ahl al-sunna* programme and its promise of real justice were indeed being forcibly expressed by the

[12] The only other reference to what may be this particular vision occurs in one of the Shehu's last works, *Tahdhir al-ikhwan* (1229 AH), a work on the coming Mahdi; a much earlier reference may be in *Amr al-sa'a* (1218 AH) when he mentions his various minor visions since boyhood but implies he had a major vision when he was 31, not 36 or 40 years old as in *Wird* (El-Masri 1978, 15). In *Ihya' al-sunna* (1794, ch.32) he warns against 'fake' visions – were they thus in fashion at this time? Fake texts in the 1950s were not unknown too.

[13] The Shehu told his *jama'a* to start arming themselves from at least 1797 ('Abdullah b. Fudi, *Tazyin al-waraqat*), but presumably for self-defence.

[14] That Muslim prisoners-of-war were sold into slavery by Muslims is a common assumption but sometimes hard to verify. Prisoners-of-war or captives taken in war could be ransomed as prisoners rather than bought back as slaves, but who could fund the ransom is problematic in Sharia law. The subject of prisoners (as distinct from slaves) is rarely discussed by historians.

Shehu, and he was attracting dissidents in huge numbers. Much was being expected of him.

Nonetheless, as the Shehu's following grew, not all his kinsmen or other scholars who knew him joined his *jama'a*. Joining was not, for free-born scholarly Muslims whether Fulbe or Hausa, an automatic response to his call.[15] We know that slaves ran away to join radical communities like that of the ba–Are Mikaila – or 'Abd al-Salam as he was later called – in Gimbana where they became Muslims and formally free.[16] We know, too, that farmers' sons in Zamfara similarly chose Islam over continued work in their family's *gandu*, in the fields or on the family weaving looms (for which Zamfara then was famous). Zamfara had just been conquered by Gobir, and one assumes conditions for refugees were especially hard there.

In short, the Muslim urban elite saw themselves as fully Muslim and in no need to fear the Shehu or any other critic; indeed many of their sons were joining the Shehu – it was more prudent to have him as a deeply respected friend. On one occasion, at an *'Id* prayer in Zamfara, the Emir of Gobir, on seeing the Shehu's thousand-strong following all gathered together, remarked that soon he the *Sarki* would be little more than a village head by comparison.[17] As the Emir knew the Shehu well, I like to think it was perhaps more a wry remark than a hostile one.

The Shehu, in his campaign to get these 'reformers' to reform even more properly, made clear what he saw were their non-Islamic practices as a Muslim government.[18] I do not doubt that there was definite oppression/exploitation and the Shehu was right to preach and write against it, and right to restore order to a problematically discordant Muslim scene. More importantly, very large numbers of Muslims from all backgrounds agreed with him, and saw in him a chance to better their lives, spiritually and (probably) also both economically and politically; ultimately they sought the rule of (Islamic) law properly implemented. But among those were some who were more willing to use violence against the oppressive authorities than was the Shehu himself.

[15] Daura scholars told the Shehu they rejected the call to jihad because their interest was the next world whereas the *mujahidun* were clearly interested primarily in *this* world's wealth and power.
[16] 'Abd al-Salam is rather enigmatic, as the only time we hear his actual words is in *Sard al-Kalam* (1817–18) where he is quoted quarrelling with Muhammad Bello (Last 1992). His original name, Mika'ila, is unusual except among Wangarawa merchant families – presumably 'Abd al-Salam started as a protégé of theirs; the Arewa, west of Kebbi, were within the Wangara trading sphere. In changing his name was he also changing sides?
[17] Last 1967a, 7, citing Gidado, *Raud al-jinan*.
[18] The key texts on this issue are, pre-jihad, *Ihya' al-sunna* (1794) and, post-jihad, *Kitab al-farq* (after 1806; see Hiskett 1960 and 1962) and *Hisn al-afham* (1810: see Siddiqi 1989). Though the Shehu labelled himself a *mujaddid, muslih and muqtadi*, he is sometimes (despite his evident Sufism) now labelled as a Salafi, in the original sense of the term: either way, he and his *jama'a* at Degel sought to follow, as exactly as possible, the ways of the Prophet, His followers and their immediate successors (see El-Masri 1978).

PHASE TWO: AN *AHL AL-SUNNA* GOES TO WAR (1804–06)

The spark that set off the conflagration we now know as the Sokoto Jihad was out of the Shehu's control. In the dry season of 1803–04 a Gobiri force was passing up the river valley east of Degel with prisoners they had taken from sacking 'Abd al-Salam's community at Gimbana. This was too much for some 'hotheads' (*sufaha'*, as Muhammad Bello called them at the time) from Shehu's Degel; they attacked the column and freed the prisoners.[19] It was a direct challenge the Gobiri authorities could not ignore. It also showed how effective and well-armed these so-called 'students' had become.

In typical dissident fashion, the Shehu then decided to move out of Degel to somewhere more remote: it was a formal *hijra*, and he had been formally elected, against his will initially, as the Imam of the *jama'a* (it is significant that till then the Shehu's people did not actually constitute a formal political unit).[20] The journey was going to be difficult: it seems they did not all set off at once, but started over a period of three days. A straggling line of people carrying all they had (and some giving birth en route) was therefore very long and exposed to attacks; water was short (it was April, at the end of the dry season), food and portable shelter had had to have been prepared. Indeed to transport his many books the Shehu had to borrow camels from a friendly Tuareg scholar, but the others may have used oxen or else carried everything on their heads: they were not ready-equipped for such a massive *hijra*. It took a week before they reached a site remote enough to stop and settle.

Underlying these actions was the model of the Prophet, the account of whose *hijra* people knew so well. The Shehu was now taking the Sunna literally: if he did exactly what the Prophet had done, then Allah might give them success. The Sunna thus governed what the Shehu and his followers did – once they reached Gudu, for example, they too dug a trench (*khandaq*) as protection. They were also to compare their battles explicitly with those the Prophet had fought.

Inevitably, the Gobiri authorities launched an expedition against the dissidents in their new encampment at Gudu and followed this up with further attacks. For the dissidents, the defensive two years, 1804–06, of

---

[19] Last 1967a, 15 citing Muhammad Bello, *Sard al-kalam*. The prisoners may well have been former runaways become Muslims.

[20] In a short manifesto seemingly written at this time to all Hausa rulers (*Wathiqat [ila jami']* ahl al-Sudan), the politico-military title of *Amir al-mu'minin* follows the Shehu's name, implying there is a widespread formal jihad in the offing. The Shehu says his jihad started in Safar (as did the Prophet's): in which case is he dating its start to May–June 1804 (1219 AH)? I assume the declaration of jihad dates to just after his election as Imam and his *hijra*. The *hijra* was in February, and the first major victory in June. No specific event is recorded for Safar 1219.

serious fighting, were marked by initial success at Tabkin Kwotto (the Prophet's 'Badr'), followed by disaster at Tsuntsua (His 'Uhud') and near-disaster at Alwasa, in addition to serious loss of life through famine and disease – more died through these than through fighting. Crucially, the high casualty rate among students and scholars led to a change in the composition of the *mujahidun* army. It seems many cattle-less young pastoralists joined in on the Shehu's side after an epizootic left them with no income except as 'mercenaries' to be paid in booty and loot. Earlier in the eighteenth century, Fulbe youths had served as free-lance fighters for the Emir of Kano – it was a job they were known to be good at (Shea 2010). But in the Shehu's jihad, the effect of these new recruits was that jihad commanders, like 'Abdullahi and Bello, could not control their own troops, who looted and kept whatever booty they liked (on one occasion they even threatened to kill Bello when he tried to restrain them). Their behaviour brought great disquiet to the original *mujahidun* as it seemed to call into question the legitimacy of the jihad. Muhammad Bello complained at the way men who were Muslims in the morning had by evening become, by their acts, *kuffar*, unbelievers.[21]

Early in this phase, when the Shehu needed all the allies and the momentum he could muster (in mid-1804), the Shehu had called on the major Emirs to submit to his leadership: the Sarkin Zazzau did so and was turbaned; the Sarkin Kano wavered awhile but was finally persuaded by his counsellors not to submit. An Emir in Kebbi accepted the Shehu – but was deposed: Muslims in these great cities were divided. Indeed, the Sarkin Zazzau who had submitted to the Shehu, was two years later replaced by an anti-jihad rival (Last 1966).

In short, the actual experience of a military jihad, born though it was out of legitimate dissent, not only transformed the *jama'a* from a group of students dedicated solely to Islam into an army of raiders ready to enslave Muslims, but through that very transformation also grew to provoke its own • Muslim dissent against it.

PHASE THREE: AN *AHL AL-SUNNA* BECOMES A CALIPHATE

This was the period of aggressive expansion and 'civil war' in Kebbi, Katsina, Kano, Zaria when a kind of 'franchise jihad' (1806–09) was instituted: military flags were given out at Birnin Gada by Muhammad Bello to would-be commanders in the east – one or two per emirate; in large emirates, the commanders had different spheres of fighting. Muhammad Bello went on from there to sack both Yandoto and Kurmin

---

[21] Muhammad Bello, *al-Dhikra*. His troops' unruliness is described in his *Infaq al-maisur* (1227/1812). 'Abdullah b. Fudi's deep disquiet is implied in his *Tazyin al-waraqat* and his *Diya' al-hukkam*, the latter written when he had abandoned the jihad and was heading east via Kano.

Dan Ranko, both ancient towns of Muslim scholars and merchants with links to Katsina. The scholar-merchants were Wangarawa: after the battle their Arabic books were found scattered over the ground by a storm's wind.[22] Their error as Muslims was remaining loyal to the Muslim Hausa Emirs of Katsina to whom over centuries they had acted as advisers and teachers; when called upon, they failed to surrender to the *mujahidun*. But as merchants their error was to monopolize the kola-nut trade: thus it could be argued that the jihad was also a struggle between two commercial groups – the Wangarawa and the Agalawa (who befriended the Shehu) – for control of the lucrative trade in kola nuts from Gonja. Whatever the case, the Wangarawa's opposition on religious grounds to the Shehu's jihad prompted the Shehu to reiterate his argument (*takfir*) that whoever is against us Muslims is thereby a non-Muslim. Later, once the Shehu decided the advent of the Mahdi was imminent and his paramountcy would last till the Mahdi came, the tone of the Shehu's books changes – he becomes much more tolerant in his legal rulings.[23] It was clear that many of those fighting on his side had divergent views of what was legally acceptable (such as wearing extra-fine clothing that had been looted). By contrast, the Shehu's brother 'Abdullahi dan Fodio was so disillusioned by how the jihad was developing that he left for Mecca; turned back by the Muslims in Kano City, he set up an old-style *tsangaya* community at Gwandu where scholarship, poetry and Sufism took precedence over government and military actions. The movement in effect was split – between a focus on scholarship in the west (Gwandu) and one on carrying through the jihad to its completion in the east (Sokoto) – even before the formal division of the Caliphate *c.* 1810.

Opening up the jihad as a 'franchise' that would-be allies could operate in their own home territories totally transformed the nature of the original campaign of dissent and dissidence. The new-style *mujahidun* in Katsina, Kano and Borno were led by former scholars and students but their forces were recruited more widely. Indeed some of their armies were labelled by enemies simply as Fellata – their status (for others) as Muslim reformers being replaced by an ethnic identity.[24] Dissidence had become political,

---

[22] This is almost a trope – books blown across the ground after a Muslim conquest of a 'Muslim' town. It is mentioned specifically for the sack of Gimbana (1803), Yandoto (1806), Kalembaina (1818); it is used in the 1950s for rulers behaving oppressively, and can still set off a riot if Christians are implicated. Yandoto never fully recovered as a town; there are no traces of Kurmin Dan Ranko left today except its site and local people's memory. The Agalawa did come to control the kola trade (see Lovejoy 1985).

[23] The key text marking the change in policy is the Shehu's *Najm al-ikhwan* (1227/1812), by which time the caliphal government was divided between Bello and 'Abdullahi, and the Shehu was teaching. For a brief analysis of the changes, see El-Masri 1978.

[24] The key promoters of the label 'Fellata' were always from Borno. The Muslim *mujahidun* saw themselves as simply Muslims and sought to ignore any ethnic or clan identities, though Muhammad Bello (in his *Miftah al-sadad fi'l-aqsam hadhihi 'l-bilad*) described them: but

not religious. In Kano, for example, the jihad in the Emirate's west began when some Fulbe shot an elderly ba-Maguje who had been left behind in his farmstead to protect the granaries and was refusing to hand over the grain.[25] His kin then appealed to their local *Sarki* (in Bebeji) who in turn passed the claim to protection on to the Emir. The religious element here seems secondary at best: *ahl al-dhimma* had rights to protection from 'bandits' however jihadi the 'bandits' claimed to be.

The final major Hausa city, Zaria, fell at the end of December 1808 when the Emir of Zaria, like the Emirs of Daura and Kano before him, withdrew from the city on (as usual) a Saturday morning to migrate south (Last 1966). A small force (70?) of *mujahidun* rode in that same morning to take over the abandoned city. Neither Emir decided to fight it out, in the fastness of their walled cities, to the bitter end: they preferred to start anew elsewhere, such was the overwhelming potency ascribed to the Shehu and his *mujahidun*. Their decision to withdraw saved many lives but I think that at root, as Muslims they recognized the Shehu was 'right' and being good Muslims they could not fight fellow Muslims; indeed, that Allah's will was being done as the world's end drew nigh. In the end, some scholars stayed behind and worked with the *mujahidun*, others emigrated with their Emir.[26] What was happening in these ancient cities, then, was not the establishment of a new state but simply a new leadership, a new elite. The courtiers changed but the notion of a court (*fada*) survived 'reform'; the title of 'Shaikh' eventually gave way to Emir (or in Kano's case 'Sultan').

THE NEW CALIPHATE *REJECTED*: THE 'SECOND JIHAD', 1817–MID-1820s

The Shehu died in April 1817 after some two years of not being well; he had moved to the town (Sokoto) where lived his son Muhammad Bello to whom the Shehu had allocated the eastern and northern 'quarters' of the Caliphate ('Abdullahi, the Shehu's brother, administered the western

---

(cont.) the Shehu was explicitly keen to keep his *jama'a* unified without such potential divisions, especially clans. But to both their enemies and the disillusioned within the ranks of the *jama'a*, the ethnic element remained: all but one of the flag-bearers, for example, was a Pullo (and even he was not given a Pullo's daughter as a bride). In contemporary lists of *ansar* (helpers of Islam) and students in the jihad period, only 19 per cent of *ansar* are non-Fulbe as are 23 per cent of students. Fulfulde soon (by mid-1820s?) ceased to be the *lingua franca* of big-city markets like Sokoto and even out in rural areas Hausa dominated simply because of the huge numbers of slaves.

[25] Maguzawa are non-Muslim Hausa who have lived in Kano and Katsina for centuries. Their name derives from the Persian term, *majus*, who in Islamic law were classed as *ahl al-dhimma*. Muhammad Bello saw them as simply *kuffar* (*Miftah al–sadad*).

[26] Those in Kano siding with the *mujahidun* now labelled themselves *lansaru* and *muhajirini* (Smith 1997, 205).

and southern quarters from Gwandu).[27] What is most striking was the way, once the Shehu was dead, very large numbers of those who had made their submission (*bay'a*) to the Shehu decided they did *not* owe allegiance either to his son or to his brother. This led to a wave of disaffection from within the large band of the Shehu's former followers; it was directed at those who had taken power after his death — in some cases it led to actual fighting, most dramatically against 'Abd al-Salam at Kware across the river from Sokoto, or against Dan Buya near Gwandu. In addition, regular, weekly campaigns in the dry season were necessary to keep the rebels ('*yan tawaye*), dispossessed into forest-land and probably including runaway Muslim slaves, simply at bay (Clapperton 1829, passim). The Shehu's enemies who had been, they said, 'paralysed' by his *baraka* (as a 'saint', *wali*), got their strength back once he was dead (Lander 1830 vol. 2, 27; 34). In Kano in particular, serious fighting recurred between Muslims where some erstwhile subordinate commanders wanted (and got) their own emirates — as at Kazaure. In the east, the leader of a still independent but much reduced Borno, the Shaikh Muhammad al-Amin al-Kanemi, sent an expedition against Kano. Hence, I think we need to see this fighting as a second jihad that is quite distinct from the Shehu's original jihad. There was a brutality to it not seen in the original fighting for the Shehu; resistance was an attempt to re-assert local autonomy which had once been (willingly, but only temporarily?) ceded to the Shehu himself. The Shehu's *takfir* of his Muslim opponents might be conceded, but not that of his heirs: this struggle was political, not religious.[28]

The wars of re-conquest were so extensive and devastating that in Kano City, as a consequence of this 'second jihad', local people in 1824 estimated (Clapperton 1829, 171) that there were as many as 30 slaves/captives to every free person (that is, 29,000 captives in a total population of some 30,000). In short, there was a massive, forced re-location of people. Not surprisingly, this generated dissent and resentment from among those who escaped this re-location.

So should we at this point assess the Shehu's original *ahl al-sunna* a failure, in that warfare and the new participants' warfare it attracted had made a proper *ahl al-sunna* an impossibility? At least his *jama'a* had survived. But was it this failure that made the Shehu recognize that the Mahdi would soon be coming and therefore decide he should instead now extend the jihad and entrust command to many others? In short, was the Shehu's vision now of a Caliphate (in which some *bida'a* was inevitable), not of an *ahl al-sunna* — he knew what strife had befallen the Prophet's

---

[27] For a map of how the Caliphate was divided in the form of an X, see Last 1997b. Bukhari, another son of the Shehu, was given the South under his uncle 'Abdullahi and took over much of the campaigning towards Nupe and its neighbours.

[28] For how the Shehu altered his position on the issue of *takfir* once the jihad was under way, see Last & al-Hajj (1965).

successors, so further killing and enslaving, and splitting irrevocably the old Muslim *umma*, might not have dismayed him: surely all he did and was doing was really Allah's work.

Later nineteenth-century dissidence within the Caliphate

Following the 'second jihad' of the 1820s, dissent in the 1830s turned sectarian rather than simply political. There was the campaign by Shaikh al-hajj 'Umar al-Futi (who was passing by Sokoto back from Mecca) to have the Tijani *tariqa* accepted as the new mode of Sufism (with himself as Shaikh) to replace the old Qadiriyya. Certain key figures in Gwandu such as Modibo Raji did join but they kept their membership secret. It was so difficult for him that Raji eventually emigrated to Yola, as did other new Tijani scholars like the poet Muhammad Tanmo'ilele from Kano (Last 1967b, 43–46). The 1840s and 1850s were a time when religious dissidence started to be serious again: not only were Tijanis becoming more numerous and foregathering in Adamawa but there was a major millenarian exodus under Liman Yamusa from Dutse in eastern Kano in the 1850s that was forcibly dispersed – some of these movements had started further west beyond the Caliphate but passed through heading east and gathering adherents as they went.[29]

It was political dissidence, however, that drove Bukhari in 1850s Hadejia to abandon his allegiance to the Caliphate – the forces sent to bring him back into the fold were inadequate for the task. The Caliphate was not so centralized that it could muster a huge army: defence had been 'franchised' out to the different Emirs. As a consequence, the level of policing of dissidents varied: it seems that rural Kano and rural Katsina had always housed dissenting communities, whereas Sokoto had a very much smaller hinterland to police: in the mid-nineteenth century it was little more than 25 miles north to south, and 10–15 miles west to east. Its south-western boundary was particularly fraught as the Muslim Kebbawa at Argungu were unwilling to recognize the suzerainty of either Sokoto or Gwandu, and though there was a truce (*amana*) for a period, fighting recurred again and again, not so much as 'dissidence' as the quest for independence. Similarly, north of Katsina, the pre-jihad Muslim regime held out as an independent Muslim state at Maradi, yet it was always ready both to raid into their former territory and to welcome dissident office-holders from jihadi Katsina. The regimes that the Shehu's jihad had ousted remained unassimilated: only Kano's Emir had been killed before

---

[29] The famines and upheavals may have led many in eastern Kano to join *c.* 1855 a massively popular, millenarian emigration eastward to Mecca led by Ibrahim Sharif al-din (or 'Mallam Dubaba', the 'Hairy'); they were massacred in Baghirmi.

he could set up his exiled statelet, though some dissident Kanawa ineffectively emigrated northwards.

Apart from millenarian and *tariqa*-based dissent, there were *ahl al-sunna*-type communities (Digawa, Salihawa or their predecessors) and individual scholars who resisted control from the centre, like M. Hamza at Tsokuwa.[30] I think it is clear that the regimes in power at the centre – like those in Birnin Kano, Birnin Katsina, Birnin Zaria – often failed to live up to the expectations aroused by the jihad; the military and political dimensions of power came to the fore, with the ruling class expanding hugely and requiring ever more revenue to sustain the life of the many 'princes' for whom occupations like trade were below their status. It is hard to quantify grass-roots dissent until it explodes into some obvious episode like an emigration, a revolt or a civil war. Runaway slaves were a feature of the administrative correspondence of the Caliphate but how much they were simply taking the chance of regaining their freedom we do not know: we do know, however, that several mixed 'maroon' communities were established on the Jos and Biu plateaus – indeed anywhere out of reach of the big horses of an emirate's cavalry. Escapees could join an existing free community like those in Tangale-Waja and become assimilated. From family histories heard today we know that happened. One millenarian Kano group, the *Isawa*, were persecuted and their leader executed; once the British missionaries came, some of them converted to Christianity as if it was what their leader had foretold.[31] They converted, it seems, as a protest against Emirate rule, and in justification offered accounts of the 'dark' side of Muslim governance (some of which I cite below). It is possible to interpret all subsequent conversion to Christianity as dissent: it certainly provoked anger among the Muslim elite which in turn provoked anxiety among colonial British.

More problematic is whether we should understand, as indications of radical dissidence, the motives of those joining the *Nasara*/British force which set out in 1902/03 to overthrow the governments of the 'Sultan' of Kano (as he then styled himself) or that of the Caliph in Sokoto: these dissidents (if that is what they were) were indeed recruited within Kano City, mainly on the Dalla side of town; when under attack by fellow Kanawa, the *Nasara*'s Kano soldiers were still able to find in the Kano countryside invaluable allies to save themselves from annihilation. We should not, I think, brand these local recruits (and their allies?) unthink-

---

[30] Complaining of Kano's excessive taxation, Shaikh Hamza left with some 15 scholars and set up an independent state among the Ningawa on Kano's hilly eastern borders (Smith 1997, 253; Patton 1987). The Salihawa were (and still are) inspired by Mahdist expectations, and remain an *ahl al-sunna*, with several dispersed communities.

[31] On the *Isawa*, see Linden (1974). They were Muslims despite their millennialist pre-occupation with the coming Prophet Isa; they for a while pinned their millenarian expectations around the missionary Walter Miller as 'their' Christian.

ingly as 'mercenaries' who were simply out for easy wages: they surely had minds of their own, and ever since the Kano civil war (*basasa*) many had lost out to the current regime. Is it too much to assume that some of these recruits wanted revenge against the Kano ruling aristocracy (*masu sarauta*) and regarded the *Nasara* as an Allah-given opportunity to wreak that revenge? We do not, of course, know what was in their minds at the time, but they almost certainly did not realize their actions would lead to some 60 years of alien, colonial rule.[32] Theirs, perhaps they thought, was only a temporary act of protest: it was Allah who brought in the *Nasara*, and it'd be He who'd drive them out again. Dissent, however brief, can have unexpected, protracted consequences.

Twentieth-century dissidence in the context of colonial rule

The take-over of the Caliphate by British Christians was reason enough for Muslims to seek opportunities to resist alien non-Muslim rule or at least to express their distancing from any association with that rule. The situation was complicated by the role of key Caliphal figures in the new 'colonial Caliphate' – the nearly blind Waziri, the new Sarkin Musulmi (confirmed by Lugard, the Governor-General) and several others who decided not to emigrate towards Mecca with the defeated Sarkin Musulmi (whose controversial appointment before the British came had split Sokoto).[33] But many 'ordinary' people did head east in the hottest part of the year when water and food are short; they had to fight to get supplies from villages and farmsteads they passed – in such demanding numbers they were not welcomed. The emigration can be seen also as a response to the belief that what had happened signified the world's end was coming very soon – in which case better to be nearer Mecca. If it was Allah who brought in the Christians, then for what purpose? Ordinary dismay at the Christians was mitigated by re-labelling them no longer as *Nasara* ('Christians') but as *Turawa* ('Europeans' or at least 'Levantines', as Whites from the Mediterranean). Exactly by whom and how that re-labelling was carried out is not known, but it was presumably to minimize daily dissent over Muslims collaborating with non-Muslims.

A second dissenting response was the increase in piety – *tariqa* membership became more important, Qur'anic schooling became

[32] The former politician and senior historian of Kano, Maitama Sule, often recalls the song sung by slaves, complaining at the too-slow coming of the *Nasara*: slaves at least wanted some change, it seems. Mercenaries (like the Azbinawa gunmen) were available for hire in the pre-colonial period as 'special forces' but the subject has been neglected by historians.

[33] The former village head of Lakwaya told me of how, as a boy, he overheard his elders discussing who should stay in Nigeria with the elderly and the herds and who should head east to Mecca. At the battle for Sokoto (15 March 1903), a key section of the Sokoto forces had stayed aloof in protest against their new Sarki.

more standard: a general re-Islamization of the Muslim *umma* would please Allah and He would then rid northern Nigeria of these Christians. Millenarian groups tried to get rid of the Christians (and their collaborators) straightaway – at Satiru in 1906 they took on both the colonial-Caliphate forces and the British.[34] It was not only millenarians either – the city of Hadejia also rose against British rule. It is of course difficult to separate the political from the religious antagonism to colonial over-rule. Dr M.S. Umar, in his book (2005), has sought to examine the subtler ways of resisting the impact of British colonialism.[35] One should, I think, add opposition to what is now called modernity (*zamani*): it is the gradual transformation of northern Nigerian society that causes disquiet as it ceases to have the old-style Muslim unity that was both moral and political.

Nonetheless, throughout the colonial period there were areas and times when possibly dissident lawlessness was rampant, but especially in the 1930s during the recession when taxation was seriously onerous. We know of highway robbers along the caravan routes through Kano; we know too of radically Islamic groups out on the borders of Sokoto as well as the continued existence of old-established networks of linked communities like the Salihawa and Digawa in rural Katsina and Kano. With the colonial Britons gone (in 1960), similarly radical groupings started to come to the big cities in the 1960s and 1970s: there were large ones like the '*Yantatsine* but also smaller bands of Muslim *almajirai* that in the evenings marched chanting through the city streets; they became very visible as dissidents vis-à-vis the established Muslim order as represented not only by the Emirs but also by the major *turuq*, the Tijaniyya and Kano's now reformed Qadiriyya under Nasiru Kabara. Similarly radical (and quite widespread now) are the *Kala Kato* who reject the Prophet's Sunna and only do (and pray) as the Holy Qur'an prescribes. The '*Yan Izala* in Jos and Kaduna represented a different, more conventional strand of dissent against the *status quo*, but it too became in a short time an established institution associated with the ruling elite.[36] In Zaria city, Shaikh El-Zakzaky's 'Muslim Brothers' have turned into Shi'ites, and have recently boomed into a vibrant, passionate economic community with large groups in Kano, Katsina and even deep-rural Sokoto.

In briefly surveying the history of dissidence within northern Nigeria's wider Muslim *umma,* I have focused neither on non-Muslims' refusal to

---

[34] See Lovejoy & Hogendorn 1990.

[35] One can also interpret the colonial period as a 'colonial caliphate', in which compromises were deemed possible for Muslims in authority (Last 1997a). It is important to recognize how transient, *c.* 1903, the occupation by *Nasara* was expected to be.

[36] These movements have been much studied, e.g. by Loimeier (1997) and Kane (2003), but scholars like Dr Mustapha Gwadabe are now re-studying a group like the '*Yan Izala* for its highly disruptive role which he compares with *Boko Haram* today.

convert to Islam nor on their military resistance (though there was much of that), but on the sort of Muslim disquiet that leads to Muslims forming an 'alternative' Islamic community (*tsangaya*) within or on the edges of a Muslim state. The latest example of such dissidence is the group nicknamed *Boko Haram*, but I suggest it is best seen within a much wider context so that a policy towards its adherents can be formed with some chance of success in the long term. Religious dissidence is a distinct phenomenon, though it can be labelled 'political' too: the element of righteousness gives a staying power to resistance but, given ideas of Judgement Day and the world's imminent end, there is also an urgency too to behaving *now* in a properly Islamic manner within a properly Islamic *jama'a*. Reform cannot be postponed; compromises defeat reform's whole purpose. Given this intransigence, governments have often resorted to violence of varying kinds in order to curb or deter the possibility of dissidence developing into insurgency.

Government's powers of dissuasion: Punishments for dissent

This is a topic that has usually been ignored by historians, yet no history of dissidence can omit what deters ordinary people from acting out their beliefs if they are contrary to the rulers' interests or ideology. There is good reason, however, for this silence: it is unusually hard to retrieve specific data from the pre-colonial period on governments' attempts to control dissent, punish it or even to deny dissidents a forum.[37] If dissidents were caught, we know one punishment was impaling (*tsire* or *yi mai tsinke* in Hausa; *kauzaqa* in Arabic) – it was a public spectacle that horrified those that saw it: a pointed stake was inserted up the prisoner's anus, angled so that its point would eventually come out either at his sternum or higher up by his throat; it was a very slow death – impaling took place on a Friday afternoon in the marketplace and the victim's groans usually ceased by noon the next day. In Kano, Alhaji Ibrahim, who had, it is claimed, once taught Kano's Emir but had later become the leader of an unorthodox Muslim sect in Kano, the *Isawa*, was impaled reportedly in Kurmi market after refusing to pray orthodoxly. But authors who never witnessed such punishments may sometimes confuse impaling with crucifixion (*salb* in Arabic; *kere* in Hausa): for example, two references to crucifixion occur in 'Abd al-Qadir dan Tafa's *Raudat al-afkar* (for years 9

---

[37] Only a few people's memories are recorded – for example, the late M. Nagwamatse as a boy in Sokoto recalled hearing the groans of a man impaled in Sokoto's old market on 13–14 March 1903; an elderly woman in Bauchi recalled the walling-up of a concubine. Textual references are rare too. But the most systematically angry note (this reference I owe to Dr Shobana Shankar) is by the missionary Walter Miller. The account of Alhaji Ibrahim's impaling and that of the *Isawa* derive from Christian sources.

and 10 when, first, Hamma was executed for claiming to be the Mahdi at Maganga, and then Salih b. Babari for leading Muslim Tuareg rebels); Alhaji Junaidu quotes them in the Arabic text of his history (using *salb*) whereas its Hausa translation (by Haliru Binji?) uses *yi mai tsinke*. *Kere* in Hausa is associated with Kontagora where it involved being strapped to a post with arms out-stretched (Abraham 1962); it was not neces-sarily fatal, unlike impaling. It is possible that impaling was introduced later in the nineteenth century; it is Ottoman practice, not a Qur'anic punishment (unlike crucifixion, *salb*). Was it felt necessary to intim-idate dissidents with even worse punishments? Whatever the case, we simply do not know how often impaling or crucifixion took place or whether in some cases the crucified prisoner was eventually cut down and released.[38] Clapperton (1828 vol. 2, 369) reports, however, that 'the wretches on the cross generally linger three days, before death puts an end to their sufferings'. In 1824 Clapperton was also told that crucifixion and impaling were reserved for 'Pagans', by which I think he meant *kuffar* – not polytheists (*mushrikun*), as these latter usually had a pact (*amana*) that was both a peace agreement and gave them *dhimmi* status (El-Masri 1978). 'Pagans' in this context would mean apostates and other renegades who opposed the new jihadi regime. Ordinary criminals (thieves, errant slaves, etc.) might be sold off south into the Atlantic slave trade.

Executions were not a great public drama. They were the sole prerog-ative of the Emir (as Sarkin Yanka; *yanka* refers, too, to any *halal*-style slaughtering), so that any subordinate ruler who executed someone was thereby declaring his autonomy and was in rebellion, as happened at Maska once. Men suspected of 'spying' (or just opposition?) had their heads cut off from behind with a sword; in one instance in the 1820s, 2000 Tuareg were killed in this way (Clapperton 1828, 369). Normally, in Sokoto, the prisoner simply walked between two escorts, with the swordsman behind, to the marketplace, and at a signal the escorts ducked and the prisoner was beheaded, with his body and head left in the marketplace's ravine. After a decisive battle, however, defeat and capture could lead to the loser being executed by having his throat slit as if he was merely an animal for sacrifice. Kiyari, as Shehu of Borno, suffered this humiliation at the hands

---

[38] Interestingly, neither extreme punishments (nor stoning) are mentioned by 'Umar al-Salagawi writing late in the century for a German in Salaga about the Kano he knew well; only amputation is described by him in detail (Ferguson 1973, 240–42). He reports (237), though, that the Emir executed two judges for being corrupt but does not say how. Was Imam 'Umar 'sanitizing' Kano, or were impaling, crucifixion and stoning actually so rare that he never witnessed one? He mentions the executioner (*hauni*; in Katsina, *horoce*) but not his methods or the site used. The main site was a large borrow-pit (*kududdufi*), presumably between the mosque and the market, whereas amputa-tions took place ('daily', says Lugard in 1902) by a borrow-pit near the Kurmi market. Lander (1830 vol. I, 200) implies bodies were left in the smelly Jakara river in mid-city. All these water-filled sites were where dead slaves' bodies were also thrown; they housed crocodiles who fed on them.

of Rabeh in 1893, but I understand it was not an unusual form of political execution; Kiyari had himself done it to others (Mohammed 2006, 64). Again, it was a way of de-humanizing anyone who dared to resist or dissent.

An alternative punishment which people today still remember was to be encased up to the neck in a city's mud wall or gate and left a few days before the head was walled in too: is it perhaps a sign of local popular dissent that the patch of wall or gate was often renamed after the victim immured inside it?[39] Some recall it being done to concubines, while others give more vague reports as indeed they do for such tortures as the removing of finger and toe nails with hot pincers and then being paraded around town; one other recorded 'punishment' was to have one's hands and then feet pounded to pieces in a mortar. These punishments are distinct from those required by the Sharia: amputations we know were carried out, for example, in Kano City, but stoning was apparently not usually done – in Sokoto there is a tradition that Muhammad Bello as *Amir al-mu'minin* sought not to order its being carried out but the victim, on the third occasion, insisted she be so punished. Instead, what is striking about these non-Sharia punishments is their almost sadistic accent on causing maximum prolonged pain, as a deterrence to intimidate any would-be dissenter. It is as if the victim, by his or her acts of dissent, had forfeited the right to be considered a human being. This may, in part perhaps, explain why records of these punishments are, it seems, excluded from history – it is not 'History'.

Long-term imprisonment (as distinct from hostage-taking) was never a feature of Islamic punishment, though 'criminals' could be held in custody until their Sharia punishment (like amputation) was carried out – the only pre-colonial 'prison' for which we have a (horrified) description was in the Emir of Kano's palace.[40] Exile was the less lethal option for a ruler to impose on those who challenged his rule. In consequence, on the margins of any polity were settlements of refugees, either awaiting a change of power in their former cities or re-orienting their loyalties to other states. But dissent remained dangerous: after one campaign in eastern Kano, many women were to be seen with an arm amputated: they had been caught up in the 'cross-fire' and one side had crippled their usefulness by removing an arm. Other punishments might involve bodies being put on poles on top of their town's old walls as a warning to

---

[39] There are references to people being sacrificed in town walls when a city (such as Maradi) was being built; sometimes fetish objects are placed in them (as in Kano: Last 1983a, 207–8). But this is for extra protection, not punishment, though who were chosen for sacrifice is not known: it could have been slaves?

[40] Lugard 1902, 88–89. Clapperton (1829, 210) mentions a large prison in Sokoto, with a deep cistern into which errant slaves were dropped (they could, once forgiven, be drawn out again). Prisons were often simply holes, in which there were many scorpions: the late Mallam Sa'id recalled being stung by several overnight when he was being deported by the British to Cameroon.

would-be dissidents; merely to be un-buried (and therefore having one's body half-eaten by hyenas) was a fearsome scenario – one that popular songs or jibes would not allow to be forgotten.[41] But some tortures may have been just rumours about, say, a particularly sadistic ruler – like the one in Nupe who, it was said, enjoyed watching in the evening men being roasted alive on a spit. Otherwise, there seems to have been little sadism involved in publicly punishing dissidents in Sokoto: dissent simply moved out of range, if it could.

Sites of dissent and dissidence

Dissent is not, of course, expressed only in violence or in some dramatic act. We need to recall and recognize some of the other ways, explicit and implicit, by which Muslims can express their disagreement with what is going on around them, especially in government. The idea is that one can 'read' dissent while observing daily life. There is bound to be much that I have missed, so that these notes of mine will spur others, I trust, into correcting and adding to them. There are, of course, very many, often subtle ways of expressing dissent – ways that put the dissident at less risk and demand much less of him (or her). Hence it is easy for the average observer to miss this 'petty dissent', but it nonetheless can be transformed in something much more dangerous by, for example, offering over time tacit support to more overt dissidents in the neighbourhood. Thus, initial sympathy with *Boko Haram* may extend to keeping silent when confronted by police or army units in search of information, or even to helping it hide weaponry.

The early stirrings of dissent can be recognized by many small signs in public. They no doubt start in the privacy of the mind, in the seclusion of the study, and no doubt too most stirrings progress no further. It is, however, the public arena which is not only more visible to the researcher but also more significant because it is where others may be attracted to listen and then to follow. Without a following dissent does not grow. So what is discussed below are some of the sites of dissent and dissidence that can be recognized today. In the past they may have included other locations, such as marketplaces which were always regarded as places of potential violence (and hence were usually sited on the west, just outside the village).[42] In major cities, they were the archetypal 'public space', where

---

[41] The dissident 'Abd al-Salam evacuated his town and fled towards Bakura where he met his end. The place name Bakura contains the homonym for hyena (*kura*), and his descendants are still teased that they had no time to dig a deep enough grave to prevent hyenas feasting on the corpse.

[42] Because spirits, like the sun, move through the day from east to west, it is wise to have butchers on the western edge of the marketplace, which is itself on the west – so no spirit, drunk on blood, will enter a house and cause a disaster; instead they move on safely into the countryside. Spirits (*aljannu, iskoki*) are recognized in Islam. For this 'alternative geography', see Last (2010).

notices were proclaimed and executions carried out; instant lynching of thieves can be carried out spontaneously by 'the market', and no-one be indicted for the crime. It is to markets that preachers (such as the *'Yan Izala*) come and harangue the people milling around on market-day – against, for example, smoking tobacco or committing other 'sins'. On occasions (in rural Zamfara and Kano), 'the market' has been known to rise up and drive the preachers out. But these are not the sites on which I want to focus here: marketplaces are sites of action, I suggest, rather than of dissenting deliberation.

MOSQUES

Mosques are not (and were not pre-colonially) state property. Lineages and individuals build them, with the mosque of the ruling lineage (i.e. the Emir's) being the main Friday mosque. Hence attendance at a different mosque, especially on Fridays, can be an act of dissent from the Emir or his informal council of *'ulama*; conversely, attending the Emir's mosque for the noon Friday prayer is an act of solidarity. Similarly, a young scholar or Sufi, to show his radical independence, may open his own mosque and no longer pray in the mosque of his Shaikh; it is not a gracious act, so it is remembered in histories. Even a single house or compound may have more than one mosque: for example, young Muslims especially if they are *'Yan Izala* might decide to pray separately from their elders in the household's main mosque – the 'refuseniks'' mosque may be no more than a small room with no obvious signs of mosque-ness, such as a cemented space in front for sitting together in the evening before the call to prayer or after the last prayer of the day. The 'radicalism' may simply be a matter of allowing into a mosque the newly pious young women (suitably covered, of course; older Muslim women, if they pray, pray inside their rooms), whereas they could not readily pray in the elders' mosque. Mosques are governed by independent committees who appoint the Imam and generally oversee policy vis-à-vis (say) the weekly *khutba* (sermon); in consequence, some mosques are known for being more radical than others, and men choose where to pray and what kind of *khutba* to listen to each week. It is a quasi-political act.

Similarly, it is not uncommon for men to stay behind in the mosque after the final prayer to chat, often politically – it is a place where one might locate key politicians informally, though there is usually a coterie that is there each night. Much 'political' business can be done there. Furthermore, it is important to recognize that the careers of many Islam-ically learned young men show that they also have qualifications from universities and colleges; rarely are they oblivious of the wider intellectual scene – nor indeed are their audience or fellow discussants. They may well dispute what passes as the 'truth' in that wider scene but they do so with knowledge.[43] Hence much more than religious politics can enter into the conversations in the mosque and be debated.

The distinction between 'public' space and private is relatively new. The colonial British, early in the twentieth century, instituted the practice of 'state' property in which the 'ownership' as well as the maintenance and running of both 'Friday' mosques and Emir's houses ('palaces') were vested in the 'Native Authorities' that formed the new administration in each emirate. By creating the notion of 'the public' the British were, unintentionally I think, emphasizing that these buildings were not in a sense the property of 'the *jama'a'*; they belonged to no-one, they were alien – like the very colonial government itself. The *jama'a* is not the 'public' in quite the same sense: the one is Muslim, the other is alien despite being staffed by Muslim Nigerians. Dissent then is, I suggest, a dimension built into the whole notion of Native Authority and its material signs such as buildings – is the same not also true of all 'government', even the United Nations?

Thus, when the new British officials saw to the building of a series of distinct 'Native Authority' premises for local government and prisons, law courts (for the newly much-enlarged professional Islamic judiciary), schools, dispensaries, etc., they gave further visible presence to a regime that many Muslims found profoundly objectionable. Pre-colonially, officials had conducted business from their family houses – courts of justice were held there, the official Gaoler kept prisoners in a part of his house (not in a public gaol), secretaries wrote the administrative letters in the Waziri's house, scholars taught in their houses and not in 'schools' (nor in the mosque). As many of the key offices were held by lineages, the lineage house was passed on to the new office-holder. When the Sokoto Caliphate was being established, its leader, the Shehu, explicitly told his new appointees (say, in Kano where they asked) to take over the houses of the pre-jihad office-holders. Where, as in Zaria, the office of Emir rotated between key lineages, the 'palace' rotated too, but elsewhere (as in Sokoto) a new branch of the ruling lineage might well continue to use his own house as the 'palace'. The palace's furniture (including its books) belonged to the lineage, however, and was removed if the palace was taken over by a different lineage. In Kano, each of the most important lineages built their own mosques, and prayed there – I think, as a gesture of their equality vis-à-vis the Emir's lineage; it was also, of course, an act

---

[43] Often northern Muslims are written off by their southern critics as 'illiterates' – thereby discounting any literacy in Arabic or in *a'jami* Hausa. This can mislead: for example, when in 1966 *Drum* magazine published an 'interview' in English with the (dead) Sardauna purportedly in 'hell', the editors presumed it would not be widely read in the north. In practice, such articles were read out aloud to ordinary people at newspaper stalls, so that it was very widely known, and strongly fuelled the hatred felt for those who were celebrating the murder of the Sardauna. Similarly radio, in Hausa (and English), reaches far into rural areas, and people listen.

of lineage solidarity (Zahradeen 1983, 57–68). If others joined them in prayer, it could be seen as an act of support for whoever was the head of the lineage. In short, the 'state' in the twentieth century became visible and separate from the *jama'a*; it was an over-powerful, alien layer which individual pious Muslims could properly resent. In today's Nigeria, when the politicians who run the 'state' are considered corrupt, the alienation from the Nigerian 'state' can be both deep-seated and widespread: a group like *Boko Haram* is thus able to tap into a rich stratum of dissent.

In any mapping of sites of dissidence (even at its mildest), it is important, then, to map a city's mosques and what each stands for – who goes where, and who does *not* go where. Mosques vary over time: some are very fashionable for a while and attract huge numbers, then a new one pulls in the crowds. A history of mosques within a city is important. During the colonial period, especially in francophone parts of West Africa, anti-colonial groups used mosques as sites for both intra-Muslim propaganda and plotting, not least because Europeans were excluded; possibly, too, weapons, documents or equipment could safely be stored there. But this was well known or at least widely suspected, and hence mosques were also a site for under-cover agents' attention.

Violence does occur in mosques, albeit rarely. In Sokoto there were scuffles recently in the main Friday mosques as radical Shi'a groups sought to preach within the mosque compound; similarly, a senior Sunni scholar when preaching there in the mosque was shot by those (from the Shi'a) he was at the time criticizing. In Kano, too, a notable Imam and preacher was shot at the dawn prayer by followers (it seems) of a rival scholar. More recently, an attempt was apparently made on the life of the Emir of Kano when he came to the mosque, but who exactly were the persons behind that attempt is not properly known though arrests were made at the time. All this is new, but there are records (e.g. in Kano) of Emirs fearing for their lives in mosques and having look-alikes praying where they would normally pray (e.g. *Kano Chronicle*, tr. Palmer, 115). Weapons are not allowed within a mosque but some Emir's bodyguards (*bayin Sarki*; 'slaves') are always there. Furthermore, extreme dissidents have been known to desecrate specific mosques, as did followers of the 'Mahdi' of Toranke in 1965 (Alkali 1968, 92–95). In short, 'sacred' violence can occur in 'sacred' space.

Emirs en route to the mosque or the *Idi* (Eid) prayer ground on horseback are vulnerable to stones (or other objects) thrown at them. On such occasions, the umbrella held above the Emir's head by palace 'slaves' can be immediately lowered to form a protective screen (this has been done in Kano). The Emir's person is not seen as sacrosanct by everyone; he needs protection, not least when crowds throng round him to touch his garments (as happened with previous Sultans of Sokoto and their heirs).

Out in the countryside there is felt to be an element of risk from 'peasants' (*talakawa*) apparently. Even the most powerful can be fearful, presumably with good reason. Dissidence is part of the scenario – despite how solid the whole political structure may seem to be to visitors.

TIMES AND MANNERS OF RITUALS

Another clear statement of dissent is the choice of a different time to start the fast of Ramadan, or more especially a different evening to end it and then celebrate *Salla* the following day. In the recent past, the vast majority of Muslims waited to hear from the Sultan of Sokoto that the new moon had been sighted. Today, it is no longer so unusual to ignore the formal announcement by the Sultan and the Nigerian Government when exactly there is to be the two-day public holiday for *Salla*; it is an act of distancing one's household from a government one does not recognize religiously – the Sultan being seen by some now as being too close to that government to be obeyed without question. In 2011 even the Saudi Government was criticized for announcing an implausible sighting of the moon, but in Nigeria it seems the breaking of the fast has now become a somewhat more personal decision: the 'public' may do as the Government prescribes but that is not necessarily for everyone – in short, the Muslim *jama'a* is no longer as publicly united as it might have once appeared to be in northern Nigeria. Dissidence can be expressed indirectly through ritual and its timing.

The exact ritual of prayer has long been an expression of difference – especially whether the arms are folded (*kablu*) or at one's side (*sadlu*) when standing in the course of prayer. After Friday prayer, there is also the issue of what *dhikr* is said and for how long – and whether, as a novelty, *bandiri* drums are used. There were thus very visible and audible differences between Qadiri and Tijani Muslims, and these could become a source of much controversy. In some emirates, the Tijaniyya clearly represented opposition to the ruling establishment when that establishment was Qadiri. Given that 'Uthman dan Fodio was a Shaikh of the Qadiriyya and his son and successor Muhammad Bello refused to abandon his father's *tariqa* in favour of the new, radical Tijaniyya (which a visitor to Sokoto, 'Umar al-Futi, was then strongly promoting), then joining the Tijaniyya was in effect an act of dissidence or at least dissent.

During party-politics in the 1950s and 1960s, voting could follow *tariqa* lines – the Northern People's Congress (NPC) being seen as more often Qadiri whereas Northern Elements Progressive Union (NEPU) was Tijani. But within Kano city, *tariqa* was not the key issue – the Emir was Tijani too; but Kanawa beyond Kano, in Qadiri-dominated areas, were noted as being both Tijani and NEPU, in a way that made the Tijaniyya seem in opposition to the establishment and their commercial interests (as in Gusau or southern Katsina). On the other hand, long-established Tijani emirates like Zaria and Adamawa were nonetheless pro-NPC; in those areas intra-Muslim dissidence took other forms, such as El-Zakzaky's *Ikhwan* who ultimately formally became Shi'i but still resided in Zaria. In short, generalizations in this field are problematic; local knowledge is crucial.

One other very significant, religiously dissenting group was the Mahdiyya which dates back to the early nineteenth century; their members piously prepare themselves in expectation of the imminent coming of the Mahdi who is an early part of the process that leads to the end of the world. There is evidence that the Shehu, *c.* 1806, believed it was important to prepare his *jama'a* for this, but by the end of the nineteenth century such beliefs were seen as dissident, not least because they led to a *hijra* of large numbers of citizens out of the Sokoto Caliphate. Major movements occurred in the 1850s, but much the largest exodus was in 1903, the year when the Christian British with their Muslim Hausa army conquered the Caliphate. The Mahdiyya challenged the authority of governments, whether pre-colonial or colonial, to the extent that the British colonial officials (and their local appointees in Sokoto) were very scared of a major rising. For the British, in Nigeria, the Sudan or more generally in the Muslim world (where in the First World War the Germans sought to mobilize it), the Mahdiyya, as an ideology, was synonymous with rebellion and its adherents were persecuted. Mahdist leaders, once they became tolerated by a less paranoid administration, were allowed to settle within cities (such as Kano) but watch was kept over both them and the quarter in which they lived. Dissidence was permitted so long as it was known – in which case, urban sites for known dissidents were a practicable solution.

DRESS EXPRESSING DISSIDENCE

Clothing for men can reveal both party-political and religious allegiance, in part as fashion perhaps but also to identify ideas held. Before the jihad, wearing a turban became *de rigeur* for a proper, reformist Muslim who was following the Shaikh 'Uthman dan Fodio or other Shaikhs under his leadership. As a consequence, the turban was banned by the Gobiri Muslim authorities. My understanding is that, as many of the Shehu's followers were runaway ex-slaves converting to Islam, these men had taken to wearing turbans as a mark of their new 'freedom' (as Muslims should not be enslaved by other Muslims); hence, to the Gobiri authorities, they had minimal right to wear a turban which otherwise was generally the acceptable mark of a senior Shaikh – thus wholly inappropriate for an escaped slave (who would normally go hat-less) or simply for a young rebellious son set on escaping his father's control. Furthermore, turbanning an official (along with putting on him a cloak, the *alkyabba*) was part of the installation procedure – so was a new Muslim follower possibly ever 'installed' by the Shehu ceremonially with a turban? Whatever the case, there were other hats one could wear that were less presumptuous of rank or status – not just the bulbous straw hat worn over a turban which not only hides the turban but is essential if one's on horseback and might need to ride fast: turbans are impracticable at a gallop, and warriors anyway prefer metal helmets. Other wide-brimmed straw hats leave no room for a turban and are more a country style (and rather idiosyncratic, unless one's a herder out all day with the cattle). In Hausaland turbans are conventionally white or dyed a dark-blue indigo (especially among Tuareg who can afford them); the latter can be signs of wealth and not just piety. Thus today a black turban denotes membership of a dissenting group.

But even today particular ways of tying a turban are especially expressive of Muslim 'radicalism' (e.g. for young *'Yan Izala* men).[44] In my experience of serious young Muslim scholars (*almajirai*), it would have been pretentious of them to wear a turban, especially when studying with a senior Shaikh. As with wearing a big gown, modesty decrees a way of wearing items of clothing unpretentiously: a fine cap is all right (men collect caps and may have over 50 in their collection), but it is a discreet (and quite expensive) style of dressing. By leaving off a turban and wearing only a particular type of cap, the wearer is also making a statement. Though wearing no head-covering at all would imply in the past at least a servile origin (especially on a young man), today's young men in town go bare-headed freely. So, too, the use of trousers or shirts reflects the wearer's 'modernity'; but calf-length trousers are now seen as Salafi and so radicals wear them. To wear a leather *bante* (loin cloth) while doing physical work might be practical (albeit now rare), but a slave was obliged to wear one as a sign of his origin. Leather clothing (esp. goats' skin) is not 'Muslim'; a good Muslim wears cotton. In short, while clothing indicates age and status, it can also declare a particular political or social stance in today's Muslim society.

Beyond the matter of head-gear is the issue of hair style. Long hair is/ was the mark of a *jarumi*, a senior warrior, whereas pious Muslims normally have their head shaved. Combed hair is very different from hair long left un-combed, the latter being considered 'wild'. Similarly a beard, such as the Prophet had, is normally reserved for an older man, but then not dyed with henna. Young *'Yan Izala* and more recently *Boko Haram* youths tended initially to grow beards, but as beards only served to identify one to the authorities or to one's opponents, cautious 'radicals' soon shaved

[44] Dr Elisha Renne is currently making a study of turbans and veils.

them off. In any case, as beards rarely grow very well in Hausaland, it is not really the easy sign of radicalism it has become today in, say, Afghanistan or in Europe or America.

On women, there were hairstyles that even the Shehu himself railed against – these were ones where the hair (sometimes with extra material tied in) is piled up in front to extend beyond the forehead. Such a style prevents the woman from touching the ground with her forehead in prayer – and so was banned. The way round the ban was to put a stone where the forehead touches the ground at prayer.[45] The Shehu also tried to stop his wives going to market – hence purdah became a mark of a good Muslim household; houses were closed to adult men unless they were servants (slaves, eunuchs) – even the rooms of adolescent sons never had a door into the inside of their home. Women were allowed to go to the mosque, but pray separately from men – it had become a matter for debate in eighteenth-century Muslim circles. The Shehu was strongly in favour of educating his women Islamically (as shown by the well-known case of his daughter Nana Asma'u), and his tomb became a place of pilgrimage for married women. They wear a normal *hijab*, not a *burqa* or *niqab*. In a city like Sokoto with its house walls made of cornstalks there was *de facto* a ban on riding on horseback through the streets on the grounds that a (male) rider could look in over the fence at the women inside.[46] It was commonplace for women, when pounding grain or other strenuous work on hot days, to wear little or nothing above the waist: privacy within the house was then essential. As it was, men peeking at women (and vice versa) through cornstalk fences was regarded as very offensive – but it happened. Some radical groups today even do not allow women's voices to be heard outside the house: instead they call their men to meals by beating a rhythm on a calabash. In short, the way a community regulates its womenfolk becomes a marker for its concern for Islamic propriety: reformers' emphasis on this is an implicit criticism of the society around them where women normally go about more freely (for example, selling milk products or marketing).

One minor point on what is suitable in a mosque: members of *Boko Haram* in Bauchi were accused of wearing shoes into their mosque. That *could* be a sign of dissent from the general rule, though, because there are very early precedents from the time of the Prophet for doing so – or else

---

[45] I am now told that modern women, unwilling to get their forehead dirty, will also use a stone as 'ground'. Normally, the site where the forehead always touches the ground in prayer can get marked permanently – and hence can become a sign of piety.

[46] There is a tradition in Sokoto that the jihad's military commander (*amir al-jaish*), Aliyu Jedo, while riding in town on his horse, was in the habit of spotting women (and seizing them?) inside their houses. The Shehu tried to discipline him, which was not easy given Aliyu Jedo's role in the jihad. However, in the division of the Caliphate *c.* 1810–12, he was given command of the northern segment under Muhammad Bello – which suggests there may have been a kind of rapprochement – and re-located out of Sokoto to his *ribat* at Binji. (*Ribats* are small towns and settlements built as fortifications along the frontier to defend the lands of Islam'.)

it might just be a malicious rumour against them. One rarely takes good shoes to the mosque (for fear of theft), but that was not the issue here.

RE-LOCATION AS AN ACT OF DISSIDENCE

The most decisive act of Muslim dissidence was (and still is) to remove your discrete community beyond the immediate surveillance of the authorities in the city – out to sites where you could not be known. Around any Hausa city is both a hinterland and a 'deep-rural' zone: beyond the latter is a wide frontier, often 'bush' which belonged to no city-state. Thus within Hausaland, particularly in the pre-colonial past but also today, there are areas of 'no-mans-land' that could be considered free from governmental control: these areas, though, suffer from poor water supply and poor soil, and are often tree-covered and home for dangerous animals like hyenas and elephants (also lions and leopards though these are rarer); they also shelter bandits and, in the past, were regular routes in and out through which invading raiders passed. Crossing these areas, even on much-travelled paths between emirates, was hazardous; to live in them securely required hill sites or wooded locations where horsemen cannot ride. Some communities 'in exile' did not go so far but settled in the 'deep-rural' zone where they lived among dispersed farming households who were pioneering the settlement of these under-populated areas. After *c.* 1920, there was major movement of farmers out from the densely populated hinterlands into these deep-rural lands which were now safe thanks to the colonial *pax*. But they remained suitable for 'radical' dissident communities too; relations with the new immigrant farmers were good and Government surveillance was light.

Radical Muslim communities therefore chose these sites to escape centralized control (in a Nigerian version of *bilad al-siba*) and live out the Islamically 'pure' lives that they preached. Although (at colonial instigation?) the Native Authorities would secretly send out under-cover agents to infiltrate them, the communities were left on their own. If Government agents did nonetheless come openly, someone from the community would be sent out to talk with them: non-members were barred from entry. They are, consequently, hard to research: the well-known groups are the Salihawa in southern Katsina and the Digawa in eastern Kano, but there are other smaller groups, for example those who pray, reportedly, only once a week and others who pray only three times a day (claiming, as Salafis, to be following original Muslim practice).[47] These groups date

---

[47] My sources on these groups include the late Alhaji Garba Sa'id on the Digawa and other Kano groups and, for the Salihawa, my hosts in Gidan Jatau and others when I lived for two years not far from a Salihawa settlement; and also the late Prof. Philip Shea, one of whose students in Bayero University wrote an essay on the Salihawa.

back, I think, to the (possibly late) nineteenth century; one of them, the Digawa, has a Hausa *a'jami* text, but more often the rules of the community are remembered, not recorded in writing. The right to behave Islamically in the purest way possible is deeply respected: it is not seen as a threat to neighbours, only to a (paranoid) government concerned about its Muslim legitimacy – for all successful rebellions have been based on claims to be re-instating for the Muslim *jama'a* a properly 'reformed' Islam.

In the pre-colonial period emigration from an emirate was a bold, decisive rejection of the Emir's right to command. Emigration might be sparked off by a perceived injustice or by some act of oppression or exploitation (*zalunci*) – or simply the failure to inherit what seemed one's rightful heritage (as a displaced heir you posed a threat and might well be murdered).[48] Emigration was the ultimate political act – it could be done by princes (e.g. out from Katsina to Maradi) or by such individual scholars as Mallam Hamza who left rural Kano for Ningi (from where he ultimately waged war against Kano). Millenarian groups like the *Isawa* similarly lived out on the frontiers (to be later mistaken by zealous, Zaria-based missionaries as early 'Christians').

Interestingly, in the nineteenth-century jihad, certain key rulers decided not to withstand a siege but emigrated out of their cities: prime examples are the Emir of Kano (who went south to Burumburum) and the Emir of Zaria who went south to Abuja; or the Emir of Daura who eventually set up in Zango. Shifting location is a symbolic act of renewal too: many a city was re-built a short distance away on a fresh site (e.g. Isa in Zamfara). So too a household, on the death of its senior man (*mai gida*), may decide it is time to move to a new site perhaps only a few hundred yards away. Re-building is not the problem: it is the sense of a new start, on a site that has been found in advance to be propitious. An un-propitious site, for example, is one that lies on a 'spirit highway' or a place associated with particular cults, for example on a rocky high place. It is possible to map sites in an area according to their propitiousness – even the value of fields can vary as to how 'safe' they are to farm (Last 2011).

Thus emigration for a dissident community, or indeed for one that has been challenged by the threat of jihad, offers a new start. As the Holy Qur'an is regarded as very 'hot', it is better studied away from a village or indeed a town: the Qur'an's power may burn out the local fetish or whatever is sustaining the local settlement and its farms. The 'bush', then, is the appropriate place for deep Qur'anic study. Indeed, more than that, a place under-

---

[48] We know little of 'special operations' conducted in the nineteenth century. Elite men and merchants so feared murder at night that they used to have a number of tents erected within the courtyards of their houses, so an assassin would fail to find where his target was sleeping. Some also kept pistols under their pillows. The Shehu too had a tent within the courtyard of his Sokoto house, but that was probably for reasons of comfort: in the hot season, rooms can be excessively warm, either for teaching or for sleeping.

ground (a cave or a hole dug out inside a house or room) may be the best site for Sufi *khalwa* (spiritual retreat) with all the power that it generates. Communities that specialize in such ritual power-generation are usually based in the deep countryside (if not in the 'desert'). But as power-centres they can be so intimidating to authorities at the centre that they are attacked and destroyed, as they were in seventeenth-century Borno (Lavers 1971, 33).

Finally, exile was the pre-colonial punishment for anyone (man or woman) convicted of a really serious crime; it was one of the punishments that the colonial British replaced by imprisonment. In that sense, one can interpret emigration out into the 'bush' as a form of self-imposed exile – there you not only are outside the jurisdiction of the authorities but are also, in a way, serving out your sentence for dissidence and dissent. One problem today is that 'exile' is no longer an option for a citizen; instead, one can escape as a 'refugee' over the border into Niger or Chad (or even Mali and at one time Libya), and 'hide' there, but the authorities, we are told, are wary of such a flow of dissidence across national frontiers, easy though it seems to be. The 'war against terrorism' has provided new funds to monitor such movements.

Today the new site for dissent is primarily urban, not rural: cities are where the young are heading for, leaving the countryside remarkably short of young men, whether as young husbands and fathers or as young *malams* (scholars) seeking alms for performing Islamic services to the public. It is in the cities that one can learn new trades, acquire new skills, take new courses and find, for oneself, the inspiring teachers and patrons. The density of population in parts of some cities makes certain quarters good places to hide in; some quarters are so run down, through multi-occupancy and decay, that the ultra-poor can squat free of charge in half-empty buildings. There one can find friends, even join gangs – whereas at home the elders keep an eye on everything that is done. At evening time, on the streets of great cities one can find groups of young Muslims moving along doing *dhikr* and chanting songs in their own style. They can earn alms enough – money or food – to sustain themselves. In a sense, then, cities are where a vibrant religious culture is to be found – and the variety of practice within that culture includes different strands of dissent. It is not for nothing that *Maitatsine c.* 1979 brought his radical *jama'a* to settle in a run-down ward of Birnin Kano ('Yan Awaki); so too, some 25 years later, Muhammad Yusuf settled his *Yusufawa* in a ward of Maiduguri. They were the first major radically Islamic groups to be urban rather than deep-rural; part of their rationale was no doubt easier access to funds, but another part, I suggest, was to attract and keep still more adherents of a certain sort – the disengaged, excluded young in search of a good cause. Both also offered economic support to those in real need and a powerful sense of belonging – more compelling than the ward-based 'gangs' and the *'yan daba* (criminal lairs) that traditionally organized city adolescents without family ties.

Conclusion

Dissent is more than violence against governments. Indeed many dissidents are often deeply against violence – I have argued that even the Shehu was initially reluctant to arm his students. But prolonged dissent, especially if it starts to attract numerous recruits, antagonises governments, who then use force to intimidate dissenters. The issue is not over power, but jurisdiction. Dissidents ultimately deny a government's jurisdiction over them, and in doing so question the legitimacy of the Government as government. Such a denial of jurisdiction thus cancels any validity the pronouncement of *takfir* might claim: dissenting Muslims are asserting a greater 'Muslim-ness'.

But by resorting to violence, even in self-defence, dissidents risk transforming their dissent: they lose control of their movement to adherents who then exploit, even glorify, the impact that war (or jihad) offers to victors. For example, in Sokoto's 'second jihad' in the 1820s there was a degree of military triumphalism against 'rebels' that suggests that for pious Muslims the moral status of the violent had already changed by then: the Shehu's daughter, Nana Asma'u, wrote long poems or songs that glorified the ferocity of battle and her soldiers' successes in killing the Muslim enemy – and she probably was not unique in taking this attitude.[49]

Some dissident groups have failed over the last two centuries, either through military defeat or disillusionment. But the use of force to stamp out overt discontent has never been wholly successful: while the nodal points around which discontent reconstitutes itself as violent protest can (sometimes) be eliminated, the aftermath is usually the dispersal of the dissidents who re-group for self-righteous revenge. Extreme piety remains both the language of discontent and the logic for political resistance as a moral act. Yet if it can, resistance exits the jurisdictions of government and remains quiet. Even in today's crowded world, I suggest, space still needs to be found to make such exits feasible.

[49] On Nana Asma'u and her poetry see Boyd and Mack, 1999. There is an explicit element of hatred (as well as triumphalism) in the war poems which may reflect local feeling among the Sokoto elite at the time. The whole issue of hatred is hard to research retrospectively except in poetry, where it may of course be more rhetorical than real – a poet's licence to dramatize? Certainly fear (and panic) among rural Muslim women was witnessed by Clapperton (1829, 226–7) in the 1820s – with some reason: if caught by the enemy, their hands were cut off (Lander 1830 vol. II, 36, 43). Today, the conflict between Muslims and Christians is generating, I think, a degree of hatred that is worrying, as hatreds not only persist but can be passed on down generations: mention of the 'Sokoto Caliphate' (and not just *Boko Haram*) today can elicit explicit fury even from academic historians and social scientists.

Bibliography

Abraham, R.C., 1962, *Dictionary of the Hausa Language*, 2nd edn, London: University of London Press.

Adeleye, R.A., 1968, 'The Dilemma of the Wazir', *Journal of the Historical Society of Nigeria*. 4 (2) 285–98.

Adeleye, R.A., 1971, *Power and Diplomacy in Northern Nigeria, 1804–1906: Sokoto Caliphate and Its Enemies*. London: Longman.

Al-Hajj, M.A., 1968, 'Asl al-Wanqariyin'. *Kano Studies*, 1 (4) 7–42.

Al-Hajj, M.A., 1973, 'The Mahdist Tradition in Northern Nigeria'. PhD thesis, Ahmadu Bello University, Zaria.

Alkali, H., 1968, 'The "Mahdi" of Toranke', *Kano Studies*, 1 (4), 92–95.

Al-Nagar, 'Umar, 1972, *The Pilgrimage Tradition in West Africa*. Khartoum: Khartoum University Press.

Batran, A.A., 2003, *Tobacco Smoking under Islamic Law: Controversy Over its Introduction*. Beltsville MD: Amana Publications.

Bello, Muhamad, 1812, (ed. C.E.J. Whitting, 1951). *Infaq al-maisur*. London: Luzac.

Bello, Omar, n.d., *Ulama' and Colonialism in Nigeria: Risalah ila'l-mu'asirin*. Sokoto: The Islamic Academy.

Boyd, J. and B. Mack, 1999, *The Collected Works of Nana Asma'u, Daughter of Usman dan Fodio (1793–1864)*. 2nd edn. Ibadan: Bookman Publishers.

Brenner, L., 1987, 'Muslim Thought in 18th Century West Africa: the case of Shaikh Usman Dan Fodio', in N. Levtzion and J.O. Voll (eds), *Eighteenth Century Renewal and Reform in Islam*. Syracuse NY: Syracuse University Press, 39–67.

Brenner, L., 1992, 'The Jihad Debate between Sokoto and Borno: Historical Analysis of Islamic Political Discourse in Nigeria', in J.F. Ade Ajayi and J.D.Y. Peel (eds) *People and Empires in African History*. London: Longman, 21-43.

Clapperton, H., 1966 [1829], *Journal of a Second Expedition into the Interior of Africa from the Bight of Benin to Soccatoo*. London: Frank Cass.

Dalen, D. van, 2012, 'This Filthy Plant: The Inspiration of a Central Sudanic Scholar in the Debate on Tobacco', *Islamic Africa*, 3 (2), 227–47.

Daumas, E., 1856, *Le Grand Désert*. Paris: M. Levy.

Denham, D. and H. Clapperton, W. Oudney, 1828, *Narrative of Travels & Discoveries in Northern and Central Africa in the Years 1822, 1823 and 1824*. London: John Murray.

El-Awa, M.S., 1982, *Punishment in Islamic Law*. Indianapolis: American Trust.

El-Masri, F.H. (ed. and trans.) 1978, '*Uthman ibn Fudi: Bayan wujub al-hijra 'ala 'l-'ibad*. Khartoum: Khartoum University Press.

Ferguson, D.E., 1973, 'Nineteenth Century Hausaland, Being a Description by Imam Imoru of the Land, Economy and Society of his People'. PhD thesis, UCLA.

Higazi, A., 2011, 'The Jos Crisis: A Recurrent Nigerian Tragedy.' Discussion paper 2 (January). Abuja: Friedrich-Ebert-Stiftung.

Hiskett, M., 1960, 'Kitab al-Farq: A Work on the Habe Kingdoms Attributed to Uthman dan Fodio', *Bulletin, School of Oriental and African Studies*, 23 (3), 558–79.

Hiskett, M., 1962, 'An Islamic Tradition of Reform in the Western Sudan from the 16th to the 18th century', *Bulletin, School of Oriental and African Studies*, 25 (3), 577–96.

Hiskett, M., 1963 (trans.), *Tazyin al-Waraqat*. Ibadan: Ibadan University Press.

Hiskett, M., 1973, *Sword of Truth: The Life and Times of the Shehu Usuman Dan Fodio*. New York: Oxford University Press.

Kane, Ousmane, 2003, *Muslim Modernity in Postcolonial Nigeria*. Leiden: Brill.

Kano Chronicle, trans. H.R. Palmer, 1928, in *Sudanese Memoirs* vol.3. Lagos: Government Printer.

Kirk-Greene, A.H.M. and P. Newman, 1971, *West African Travels and Adventures: Two*

Autobiographical Narratives from Northern Nigeria. New Haven CT: Yale University Press.

Lander, R.L., 1830, 1967, *Records of Captain Clapperton's Last Expedition in Africa*. 2 vols. London: Colburn & Bentley; reprinted, F. Cass.

Last, M., 1966, 'A Solution to the Problems of Dynastic Chronology in 19th century Zaria & Kano', *Journal, Historical Society of Nigeria*, 3 (3) 461–69.

Last, M., 1967a, *The Sokoto Caliphate*. London: Longman.

Last, M., 1967b, 'The Arabic-Script Literature of the North: vol. 2. Fulfulde Poetry, 43–46'. *Second Interim Report, Northern History Research Scheme*. Zaria: Ahmadu Bello University.

Last, M., 1980, Last, M. 1983a. 'From Sultanate to Caliphate: Kano, 1450–1800', in B.M. Barkindo (ed), *Studies in the History of Kano*. Ibadan: Heinemann, 67–91.

Last, M., 1983b, 'A Kano Anomaly: A Terracotta Figurine' in B.M. Barkindo (ed), *Studies in the History of Kano*. Ibadan: Heinemann, 207– 8.

Last, M., 1992, 'Injustice and Legitimacy in the Early Sokoto Caliphate', in J.F.A. Ajayi, J.D.Y. Peel (eds), *Peoples and Empires in African History: essays in memory of Michael Crowder*. London: Longman, 45–57.

Last, M., 1993, 'History as Religion: Deconstructing the Magians ('Maguzawa') of Nigerian Hausaland', in J.-P. Chrétien (ed.), *L'Invention Religieuse en Afrique: Histoire et Religion en Afrique Noire*. Paris: Karthala, 267–96.

Last, M., 1997a, 'The 'Colonial Caliphate' Of Northern Nigeria', in D. Robinson et J-L. Triaud (éds), *Les Temps des Marabouts: Itinéraires et Stratégies Islamiques en Afrique Occidentale Française v. 1880–1960*. Paris: Karthala, 67–82.

Last, M., 1997b, 'Sokoto' in *Encyclopaedia of Islam*, vol. 9, 711–12. Leiden: Brill.

Last, M., 2000, 'Shaikh 'Uthman b. Fudi', *Encyclopaedia of Islam*, 10, 949–51, Leiden: Brill.

Last, M., 2011, 'Another Geography: Risks to Health as Perceived in a Deep-rural Environment in Hausaland', *Anthropology & Medicine*, 18 (2), 217–29.

Last, M. and M.A. al-Hajj, 1965, 'Attempts at Defining a Muslim in 19th Century Hausaland & Bornu', *Journal, Historical Society of Nigeria*, 3, 2, 231–40.

Lavers, J.E., 1971, 'Islam in the Borno Caliphate', *Odu*, 5, 27–53.

Linden, I., 1974, *The Isawa Mallams c. 1850–1919: Some Problems in the Religious History of Northern Nigeria* (Occasional paper). Zaria: Ahmadu Bello University.

Loimeier, R., 1997, *Islamic Reform and Political Change in Northern Nigeria*. Evanston IL: Northwestern University Press.

Lovejoy, E., 1985, *Caravans of Kola: The Hausa Kola Trade, 1700–1900*. Zaria: ABU Press.

Lovejoy, E. and J.S. Hogendorn, 1990, 'Revolutionary Mahdism and Resistance to Colonial Rule in the Sokoto Caliphate 1905-6,' *Journal of African History*, 31 (2) 217–44.

Lugard, F.D., 1902, *Northern Nigeria – Annual Report*. London: HMSO.

Mohammed, K., 2006, *Borno in the Rabih Years 1893–1901* (BSS Series 2). Maiduguri: University of Maiduguri.

Muhammad, Junaid b., 1957, *Tarihin Fulani* [Hausa trans.], *Dabt al-Multaqatat* [n.d. Arabic]. Zaria: NRLA.

Patton, A., 1987, 'An Islamic Frontier Polity: The Ningi Mountains of Northern Nigeria, 1846-1902', in I. Kopytoff (ed.). *The African Frontier: The Reproduction of Traditional African Societies*. Bloomington IN: Indiana University Press, 195–213.

Saeed, A.G., 1992, 'A biographical study of Shaykh Sa'id b. Hayat (1887–1978) and British Policy towards the Mahdiyya in Northern Nigeria 1900–1960'. PhD thesis, Bayero University, Kano.

Shea, J., 2010, *The Ada Tradition in Kano Historiography*. Katsina: Lugga Press.

Siddiqi, F.R., 1989, *Shaykh 'Uthman ibn Fudi: Hisn al-Afham Min Juyush al-Awham*. Kano: Quality Press.

Smith, M.G., 1997, *Government in Kano 1350–1950*. Boulder CO: Westview Press.

Umar, M.S., 2005, *Islam and Colonialism: Intellectual Responses of Muslims of Northern Nigeria to British Colonial Rule*. Leiden: Brill.

Usman, Y.B., 1981, *The Transformation of Katsina 1400–1883*. Zaria: ABU Press.
Wagemakers, Joas, 2012, 'The Enduring Legacy of the Second Saudi State: Quietist and Radical Wahhabi Contestations of Al-Walā' Wa-l-Barā", *International Journal of Middle East Studies*, 44 (1), 93–110.
Wilbert, J., 1987, *Tobacco and Shamanism in South America*. New Haven CT: Yale University Press.
Zahradeen, M.S., 1983, 'The Place of Mosques in the History of Kano', in B.M. Barkindo, *Studies in the History of Kano*. Ibadan: Heinemann, 57–66.

3

Contemporary Islamic sects & groups in northern Nigeria

ABDUL RAUFU MUSTAPHA
& MUKHTAR U. BUNZA

Introduction

A major bone of contention in the politics of religion in Nigeria is the relative sizes of her Muslim and Christian populations.[1] What is not in doubt, however, is that in the 19 states that make up the three northern geo-political zones of the country, Muslims are a majority, along with a significant Christian minority and a generous sprinkling of followers of African Traditional Religions. However, as Map 3.1 shows, there are significant variations in the distribution of Muslims between these states. The states in the north-west zone have the highest percentage of Muslims in their total population, followed by the states in the north-east and the north-central zones in that descending order. The divisions *within* this Muslim population are the subject of this chapter.[2]

At the start of the Sokoto Jihad in 1804, virtually all Muslims in northern Nigeria subscribed to Sunni Islam of the Maliki School, with most elites also belonging to the Qadiriyya *tariqa*, or Brotherhood. By 1830, however, we see the introduction of the rival Tijaniyya *tariqa*. In the contemporary period, the Islamic doctrinal landscape has further fragmented into a myriad of competing sects and groups, including different groups of Sufis, Salafists, jihadists, Shi'ites, Islamic women's organizations, ethnic Yoruba Muslim organizations and a host of idiosyn-

[1] For an extended discussion of the issues in contention between Muslim and Christian communities in Nigeria see the companion volume to this one: Mustapha & Ehrhardt (eds), forthcoming, *Creed & Grievance: Muslims, Christians & Society in Northern Nigeria*, James Currey.

[2] According to the Pew Forum on Religion & Public Life, the Sunni constitute 38% of the national Muslim population, with the Shi'a (12%), the Ahmadiyya (3%), the 'something else' (2%), the 'Just a Muslim' (42%), and the 'Don't Know' (4%) (Pew 2010, 21). Most of the 'Just a Muslim' are also likely to be Sunni-inclined. For a discussion of the sizes of the different affiliations, see Ostien (2012).

Map 3.1 Nigeria, showing various boundaries, and percentages of
Muslims by current state per 1963 census
(courtesy of University of Wisconsin-Madison African Studies Program and Cartographic
Laboratory; percentages of Muslims by current state from Ostien 2012)

cratic sects, some oriented towards violent politics. This process of the
fragmentation of Muslim identities has resulted in the individualization
of religious affiliation and heightened competition for followership in a
'prayer economy' led by the *'ulama*. The result of this long process is the
rise of contentious religious politics which is the subject of this chapter.
In this chapter we examine all the major groups and actors within the
Muslim communities of northern Nigeria, their doctrinal positions and
ritual practices, their claims on Muslims and others, and their political
orientation towards the wider Nigerian society. We emphasize both the
ways these Muslim groups perceive themselves and how they are perceived
by others. Sometimes, there might be contradictions between the two,
but such contradictory perceptions are nevertheless important as, right or
wrong, they frame the interactions between the different Muslim groups.

Islamic sects: histories, beliefs, rituals & social composition

The formation of associations to advance the cause of the religion is not new in the historical evolution of Islam. Different sects, ideologies and schools of thought have emerged within the religion throughout Islamic history. Within the context of the macro split between Sunni and Shi'a Islam, there are four Sunni and three Shi'a Schools of Law (*fiqh*) and about 313 Sufi Brotherhoods throughout the Sunni Muslim world. Historically, therefore, Islam has been characterized by the pluralism of its expression in specific geographical, historical and social contexts. An important issue raised in this chapter is the challenge to this pluralism by the competing doctrinal claims of different contemporary Muslim groups in northern Nigeria.

In northern Nigeria, the first Islamic ideology was the Sunni version of Islam based on the Maliki School of *Fiqh*. Thereafter, Qadiriyya and Tijaniyya Sufi Brotherhoods or *tariqa* (pl. *turuq*) emerged. More recently – from the 1970s – Sunni reformists, vehemently opposed to the *turuq* and followers of Shi'a thought, have also emerged. Historically, therefore, there has been a tendency of fragmentation and individuation of Islamic identities in the region over time, especially after the dislocations caused by colonial conquest (see Umar 2005). Our objective in this chapter is to make clear some of the doctrinal differences between these groups who compete, sometimes fiercely, for the allegiance of the Muslim community. In analysing these groups, we place emphasis on four things:
  (a) their historical background;
  (b) their doctrinal beliefs;
  (c) their ritual practices; and
  (d) their social composition and connections with the wider society.
Furthermore, as indicated earlier, we seek to capture both the self-perception of the groups, and the way they are perceived by others, since both are important in defining their roles in society.

SUFISM

The Sufis remain the majority group within northern Nigerian Islam. Sufism is the individual spiritual quest to get closer to God. It can also be defined as an attempt to interpret Islam in the context of the prevailing – often seen as corrupting – times. According to Shaikh Ibrahim Niasse, the 'Sufi is the son of his hour (*ibn waqtihi*)' (Cisse 1984). Sufism, or *tasawwuf*,

aims, by purifying man's heart and employing his senses and faculties in the way of God, to live a life at the spiritual level. *Tasawwuf* also enables man, through constant performance of the acts of worshipping God, to deepen his consciousness of being a servant of God. It enables him to renounce the world with respect to its transient dimension and the face of it that is turned to human desires and fancies, and awakens him to the other world and to the face of this world that is turned toward the Divine Beautiful Names. (World of Tasawwuf 2008)

In short, Sufism is the cultivation of good character, awareness of God and surrendering to God's will, often in the context of a challenging environment. The Sufis are therefore defined as:

Muslims who take seriously God's call to perceive his presence both in the world and in the self ... [and] stress inwardness over outwardness, contemplation over action, spiritual development over legalism, and cultivation of the soul over social interaction. (J. Esposito, cited in Hill 2010, 16–17)

Based on this philosophical outlook, certain ritual practices are common to the Sufis. These include the rigorous fulfilment of all obligatory religious duties, the undertaking of additional voluntary prayers day and night, the constant remembrance (*zikr* or *dhikr*) of Allah, the unceasing *salawaat* (invocations of blessings) on Prophet Muhammad, fasting, charity, *zuhd* (abstinence) and *juhd* (exertion in the way of Allah) as exemplified by the Prophet (Qadiriya n.d.). The Sufi organizations therefore performed rituals and rites through which the purification of the self is given prominence over the wholesale transformation of society. However, many Sufi orders are identified with specific ritualistic practices which constantly seek 'to realise the presence of God' (World of Tasawwuf 2008). Sufi emphasis was therefore on the transformation of the individual on the premise that the society can hardly be reformed if the individual's mind remains corrupted. The Sufis tend to favour *jihad al nafsi* (internal struggle to conquer the self) to *jihad al-kharij* (external jihad targeted at the conquest of others) (Laremont 2011, 164). Another important aspect of Sufism is the key distinction between the Shaikhs and their disciples. The Shaikhs are seen as God's chosen spiritual guides for the people, blessed with *Baraka* (charisma or grace), the fruits of which can be transmitted to their followers who seek *tarbiyat al-nafs*, or guiding of the soul. These Shaikhs command considerable reverence with important political and social ramifications as exemplified by the politics of modern Senegal and northern Nigeria. Among the key characteristics of Sufi groups are their mysticism and their veneration of saints. This reverence for saints and Shaikhs is an important distinction between the Sufis and the more iconoclastic Salafists.

Qadiriyya

The Qadiriyya Order was named after Abd al-Qadir al-Jilani (c. 1077–1166), a Sufi teacher of enormous prestige and learning whose family lineage is said to go right back to the Prophet, conferring on him the position of a *quṭb* (pole or axis) (Ben Amara 2011, 76). He was buried in Baghdad and his tomb is a pilgrimage site (Spencer 1998; Schimmel 1975). Shaikh 'Uthman dan Fodio identified with the Qadiriyya Order. In fact, so strong was this identification that his followers were sometimes referred to as 'Qadirawa' – followers of Qadiriyya. The Qadiriyya is therefore the oldest of the Sufi orders in northern Nigeria. In a major work, *Ihya' as-Sunna*, Shaikh 'Uthman dan Fodio 'took pains to distinguish Sufism from *bid'a*' (evil innovations) (Loimeier 1997b, 20). As we shall see, subsequent anti-Sufi reformers took a different view. There are a few characteristics which distinguished the Qadiriyya from the other Sufi orders. For example, they are less centralized in their approach to organization and are often flexible in the adaptation of their Sufi rituals to changing circumstances. Followers of Qadiriyya are therefore invariably less rigid in ritual practices, compared, for instance, to the Tijaniyya. Kano City has the largest number of Qadiriyya followers, despite the roots of the order in Sokoto. Important rituals also distinguish the 'traditional' Qadiriyya of Sokoto from the better organized 'reformed' Qadiriyya of Kano.

In contemporary northern Nigeria, the dominant Qadiriyya sect developed around the Kano-based scholar, Shaikh Nasiru Kabara (Loimeier 1997b). The Qadiriyya-Nasiriyya came under pressure from the dynamic expansion of the Tijaniyya-Ibrahimiyya (the Tijaniyya Order affiliated to Shaikh Ibrahim Niasse of Kaolack, Senegal) in the mid-twentieth century. To revitalize the Qadiriyya, Nasiru Kabara adopted some rituals and rites similar to the Tijaniyya. These helped him to strengthen the Qadiriyya which was thereby transformed into a religious mass movement along the lines of the Tijaniyya-Ibrahimiyya. Shaikh Kabara's important contribution from the 1930s was the transformation of an elitist, cerebral, 'traditional', religious order, as in Sokoto, into a 'reformed' mass movement, based on expressive group rituals, as in Kano. When the Emir of Kano Abdullahi Bayero went on *hajj* to Mecca in 1937, Kabara used the opportunity to give a senior member of the Emir's entourage, Wali Suleiman, a letter for the Khalifa of the Qadiriyya-Samaniyya in Mecca, Shaikh Abu-I-Hassan as-Sammani. Shaikh Kabara requested the Samaniyya leader to initiate him into his organization and make him his *Muqaddam* (authoritative representative, propagator and spiritual guide to other disciples) in Kano. Abu-I-Hassan was reported to have been so impressed by Shaikh Kabara's versatility in Islam that he granted his request by appointing him the leader of the Qadiriyya-Samaniyya in Kano. Kabara subsequently established direct contact with various other original centres of the different branches of the Qadiriyya and once in possession of the various *Silasil* (pl. – spiritual chain of authority) became the focus of attention for other followers and *mallamai* – scholars – of the Qadiriyya in Kano and Nigeria who wanted to renew their *Silsila* (sing,) through him.

Between 1937 and the late 1950s Kabara's bid for a unified leadership within the Qadiriyya in Kano and Nigeria was essentially successful (Paden 1973). Qadiriyya is therefore not just an important religious group within Nigerian Islam; it also has the distinction of claiming an unchallenged direct connection to the past through the Sokoto Caliphate. From the patterns of authority and community within Qadiriyya in Kano several important points can be deduced (cf. Adamu n.d.). First, association with Qadiriyya in the nineteenth century was limited to Fulani *mallamai* (traditional Muslim scholars/clerics) and administrators (who derived their authority from the Fulani leaders of the jihad) and to North African Arabs (who did not integrate themselves religiously into the Kano milieu). At this point, Qadiriyya was not a mass phenomenon, but an ethnically segmented religious orientation. Second, with the establishment of colonial rule, elements in the Kano Arab community re-affirmed their own direct spiritual links with North African sources of spiritual authority. Third, members of the Hausa *mallamai* class began to associate with this renewed form of North African Qadiriyya and were recruited into leadership positions within one generation. Fourth, part of the success of Qadiriyya in the Hausa sector of society was due to an emphasis on group worship and the focusing of activities within local mosques. Last, the 'legitimate' successor to the leadership of traditional Fulani Qadiriyya in Kano (Nasiru Kabara) affiliated with various independent lines of Qadiriyya authority as a reinforcement of his 'inherited' authority and through this 'achieved status' consolidated the Arab, Hausa and Fulani strands of Qadiriyya in Kano into a single organizational structure – 'reformed' Qadiriyya (Paden 1973).

This consolidation was accomplished partly by extending Qadiriyya from an elite base to a mass base. And in this process, the support of wealthy Hausa merchants was essential. At the mass level, Qadiriyya-Nasiriyya was also a redirection of the emerging tide of local Kano nationalism which increasingly demanded that religious – and by extension political – authority and focus be shifted from Sokoto and North Africa to Kano itself. However, because of the mass base of Qadiriyya-Nasiriyya, it was no longer possible for the Qadiriyya elite to identify completely with the Kano ruling aristocratic class. Thus, while brotherhood leaders might act as advisers to the aristocratic class, they have also tended to guard their independent status as autonomous actors. Perhaps as a consequence of this shift from elite to a mass base, the brotherhood leadership became involved in two relatively new functions: the interpretation of doctrine specifically for local use and the inspiration, through rituals and ceremonies, of mass worship and following (Adamu n.d.). Important rituals include *wird* (litanies), *dhikr* (remembrance and praising the Prophet), *bandiri* (religious music and incantations accompanied by drumming – this ritual is very specific to Qadiriyya-Nasiriyya), *maukibi* (processions of thousands of followers to the graveyard of Qadiriyya saints in Kano), *ashafa* (special congregations during Ramadan for the Hausa interpretation of *al-Shifa'*, a hagiographic book on the Prophet Muhammad) and, most importantly, the *maulid annabiyyi* (the birthday of the Prophet) celebrated on the eleventh night of the Islamic month of *Rabiul Auwal*.

Through these rituals, the Qadiriyya masses gained concrete social and organizational form in Kano and other centres of Islam in northern Nigeria. There was also the sewing of distinct uniforms, often of modern para-military design, by the leadership and members. These group activities reinforce the intimate bonds of loyalty between the leaders and their followers. However, the most distinctive aspect of Qadiriyya-Nasiriyya rituals is the celebration of the birthday of its founder, Abd al-Qadir. This was an innovation introduced by Shaikh Nasiru Kabara. According to Adamu (n.d.):

> Reformed Qadiriyya has placed a special emphasis on group celebration of the founder's birthday (Maulidin Abdulkadir). It serves as a yearly meeting for brotherhood leaders and members from throughout northern Nigeria. Delegations from each of the major northern cities congregate in Kano for a full day of prayers and activities. The central feature of the day is a group procession, arranged by area delegations, from the home of Nasiru Kabara in the Jarkasa area of Kabara ward to the Kano Qadiriyya burial ground west of Kano City, where prayers are said over the graves of Kano Qadiriyya saints. The procession also serves as the only time in the year when men, women, and children all participate in the same worship service. The order of procession indicates roughly the hierarchy of authority within the Qadiriyya elite.

In spite of the fact that the Qadiriyya led by Kabara claims connection with Shaikh 'Uthman dan Fodio and the Sokoto jihad movement, there is a very wide gap between the Qadiriyya practised and led by Nasiru Kabara, on the one hand, and what is conceived as Qadiriyya in Sokoto. Important rituals separate the two contemporary versions of Qadiriyya. In the Sokoto version of Qadiriyya there is no *bandiri*, no *maukibi* procession, no celebration of *Maulid* (birthday) of Abd al-Qadir and no distinct uniform of any kind for rituals or celebrations. These bonding and emotional rituals, through which Qadiriyya-Nasiriyya in Kano became a mass movement, are completely lacking in the version of Qadiriyya still practised in Sokoto.

Shaikh Nasiru Kabara died in October 1994 and his son, Shaikh Qaribullah Nasiru Kabara took over the leadership of the community. As Adamu (n.d.) noted, the chief functions of the Qadiriyya leadership remain those of initiating new members, training of a new generation of scholars, spiritual intermediation on behalf of members, financing and organizing the various activities of the brotherhood, and communicating with all segments of the brotherhood, local and international. Equally important is the administration of rituals from the weekly *Zikr* gatherings to the group *wird*. Some Qadiriyya Imams also lead twice weekly *bandiri* sessions.

Tijaniyya

The Tijaniyya is possibly the largest Sufi order in Nigeria. The composition of membership tends to be biased towards males of all ages, regardless of social and economic status. Historically, the Tijaniyya followers are said to be relatively strict in religious rituals but more radical in their political orientation, compared to the Qadiriyya which is regarded as more relaxed in ritual matters but more conservative and pro-establishment in its politics. The political radicalism of Tijaniyya has a long history; during colonial occupation in the late nineteenth century, more Tijaniyya Emirs waged wars of resistance against the British, compared to the Qadiriyya Emirs (see introduction to this volume). It has also been argued that in the colonial period, the social basis of the Tijaniyya was the mercantile classes and the relatively rich farmer-traders in Kano, Zaria and southern Katsina Provinces, who supported the radical populist anti-establishment party, the Northern Elements Progressive Union (NEPU), while the Qadiriyya tended to support the traditional aristocracy and its party, the Northern People's Congress (NPC). In the 1960s the Tijaniyya were virtual sworn enemies of the NPC-led Northern Regional Government led by the Sardauna of Sokoto. This was partly due to the non-aristocratic social basis of Tijaniyya, to its long history of political and social radicalism and to its ties to Emir Sanusi of Kano – another thorn in the Sardauna's side.

The Tijaniyya Brotherhood was founded in 1781 by Shaikh Ahmad Tijani (1737–1815), an Algerian scholar who migrated to the Moroccan city of Fez – many Tijanis continue to go on pilgrimage to Fez. The Order became very popular in North Africa in the nineteenth and twentieth centuries from whence it spread into West Africa. Al-Hajj Umar Tal Al-Futi of Futa Jalon introduced the Tijaniyya Sufi brotherhood into West Africa, and he was made the Khalifa of Tijaniyya in Sahelian West Africa in 1830. He was in Sokoto and Borno on his way from Makah in the 1830s – spreading Tijaniyya ideology within the predominantly Qadiriyya Sokoto Caliphate. With the introduction of Tijaniyya, the Qadiriyya gradually lost its spiritual monopoly in the Sokoto Caliphate (Robinson 1985). The dominant Tijaniyya Order in Senegal is based in the Holy city of Tivaouane. A secondary Senegalese Tijaniyya Order, founded by the Niasse family and based at Kaolack, has followers in the millions right across West Africa. It is this Niassene Order, also known as Tijaniyya-Ibrahimiyya – after its leader Shaikh Ibrahim Niasse – that is particularly powerful across Nigeria. Some have described Tijaniyya-Ibrahimiyya as the 'largest single Muslim movement in West Africa' (Cisse 1984). Kaolack is also an important centre of religious pilgrimage, just below the Moroccan city of Fez in the Tijaniyya pecking order.[3]

For the Tijani adept, Islam consists of three interlocking parts. The first is Sharia, containing *l'itiqaadaat* (sets of core beliefs about the Prophet, the Holy Books, the Day of Judgement and the Hereafter), *ibadat* (worship rituals performed in glorification of Allah including salat, zakat, fasting, *hajj* and jihad), *muamalat* (contractual obligations between the faithful and all of Allah's creatures – including marriage contracts, settlement of disputes, contractual terms for trade and loans), *kaffarat* (expiation of sins against God and his creatures) and *uqubaat* (grave sins requiring capital punishment). The second is *al-Iman*, concerned with the spiritual purification of the heart of the faithful, while the third is *al-Ihsan*, the search for the highest stage of religious consciousness signifying closeness to God.[4] Contrary to Salafist emphasis on *ibadat*, the Tijaniyya see it as a precondition for *zuhd* (asceticism) which then leads to the right *al-Iman*. Within this Tijani emphasis on *al-Iman*, members of the Order must accept three obligations: *Lazimi, Wazifa and Dhikr Jumu'at. Lazimi* is the most important work of the initiate through which he tries to emulate the ways of the Prophet and his Companions. The ritualistic aspect of *lazimi* involves the recitation of three liturgies – asking forgiveness for sins, praising the Prophet and seeking God's grace – on a daily basis. While *lazimi* is recited on an individual basis, the *wazifa* is a group recitation, also performed on a daily basis. *Dhikr Jumu'at*, by contrast, is a group recital conducted only on Fridays. Within Tijani practice of *al-Ihsan*, the initiate must locate himself on a nine-step scale of self-purification, starting from step one, *al-taubah* (repentance) to step nine, *al-ma'arifah*, connoting a high level of understanding of, and identification with, God's powers to such an extent as to become capable of defying the conventional laws of society and nature.

Central to the appeal of Tijaniyya-Ibrahimiyya is the concept of *fayda* (in some parts of northern Nigeria, the group is known by this term), literally

---

[3] For details of the evolution and rapid expansion of the Tijaniyya during the colonial era see Paden (1973), Loimeier (1997b) and Umar (2000).
[4] Interview with Shaikh Mukhtar Adam Abdallah, Jos, 18 April 2014.

meaning flood, effusion or superabundance. It is interpreted as the 'flux of Divine grace, mercy and love passing through the Prophet to God's creation':

> God is said to be a well, 'whose Being is continuous and without end'; knowledge of God is the water, 'so precious it cannot be thrown away and yet cannot be put back into a well already overflowing'; the Prophet is a bucket 'that never wants repair' drawing the water from the well; Shaykh Ahmad Tijani is the 'tireless worker who continually draws water from the well'; and Shaykh Ibrahim himself is a basin next to the well, 'an extraordinary spiritual adept who has received so much in the way of Divine Gnosis that he must communicate this Gnosis to others or it will overflow'. (Wright n.d.)

Through his possession of *fayda*, Shaikh Ibrahim Niasse is seen by his followers as the connection to God's all-powerful grace. For the Qadiriyya, Tijani emphasis on *fayda* and the resulting claim of rebirth or union with God (*wusul*) was condemned as an 'innovation' fuelled by 'emotional excess' (Paden 1973, 132).[5] Another significant Tijani belief is the recitation of the litany of *salat al-fatih* in praise of the Prophet. According to Shaikh Ahmad Tijani, the founder of Tijaniyya, reciting the litany once was equivalent in benefits to 'all the praises to God made in the universe ... to the recitation of the Koran six thousand times' (Kane 2003, 133).

Within the Nigerian context, multitudes of locally competing networks have emerged within Tijaniyya-Ibrahimiyya. In Kano, the stupendously wealthy scholar-trader Shaikh Isyaku Rabiu is an acknowledged leader, though some factions dispute his claim; some other factions align with Shaikh Dahiru Bauchi. The Tijaniyya has a headquarters located within Shaikh Isyaku Rabiu's house. Another leader is Khalifa Ismaila Ibrahim. Two major social values of the Tijaniyya are the veneration of its pantheon of Shaikhs and the pursuit of education through its *Zawiya* (local networks of initiates).The group has uniforms for its members which are used during special occasions/celebrations, although uniforms are not used during everyday worship. Being a Sufi group it has specific ritual practices that distinguish members from the followers of other Islamic sects, the veneration of its Shaikhs being one of them (Spencer 1998).

SALAFIST – ANTI-SUFI GROUPS

Jama'atu Izalatil Bid'a wa Iqamat al-Sunna (Izala or JIBWIS)

Though the two Sufi orders share the introspection of Sufism, they differ in terms of their pantheons of saints, their social basis and their

---

[5] See also Hiskett (1980) and Seesemann (2011) for more detailed analysis of *fayda* and the criticisms against it.

ritual practices. Importantly, they also competed for followership and influence in the 'prayer economy', with the Qadiriyya accusing the Tijaniyya of 'emotional exuberance'. Furthermore, even within each *tariqa*, especially within the Tijaniyya-Ibrahimiyya, there were frequent factional disputes for clerical supremacy. However, all these differences paled into insignificance when the Sufis were challenged in the 1970s by reformist Salafists, who were fellow Sunnis, but were bitterly opposed to Sufism. Until the 1970s, much of the internal politics of the Muslim communities of northern Nigeria was shaped by the competition between the different networks of the *turuq* (see Paden 1973). The Salafist groups have made substantial inroad into the followership of the Sufi orders (Loimeier 1997b), but the Sufi followers are still the majority within the Muslim community. The nature of this Salafist challenge to the established Sufi order is key to understanding the nature of doctrinal fragmentation and social disorder in contemporary northern Nigeria.

In the face of the competition between the Sufi orders in the 1960s, the *Jama'atu Nasril Islam* (JNI) was formed in 1962 at the initiative of Premier Ahmadu Bello, the Sardauna of Sokoto, ostensibly to enlighten and unify the Muslim *umma*. With the death of Ahmadu Bello in 1966, the JNI broke into factions and by 1971 the gulf between the factions became insurmountable. A key figure in these disputes was Shaikh Abubakar Gumi, adviser to Premier Ahmadu Bello on religious affairs. In 1972, Gumi published a book, *al-Aqida as-sahiha*, in which he sets out a frontal attack on the core principles of the two Sufi orders. For the first time in the history of northern Nigerian Islam, established Sufi beliefs and rituals were subjected to a scathing rejection. An important concept in Shaikh Gumi's thought is that the era of *Jahiliyya* (Era of Ignorance), which was commonly used within Islam to refer to the historical period preceding the appearance of Prophet Mohammed, was actually a contemporary condition of society in many parts of the world including the Islamic states. Unlike the Sufi emphasis on personal purification, Gumi set out an agenda for the transformation of a society he believed was caught up in this ignorance. Furthermore, consistent with Wahhabi thinking, Gumi emphasized the importance of *ibadat* (ritual practices), *taoheed* (the uniqueness of God) and the rejection of a special role which the Sufis have ascribed to the Prophet. From this doctrinal critique, Gumi condemns a number of rituals associated with the Sufi orders and at a public sermon in Kaduna on 11 April 1977, he pronounced that anyone who recited the key Tijani litany, *salat al-fatih* was an apostate who was eligible to be killed. Marriage to a Tijani was also declared illegal, since according to his logic, an apostate is not a Muslim (Laremont 2011, 157–8). According to the Tijaniyya leader, Shaikh Dahiru Bauchi:

Before the white man came, any town you went to, all you had to do was do ablution and go into a mosque and say your prayers. You had no need to ask who was the Imam. [...] Gumi has brought his new religion which is called *Izala* and they say that we are infidels. (Laremont 2011, 146)

While Shaikh Abubakar Gumi was venerated by his followers as a *mujaddid* (reformer of the religion), 'he was attacked by his opponents as the personification of Satan' (Loimeier 1997b, 179).

In March 1978 in Jos, the capital of Plateau State, disciples of Shaikh Gumi, led by Shaikh Ismaila Idris, established a new association, the *Jama'atu Izalatil Bid'a wa iqamat al-Sunna* (Society for the Eradication of Innovation and the Reinstatement of Tradition), popularly known as *Izala* or JIBWIS. There is a rich and extensive literature on the *Izala*, (Loimeier 1997a, 1997b; Umar 1999; Kane 2003; Ben Amara 2011; and Brigaglia 2012). Ideologically, *Izala* is vehemently opposed to Sufism, considering many of the Sufi beliefs and practices to be heretical innovations, if not outright idolatrous. According to Shaikh Idris, by associating their Shaikhs with Allah in worship, the *turuq* are guilty of *shirk* (polytheism) (Umar 1993, 47). The Sufis, by contrast, believe that the Qur'an (Chapter 43:48–49) affirms the role of mediators (*walis*), 'saints to whom God has granted knowledge and Divine wisdom. They address different levels of intervention by spirits' (Lawrence 2006, 185–6). *Izala* also condemned many *turuq* rituals and practices, such as bowing and showing deferential respect to Shaikhs and parents in a way that allegedly elevated such individuals to a status approaching that of God. For its literalist interpretations of Islam, *Izala* borrows heavily from Muhammad ibn Abdulwahhab's *Kitaab At-Tawheed*, and selectively from Shaikh 'Uthman dan Fodio. *Izala* is also vehemently opposed to the Shi'a group that has emerged in northern Nigeria since the late 1970s.

To drive home this doctrinal differentiation between the 'right' and 'wrong' paths, *Izala* developed ritual practices which marked it out from the rest. One set of changes challenged the established patterns of praying. *Izala* challenged the commonly agreed time for praying the first afternoon congregational prayer, *zuhur*. The specified timing for this prayer is a range between 1 p.m. and 3 p.m. By common consensus in northern Nigeria, most people said this prayer at 2 p.m., but *Izala* insisted on saying the prayer at the earliest opportunity at 1 p.m. *Izala* also changed the timing for the voluntary prayers – *rakatani fajr* – associated with the early morning *subuhi* prayers. Furthermore, *Izala* changed the established tradition of calling the *subuhi* prayers. Traditionally in northern Nigeria, two calls were made for the *subuhi* prayers. While the first alerted the faithful to the approaching time for the prayer, the second was the definitive call to prayers. Traditionally, the phrase '*asalat khairun minan noaum*' (salat is better than sleep) is only said during the second, final, call. However, *Izala* transferred this phrase to the first call to prayers, arguing that prayers must always be better than sleep. For others, however, this is so only when the time for the prayers in due, not before. This rearrangement of phrases often confuses the unwary regarding when it is time to pray. It is especially problematic in the month of Ramadan, when the start of the daily fast coincides with the *subuhi* prayers. *Izala* also adopted the style of restive sitting during prayers – *jalasat isteraha* – which is not a common practice in northern Nigeria. Finally, traditionally in northern Nigeria, Muslims have used rosaries or counting beads (*tesba*) to count out their recitation of various litanies. The Tijaniyya have the most elaborate rosaries of all. *Izala* condemned the use of the *tesba*, claiming it is of Buddhist origins. It was also argued that the Prophet prayed by counting on his fingers. *Izala* adherents now prefer to use Chinese-made electronic counters which they strap to one finger! These ritualistic changes, along with others, such as the 'democratization' of the authority to slaughter the ram during festivities, and changes in the definition and nature of performing the *hajj*[6], had the effect of setting the *Izala* apart from the rest of the Muslim community. There developed a profound process of mutual 'othering' within the Muslim community – the Salafist set against the Sufis. While the *Izala* referred to the Sufis as the *Ahl al-bid'a* (the people of the harmful innovations) the Sufis referred to *Izala* members as the *Ahl al-Ahwā* (people of the [unreasonable?] passions) (Ben Amara 2011, 222).

Izala readily found support among certain groups within northern Nigerian Islam. First, it provided Western-educated Muslims with 'a more rational religion'(Loimeier 1997b, 258), along with providing this middle class, threatened with economic hardship since the late 1970s, with the religious justification for avoiding costly religious rituals and contributions. Second, it appealed to the poor, who could now renounce the high expectations traditional society placed on ceremonies like weddings and child naming without feeling like social failures. Third, it appealed to the youth, increasingly frustrated by lack of opportunities and the hierarchies of deference within traditional society. Fourth, *Izala* appealed to women,

---

[6] Amongst the Sufis, the *'ulama* or those in high religious standing tend to monopolize the ritual slaughter of rams, in the process, keeping the neck of the animal as their 'reward'. *Izala* asserted that every male Muslim was qualified to slaughter rams and kicked against the 'extortion' of parts of the animal. With respect to the *hajj*, there are three types of *hajj*, based on the initial declared intentions of the pilgrim: *Ifrad*, the common type in the Maliki *fiqh* practised in northern Nigeria; *tamatt'ui*, preferred by the Hanbali *fiqh* in Saudi Arabi; and *qiran*. While most northern Nigerian Sufis still practise *ifrad*, *Izala* tends to promote *tamatt'ui*.

especially through the active propagation of women's education which provided these women access to the public domain. Last, it appealed to migrant populations in new colonial cities like Kaduna and Jos, and to those in sections of old cities like the 'settler' quarters in cities like Kano. These settler communities were poorly integrated into the networks of the *turuq* based in the traditional cities, and frequently faced discrimination at the hands of the 'indigenous' Muslims. In many respects, therefore, *Izala* was embraced by a 'modernist' tendency within northern Muslim populations – university academics, dynamic traders in the settler quarters of northern cities and modern-orientated functionaries of state institutions at various levels – desirous of moving beyond the routines and strictures established by the *turuq*.

As Masquelier (2009, 78) noted for Niger Republic, 'Islam has become a medium for expressing ideological, political, and even socio-economic cleavages'. This is true of the rise of *Izala* in both Nigeria and Niger, as dwindling economic opportunities and growing marginalization and feelings of disempowerment fuelled competing Islamic visions of society and the moral order with many gravitating to the belief that the 'economic problems are rooted in immorality and that widespread moral reforms must be instituted before the debilitating effects of poverty and underdevelopment can be reversed' (Masquelier 2009, xvii). By preaching 'individualism, conservation, and the rational utilization of resources' (Masquelier 2009, 89), *Izala*'s social message amounted to the 'reorientation from communal to an individualistic mode of religiosity that seems to be more in tune with the rugged individualism of capitalist social relations' (Umar 1993, 178). While this message resonated with the marginalized or modernist social groups identified above, there are also those 'Muslims for whom Izala's assertive individualism and egalitarianism were a threat to society and family' (Masquelier 2009, 94).

True to its modernist orientation, and unlike the informal networks of the *turuq*, *Izala* registered with the state as a formal organization with a constitution and statutes. The organization had four pillars of authority within it: the administrative cadre based originally in Jos; the leaders of the regional branches; the intellectual supporters in the universities; and supporters in trades, banking and industry. These pillars were not oriented towards each other, but were instead directed towards the person of Shaikh Abubakar Gumi 'who presided as inspiration, advisor, leader, guide, mediator, and "national Patron" above the whole movement' (Loimeier 1997b, 228). The spread of *Izala* ideology was accompanied by the opening of new mosques and schools, which its clerics control. *Izala* says it is opposed to all kinds of violence, protest or demonstration against government. This is the orientation of societal 'reform without violence' advocated by Shaikh Abubakar Gumi.[7] However, while *Izala* may not have advocated violence against the state, many accused it of intolerance, provocation and aggressive behaviour towards other Muslims; in many northern cities, irreverent and scathing *Izala* criticism of cherished Sufi Shaikhs, the forceful seizure of mosques by *Izala* adherents and the attempt to prevent the conduct of Sufi rituals, opened the door to violent *intra*-Islam conflict.

From Izala to Ahl al-sunna wa'l-jama'a

Izala members saw themselves as followers of the 'righteous ancestors' (*as-salaf as-salih*), and tended to divide the Muslim community into three categories. In the first category were themselves, the *Ahl al-Sunna*, followers of the path of the Prophet, though technically, this appellation applied to all Muslims. In the second category came the Sufis, whom they condemned as the *Ahl al-Bid'a*, or those who have corrupted their worship with dangerous innovations. In the final category came the Shi'a, whom the *Izala* barely acknowledge to be Muslims. However, despite *Izala*'s formidable doctrinal arsenal, and Gumi's towering personality within the group, the organization was not immune to internal rivalries, power struggles and factionalism (see Ben Amara 2011)[8]. This development is partly explainable by the importance of personalities in the evolution of jihadist movements. According to Gerges (2005, 34) 'personalities, not ideals or organisations, are the drivers' behind such movements. Within *Izala*, despite the doctrinal position on egalitarianism and the organizational apparatuses of the constitution, Gumi was the main personality driving the group. However, some ambitious members of the group increasingly demanded a greater role and influence in the leadership of the group. Scholars like Aminu Din Abubakar and Sidi Attahiru Sokoto soon broke away from the *Izala* fold to found their own organizations with similar aims. Between 1980 and 1990, *Izala* witnessed serious internal dissension, and matters soon came to a head with the accusation of embezzlement levelled against the formal head of the organization,

[7] Interview with Sheikh Abbas Jega, Chairman, Izala 'Ulama's Council, Kebbi State Chapter, on Thursday, 10 March 2012, at Jega town, Kebbi State.

[8] 'The late Sheikh Jaafar Mahmud Adam of Kano, who underwent a transformation from a member of Izala to a Salafī scholar after he studied in Medina, remarks that both factions of Izala in Jos and Kaduna as well those who left the movement are similar in the 'way they act and in their religious outlook and goals. According to him they all practise *da'wa* for the Qur'ān and the Sunna of the Prophet. He called all of them *Ahl al-sunna wa'l-Jamā'a*' (Ben Amara 237) ... The reasons for Izala split are therefore not doctrinal, but due to 'an attempt to use Izala as a "channel of negotiation with the state". Another reason leading to the break of the Society can to be explained given the fact that "patrons of the movement" who were also part of the state apparatus tried to exercise power over Izala ... It was a kind of struggle for power within the movement. The monetary aspect also seemed to play a critical role in the division. In the year 1991, the two parties of Izala started "discrediting each other"' (Ben Amara 2011, 245).

Shaikh Ismaila Idris. The resulting political tussle split *Izala* first into two (Loimeier 1997b, 222–3), and then three (Ben Amara 2011, 267).

Izala A, based in Jos, was dominated by the old brigade; and *Izala* B, based in Kaduna, was dominated by the younger generation. Importantly, the 'emerging conflict between the first and second generations was articulated in the language of religious discourses' (Anon. 2012, 121) with the younger generation softening the core Salafi/Wahhabi doctrine that had hitherto characterized *Izala*. With each faction of *Izala* accusing the other of the same *bid'a* deviations they had previously flung at the Sufis, the 'controversy demonstrates how dynamic and unstable religious concepts are' (Ben Amara 2011, 270).

Since this division within *Izala*, important doctrinal and ritual practices have developed to differentiate the two wings. For instance, *Izala* A believes strictly in the application of Maliki *fiqh* as the only reference point on legal issues, while *Izala* B places emphasis on *hadith* (traditional teachings) and on individual *ijtihad* (interpretative application of Islamic law by experts learned in the Qur'an and *hadith*, through independent reasoning), meaning that individuals are free to use their reason, applied through any acceptable and appropriate Islamic texts, to determine their position on any specific issue. This autonomous approach to *fiqh*, while not rejecting Maliki *fiqh*, makes the *Izala* B part of the *Zahiriyya*, a school of law defined by its emphasis on self-*ijtihad*. Furthermore, there are some differences in the styles of prayers between these two wings of Izala. While *Izala* A prays in the *sadlu* style (arms to the side), *Izala* B prays in the *Qablu* style (arms across the chest). At the organizational level, while *Izala* A insists on centralized discipline, *Izala* B gives more room for individual judgement in the conduct of its affairs. Finally, while the clerics of *Izala* A always wear turbans, those of *Izala* B frequently do not. The two groups also differed on their reading of Saddam Hussein's invasion of Kuwait in 1990 with the *Saddamawa* (supporters of Saddam Hussein) and *Bushawa* (named after George H. Bush; supporters of the Saudis) (Ben Amara 2011, 246).

The death of Shaikh Abubakar Gumi in 1992 accelerated this process of factionalism. Some analysts speak of a 'third group C' in *Izala*, made up of younger members sent to the University of Medina for higher degrees who, on their return to Nigeria, constituted this third faction, the *'Yan Medina* (people of Medina; meaning those who studied in Medina). This third 'group' of *Izala* is only so in name, as it is more heterogeneous than the two other factions, is more focused on individuals, and it is neither organized under one name nor does it have visible or well-known leaders. Under this category are scholars like Shaikh Jaafar Mahmud Adam (Ben Amara 2011, 267). *Izala* factionalism therefore resulted in the emergence of *Izala* A, seen as extreme in its interpretation and application of Islam and uncompromising in its outlook; *Izala* B, called '*Yan Tawaye* (the seceders) who are seen as liberal and moderate; and *Izala* C, a loosely defined group trying to maintain some sense of doctrinal neutrality (Ben Amara 2011, 267).

In the contemporary period, the *Ahl al-sunna* are divided into at least four camps. First, there are the *Izala* A and B. Second there is the Salafiyya Movement, which is more doctrinally strict than the two wings of *Izala*. The movement restricts itself only to those things traceable to the period of the Prophet and his Companions, and rejects such modern things as the taking of pictures and the watching of television. Last, there are independent actors and organizations like the *Al-Garkawi* in Kaduna, who have developed their own distinct doctrines and rituals. As we shall see, it is within this context of self-*ijtihad* and the formation of competing organizations within the 'prayer economy' that *Boko Haram* emerged out of the broad Salafist tendency.

THE SHI'A

Islamic Movement of Nigeria (IMN), or Muslim Brothers

The Shi'a sect is one of the earliest branching away from the established Sunni order in Islamic history. It started to take root after the death of the Prophet and the choice of Abubakar as the First Caliph by a gathering of religious and clan elders around 632–633 AD. This choice led to the split between the Shi'a and the Sunni establishment. While Sunnis choose their leaders through community consensus, *ijma'*, Shi'ites on the other hand, observe *nass,* literally 'condition' or 'arrangement', through which a rightly-guided leader designates his successor (see Momen 1987; Winters 1996; Sachedina 1998; Mottahedeh 2008; Daftary & Miskinzoda 2014). From this point of view, while the Shi'a, like other schools of thought in Islam, believe in the Qur'an and that Prophet Mohammed is the Seal of the Prophets, they nevertheless reject the notion of choosing leaders for the Islamic community by consensus. The Shi'a believe that only God can designate the leader for His community on earth. According to Shi'a beliefs, the Prophet's family and descendants, the *Ahl al-Bayt* 'the People of the House', have special divinely inspired spiritual and political claims to authority over the community. Accordingly, the Shi'a believers prefer *hadith* attributed to the *Ahl al-Bayt*, and have their own separate collection of *hadith*, different from the dominant Sunni texts. Because of the divine source of the choice of the Imam, the Shi'a also believe that their Imams or leaders are divinely guided, and are therefore free from error and sin. By definition, therefore, the Shi'a Imam is infallible. The original Shi'a splinter group fragmented into many minor sects up to the present Shi'a Imamiyya Khomainiyya of contemporary Iran established after the Islamic revolution of 1979.

This revolution precipitated the incursion of Shi'a thought into Nigerian Islam which had hitherto been uniformly Sunni. A key transmission belt was the Muslim Brothers, a group led by Shaikh Ibrahim El-Zakzaky. While the religious debates within the Muslim community in the 1970s demystified religion, undermined the established Sufi networks, and encouraged the individuation of belief, the economic crises of post-Civil War Nigeria from the late 1970s, and the corruption and authoritarianism of various military regimes all contributed to the radicalization of Muslim students in the universities, organized around the Muslim Students Society (MSS). Within this condition of social and religious ferment, some Muslim students embraced political Islam because in 'their way of thinking, the crisis that African countries face can be resolved only by a return to Islam as the supreme moral, legal and political code' for the organization of the state (Soares & Otayek 2007, 16). Ibrahim El-Zakzaky was one of such students at Ahmadu Bello University, Zaria, and he was expelled in 1979 after being charged with setting fire to the Vice-chancellor's office and the Senior Staff Club, and attacking fellow students of the palm wine drinkers' clubs (Kane 2003, 95). Initially, there was no Shi'a ideology attached to the *Movement for Jihad and the Restoration of the Caliphate* which Shaikh El-Zakzaky formed (Bunza 2004a; 2004b). Instead, the turban-clad radicals organized demonstrations in northern cities, at which slogans like 'Down with the Nigerian Constitution' and 'Islam Only' were proclaimed. Advocating a campaign of civil disobedience against the '*kufr*-oriented system', Shaikh El-Zakzaky 'is said to have encouraged the youth to refuse to attend schools and to abstain from working in any public or private institution whatsoever as long as Nigeria remained a secular state' (Kane 2003, 95).

With time, however, the radical Islamists of the MSS soon broke into two factions – the pro-Saudi Wahhabi-inclined *Da'wa* group, dedicated to missionary work, and the pro-Iranian *Umma* group, dedicated to the enthronement of Sharia and the establishment of an Islamic state.[9] The *Umma* subsequently split into the *Hodabiyya*, which favoured accommodation with the state, and the '*yan Shi'a*, who gravitated towards Iranian Shi'ism (Casey 2008, 77). From these humble beginnings, El-Zakzaky's group, the IMN, has expanded beyond its initial students' base to include about 12 per cent of the Muslim population of the country (Pew 2010, 21). Some members of the group now openly claim to be *Jafariyya*, followers of the sixth Shi'a Imam, Ja'far as-Sadiq.[10] This Shi'a bent notwithstanding, the IMN still claims to be part of the legacy of

[9] Kane (2003, 94–95) writes of the partial domestication and co-option of some of the Islamist radicals through the formation of organizations like the Light of Islam Association (LISA) in Maiduguri and the Islamic Trust of Nigeria (ITN) in Zaria. These organizations continued the tradition of active proselytization, but without challenging the state.

[10] On the importance of Ja'far 'The Truthful' within Shi'ism, see Lawrence 2006, Chapter 5.

Shaikh 'Uthman dan Fodio and has established a network of *Fudiyyah* schools, named after him.

Deriving from Shi'a history, the concept of martyrdom (*shahada*) is an important element in IMN doctrine. Shaikh El-Zakzaky argues that martyrdom is a necessary part of the struggle to Islamize state and society. He identifies three aspects of what he terms the unalterable tradition (Sunna) ordained by God for all His prophets: 1) only the youth and the weak in society readily accept the message of God's prophets; 2) the mighty ones in society lead the majority to oppose God's prophets and their small band of youthful and weak followers; and 3) God causes the two opposed groups to clash, leading to the victory of the prophets and their groups of previously vulnerable followers. According to Shaikh El-Zakzaky, loss of life, including that of prophets, is also an ineluctable feature of each of these three aspects of the correct path prescribed by God for the struggle to Islamize societies, hence his claim that 'religion cannot be established without bloodshed' (Bunza 2002). By definition, this is a very confrontational ideology, with its focus on radical societal conversion, contrary to the Sufi search for redemption through personal reformation and perfection. If the IMN emphasizes the importance of *shahada* in its ideology, other Muslim groups in Nigeria, especially of the Salafiyya tendency, tend to emphasize its embrace of *taqiyya* (religious dissimulation and deceit), suggesting that the IMN cannot be trusted. At the level of ritual practice, while other Muslims wash their feet during ablution, the Shi'a only rub water on their feet, instead of washing them. Another distinguishing feature of the IMN is the very prominent part women play in the movement.

Shaikh El-Zakzaky and his followers were nevertheless some of the few known Islamic sects that opposed the introduction of full Sharia law in 12 far-northern states of Nigeria in 1999. According to him, no real Sharia can come through the administrative act of politicians and legislatures. The only way to actualize Sharia was through jihad, not through piggy-backing on powers conferred by a secular constitution. The Shi'a in Nigeria generally condemn the Nigerian state as *Tagut* (satanic demons intent on leading people away from God) and Muslims who subscribe to their teaching must not obey the un-Islamic government (Bunza 2004a, 2004b). Their dislike of the Nigerian state is only surpassed by their virulent anti-Americanism. The connection between this sect and Iran, politically and religiously, is very strong. It was this Iranian-Shi'ite connection, according to Tahir Gwarzo (2007) that resulted in the break in the ranks of the movement, and the establishment of *Jamat al-Tajdeed al-Islami* (JTI) in 1994. The JTI, with its base in the *Hodabiyya* group, is less enamoured of Iran and generally less confrontational towards the Nigerian state. The national headquarters of the IMN is in Zaria city, the birth-place of its leader in Nigeria, Shaikh

Ibrahim El-Zakzaky, with branches in almost all states in northern Nigeria and in Niger Republic.

Though they have been known to boast that they can organize processions with as many as 500,000 people (Hill 2010, 24), the Shi'a nevertheless constitute a significant minority of Muslims, and are mostly located in the cities of the north. In recent years, however, they have started an active programme of rural recruitment. Many of the demonstrations and processions held by the movement are to mark important Shi'a dates like the Ashura and Al-Quds Day. In early December 2011 the IMN mobilized over 20,000 Muslims in Kaduna to join 'the rest of the world in staging a peaceful demonstration to mark the day of Ashura in remembrance of the martyrdom of late Imam Husain, the grandson of Prophet Muhammad'. In his speech at the occasion, a leading lieutenant of Shaikh El-Zakzaky, Malam Muhammad Mukhtar Sahabi argued that

> through the Ashura tragedy, we have learnt that the victor and the vanquished cannot be determined by the immediate results of a battle or war, but by the long-term repercussions of the clash of their ideologies on the course of events and influence on the minds of men. [...] We hold firm the belief that to uproot evil, one must act like the candle, who burns itself to give others light. True love for martyrdom is the one and only way of genuine revolution. While we feel afresh the anguish and pain inflicted on the Household of the Holy Prophet (SAW) on Ashura day, we re-echo the sayings of Imam Khomeini (QS): 'Every day is Ashura, every land Karbala'. (Cited in Isuwa 2011)

In September 2012, the IMN was the only Muslim group in Nigeria to get directly involved in the world-wide Islamic demonstrations of anger against the blasphemous movie *Innocence of Muslims*. It mobilized several thousands of demonstrators in Kano, Zaria and Kaduna against the film, with some of the demonstrators already wearing their burial shrouds in readiness for martyrdom. Despite the large number of people in attendance, most of the IMN demonstrations have been very peaceful, partly due to the tight discipline of the members. Surprisingly, despite the confrontational tone of its fiery rhetoric, the IMN has 'resorted to violence only exceptionally (Kane 2003, 97).[11] Indeed, the organization actively pursues inter-faith dialogue for peaceful co-existence with Christians; in August 2012, Shaikh El-Zakzaky even received

[11] On Friday 25 July 2014, the sect organized its annual Al-Quds procession in Zaria. A conflict arose over the right of way between the procession and a military convoy. This allegedly led to the shooting and killing of 35 members of the sect by soldiers. The dead included three sons of Shaikh El-Zakzaky, two of whom were allegedly arrested alive but subsequently killed in detention. While the army claimed that it was first shot at, there is no report of any casualty amongst the soldiers or the seizing of any weapons from the sect (see: Tukur 2014; NAN 2014).

a delegation from the Christian Association of Nigeria (CAN) in his headquarters, noting in his speech that

> there is a saying of imam Ali (AS) that there are two types of humans, they are either your brothers in religion or your brothers in creation. No man is an island and so everyone has to live with the other and not alone because it is virtually impossible to live alone ... If we know that we have to live together why then don't we stop the fight and come and understand how to live together. (Cited in Islamic Movement 2012)

The IMN even has a Christians' Forum through which it is in constant dialogue with Christian clerics and youths who are regularly invited to IMN activities.

Jamat al-Tajdeed al-Islami (JTI)
In 1994, Shaikh El-Zakzaky's Muslim Brothers split. A group that was not satisfied with the increasing tilt towards *Shi'a* ideology and Iran founded a new association which they named *Jamat al-Tajdeed al-Islami* (Movement for Islamic Reform) – also known as *Ahl al-sunna wa'l-jama'a, Ja'amutu Tajidmul Islami* (Movement for the Islamic Revival – MIR). The Association is largely based in Kano, and led by Abubakar Mujahid. To buttress their disagreement with IMN, Abubakar's group cited as evidence the books and magazines that came from Iran, which are allegedly anti-*Sahaba* (the Prophet's Companions) and which often make derogatory remarks against the *Sahaba*. JTI's presence can be found in many states in the north, though it has particularly strong followership in Kano and Zamfara states. The group maintains a cordial relationship with all Islamic groups irrespective of sectarian divide with the exception of its parent Shi'ite group. The group has both male and female members although men are in the majority. Membership cuts across all ages and ethnic identities, and at all levels of economic and social statuses. JTI members are now part of many Sharia implementing agencies in the Sharia states.

YORUBA MUSLIMS

In addition to the three main categories of Sunni Muslims and the Shi'a in northern Nigeria, there are several smaller groups that are generally considered part of the larger Muslim community. Some of these groups are differentiated along *ethnic* or *doctrinal* grounds. For example, ethnic Yoruba Muslims can be found in some ethnically-specific Islamic groups such as the *Nasrul-Lahi Fathi* Society of Nigeria (NASFAT), described by Soares (2009, 190) as 'a Yoruba Muslim organization, arguably even a form of Yoruba Muslim cultural nationalism'. The organization is found 'anywhere where there are large concentrations of Yoruba in Nigeria'. Numerically NASFAT has over one million members all over the Federation.

NASFAT arose as a response to threats to Yoruba Muslim identity perceived by the Yoruba Muslim elite in Lagos. Rising levels of materialism in society, Christian proselytization, especially by the Pentecostal Churches, and laxity among practising Yoruba Muslims constituted threats to the future of the faith according to this elite. It was also felt that the efforts of earlier Muslim organizations in Yorubaland such as the Ansar al-Deen, Nawairrudden, Nurudeen and Umaruddeen societies needed to be complemented especially in the provision of basic Islamic education to Muslims. On Sunday 5 March 1995 NASFAT came into existence with Alhaji Abdullateef Wale Olasopu as national Chairman and Chair of the Board of Trustees. Some of the aims and objectives of the Society are to establish strong prayer groups, create exemplary leadership, provide assistance and care to the needy and provide sound Islamic education to its members and beyond. The activities of NASFAT include weekly prayer/ lecture on Sundays, observance of late night prayers, economic empowerment schemes and skill building to uplift its members, promotion of peaceful co-existence, publication of NASFAT news bulletin and quarterly magazine – 'The Victory' – among other things (NASFAT 2006). It also runs an Islamic university.

NASFAT advocates modernist and reformist views, and emphasizes the 'equality of all Muslims', contrary to the hierarchy of the Sufis or the sectarianism of the Salafis. Its key focus is on matters of individual piety and ethics, along with the education and socio-economic empowerment of its members. Its membership is dominated by the Yoruba as only a few non-Yoruba are members (Nurudeen 2004). Contrary to the practice of the dominant patterns of Hausa Islam in the north, women play an active role in NASFAT. NASFAT villages were created especially outside major towns, consisting of mosque and multi-purpose lecture hall, instead of the usual practice by other groups of erecting only mosques or secretariats. The multi-purpose hall allows the society to engage in a wide spectrum of religious, social and economic activities. Ideologically, it is an open society where members can come from any other organization or tendency within Islam, provided one is ready to uphold the teachings of the Qur'an and the Sunna of the Prophet, and observe basic rules of non-discrimination against other Muslims. Fundamental principles of the society are prayers and charity to the destitute. It is one of the fastest growing Muslim organizations in Nigeria.

Other ethnic Yoruba Muslim organizations active in the north include the, Nurudeen, Ansarudeen and Nawairudeen groups. Though the Ahmadiyya is not strictly speaking an ethnic Yoruba organization, the majority of its members are Yoruba. These groups run mosques, schools and social activities. Apart from their ethnic particularity, they are also noted for women's active participation in their activities. But they are not as dynamic or as influential as NASFAT which has Yoruba professional elite at its core. The Ahmadiyya are particularly noted for their missionary zeal in spreading access to Western education and health services. But many Muslims do not consider the Ahmadiyya to be Muslims because the group's founder is alleged to have claimed to be a prophet, contrary to basic Islamic precepts.

MARGINAL SECTS

There are also many small sects within northern Nigerian Islam. At the more heretical end of the doctrinal spectrum lies the *Maitatsine* sect, whose members are not publicly visible at the time of writing. Violent conflict between the sect and state authorities in Kano in December 1980 led to the death of over 4,000 people (Clarke & Linden 1984, 119). The sect was noted for many heretical views, including the suggestion that Muslims could pray facing any direction, instead of the orthodox belief in facing Mecca. The group also believed that any Muslim who wore a watch or a button, went to bed at the end of the day with more than a tiny amount of money in his pocket, ate the popular local Hausa soup called *kuka* or smoked a cigarette, was a *kuffir* (unbeliever). Mohammed Marwa, alias *Maitatsine*, 'The Anathemizer', (Hiskett 1987, 209), the Cameroonian leader of the sect was noted for his quirky interpretations of the Qur'an, based on a 'culturally-tied form of … hidden Qur'an exegesis' which appealed to his 'largely non-literate congregation'. Furthermore, *Maitatsine* denied that the Sunna of the Prophet had the authority of revelation, preferring instead to rely solely on his interpretation of the Qur'an. It is even claimed that 'copies of the Qur'an found in the ruins of his house had the name of [Prophet] Mohammed deleted and his own name inserted' (Hiskett 1987, 220).

Some scholars have linked the rise of *Maitatsine* to the socio-economic stresses caused by the collapse of peasant agriculture in the north, the rise of an individualistic ethos associated with the semi-industrial capitalism that accompanied the oil boom of the 1970s, and the collapse of long-established rural-urban integration processes that responded to ecological and demographic shifts in the countryside (Lubeck 1985). Others explain the rise of *Maitatsine* in terms of the prevalence of non-Muslim belief systems peculiar to some marginalized social groups within northern society (Hiskett 1987). Either way, it is agreed that *Maitatsine* was a movement of different segments of the marginalized within northern semi-industrial capitalist society. These groups faced both economic deprivation and cultural alienation from the Muslim mainstream. Though *Maitatsine* started in Kano, it quickly spread to other northern cities like Maiduguri, Kaduna, Gombe, Funtua and Yola and its sporadic violence against the state lasted from 1980 to 1993 (Loimeier 1997b, 220).

Darul Islam is another marginal sect made up largely of poor people from the drought-stressed Sahelian regions of northern Nigeria. It expanded from 300 persons to 7,000 in three years (Orintunsi & Olatunbosun 2014a). The group lived in a secluded farming commune near Mokwa, in Niger State, before it was forcibly disbanded by the Niger State Government in 2009 after the *Boko Haram* clash with security forces in Maiduguri. Its members were forcibly repatriated to their states of origin. As far as can be observed, the puritanical movement is pacifist in orientation, preferring to live in isolation in its farming communes, away from the corrupting influences of modern society. Salvation is sought through avoiding 'contaminating' contact with the outside world and leading a 'virtuous' life in isolation. According to the leader of the group, Malam Bashir Abdullahi Suleiman, the group's isolationism derived from the urge to practise their faith 'in the most discreet form ... possible', without mixing with the many sinful people one encounters in the wider world. Furthermore, the group is opposed to sending its children to Western-education schools, because, according to their leader,

> they believe that what obtains in such schools is *haram* ... For instance, children ... are taught that man originated from an ape; this differs from the knowledge we believe in, i.e. that man was created by God, through Prophet Adam. (Anon. 2012, 120)

Attempts to link the *Darul Islam* to *Boko Haram* have not been supported with credible evidence. In June 2014, 240 members of another sect named *Nibrassiya Huda* headed by Shaikh Mohammed Abubakar were dislodged from a forest enclave on the outskirts of Cheche village near Lapai in Niger State. The sect, which has been in existence since 2008, claims to be preaching the 'true teachings of Tijjaniyya' (Hamagam 2014). According to their spokesperson: 'We have nothing to do with *Boko Haram*. We don't share the same belief and have nothing in common. *Boko Haram* has its agenda of destruction. We are peaceful Islamic scholars and farmers' (Orintunsi & Olatunbosun 2014a). However, according to the traditional authorities in the area and State Government officials, the sect is propagating doctrines that have no basis in Islam, fomenting trouble, attacking people who do not share their views, engaging in promiscuous activities and forcefully conducting marriages and dissolving them at will (Orintunsi & Olatunbosun 2014b). They were also alleged to be disdainful of other Muslims and preparing to use their forest enclave 'as a training ground for a new sect of Islamic fundamentalists' (Mosadomi 2014).

The *Mahdiyya* is another marginal Muslim sect, based largely in Kano. These are followers of Muhammad Ahmad b. Sayyid of Sudan, who proclaimed himself as the long-expected Mahdi, the God-guided One, sent as the Saviour of Muslims as the End of Time approached in the late nineteenth century. Though Sayyid died in 1885, his followership in pre-colonial northern Nigeria remained a thorn in the flesh of the British colonial administration which saw a Mahdist threat behind every bush. This movement was particularly strong in Adamawa and Kano in the colonial period. A tiny section of the movement remains active in Kano today (see Saeed 1992a, 1992b, and Saidu 1983).

The *'Yan Hakika* is a small idiosyncratic sect within Nigerian Islam. As noted earlier, the highest spiritual level for the Tijaniyya is the realization of *al-Ma'arifah* – deep spiritual knowledge of God. The local Hausa term used for this realization is *Hakika* (Reality). The *'Yan Hakika* claim, on the basis of their practice of the Tijani *al-Ihsan,* to have reached a new level of consciousness characterized by closeness to God, and a realization that everything is of God and therefore *halal,* meaning that technically, nothing can be considered as *haram* or forbidden. Based on this logic, the *'Yan Hakika* practise many things forbidden in mainstream Islam such as drinking alcohol, fornication and the eating of dog meat. A second plank in the doctrinal platform of the *'Yan Hakika* is the argument that they no longer need to say the five daily prayers practised by mainstream Muslims. They (mis)interpret a verse in the Qur'an which commands Muslims to worship God until '*Yeqin*'. Literally, *Yeqin* means 'certitude'. While mainstream Muslims interpret the command to mean worshipping God until the final certitude of death, the *'Yan Hakika* interpret it to mean worshipping God until they reach the state of *Hakika*[12], after which, they are absolved from any further obligations to say the daily prayers.

By most definitions within mainstream northern Nigerian Islam, these are highly heretical views. The *'Yan Hakika*'s leading cleric, Shaikh Baban Salma, lived in Jos, and was reputed to be well-versed in the magical arts. He was credited with the ability to wall himself up in a room for months on end with only water for sustenance. He was also rumoured to have married his daughter to the consternation of other Muslims. He was subsequently expelled from Jos by the Muslim community leaders, and moved to Lafia in Nasarawa State, from whence he was again expelled by the resentful Muslim community. Shaikh Baban Salma and his followers then founded their own settlement in the Lafia countryside, called Muhajir. Like the *Isawa,* a group of millenarian Muslims, pre-occupied with the second coming of Prophet Isa (Jesus Christ), the *'Yan Hakika*

[12] For an earlier controversy on the Tijani conception of *Hakika,* see Hiskett 1980.

are also alleged to occasionally display pictures of Mary and Jesus at their functions.

The *Qur'aniyyun* are Muslims, who like the *Maitatsine*, reject the significance of the teachings of the Prophet (the *hadith*) and accept only the Qur'an as the revelation of Allah. They are similar to the equally scripturalist loose grouping called the *Kala Kato*, meaning 'A mere man (i.e. Prophet Muhammad) said it'. The followers of *Kala Kato* rely exclusively on traditional, Qur'anic education, to the exclusion of all other forms of knowledge. The *Qur'aniyyun*, often well educated in Western-education schools, believe that there is mathematical harmony embedded in the Qur'an. They have their own mosque in Kaduna, and are to be found in most northern Nigerian cities. By contrast, the *Kala Kato* are largely young and poor, eking out a living peacefully in the margins of society. *Kala Kato* and *Darul Islam* are often difficult to differentiate from each other; and both can easily be confused with the violently millenarian rabble of *Maitatsine* or the insurgent *Boko Haram*.

Boko Haram, or *Jama'atu Ahlul Sunna li Da'awati wal Jihad* is a group that started in Maiduguri in the north-east zone in the early 2000s, but its influence has spread to all parts of the north. Given its violent attacks over the past few years, there has been considerable academic and journalistic interest in this group. According to Anon. (2012, 120), the doctrinal genealogy of *Boko Haram* derives from two sources: the longstanding negative attitudes toward Western education among the Muslims of northern Nigeria, and the further development of Salafi-Wahhabi doctrine associated with Shaikh Abubakar Gumi and *Izala*. Earlier, we discussed the organizational and doctrinal schism that arose within *Izala*. Anon. further states that *Boko Haram* arose in the context of yet another schism, this time, within the ranks of the Salafiyya tendency within *Izala*. Given the crowded 'religious marketplace' the struggle for a followership and influence necessitated the starting of a new religious discourse 'that would be distinctively different from the established doctrines of Izala' (Anon. 2012, 121–2). Mohammed Yusuf, the first leader of the *Yusufiyya* movement

> successfully followed the shortcut to prominence by articulating a new discourse that stridently emphasized Salafi doctrines on a host of issues. Only two distinct positions brought disagreement from fellow Salafis: 1) modern western education was religiously forbidden to Muslims, and 2) employment in the Government of Nigeria was also religiously forbidden. (Anon. 2012, 122)

According to a key eye witness to the rise of *Boko Haram*, the journalist Ahmad Salkida:

In early 2002, Yusuf was seen by many as a likely heir to the renowned late Sheik Ja'afar Mahmud Adam in Maiduguri on account of his brilliance and closeness to the late renowned scholar. But all that changed shortly when one late Mohammed Alli approached late Yusuf with reasons to boycott democracy, civil service and western oriented schools. Late Yusuf then disengaged his service with the Yobe state government. Then, in a 2006 press release signed by the sect's *Shura* (Consultative) Council, they stated that, Islam permits them to subsist under a modern government like Nigeria but has explicitly prohibited them from joining or supporting such governments in so far as their systems, structures and institutions contain elements contradictory to core Islamic principles and beliefs. (Salkida 2013a)

Yusuf undertook the task of this doctrinal articulation at two levels, the scholarly and the polemical. At the scholarly level, he wrote *Hadhihee aqidatuna wa manhaji da'awatina* (This is Our Creed and the Basis of Our Preaching)[13] in which he tries to trace his stance all the way back to the *al-Salaf*. He discusses modern democracy and rejects it as un–Islamic. Then he discusses Western education and concludes that it is *haram*, and any Muslim who partakes in it must be a *kuffir*.[14] Third, he discusses the security apparatus of the Nigerian state, asserting that these state institutions draw their powers, not from the Qur'an, but from a secular constitution. He concludes, therefore, that it is *haram* for any Muslim to belong to any of these state institutions. Fourth, he discusses the presence of the Shi'ites within northern Nigerian Islam. He criticizes their attitudes towards the *Sahaba* (the Companions of the Prophet) and their understanding of the notion of leadership within Islam. He concludes that the Shi'ites are not Muslims. Finally, he discusses the Sufi Brotherhoods, and similarly concludes that their creeds are un–Islamic. Mohammed Yusuf therefore defined most northern Nigerian Muslims as being non-Muslims, except for the narrow group surrounding him.

In his discussion of Western education, Yusuf delves into the generally accepted Islamic concept of *Darura* (Necessity). As it is understood in northern Nigeria, *darura* makes it possible for Muslims to lead a meaningful life under a non-Islamic government. The concept dictates that in the

---

[13] We are grateful to Dr Yusuf Abdullahi Yusuf for the translation of this book.

[14] Ironically, after the Nigerian military destroyed Mohammed Yusuf's enclave in Maiduguri in July 2009, a Nigerian newspaper published a picture of some of the classrooms in the enclave in which sect members were taught *boko* subjects. The caption for the picture read: 'Two of the classes in a school discovered in the Boko Haram enclave. Mathematics and English were last taught on 2/7/2009 as reflected on the Blackboard', *Leadership*, Sunday 9 August 2009, cited in Mustapha Shehu, 'Almajiri: The Boko Haram in the Northern Elite', www.gamji.com/article8000/NEWS8741.htm. Ahmad Salkida (2013a), claimed that the late 'Yusuf's teaching was an abuse to Algebra, reproductive health and the science of astronomy that has its roots in Islam [*sic*]'.

absence of the Islamic state, the Muslim *umma* must make compromises with the extant status quo in order to ensure that the community's interests are not harmed beyond what is already subsisting under the non-Islamic state. According to Yusuf, the constraints and compromises implied by the concept must be rejected by individual Muslims who are denied the opportunity to invoke *darura* to justify their engagement with the institutions of the state. Muslims, he asserts, must reject the current Nigerian state, built on a Western democratic model, and replace it with an Islamic state built on the Sharia. This position is in sharp contrast to the position of *Izala* which recognizes the validity of the Nigerian Constitution, and harps on the importance of the constitutional provision which guarantees the freedom of thought and worship to all irrespective of religious affiliation (Loimeier 1997b, 229). In justification of *darura*, another scholar pointed out to Yusuf that for 21 out of the 23 years of the prophetic career of Prophet Mohammed 'idols on the Ka'ba were not removed, even though the Prophet had already received God's command for waging jihad'(Anon. 2012, 135).

If Yusuf adopted a semi-scholarly tone in *Hadhihee*, his tone in his lectures and speeches to his followers was more belligerent and polemical, filled as they were with sarcasm and ridicule against his opponents. In these speeches and interviews, he elaborated his disagreements with aspects of Western education such as the explanation for rainfall in geography, Darwinist theory of evolution, the notion that the earth was round, the naming of planets after Greek pagan gods, and the distinction in sociology between rationality and belief (Boyle 2009). He also developed an 'expansive conception of the religiously forbidden' which included watching football matches and movies (Anon. 2012, 124–6). In one of such sermons, he also asserted that all *Ahl al-sunna* (Salafi) groups who refuse to follow his creed deserved to be killed because they knew the truth, but refused to preach and proclaim it. These groups he termed the *"yan bid'an zamani"* (practitioners of modern dangerous innovations), distinct from the 'old' *bid'a* associated with the so-called innovations of the Sufi Brotherhoods. Because Gumi held the view that it 'has always been to my conviction that the best way to effect change in the society is to educate those who have power, about the virtue of justice and the fear of God' (Gumi 1992, 130), he was denounced 'as a government Mallam' by Mohammed Yusuf according to the assassinated Shaikh Albani of Zaria (Omipidan 2009).

As for the Brotherhoods, since they were not really Muslims, Mohammed Yusuf intended to invite them to 'join' Islam; should they refuse the call, then he considered them to be legitimate targets for elimination. This 'largely self-educated' cleric spewed out a constant stream of ultra-Salafi doctrines and developed an 'incredible ability to

solidly marshal Salafi arguments in support of his seemingly preposterous positions' (Anon. 2012, 122). His main model was the thirteenth-
century Islamic scholar, Ibn Taymiyya, noted particularly for his
advocacy of violent jihad against 'nominal Muslims' (Lawrence 2006,
179). The *Yusufiyya* mosque and headquarters in Maiduguri was called
the Ibn Taymiyya Mosque.

Key to understanding Mohammed Yusuf is his motivation. According
to Anon. (2012, 119), preachers like Mohammed Yusuf were driven by
'the will to appropriate the absolute power of God', demonstrated in
the authoritativeness and vehemence with which he condemned many
things. His denunciation of the concept of *darura*, his consequent refusal
to recognize the Nigerian constitution, and his declaration that 'he and
his followers would not obey the laws of the land' (Anon. 2012, 129), all
combined to betray the scale of his ambitions. On the two key questions of
Western education and employment in government, the mainstream *Ahl
al-sunna* groups disagreed with Mohammed Yusuf's position and between
2003 and 2004, some tried unsuccessfully to make him see the fallacies in
his positions. After eight unsuccessful meetings with Mohammed Yusuf,
these scholars began to question his integrity, sincerity and motives.
According to the leading *Ahl al-sunna* scholar, and former patron of
Mohammed Yusuf, Shaikh Jafar Adam, 'some of the people saying *boko* is
haram are sincere but lack sufficient religious knowledge and these are the
bulk of the followers, while others are colluding with enemies of Muslims'
(Anon. 2012, 139). In a similar vein, another leading *Ahl al-sunna* scholar,
Shaikh Muhammad Awwal Adam Albani of the Salafiyya Movement in
Zaria denounced those preaching 'shallow doctrines' for the sole purpose
of 'assuming leadership and followers' (*SaharaReporters* 2014).[15] Both Jafar
and Albani were subsequently gunned down in 2007 and 2014 respectively, with *Boko Haram* claiming responsibility for Albani's killing.
Boko Haram is therefore a jihadist and Salafist group, wedded to the use
of violence against opposing Muslims, Christians and state institutions
(Mustapha 2012; Anon. 2012).

We now turn our attention to the membership of *Boko Haram*.
Membership of the group includes a small number of well-educated,
but alienated, young Muslim men who spoke fluent English and had
university degrees which they agreed to burn on joining the sect. One of
such young men is Aminu Sadiq Ogwuche, accused of bombing the Abuja
suburb of Nyanya in April 2014 (see Vanguard Media 2014; *Punch* Nigeria
2014). Some members could even be regarded as well-to-do by Nigerian

[15] According to Mohammed (2010, 41), 'Sheikh Muhammad Auwal Albany knew Mohammed
Yusuf intimately. In fact Yusuf was his student. He described the late sect leader as a mere "gardi"
[semi-literate rural bumpkin] who just read the Qur'an without knowing its translation. He said:
"With his limited knowledge, Mohammed Yusuf started dabbling into what he knew little about,
saying that science was incompatible with Islam"'.

standards.[16] However, the bulk of the membership are drawn from people from far less privileged backgrounds, most of whose ambitions in life have been stymied by the corruption and mis-governance that have characterized Nigeria since the 1970s. Nigerian federalism was unusual in the sense that the Northern Region had more people than the southern regions combined. Through this demographic advantage, the region controlled political power, while the southern regions were more economically and educationally developed, and so controlled the economy and the bureaucracy. Between 1954 and 1966 the various regions engaged in 'competitive ethno-regional modernization', which ushered in substantial social and economic development, especially for the majority ethnic groups. From 1966, with the ascendancy of the military, and the rise of oil rents from 1970, there has been a corrosion of regional autonomy and a centralization of political power and oil rents at the centre. Northern political and military elites have had privileged access to the federal centre and gradually abandoned any systematic concern for developing their region, contenting themselves to be, with their presumed supremacy, at the centre. Personal class-based accumulation strategies replaced erstwhile collective regional strategies. The result is that the northern states, which have historically had the worst social indicators even under British colonial rule, fell further behind, compared to the southern states. In Nigeria today, every social indicator shows the northern states to be far worse off; if different parts of Nigeria were individual countries, many southern states would be middle income countries, while most northern states would be at the bottom of the Human Development Index scale.

This failure of political leadership in the north has been compounded by wider economic and political developments. Neoliberal policies of structural adjustment policies in the 1980s and 1990s affected the north more by triggering a process of rapid de-industrialization, while privatization policies since 1999 have strengthened the southern grip on the commanding sectors of the economy. Meanwhile, democratization in 1999 ushered in a political swing away from the north as well. All these dynamics have fuelled unease and disorientation amongst a northern political elite long since disconnected from its societal moorings. However, the consequences of these economic and political changes for the ordinary citizenry in the north have been more stark, intensifying poverty and the lack of basic facilities, and heightening social dislocation. Apart from the regional

[16] According to Salkida (2011), 'The man who bombed the Nigeria Police Force headquarters in Abuja on June 16 was a fairly well-to-do businessman who was actually on a suicide mission on behalf of the Islamic sect the Boko Haram ... Mohammed Manga was a 35-year-old married man with five children who drove overnight from Maiduguri to Abuja in order to carry out the morning attack which left about five people dead, including a police officer, and many cars incinerated in the blast. He had left N4 million in his will for his five children – two girls and three boys – before embarking on the fateful journey to the nation's capital.'

dimension of inequality, the cheek-by-jowl existence of conspicuous consumption by a tiny northern elite and increasing poverty for the majority has religious and political implications. At the religious level, the 'greed', corruption and self-centred accumulation and consumption by the narrow class of northern political, military and bureaucratic elites is seen as contradicting 'Qur'anic economics':

> At its heart was a notion of property circulated and purified, in part, through charity. Thus did donors imitate God, who made a gift of his surplus (*fadl*) and sustenance (*rizq*), without ever expecting it to be returned. Donors were to provide for the needy freely and unstint- ingly. These Qur'anic notions of the 'purification' and 'circulation' of property illustrate a distinctively Islamic way of conceptualizing charity, generosity, and poverty markedly different from 'the Christian notion of perennial reciprocity between rich and poor and the ideal of charity as an expression of community love.' (Bonner 2005, 392)

Increased poverty and inequality in the north also had political ramifi- cations. According to Nigeria's first High Commissioner to Pretoria and the holder of the high Sokoto Caliphate aristocratic title of *Sarkin Sudan* of Wurno, Alhaji Shehu Malami, the nation should expect more *Boko Haram*s because of the breach of the social contract between the ruling class and the citizenry in much of Nigeria, but particularly in the northern Muslim states. He argued that there 'is a permanent binding social contract between the nation and its citizens; the nation is to look after the welfare of the citizens and they, in return, are expected to behave like responsible citizens; and that contract has been broken woefully'. He pointed out that the ordinary citizen faced 'criminal neglect' characterized by general infrastructural decay, and the lack of basic social amenities like water, medicine, power supply and education. At the same time, the political class 'are very busy rehearsing how to steal more, how to further corrupt the system to serve them more' (see Malami, 2009).

Some have argued that since not all the poor embrace radical Islam, then poverty cannot be an explanation for the rise of groups like *Boko Haram*. While former Central Bank of Nigeria Governor Sanusi Lamido Sanusi blamed growing terrorism in the north on the high level of unemployment and poverty (Onuba & Adesomoju 2013), others like President Goodluck Jonathan and his People's Democratic Party (PDP) argue that 'poverty and misrule were not responsible for the insurgency … poverty was not a recent phenomenon in the country and therefore cannot form the basis of the sudden wave of criminal attacks on innocent victims, most of whom live within the poverty bracket' (Umoru 2013).

This latter point of view misses the point; while it is true that not all the poor are radicalized, poverty and inequality are important factors in the radicalization of some of the poor and the non-poor (see Chapter 6). In the context of northern Nigeria, the neglect of the wellbeing of the poor by the northern elite undermined its religious credentials, destroyed its 'social contract' with society, and thereby expanded the opportunity for religious sectarianism and obscurantism which claim to provide an alternative vision of society. This is the context for the emergence of hordes of angry young men, ready to buy into the ideology of *Boko Haram*. The rise of the sect must therefore be understood partly in terms of the intra-Muslim sectarian doctrinal work which we have traced in this chapter, on the one hand, and on the other, the festering socio-economic context of increasing poverty, rising inequality and thwarted hopes of most young people.

It is instructive that in tracing the rise of *Boko Haram* in his state, Borno State Governor Kashim Shettima said that the late *Boko Haram* leader Mohammed Yusuf, 'despite his misguided ideology, retained the loyalty of his supporters by providing one meal a day to each of his disciples. He also had a youth empowerment scheme, under which he helped his disciples to go into petty trading and wheel barrow pushing. He also arranged cheap marriages between sect members, which enabled many of them to marry, which gave them personal dignity and self-worth' (Abdallah 2012). The connection between initial *Boko Haram* recruitment and the dashed socio-economic hopes of the youth has been attested to by key eye witnesses who observed the growth and expansion of the sect. According to Ahmad Salkida, the sect:

> took advantage of the poor quality of our educational system, the incessant strikes, cult activities, widespread malpractices and prostitutions that is [*sic*] made worse with no offer of jobs after graduation to wheedle many youth to abandon school and embrace Yusuf's new and emerging state that promises to offer them a better alternative ... Late Yusuf also took advantage of the irresponsible leadership at all levels of government as unemployment, poverty, corruption and insecurity become the order of the day. And, as he points out such failures, citing verses of the Qur'an and the sayings of the Prophet, the youth see him as the leader that will indeed deliver them from malevolence to the promised land ... Were it not for a country like Nigeria, where government have [*sic*] failed to provide basic life support for its citizens, late Yusuf may have never thrived.' (Salkida 2013a)[17]

[17] 'Another resident, Mallam Aisami added, because of the revolutionary nature of the preaching; castigating leaders and promising Islamic government based on the Sharia, where the rights of all would be protected and everyone would be equal before the law, Mohammed Yusuf was able to

With their full beards, trousers that stopped above the ankle, knee-length jumpers, red, white or green turbans worn according to their rank within the sect, a waist coat (*farmala*) with many pockets, a particular type of sandals bought from second-hand clothes dealers, and wielding sticks (Gana 2013), the rabble that was to transform into the dreaded *Boko Haram* assembled in Maiduguri between 2002 and 2006.

By 2009, *Boko Haram* was involved in a series of violent confrontations with the Nigerian state and by 2010 it had launched an insurgency responsible for the death of thousands of Christians and Muslims across northern Nigeria. This was the context for the emergence in 2011–2012 of a splinter group from *Boko Haram* called *Ansaru*. The new group's full name is *Jama'atu Ansarul Muslimina fi Biladis Sudan* (Vanguards for the Aid of Muslims in Black Africa), also known as JAMBS. The group claims to be fighting an armed jihad to reclaim 'the lost dignity of Muslims of black Africa' and to create an Islamic Caliphate covering Niger Republic, Cameroon and northern Nigeria (Emmanuel 2013). *Ansaru* is a dissident faction that rejects the post-2009 leader of *Boko Haram*, Abubakar Shekau, as 'too reckless'. *Ansaru* first announced its existence publicly on 26 January, 2012 in Kano, after *Boko Haram* attacked the city and killed about 150 Muslim civilians in the process. In a June 2012 video, *Ansaru* explained that the sin of killing a fellow Muslim was second only to the sin of accepting laws other than the Sharia and in another video in November, it described the killing of Muslims as 'inexcusable' (Zenn 2013). *Ansaru* also accused Shekau of maintaining his leadership through 'extreme actions'.

Matthew Bey and Sim Tack (2013) highlight the key differences between *Boko Haram* and *Ansaru*, arguing that both have distinct agendas and different tactics and target sets. First, while *Boko Haram* was more focused on Nigerian national issues, *Ansaru* had a more pan-West African orientation. Bey and Tack write of a split within *Boko Haram* between 'nationalist factions' aligned with Boko Haram leader Abubakar Shekau and 'transnational factions' in *Ansaru*. Because of its transnational orientation, *Ansaru* is said to have closer ties with Islamist groups in other countries, including Al-Qaeda in the Islamic Maghreb (AQIM) and the Movement for Unity and Jihad in West Africa (MUJWA). Second, while abhorring *Boko Haram*'s indiscriminate killings of both Muslims and Christians,[18] *Ansaru* has specialized in targeted attacks on the security forces, and especially, the kidnapping of Western hostages similar to

(cont.) win the hearts of the teeming under-educated, unemployed youths who thronged his HQ in large numbers. He himself was a youth who had overcome what he called the trappings of *boko* which include modernization, globalisation, western education etc to realise his "full potentials" he told them' (Gana 2013).

[18] For example, in April 2013, *Ansaru* (JAMBS) released a statement in which it restated its condemnation of 'Boko Haram's attacks on Churches which JAMBS and the entire Muslims condemned' (Adamu 2013).

those carried out by AQIM. *Boko Haram*'s targets, on the other hand, are typically churches, the police, the military, religious leaders and political institutions. *Ansaru*'s first claimed attack was in November 2012, when 40 gunmen assailed the Special Anti-Robbery Squad detention facility in Abuja. Though the police claimed that only five prisoners escaped, *Ansaru* alleged that it freed 37 members and 286 other prisoners (Zenn 2013). The next attack was by 30 gunmen on a French company's compound in Katsina, resulting in the kidnapping of a French engineer. In January 2013, *Ansaru* ambushed a military convoy bound for Mali and in February, it abducted seven foreign nationals in Bauchi. According to Bey and Tack (2013) while *Boko Haram*'s tactics can be broken down into two categories: suicide bombings (typically using vehicle-borne explosives) and motorcycle ambushes, *Ansaru*'s attacks have consisted of raids by platoon-sized gunmen against hardened targets, be they government facilities or protected dwellings of Western foreigners. Explosives are hardly used in *Ansaru* attacks, except to breach barriers. According to a senior counter-terrorism official, Maj. Gen. Sarkin-Yaki Bello, *Ansaru* is a more sophisticated version of *Boko Haram*, the group that spawned it: 'They speak Arabic better, and they have more international connections' (cited in Nossiter 2013). While *Boko Haram*'s core area of operations is in the north-east, *Ansaru* tends to be more active in the north-west.

NON-SECTARIAN CLERICS

Tired of the disunity and squabbling caused by sectarian divisions within the Muslim community, an increasing number of Muslims are regarding themselves as 'neutral' Muslims, free of any sectarian allegiance (Loimeier 1997b, 312; Ostien 2012). Within this group is a class of very influential clerics. Shaikh Abubakar Jibril is one of such independent clerics. He joined *Izala* in 1978 and rose to fame as the Imam of the influential Farfaru Jumu'at mosque in Sokoto. Indeed, his oratory and outspokenness made him a very popular scholar especially among the youth. Shaikh Abubakar Jibril was elected the Chairman, Council of 'Ulama of *Izala* in Sokoto State in 1979. He remained in that post until a leadership crisis erupted between him and the late Sidi Attahiru Ibrahim in 1983–85. Consequently, he left *Izala* and subscribed to the Iranian model of *daawa*. Around 1995, when Shaikh El-Zakzaky declared his leaning towards Shi'ite ideology, many erstwhile pro-Iran clerics changed to *Tajdeed* (TJI). However, Jibril did not subscribe to *Tajdeed*, but instead developed his own idiosyncratic blend of Saudi theology and Iranian political philosophy. He used to say '*A Aqeedah muna tareda Saudi Arabiya, amma a Siyasa muna tareda kasar Iran*' (On matters concerning theology and creed, we are with Saudi Arabia, but on matters of politics, we are with Iran).

His sermons are essentially aimed at conscientizing Muslims on political and international affairs, themes that are often neglected in other mosques. In his serialized sermons 1997–1999 entitled, *Tabargazar Manyan Arewa* (Political Blunders of Northern Nigerian Leaders), he criticizes northern political leaders for their political miscalculations and moral lapses in the context of competitive Nigerian national politics. Shaikh Jibril was also very critical of the Bafarawa administration in Sokoto State from 1999 to 2007. In fact, the Imam used to analyse and critically examine even the contracts awarded by the Government, and sought to expose Government inaccuracies, misappropriation of public funds, and general lack of sensitivity on religious and moral matters. Because of his power and influence, the State Government under Governor Magatakarda Wammako appointed Shaikh Jibril to various committees in the administration. He was the Chairman of the Ramadan Iftar Committee and Member of the *Hajj* Committee. Shaikh Jibril is one of the rare Muslim scholars who are fearless, and always speak their mind. In the 2011 Presidential election campaigns, he was arrested along with four of his sons, for vandalizing President Jonathan's campaign billboards. The cleric confirmed that he did disfigure President Jonathan's campaign pictures in order 'to register his opposition to President Jonathan's contest for the Presidency and to damage his political future, at least in Sokoto'.[19]

Another example of an influential but non-sectarian cleric is Malam Muhammad Sani Isah. He studied at the Jama'atu College for Arabic and Islamic studies, Kaduna, from 1982 to 1986, before proceeding to Islamic African Center, now International University of Africa, Khartoum, from 1987 to 1991. He is very open in his attitude towards other Islamic groups. This is demonstrated by his being a member of different Islamic groups in Kaduna State. For example, he is a member of the Council of Imams and 'Ulama, the Supreme Council of Sharia, the *Jama'atu Nasril Islam*, the Kaduna State Pilgrims Welfare Board, the Assembly of Muslims in Nigeria, and of Religious Leaders' Network on Reproductive Health. He is also the Joint National Coordinator, Interfaith Mediation Centre for Muslim – Christian Dialogue Forum in Kaduna. His orientation towards other religious faiths in Nigeria is one of accommodation and tolerance.[20]

A final example of a non-sectarian cleric is Shaikh Dr Yusuf Ali from Gaya in Kano state. Combining Western and Islamic education, he obtained his PhD in Islamic and Arabic Studies from Bayero University, Kano. Shaikh Yusuf Ali has a large following spread across all the states in the north. He runs several religious programmes on radio and television, including *Dausayin Musulunci, Gyadar Dogo, Maigida Kan Gida, Ilimi Kogi Ne, Nurul Islam, Ihya Us Sunna* and *Ibadat*. Some of the radio

---

[19] Interviewed at his house at Minanata area, Sokoto city, on Saturday 19 March 2011.
[20] Interviewed at Kaduna on 18 March 2011.

and television stations that air his programs include Radio Kano, Radio Jigawa, Federal Radio Corporation of Nigeria, Kaduna, Radio Zamfara, National Television Authority, Kano, Sokoto, Kaduna, Kogi and Kano State Television. Being a non-sectarian, he tries to be cordial and in good terms with other Islamic scholars. He is also an Upper Area Court judge.

MUSLIM WOMEN'S ORGANIZATIONS

Muslim Sisters Organization (MSO) & Federation of Muslim Women's Associations of Nigeria (FOMWAN)

Though the dominant cultural understanding of Islam in the north tends to encourage the marginalization of female participation in important public spaces in the name of preventing the mixing of the sexes, Nana Asma'u's example of scholarship, service and active engagement with public affairs during the Jihad of 1804 remains a relevant model for modern Muslim women in the north. Furthermore, despite the culture of patriarchy, traditional Hausa-Fulani female scholars of the Sufi orders continue to initiate other women into their orders or to organize pilgrimages to Mecca (Hutson 1999; Werthmann 2005). Women belonging to the ethnic Yoruba Muslim communities also play an active, if secondary, role in the religious life of their communities and frequently organize women's wings of their various religious organizations. Significantly, Yoruba Muslim women are encouraged to go to the mosque, especially on Fridays, something not encouraged for the majority of Hausa-Fulani women. Within Hausa-Fulani Islam, only women belonging to the Shi'a community are active within their religious organization, taking prominent roles in meetings, demonstrations and processions.

However, following in the footsteps of Nana Asma'u, modern Hausa-Fulani Muslim women seek both religious and secular education as a means of rendering service to their families and communities and in fulfilment of their religious obligation to learn as enjoined by Shaikh 'Uthman dan Fodio. But:

> Acquiring a Western education does not ... mean basing their own lives on Western role models and gender norms. Rather, women try to modify their roles and the options available to them within the standard context of their culture and religion ... Women in Northern Nigeria are expanding their options by stressing their Islamic right – and even obligation – to become educated in order to live up to their family duties. (Werthmann 2005, 110–11)

It is in this spirit that Western-educated Muslim women have set up women's Islamic organizations to promote their interests. As Paden

(2002) notes, in the mid–1980s, the impact of the greater spread of Western education began to be felt more clearly among Muslim women in northern Nigeria. As a consequence, many Muslim women became active in the public sphere with some participating in the secular oriented, gender organization, Women in Nigeria (cf. Imam 1985). Others preferred to organize within the context of their Muslim identity, leading to the formation of the Muslim Sisters Organization (MSO) in Kano in 1983. The MSO was established by a core of women activists with a background in the Muslim Students Society of Nigeria who wanted to continue Islamic activism even after leaving school. It convened the first International conference for Muslim Women in Kano where the decision was taken to establish a national Muslim Women's organization. This led to the founding of the Federation of Muslim Women's Associations of Nigeria (FOMWAN) in 1985. FOMWAN sought to give coherence to Muslim women's organizations throughout Nigeria and 'focused on the need to counteract the role of 'custom' in Nigerian Muslim societies' (Paden 2002, 5). By the early 1990s, FOMWAN had about 400 member organizations throughout Nigeria, forming an important bridge between Western–educated ethnic Hausa-Fulani and ethnic Yoruba Muslim women across Nigeria.

The mission of FOMWAN is to propagate Islam, educate Muslim women and ensure that they live in accordance with the tenets of Islam. It has established primary and tertiary schools with a bias for Islamic studies in all the state capitals in the north and in some local government areas (FOMWAN 2011). FOMWAN actively campaigns against issues such as forced marriage, genital mutilation and the exclusion of women from education and public life. Some other aims and objectives include: promoting the understanding and practice of the teachings of the Qur'an and Sunna, education of Muslim women at all levels, provision of health services especially in reproductive health, and the intellectual and economic empowerment of women through capacity building. Each state in Nigeria sends representatives to a national committee which runs the organization and publishes a magazine (*The Muslim Woman*). State and National committees of the organization are headed by *Amirah* (female Emirs or Heads). Conferences on topics of special concern to Muslim women are periodically held. The main language of communication is English. FOMWAN also acts as a liaison with other national and international Muslim women's organizations. It collaborates with international development agencies in carrying out programmes of interest to Muslim women. The provision of education, especially to women, the girl–child and children generally, has been the main preoccupation of this association. It is beyond doubt that FOMWAN has contributed significantly to the development of Islamic education in the north.

Conclusion

The evolution of Islamic identities in northern Nigeria has important implications for the country. They affect the interaction between the various Muslim communities. Importantly, they also affect inter-faith relations with followers of other faiths, and the development of a national multi-religious culture. There is a historical consciousness within the Muslim communities we have explored, which provides both models of actions and past institutional templates which Muslims are able to mobilize in the contemporary period. Beyond these historical factors, however, are other contemporary ones which have an equally strong pull on the imagination. As a commentator noted:

> Religious piety and mundane interests are both relevant in understanding radical and counter-radical trends. The reality of contemporary religious movements in Nigeria is that an individual religious entrepreneur stands to benefit materially by building mass followers who contribute donations for the upkeep of their religious leader; similarly, the larger the number of followers, the more influence and prestige the leader holds. Such religious influence can easily be converted into political influence and access to influential figures in government, which can in turn yield material rewards. However, the assets needed to build a mass following include deep Islamic knowledge as well as demonstrated piety and zeal for Islam. (Anon. 2012, 141)

For both historical and mundane reasons, therefore, the Muslim actors and sects in northern Nigeria are bound to play important roles in the development of the region and the evolution of inter-faith relations in the country as a whole.

A second important point is that Nigeria's difficult inter-faith relations often present a beguilingly simple picture of Muslims against Christians, sometimes presented as 'Muslim north' against 'Christian south'. As we have tried to show, the north contains important and large – albeit minority – Christian communities, and besides, there is no singular 'Muslim' identity in the region. Instead, what we wish to emphasize is a historical process of identity fragmentation within the Muslim community. Differing interpretations of Islamic doctrine, different attitudes towards the need for reform and rejuvenation, opposing conceptions of the 'virtuous life', different ritual practices and competing mundane interests, have led to tensions and fragmentation within the Muslim community. While Muslim/Christian conflicts cannot be wished away, the idea of a unitary block of Nigerian Muslims confronting an equally unitary block of Christian opposition is a figment of the imagination of journalists and religious entrepreneurs which can endure only if we fail to look closely at the fissures – and conflicts – within both the Muslim and Christian communities. Through our categorization of the different sects, actors and institutions we show how conflicts have been as much a defining feature of *intra*-Muslim relations over the centuries in northern Nigeria, as they have been in the recent history of Muslim/Christian relations.

Third, great changes and transformations in the ecological, demo-graphic, socio-economic and political fields have taken place in the north since the late 1960s. The powerful Native Authority administra-tions were disbanded from 1967, diminishing the position and authority of the Emirs. Furthermore, state creation in 1967 fractured the insti-tutional edifice and sense of solidarity of the pan-northern Western-educated elite, while military rule from 1966 and the civil war from 1967 unleashed unprecedented social and political changes. These included the centralization of political power at the national level. The oil boom from 1970 transformed, not only the revenue basis of the state, but also the nature and quality of governance while the deterioration of the agricul-tural economy and the severe Sahelian droughts of the 1970s put rural communities under acute stress. These changes, along with other trends such as the widening gap between the north and south, women's increasing access to education and employment, and the greater prominence of the federal centre in local lives, were bound to cause a measure of social dislo-cation and friction. In this context of rapid flux, it is not surprising that Islam increasingly became the medium for articulating grievance and dissent. In the face of rising poverty and discontent since 1982, and the diminishing coherence and effectiveness of the state in responding to the challenges facing state and society, Islam has become a potent tool, both for those seeking positive responses to the challenges and those seeking more narrowly to profit from the situation.

There is not one homogeneous Islam in northern Nigeria, neither do we have a single Islamic response to the challenges of modern life. Instead, traditionalists, modernists and radicals, organized in different sects and groups, compete for followership and influence. In the process, they have converted the sacred sphere into something akin to a market. Collective action within these Muslim sects and groups can best be understood by studying their historical antecedents, the structural strains within the community as a whole, each group's (re)interpretation of established Islamic precepts in the context of rapid social change, and their strategies and motivations for mobilizing a followership. Only by adopting such a grounded historical and sociological approach can we begin to understand the complex connections between faith and conflict in northern Nigeria.

Bibliography

Abdallah, Nurudeen M., 2012, 'Shettima: How to end Boko Haram menace', *Daily Trust*, http://dailytrust.com.ng, accessed 20 February 2012.

Adamu, Lawan Danjuma, 2013, 'Ansaru warns MEND against attacks on Muslims', *Daily Trust*, 17 April, http://dailytrust.com.ng, accessed on 17 April 2013.

Adamu, Uba Abdalla (ed.), n.d., *Darul Qadiriyya*, Official website of Qadiriyya, Kano, edited by Abdalla Uba Adamu, www.kanoonline.com/religion/qadriyya/publications.html, accessed on 22 September 2011.

Alhajj, M.A., 1973, 'Mahdist Tradition on Northern Nigeria', Ph.D. thesis, Abdullahi Bayero College, Kano.

Alkali, N.M. (ed.), 1993, 'Islam in the Central Sudan and the Emergence of Kanem', in his *Islam in Africa: Proceedings of the Islam in Africa Conference*, Ibadan: Spectrum Books.

Anon., 2012, 'The Popular Discourses of Salafi Radicalism and Salafi Counter-radicalism in Nigeria: A Case Study of Boko Haram', *Journal of Religion in Africa*, 42 (2), 118–44.

Ben Amara, Ramzi, 2011, 'The Izala Movement in Nigeria: Its Split, Relationship to Sufis and Perception of Sharī'a Re-Implementation', A dissertation submitted in partial fulfilment of the requirements for the degree of Doctor of Philosophy (D.Phil.) at Bayreuth International Graduate School of African Studies, BIGSAS, Universitat Bayreuth, Germany.

Bey, Matthew and Sim Tack, 2013, 'The Rise of a New Nigerian Militant Group', *Stratfor Global Intelligence*, 21 February.

Bonner, M., 2005, 'Poverty and Economics in the Qur'an', *Journal of Interdisciplinary History*, 35 (3 Special Issue, 'Poverty and Charity: Judaism, Christianity, and Islam'), 391–406.

Boyle, Joe, 2009, 'Nigeria's "Taliban" Enigma', BBC, 28 July, www.bbc.com/news/world, accessed on 31 July 2009.

Brigaglia, Andrea, 2012, 'A Contribution to the History of the Wahhabi Da'wa in West Africa: The Career and the Murder of Shaykh Ja'far Mahmoud Adam (Daura, *c.* 1961/1962 – Kano 2007)', in *Islamic Africa*, 3 (1), 1–23.

Bunza, M.U., 2002, 'Political Islam Under British Colonial Administration In Sokoto Province: 1903–1950s', in *Journal for Islamic Studies*, University of Cape Town South Africa, (Special Issue) 22.

Bunza, M.U., 2004a, 'Muslims and the Modern State in Nigeria: A Study of the Impact of Foreign Religious Literature, 1980s–1990s', *Islam et Sociétés au Sud du Sahara*, 17–18, 49–63.

Bunza, M.U., 2004b, 'The Iranian Model of Political Islamic Movement in Nigeria', in Gomez-Perez, M. (ed.) *L'Islam Politique au Sud du Sahara: Identities, Discourse et Enjeux*, 227–42.

Bunza, M.U., forthcoming, 'Migration, Itinerancy and the Making of Trans-National Muslim Intelligentsia in Nigeria' in Harrak, Fatima, and Ross, Eric (eds), *Religion and Migration*, proceedings of Conference, Rabat.

Casey, C., 2008, '"Marginal Muslims": Politics and the Perceptual Bounds of Islamic Authenticity in Northern Nigeria', *Africa Today*, 54 (3), 67–92.

Cisse, Hassan 'Shaykh al-Islam Ibrahim Niasse', 1984, http://tijani.org/shaykh-al-islam-ibrahim-niasse, accessed on 4 January 2012.

Clarke, Ian and Peter Linden, 1984, *Islam in Modern Nigeria: A Study of a Muslim Community in a Post-Independence State (1960–80)*, Mainz: Gruenewald.

Daftary, F. and G. Miskinzoda (eds), 2014, *The Study of Shi'i Islam: History, Theology and Law (Shi'i Heritage)*, London: I.B. Tauris.

Emmanuel, Ogala, 2013, 'Five things you should know about new extremist sect,

ANSARU', *Premium Times*, 23 February, www.premiumtimesng.com, accessed on 23 February 2013.

Enwerem, I.M., 1998, *A Dangerous Awakening: Politicization of Religion in Nigeria*, Ibadan: IFRA.

FOMWAN (Federation of Muslim Women's Associations in Nigeria), 2011, Mission statement, http://fomwan.org, accessed on 12 May 2011.

Gana, Ibrahim, 2013, 'The fall of Boko Haram in Maiduguri' *Leadership*, 26 July, http://leadership.ng, accessed on 26 July 2013.

Gerges, F.A., 2005, *The Far Enemy: Why Jihad Went Global*, Cambridge: Cambridge University Press.

Gumi, Abubakar with I.A. Tsiga, 1992, *Where I Stand*, Ibadan: Spectrum Books.

Gwarzo, T., 2007, 'The State and Islamic Civil Society: A Case Study of JTI, MSO, *Manarulhuda* and *Sabilurrashad*', Ph.D. Bayero University, Kano.

Hamagam, Aliyu, 2014, 'Niger sacks another Islamic sect', *Daily Trust*, 5 June, http://dailytrust.com.ng, accessed on 5 June 2014.

Hill, Jonathan, 2010, 'Sufism in Northern Nigeria: Force for Counter-Radicalization?' Strategic Studies Institute, Carlisle PA: U.S. Army War College, www.StrategicStudiesInstitute.army.mil, accessed 24 July 2011.

Hiskett, M., 1987, 'The Maitatsine Riots in Kano, 1980: An Assessment', *Journal of Religion in Africa*, 17 (3), 209–23.

Hiskett, M., 1980, 'The "Community of Grace" and its Opponents, the "Rejecters": A Debate about Theology and Mysticism in Muslim West Africa with Special Reference to its Hausa Expression', *African Language Studies*, 17, 99–140.

Hutson, Alaine S., 1999, 'The Development of Women's Authority in the Kano Tijaniyya, 1894–1963', *Africa Today* 46 (3–4), 43–64.

Imam, A., (ed.), 1985, *Women in Nigeria Today*, London: Zed Books.

Islamic Movement in Nigeria, 2012. www.islamicmovement.org/index.php?option=com_content&view=article&id=431:christianmuslim-group-visit-sheikh-zakzaky-h&catid=41:frontpage. Accessed 2 January 2012.

Isuwa, Sunday, 2011, 'Nigeria: Over 20,000 Muslims Observe Ashura in Kaduna', *Daily Trust*, 7 December, http://allafrica.com/stories/201112071029.html, accessed on 7 December 2011.

Kane, Ousmane, 2003, *Muslim Modernity in Postcolonial Nigeria: A Study of the Society for the Removal of Innovation and Reinstatement of Tradition*. Leiden: Brill.

Larémont, Ricardo R., 2011, *Islamic Law and Politics in Northern Nigeria*, Trenton NJ: Africa World Press.

Lawrence, B., 2006, *The Qur'an: A Biography*, London: Atlantic Books.Loimeier, R., 1997a, 'Islamic Reforms and Political Change: The Example of Abubakar Gumi and 'Yan Izala Movement in Northern Nigeria', E.E. Rosander and D. Westerlund (eds), *African Islam and Islam in Africa: Encounters Between Sufis and Islamists*, London: Hurst & Company.

Loimeier, R., 1997b, *Islamic Reform and Political Change in Northern Nigeria*, Evanston IL, Northwestern University Press.

Loimeier, R., 2012, 'Boko Haram: The Development of a Militant Religious Movement in Nigeria', *Africa Spectrum*, 47 (2–3), 137–155.

Lubeck, Paul M., 1985, 'Islamic Protest under Semi-Industrial Capitalism: 'Yan Tatsine Explained', *Africa*, 55 (4), 369–89.

Malami, Shehu, 2009, 'Expect More Boko Harams', *Leadership*, www.leadership.ng, accessed on 2 August 2009.

Masquelier, Adeline, 2009, *Women and Islamic Revival in a West African Town*, Bloomington IN: Indiana University Press.

Mohammed, Abdulkareem, 2010, *The Paradox of Boko Haram*, Kano: Moving Image.

Momen, Moojan, 1987, *An Introduction to Shi'i Islam: The History and Doctrines of Twelver Shi'ism*, New Haven CT, Yale University Press.

Mosadomi, Wole (2014) 'Niger govt, security operatives dislodge Islamist sect from forest', *Vanguard*, 5 June. www.vanguardngr.com, accessed on 5 June 2014.

Mottahedeh, Roy, 2008, The Mantle of the Prophet, Oneworld Publications; Second Edition edition, London.

Mustapha, Abdul Raufu, 2012, 'Boko Haram: Killing in God's name', *Mail & Guardian*, 5 April, http://mg.co.za/article/2012-04-05-boko-haram-killing-in-gods-name, accessed on 5 April 2012.

NACOMYO (National Council of Muslim Youth Organisations), n.d., *NACOMYO at a Glance*, National Mosque Abuja: NACOMYO National Secretariat.

NAN (News Agency of Nigeria), 2014, 'Zaria procession killings: Army opens probe, but says soldiers were fired upon', *Premium Times*, 27 July, www.premiumtimesng.com, accessed on 27 July 2014.

NASFAT (Nasrul-Lahi-L-Fatih Society), 2006, *Prayer Book/Manual*, Lagos: NASFAT World Headquarters.

Nossiter, Adam, 2013, 'New Threat in Nigeria as Militants Split Off', *New York Times*, 23 April, www.nytimes.com, accessed on 23 April 2013.

Nuhu, D., 2004, 'Crisis in the Izala Movement: A Case Study of Sokoto, 1986–2002', B.A. History, Usmanu Danfodiyo University Sokoto.

Nurudeen, A., 2004, 'Nasrul-lahi lil- Fah (NASFAT), in Sokoto, 1995–2003', B.A. History dissertation, Usumanu Dan Fodio University, Sokoto.

Omipidan, Ismail, 2009, 'Boko Haram: How Yusuf imported arms into the country', *Sun News*, 10 October 2009, http://sunnewsonline.com/new.

Onuba, Ifeanyi and Adesomoju, Ade, 2013, 'Unemployment, poverty responsible for terrorism in North – Sanusi', *Punch*, 16 January 2013, www.punchng.com, accessed on 16 January 2013.

Orintunsi, Jide and Olatunbosun, Yinka, 2014a, 'Military dislodges another Islamic sect in Niger' *Nation*, 5 June 2014, http://thenationonlineng.net, accessed on 5 June 2014.

Orintunsi, Jide and Olatunbosun, Yinka, 2014b, 'Terrorism: Niger dislodges radical Islamic sect camp', *Nation*, 4 June 2014, http://thenationonlineng.net, accessed on 4 June 2014.

Ostien, P., 2000, 'Islamic Criminal Law: What it means in Zamfara and Niger States', in *Journal of Public and Private Law*, 4 (4), 1–18.

Ostien, P., 2001, 'Ten Good things about the Implementation of Sharia taking Place in some States in Northern Nigeria', *Newswatch* (Lagos) July 9, 61–64.

Ostien, P., 2012, 'Percentages By Religion of the 1952 and 1963 Populations of Nigeria's Present 36 States', IRP–Abuja: Background Paper 1, NRN, Department of International Development, University of Oxford.

Paden J.N., 1973, *Religion and Political Culture in Kano*, Berkeley CA, University of California Press.

Paden, J.N., 2002, 'Islam and Democratic Federalism in Nigeria', CSIS, *Africa Notes*, 8 March, Washington DC: Center for Strategic and International Studies, http://csis.org/files/media/csis/pubs/anotes_0203.pdf, accessed on 12 April 2002.

Pew Forum on Religion & Public Life, 2010, 'Tolerance and Tension: Islam and Christianity in Sub-Saharan Africa', Washington DC: Pew Research Center. www.pewforum.org/files/2010/04/sub-saharan-africa-full-report.pdf, accessed 3 May 2014.

Post, K.W.J., 1963, *The Nigerian Federal Elections of 1959: Politics and Administration in a Developing Political System*, Oxford University Press, Oxford.

Punch Nigeria, 2014, 'Allah's enemies should be maimed, killed – Ogwuche, Nyanya bomb mastermind', *Punch*, 17 May, www.punchng.com, accessed on 17 May 2014.

Qadiriya, www.sufizikr.org/?page_id=93, accessed on 4 January 2012.

Robinson, D., 1985, *The Holy War of Umar Tal*, Oxford: Clarendon.

Sachedina, Abdulaziz Abdulhussein, 1998, *The Just Ruler (al-Sultan al-Adil) in Shi'ite Islam: The Comprehensive Authority of the Jurist in Imamite Jurisprudence*, Oxford: Oxford University Press.

Saeed, A.G., 1992a, 'British Fears over Mahdism in Northern Nigeria: A Look at Bormi

1903, Satiru 1906 and Dumbulwa 1923', *Frankfurter Afrikanistische Blätter* 4, 35–37.

Saeed, A.G., 1992b, 'A Biographical Study of Shaykh Sai'd Bin Hayyat (1887–1978) and the British Policy towards the Mahdiyya in Northern Nigeria, 1900–1960', Ph.D. Thesis, Bayero University, Kano.

SaharaReporters, (2014), 'How terrorists trailed Sheik Albani and family from his school before killing them', *SaharaReporters*, New York, 2 February, http://saharareporters. com, accessed on 2 February 2014.

Saidu, A.G.A. 1983, 'Mahdiya: Its Doctrines, Spread in West Africa and Encounter with Imperialists', paper presented at the Department of Islamic Studies, Bayero University, Kano.

Salkida, Ahmad M., 2011, 'The story of Nigeria's first suicide bomber', *Blueprint*, reproduced in *SaharaReporters*, 26 June, http://saharareporters.com, accessed on 27 June 2011.

Salkida, Ahmad, 2013a, 'Genesis and consequences of Boko Haram crisis', *Kano* Online, http://kanoonline.com, accessed on 30 April 2013.

Salkida, Ahmad, 2013b, 'How to end Boko Haram crisis', reprinted in *Nairaland Forum*, 17 May 2014, www.nairaland.com/1294203/time-pay-attention-ahmad-salkida, accessed on 3 October 2014.

Schimmel, Annemarie, 1975, *Mystical Dimensions of Islam*, Chapel Hill NC: University of North Carolina Press.

Seesemann, Rudiger, 2011, *The Divine Flood: Ibrahim Niasse and the Roots of a Twenti-eth-century Sufi Revival*, Oxford: Oxford University Press.

Soares, B.F., 2009, 'An Islamic Social Movement in Contemporary West Africa: NASFAT of Nigeria', in S.D.K. Ellis and I. van Kessel (eds), Movers and Shakers: Social Movements in Africa, Leiden: Brill.

Soares, B.F. and Otayek, R. (eds), 2007, *Islam and Muslim Politics in Africa*, Basingstoke: Palgrave Macmillan.

Spencer, T.J., 1998, *The Sufi Orders in Islam*, New York and Oxford: Oxford University Press.Sulaiman, H., 2011, 'The Imperative of Judicial Reform in the Implementation of Sharia', presented at the 5th National Conference of Sharia Implementing States, Sokoto, 23–25 March.

Tsiga, I.A. and Adamu A.U., (eds), 1997, *Islam and the History of Learning in Katsina*, Ibadan: Spectrum Books.

Tukur, Sani, 2014, 'Zakzaky speaks: my sons were taken alive, then summarily executed by soldiers', *Premium Times*, 26 July www.premiumtimesng.com, accessed on 26 July 2014.

Umar, Muhammad S., 1993, 'Changing Islamic Identity in Nigeria from the 1960s to the 1980s: From Sufism to Anti-Sufism', in Brenner, Louis (ed.), *Muslim Identity and Social Change in Sub-saharan Africa*, Bloomington IN, Indiana University Press.

Umar, Muhammad S., 1999, 'Sufism and its Opponents in Nigeria: The Doctrinal and Intellectual Aspects', in F. de Jong and B. Redtke, (eds), *Islamic Mysticism Contested: Thirteen Centuries of Controversies and Polemics*, Leiden: Brill, 357–85.

Umar, Muhammad S., 2000, 'The Tijaniyya and British Colonial Authorities in Northern Nigeria', in Triaud J.-L. and Robinson, D. (eds), *La Tijâniyya: Une Confrérie Musulmane à la Conquête de'Afrique*, Paris, Karthala, 327–55.

Umar, Muhammad S., 2005, *Islam and Colonialism: Intellectual Responses of Muslims of Northern Nigeria to British Colonial Rule*, Leiden: Brill.

Umoru, Henry, 2013, 'Poverty, misrule, not responsible for Boko Haram – PDP', *Vanguard*, 26 January, www.vanguardngr.com, accessed on 26 January 2013.

Usman, Y.B., 1983, ' A Reflection of the History of Relations between Borno and Hausaland before 1804', in Usman, B. and Alkali, N. (eds), *Studies in the History of Pre-Colonial Borno*, Zaria: Northern Nigerian Publishing.

Vanguard Media, 2014, 'Boko Haram members burn their university certificates – Shehu Sani', *CNN*, republished in *Vanguard*, 14 May, www.vanguardngr.com, accessed on 16 May 2014.

Werthmann, K., 2005, 'The example of Nana Asma'u', *D+C Development and Cooperation*, 32 (3), 108–111.

Winters, Jonah, 1996, 'Origins of Shi'ism: A Consensus of Western Scholarship', http://bahai-library.com/winters_origins_shiism, accessed on 5 January 2012.

World of Tasawwuf, 2008, www.spiritualfoundation.net/sufism.htm#97635302, accessed on 4 January 2012.

Wright, Zakariya, nd. 'The Concept of the Spiritual Flood (fayda) in Tijani Doctrine', http://tijani.org/the-concept-of-the-spiritual-flood-fayda-in-tijani-doctrine, accessed on 4 January 2012.

Zenn, Jacob, 2013, 'Ansaru: a profile of Nigeria's newest jihadist movement – Jamestown Terrorism Monitor', *SaharaReporters*, 12 January, http://saharareporters.com, accessed on 12 January 2013.

4

Experiencing inequality at close range
Almajiri students & Qur'anic schools in Kano

HANNAH HOECHNER

Introduction

The *almajirai*, boys and young men enrolled in 'traditional' Qur'anic schools rather than formal (Western-style) education, have become an issue of growing concern in northern Nigeria. The students of such schools have attracted attention in the context of increased attempts to achieve universal primary education and growing concerns about child welfare. In the context of growing violent conflict, they have also been associated with Islamic radicalization and militancy. The current spate of *Boko Haram* violence in northern Nigeria has carried such modes of thinking to the extremes. The *almajiri* education system is described as 'Nigeria's ticking time bomb' (Kulutempa 2011) and as a threat to the national security (Lawal 2011). Similarly, Nobel laureate Wole Soyinka declared in an article in the *Newsweek* Magazine about *Boko Haram* that the 'butchers of Nigeria' have 'been deliberately bred, nurtured, sheltered, rendered pliant, obedient to only one line of command, ready to be unleashed at the rest of society. They were bred in madrassas and are generally known as the almajiris' (Soyinka 2012). 'Traditional' Qur'anic students are one group of young Muslims that seem, within some popular imagination, to personify the potential for violence within northern Muslim society. This chapter explores the position of this ubiquitous social group in Kano.

As the *almajirai* are thought about first and foremost as a threat, policy recommendations concerning them are often cast in terms of containment, quarantine and even eradication. Several states and also federal bodies consider legislative action against the *almajiri* system, either under anti-trafficking legislation or by putting a ban on begging (e.g. Hassan 2013; Salihi 2013). Abolitionist and punitive approaches are based on the idea that problematic outcomes are produced within the (narrow) confines of

98

'traditional' Qur'anic schools where 'backward' and 'neglectful' parents abandon children they do not want to take responsibility for (e.g. Kumolu 2012). Qur'anic schools are considered sites where children suffer abuse at the hands of exploitative teachers and where they learn radical doctrines. This chapter shows the problems of such reasoning. The *almajirai* are often portrayed as a distinct and clearly circumscribed demographic. This is misleading. In terms of skills and future prospects, little differentiates them from other poor undereducated youths from rural households. Young people frequently move between different educational systems, which means few children are 'pure' *almajirai*. The tale of 'backward' and 'negligent' parents moreover cuts a complicated story too short to be meaningful. Various economic, social and religious reasons play together to motivate parents to enrol children as *almajirai*.

I also argue that it is not enough to look at the school setting in the strict sense to find out what *almajirai*'s experiences are like, including what might be problematic about them. There are clearly problems with the way children grow up in 'traditional' Qur'anic schools. The difficulties the *almajirai* face in terms of accessing food, shelter and health-care for example are well known. But the *almajirai* also encounter difficulties that cannot be understood by focusing on Qur'anic schools alone. Such schools operate in a social context where inequalities are pervasive, giving rise to experiences of exclusion. Where inequalities are large, the better-off may seek to distinguish themselves from poorer segments of society so as to justify differences. It is important to take this context into account when evaluating sources of risk for the *almajirai*.

Katz says about her field site in rural Sudan that in the wake of its incorporation into the capitalist global economy 'greater awareness of what is to be had not only increased desire, but made not having more apparent and painful than before' (2004, 227). Ferguson compares people's experiences of modernity in the Zambian Copperbelt with the experience of being hung-up on in the course of an aborted telephone conversation: it 'is not the same as never having had a phone' (1999, 238). What is 'to be had' is constantly within eyeshot but none the less solidly out of reach. This is the case in Nigeria where income inequality has risen dramatically since the beginning of World-Bank-imposed structural adjustment in 1986, especially in the north-west, evidenced by the rise in the percentage of people living on less than two-thirds of mean per capita expenditure from 27 per cent in 1980 to 54 per cent in 2004 (Aigbokhan 2008, 11–14).

It has been argued that growing inequalities tend to enlarge the physical distance between different socio-economic strata through processes of gentrification and ghettoization (e.g. Lees et al. 2008; Wacquant 1999). The *almajiri* system reverses such trends. Most *almajirai* come from poor rural households. Enrolment as *almajiri* entails work for wealthier strata of society, and sojourns in urban areas, at least during the agriculturally unproductive dry season. This brings the *almajirai* close, both physically and emotionally, to people who have much more than them in terms of material possessions as well as opportunities (e.g. to acquire knowledge). Where neighbourhood children attend secular school in the morning and *Islamiyya* school in the afternoon, employment niches open up for *almajirai*, including in households that would for economic reasons rather rely on their own children's work if it was available during the day.[1] This means the *almajirai* are daily reminded that other children attend forms of education from which they are excluded. Being excluded is an experience they struggle to come to grips with. Employment in urban middle/upper-class households entails additional challenges for *almajirai*, which are both particularly problematic and formative.

Domestic work arrangements have been described as 'the most intense, sustained contact with members of other classes that most of their participants encounter' (Dickey 2000, 463). Such arrangements are tricky because they juxtapose a spatial and emotional 'intimacy based on the worker's closeness to the family and a distance based on class and other hierarchies' (Adams & Dickey 2000, 3). Unlike in most other work settings, relationships between workers and employers are forged 'at close range, creating a more intense dynamic of self-other contrast' (ibid., 2). A way must be found 'to create difference and otherness to justify workplace hierarchies' (ibid., 17). For the *almajirai* this often means that they feel looked down upon and disrespected by the people they work for. If we are worried about the extent to which *almajirai* become frustrated with or alienated from mainstream society, our concern has to be with problematic experiences like these.

The next section discusses methods and data. I then introduce the *almajiri* system, including the reasons why families opt to enrol children in it today, even though the system promises no longer access to high status or even a sustainable livelihood. After that, I describe how the *almajirai* are incorporated into urban neighbourhoods on highly unequal terms. I conclude by evaluating the risks the *almajirai* face in their lives – and the risks they presumably pose to society. I discuss appropriate policy responses to the system in light of that and second the *almajirai*'s call to conceive of their upbringing and wellbeing as a collective responsibility.

Research methods, data and remaining questions

The material for this chapter stems from media records, that is, national and international English-language news, and Internet sources including

---

[1] For want of alternatives, *almajirai* often accept non-monetary offerings – a place to sleep in the entrance room (*soro*) or a meal – as payment.

blogs and online forums. I also draw on official narratives, institutional publications from local and international organizations working with children, and local academic production. In addition, I build on 13 months of fieldwork that I carried out in Kano State between 2009 and 2011. My fieldwork included four months in Albasu, a small rural town in Albasu Local Government Area (LGA) in the east of Kano State. For the remaining time, I lived at Sabuwar ☐ofa within Kano's Old City. I collected data in the form of fieldwork observations, as well as semi-structured interviews, group conversations and casual interactions with *almajirai*, their parents, caregivers and teachers as well as some former *almajirai*. Furthermore, I use translated and transcribed 'radio interviews' the young *almajirai* conducted amongst each other with my tape recorder and discussions of the photographs they took with disposable cameras. I also draw on data from the production process of a participatory documentary film/docu-drama about the perspectives of *almajirai* on their lives and the challenges they face.[2] This includes stories narrated or written down during the script-writing process, as well as discussions about the way they would like to see their lives and identities represented on screen. The nine participating youths were aged between 15 and 20 years, and came from three different Qur'anic schools in both urban and rural Kano.

While the *almajirai* and their families are often talked and written about, they are rarely listened to on their own terms. Throughout my research, I sought as much as possible to create a space where they can voice their concerns. Inevitably, such an endeavour poses particular methodological challenges. Jeffrey finds 'a methodological bias built into [anthropological] researchers' sample of youth in the global south' and queries '[t]o what extent researchers [are] inevitably drawn to more outgoing, charismatic youth – those who survive and "get on"'? (2011, 794) I encountered neither the 'gullible children' (Awofeso et al. 2003, 320) nor the 'angry youth' (*Weekly Trust* 13 December 2002, in Adamu, n.d.) which is how the *almajirai* are often described. But can we conclude from this that they do not exist? Logistical challenges make it difficult to trace the trajectories of 'problematic' *almajirai*. If they are resentful of Westerners, they are unlikely to respond to my requests for information. If they are truant, they are unlikely to be accessible through their schools. One of the burning questions that my research does not directly address is that of the relationship between *Boko Haram* and the *almajirai*. I did not encounter *Boko Haram* sympathizers in the Qur'anic schools where I conducted my research, and to pursue them more energetically on the topic would likely have alienated my informants and jeopardized their trust. It remains for future research to establish whether the *almajiri* system contributes

---

[2]   *Duniya Juyi Juyi*, available online at: www.qeh.ox.ac.uk/research/video/odid-student-research/video-hlg, accessed 3 October 2014.

to the *Boko Haram* insurgency, and if so in what ways.[3] However, what seems clear from available evidence is that depictions by people like Wole Soyinka of *almajirai* as creatures 'bred' for perpetuating violence are both sweeping and unsubstantiated.

Who are the Almajirai?

The *almajirai* are boys and young men from primary-school age to their early twenties who are enrolled in 'residential colleges' beyond the state's purview and regulatory interventions. Many schools lack physical infra-structure beyond a canopied forecourt where the teaching takes place, compelling their students to cohabit other spaces like mosques or neigh-bours' entrance halls (*soro*). The *almajirai* learn to read, write and recite the Holy Qur'an. Modern/secular or Islamic subjects other than the Qur'an do not form part of their curriculum. During the lesson-free time, the *almajirai* earn their livelihood by doing menial jobs for neighbours or in markets and motor parks, or through begging (*bara*). The 'traditional' Qur'anic school system is widespread in Muslim West Africa and is used mostly by poor rural families. Children are handed over to the teacher (*malam*, pl.: *malamai*), who receives no salary but lives off the support given by the local community, the alms received in exchange for his spiritual services, the contributions of his students and supplementary income-generating activities. Most teachers are themselves products of the *almajiri* system. While many students return home at least once a year (for the major holidays or to help their parents farm), others do not see their parents for years. Some teachers migrate with their schools following seasonal agricultural patterns.

Enrolment in Qur'anic schools all over Nigeria is estimated to exceed 9.5 million, with more than 8.5 million in the northern part of the country (UBEC 2010). How many of these students are *almajirai* is, however, subject to speculation, as the existing statistics do not differ-entiate between day students (who stay with their parents, potentially attend modern school in addition to Qur'anic school, and include females) and 'boarding' male students (*almajirai*). A census carried out in Kano State in 2003 found over 1.2 million students enrolled in 'traditional' Qur'anic schools in the state. However, this figure again includes girls as well as boys who are day students, suggesting that the actual number of *almajirai* is significantly lower (Office of the Special Adviser 2005). Since modern, Western education was introduced in Nigeria under British colonial rule, the prestige and political influence of 'traditional' Qur'anic

---

[3] For a discussion of possible – contradictory – trends, see the introductory chapter to this volume by Mustapha.

scholars have gradually diminished. Economic decline since the 1980s affected the *almajirai* as it reduced both their income opportunities and the ability of others in society to support them through alms (see Lubeck 1985). The emergence of reform-oriented Islamic movements in Nigeria marginalized the *almajiri* system further (see Kane 2003; Loimeier 1997). Increasingly, it attracted criticism as a Hausa cultural accretion to Islam. Many object to the *almajirai*'s practice of begging which, in their view, Islam permits only in acute emergencies (see Bambale 2007). Prestige and status increasingly derive from mastering the 'modern'/reformed forms of knowledge associated with 'high culture' Islam. Not only has the respect available for the *almajirai*'s learning decreased, but they also feel the brunt of religious differences: followers of the reformist *Izala*[4] would not only refuse begging *almajirai* food, but may even beat them, *almajirai* told me.[5]

Particularly since the *Maitatsine* crisis in the 1980s the *almajiri* system has moreover been declared responsible for religious violence. The *Maitatsine* insurgents were believed to be mainly 'traditional' Qur'anic school students (Hiskett 1987; Lubeck 1985; Winters 1987). In the context of the current *Boko Haram* Islamist insurgency with its attacks on government institutions including modern/secular schools, 'traditional' Qur'anic students are accused of furnishing the 'cannon fodder' for violence (234NEXT 2011). Today, the *almajiri* system promises neither access to political power nor high social status, its former economic viability has largely been undermined and its religious merit has come under attack. Students are moreover vilified as presumed perpetrators of violence. Yet, demand for the system persists. Many believe that this is because parents enrolling their children as *almajirai* are 'backward' and 'negligent' and do not appreciate secular knowledge (see Kumolu 2012; Salihi 2013; Sule-Kano 2008). My research suggests a more complex story though.

Relic from the past or coping strategy of the poor?

Throughout my research I have not actually met anyone who considered secular education as principally *haram* (forbidden) and met very few who thought it not particularly desirable (cf. Brigaglia 2008). Appreciation of different forms of knowledge is reflected in children's educational trajec-

---

[4] 'Society for the Removal of Innovation and Reestablishment of the Sunna' (see Loimeier 1997).
[5] While the students and teachers of the *almajiri* system are unlikely to embrace reformist ideas, not all necessarily belong to one of the Sufi brotherhoods (*Tijaniyya* or *Qadiriyya*). But stickers with the bust of *Tijaniyya* shaikh Ibrahim Niass decorate many *almajirai*'s phones and begging bowls. Which *tariqa* (brotherhood) one identifies with is not a divisive issue, however, and I met *almajirai* who did not share their *malam*'s *tariqa* affiliation.

tories. Many young people do not live as *almajirai* all way through their childhood and youth, but – voluntarily, or forced by circumstances – switch between different educational options. Their schooling trajectories may for example include episodes in so-called *Islamiyya* schools. These are modernized Islamic schools that teach the Qur'an, but also other Islamic and in some instances modern/secular subjects. But many *almajirai* also attend secular school for a couple of years before enrolling as Qur'anic students, and are planning to further their secular education in the future. Former *almajirai* are likely to make up a large part of the clientele of adult evening schools.[6]

Various people in my rural field site Albasu stated to me that in the past, people did not value secular education, but that now most had come to understand its benefits. Yet, increasing acceptance on principle has been thwarted by state withdrawal from the education sector since structural adjustment (Baba 2011; Umar 2003). While basic education is officially free, in reality it implies recurrent expenses: for text books and writing materials, uniforms, transportation where necessary, contributions to the rehabilitation of school facilities which are often in a deplorable state, levies to buy chalk, brooms, report cards and other such sundry running costs. Especially post-primary education has its price – starting with the bribe sometimes required to secure one of the limited places[7] – and often requires students to commute/board. Poor-quality teaching (see Johnson 2011), costs, including opportunity costs in terms of forgone children's work (see Tomasevski 2005), insecurity about the transitions to the next level of schooling, and more-than insecure pay-offs in terms of future opportunities make parents wonder whether secular school is quite worth the investment.

Admittedly, my research might underestimate remaining resentments against secular education on ideological grounds as people opposed to anything 'Western' might have avoided meeting me/talking to me, and as interviewees may have concealed critical views thinking they would make me, a secular school product, uncomfortable. Several people I spoke to felt that secular knowledge comes second in importance to religious knowledge. Whereas parents may find it excusable to let their children's *boko* education slide, most felt strongly about ensuring their wards acquire at least a modicum of Qur'anic knowledge. But whatever the role of remaining resentments against *boko* education, given the financial diffi-culties poor parents face trying to enrol and sustain their children in secular education, we cannot jump to the conclusion that it is necessarily a dislike

[6] This impression is based on visits to two different adult evening education centres in Kano City and on information from older/former *almajirai*.

[7] I was told on several occasions that children did not proceed to secondary school even though they would have liked to and performed well in primary school, because they could not secure admission. Admission letters are often distributed based not on merit, but on 'purchasing power'.

for secular education that makes children drop out of secular school and enrol as *almajirai*. Also, to dismiss critical views on *boko* education out of hand as 'backward' is problematic. It ignores that negative attitudes towards *boko* education originate in part at least in contemporary social and political conditions. *Boko Haram*, for example, links its rejection of '*boko*' to the corruption and depravity of today's elites, most of whom are modern school products (e.g. Last 2009).

People make reasoned decisions based on the options available to them, and costly and poor-quality secular education may not make for a particularly attractive choice. The *almajiri* system is valued for the character training and life skills it is believed to impart. A certain degree of hardship is considered educative as it teaches boys endurance and steels their character. The system moreover offers redress for a number of difficult situations. Gathering the resources to launch an adult career – that is to build a room for prospective bride(s) and children, and to marry – affords a real challenge to adolescent boys and young men in a largely eroding rural economy where opportunities to earn cash income are scarce. Seasonal or permanent migration to the cities, which offer petty income opportunities as street vendors and odd-job men, promises redress. Migration, especially during the agriculturally unproductive dry season, is indeed a common strategy of Sahelian peasant households to reduce their subsistence burden and allows boys to acquire livelihood skills appropriate to the ecology of the region (e.g. Mortimore 1998; Mustapha & Meagher 1992).

Divorce is frequent and easy to achieve in Hausaland. In 1959, Smith wrote that '[t]he average Hausa woman probably makes three or four marriages before the menopause' (p. 244). The repeated efforts of Kano State Governor Rabiu Kwankwaso to marry off divorcees suggest that divorce continues to be pervasive (NAN 2013). Many marriages end in divorce because husbands fail to take care of the basic subsistence needs of their families, or because of fights between or over co-wives. In the case of divorce, the need may arise to 're-accommodate' children. Divorced mothers, who are expected to re-marry soon on religious grounds, can rarely move into new marriages with children from previous ones. Children left with fathers are at risk of suffering neglect, and abuse from stepmothers. High maternal mortality also renders children motherless (Federal Ministry of Health 2011). For boys, the *almajiri* system offers a way out under such constrained familial circumstances.

In sum, multiple economic, cultural and religious factors play together to make some parents prefer the *almajiri* system to other options. Poverty is a major factor constraining choice; modern secular education often does not constitute a meaningful option; high divorce rates necessitate the 're-accommodation' of children. Norms about the gender-appropriate upbringing of children, religious beliefs in the need to prepare for the hereafter, and a concern with boys' acquisition of livelihood skills appropriate to the peasant economy and ecology of the region all also play a role for enrolment decisions. *Almajiri* enrolment thus cannot be reduced to parental 'backwardness' or negligence. Equally, an exclusive focus on the *almajiri* system as a putative radicalizing agent in young people's lives simplifies matters. It overlooks that the *almajirai* do not constitute the neatly separable social category as which they are often portrayed. Many young men are not 'pure' products of the *almajiri* system, but have also experienced other strands of education. Educational disadvantage in northern Nigeria extends far beyond the *almajirai*, as the low secular school enrolment rates for girls, or the poor achievements of even those children who do attend secular school, attest. According to the Nigerian Demographic and Health Survey, 35 per cent of school-aged girls and 47 per cent of school-aged boys attend primary school in the north-west. In Sokoto State, 91 per cent of children aged 5–16 years cannot read a simple sentence in Roman script in their preferred language at all. Only 14 per cent of children of that age group in Sokoto manage to add two single-digit numbers correctly on paper (National Population Commission 2011 44–59; 159–77).[8] The skills poor youths from rural families acquire are thus limited and their future prospects drab whether or not they enrol as *almajirai*.

Incorporation into urban neighbourhoods on adverse terms

As Qur'anic students who come to town first and foremost to pursue their religious education, *almajirai* relate to the people in their neighbourhoods on complex terms. As religious scholars without means they are habitual recipients of alms. Yet, it has become very much impossible for *almajirai* today to survive on the basis of charity only. Begging, moreover, exposes *almajirai* to abuse. Almost all *almajirai* have already been insulted and chased away when begging. Some even describe physical assaults.[9] Domestic work for neighbouring households can constitute a comparatively easy way of earning money as it allows children to exploit skills they have learned at home (Bourdillon 2009, 2). Towards the end of puberty,

---

[8] As the statistics are based on written tests in Roman script, they test a particular set of skills: the ability to read and write in Roman script and to do paper-based calculations using Roman numbers. We cannot conclude from them that children lack literacy and numeracy altogether, as results may well have been different if tests had been administered in *a'jami* (Hausa written in Arabic script), or if children had been asked to add numbers in their heads rather than on paper.

[9] In a radio programme organised by UNICEF, NAPTIP (National Agency for the Prohibition of Trafficking in Persons and Other Related Matters) and CAESI, the participating *almajirai* for example recount how people pour water over them when they beg to make them leave. Available online at: www.unicef.org/nigeria/A_saurare_mu_2.pdf

adult gender norms begin to govern the *almajirai's* behaviour fully, thereby ruling out forms of employment that involve entering a house other than their own. But until they reach this age, almost all *almajirai* work as household help for some time, my research suggests. *Almajirai* enter a symbiotic relationship with the people in the neighbourhoods of their schools. Townspeople can gain religious standing by supporting *almajirai*. Simultaneously, the *almajirai* constitute a readily available and close-by pool of cheap labour that people can draw on for various household tasks. In Hausa society where many women practise *purdah* (seclusion), and thus are largely confined to their compounds, children make the daily activities of the household possible as they are sent to buy foodstuffs, fetch water or run errands (see Robson 2004; Schildkrout [1978] 2002). Some households establish fairly durable relationships with individual *almajirai*, who may be in charge of washing and ironing clothes, of cleaning around the house, of fetching water each day, and of doing the daily shopping. Others employ *almajirai* on an ad hoc basis for all sorts of odd jobs and errands, e.g. to catch runaway chickens, to repair a mud wall that has crumbled under the rain or to clear out a blocked sewer.

Ideas about what it means to be 'civilized,' 'moral' or 'pious,' play an important role in how *almajirai* and their employers conceive of one another and of their relationship (cf. Shah 2000, 95). Hansen observes that many employers think of their servants as material-minded and exploitative, and of themselves as fair-minded and generous (2000, 37, 47). Similarly, people employing *almajirai* sometimes interpret their actions as a means of honouring their religious commitments through 'facilitating' the *almajirai's* religious studies, or as a way of taking responsibility for the needy, rather than as a labour contract.[10] In one scene in the film/docu-drama that we produced, two upper-class women discuss their opinions on *almajirai*. One of them states:

> Their parents grew tired of them, they farm, grow food, sell it to us, then they send their children and want us to feed them?

While the protagonist of the film Aminu is providing crucial services to her household, his employer dismisses this, and casts their relationship as one in which she is expected to feed him magnanimously. Surely, this scene caricatures upper-class behaviour. Nonetheless, it originates from a shared understanding between the *almajirai* and the professional actresses involved of how some people define themselves vis-à-vis the *almajirai*

---

[10] Some people support *almajirai* unconditionally. Yet, most *almajirai* are expected to reciprocate the 'charity' they receive in some way or the other, be it through prayers for a 'benefactor's' benefit, through the provision of other spiritual services or by carrying out the sorts of domestic work described above.

working for them. The better-off employers of *almajirai* that I interacted with frequently during my fieldwork certainly cast themselves as granting rather than seizing opportunities when I asked them about the *almajirai* in their households.

According to Hansen, many employers justify difference as morally acceptable through collapsing character and socio-economic status into one concept (2000, 55–56). Shah echoes this, arguing that urban employers in Nepal want domestics from rural areas as these are considered honest, loyal, meek and obedient. Incidentally, such qualities make it easier to appropriate their labour. However, as a flipside of their association with meekness and loyalty, rural children are stereotyped as 'ignorant, dirty, and ... uncivilised', which 'provides urbanity with a civilizing role and further adds a cultural dimension and rationale for the servant's subordination' (Shah 2000, 95). The *almajirai* are frequently labelled backward, gullible and dirty. 'Typical *Almajirai* are identifiable by their awful state of hygiene, unkempt tattered clothes, diseases-afflicted and ulcerated skins', Aluaigba writes (2009, 19, citing Usman 2008, 67). According to Amzat, '[i]t has become a common abuse to call anyone looking ... dirty an almajiri' (2008, 59–60, citing Bashir 1994). Tellingly, Aminu's employer in our film admonishes him when he first comes to her house and is offered employment on the condition that 'from now on, you'll bathe, and wash your clothes, so you look like other people too'. The employment arrangement is thus garnished with 'civilizing' overtones.

While employers may portray themselves as magnanimous benefactors, the *almajirai* emphasized the value and importance of their work for the wider public good. The youths involved in the film project, for instance, expressed frustration that their contributions to the smooth functioning of society often went unrecognized and undervalued. What would happen if there were no *almajirai* to do all the work they are currently shouldering, they asked. One boy[11] said he wanted to take a long holiday at home after the Muslim festival of *Eid al-Kabir* so the family he was working for would have to fetch their water themselves for a while. He was hoping they would realize how demanding his work was – for which he got paid with a place to sleep and occasional meals.

Market transaction or patron-client relationship?

Shah (2000) argues that employers strategically maintain ambiguity about the nature of the relationship between them and their servants so as to

---

[11] I anonymized informants where I felt it necessary to protect their identity. Where informants were comfortable with statements being publicised in their name and where I considered this safe for them, I left names and identifying information unchanged.

mystify relations of domination. Domestics defy the analytical categories commonly used to theorize class relations. They are neither exclusively wage labourers nor exclusively serfs in the Marxist sense, and yet they combine elements of both. '[T]he domestic,' Shah writes for the Nepalese context, 'by the liminal zone he or she occupies, is appropriated in labor as well as in person' (2000, 89). Domestic work often occupies the grey area between intimate personal relationships (based on affection), and labour contract (based on the exchange of services for compensation). Klocker describes how child domestic workers in Tanzania, 'attained neither the benefits of familial membership (protection, security, love, nurturance, and access to education) nor the advantages of being an employee (set working conditions and wages)' (2011, 214). Nonetheless kinship ideology is often used to subordinate child domestics as employers make use of it to 'instil loyalty and diligence in their servants while disabling full incorporation' (Shah 2000, 111).

Ambiguity finds expression in a lack of explicit arrangements concerning working hours and pay. The *almajirai* for example complained that often employers would not respect the timetable of the Qur'anic school and demand that a boy works for them during school hours:

> Some of our employers ... mistreat you. Some send their own children to [secular] school. But you, you're expected to stay and work for them. If you say it's time for your own studies, they'll complain: 'we're helping you, you good-for-nothings, first you go to the market, then you can go to your school.' If you tell them, you'll be late, they don't care.

Shah writes that being remunerated through gifts and tips rather than a contractual wage 'necessarily relegate[s child domestics] to a subordinate position where they have to be obliging and servile to their masters beyond what is required in contractual wage relations' (2000, 101). This was the case for *almajirai* as the payment they received was often minimal, and seldom fixed. One *almajiri* I was close to in Kano for example received no formal payment from the household in whose *soro* (entrance hall) he slept, and for whom he fetched water every day. Instead, they stepped in on different occasions to cover his expenses, such as the transport costs to visit home or the money needed to sew new clothes on *Salla* (*Eid el-Fitr* and *Eid el-Kabir*).

In many respects the *almajirai* stand to lose from work arrangements whose terms are vague and personalized, as these put them at the mercy of their employers. Yet, one-off impersonal monetized transactions do not serve their interest either. The *almajirai* participating in the film project for instance lamented that their provision of spiritual services[12] becomes more

---

[12] Such as saying specific prayers for a 'benefactor's' benefit or providing *rubutun sha*, spiritual medicine consisting of Qur'anic verses washed off a slate to be drunk.

and more commodified: in the past, it was based on long-term reciprocity within the community. Today, it was turned into a one-off exchange of cures for cash in which the affluent shun any longer-term responsibility for the *almajirai*'s wellbeing. One of the youths participating in the film project said:

> There are people that won't stop to help you until they have some problem themselves. That's when they'll call upon you. When [someone] is well, he doesn't care about you, but when he's unwell, you'll see him gather 70 or 50 *almajirai*, and give them 1500 or 2000 Naira [to say prayers for him].

In an ideal case, the *almajirai* argued, households would take an *almajiri* in as a 'son of the house' (□*an gida*). They would offer him a space to socialize and relax during the day and a place to sleep at night, provide a reliable food supply and listen to his worries and difficulties. They would sponsor him through secular education, sew clothes for him on *Salla*, and help him find better-paying income opportunities once he grew older. During script-writing, the participating *almajirai* described such an ideal-case scenario:

> An *almajiri* enjoys his life when he becomes a □*an gari* [literally, son of the town], when he finds a kind *uwar* □*aki* [female employer], who will take him in like her son ... He gets food in the morning, at midday and at night. She gives him soap to wash and bath, she buys him clothes, if the clothes of her husband are too small for him, she passes them on to him. At *Salla*, she will have clothes sewn for him. And he, he shows them respect and obedience/loyalty [*biyayya*]. When it's time for his studies, they will tell him to go to school. If she sees he is upset, she will ask him what upsets him. If he has some small favours to ask, they will help him out.

What the *almajirai* were seeking is best understood as a durable form of patron-client relationship. Smith describes the Hausa cultural 'blueprint' for such relationships:

> Clientage is a relation between two persons and their dependents, which presupposes status inequality of the principals, and consists in ties of mutual loyalty, interest and assistance. The inferior or client frequently performs political or domestic services for his superior or patron, while the latter takes care of him politically, by protecting him from interference by other officials or aristocrats, and also assists him economically (1957, 13).

Clientage is not limited to the political sphere. Smith also describes 'domestic' forms of clientage, or *barantaka* (literally, service), where a servant farms and runs errands for a patron (see Morgan et al. 2010, 84). Such relationships are formed amongst commoners (that is, they do not necessarily involve nobility), and can provide a substitute for kinship networks for those, including immigrants, who lack 'effective support from kinsfolk in the community ... But whereas kinship is a permanent relation, clientage is an association terminable at the wish of either party' (M.G. Smith 1954, 32). Smith draws our attention to the pervasive use of kinship terms to express such relationships. Patrons for example are frequently referred to as 'fathers' or 'mothers of the house' (*uban ☐aki* or *uban gida* for male patrons; *uwar ☐aki* or *uwar rana* for female patrons), and their respective clients figure as 'sons' or 'daughters' (*☐an arziki*, *'yar arziki*, *☐an gida*).

Patronage and clientelism have long been discussed as the bane of African politics and social relations, stalling social mobility and trapping poor clients in relationships of dependence and servitude (e.g. Chabal & Daloz 1999). Yet, recent scholarship has called for a more nuanced examination of the actual power relations ensuing, and urged us to pay attention not only to the agency of patrons but also to that of clients (see Mustapha & Whitfield 2009). Clients may strategically enter patronage relationships to access social and financial resources through their patrons (e.g. Morgan et al. 2010; Wasiuzzaman & Wells 2010). Hickey and du Toit point out that 'there may be elements of clientelism that have much to offer the poorest people, at least in the short-medium term' (2007, 9). Rather than jumping to conclusions about the detrimental nature of patronage/clientelism, we should examine poor people's actual experiences of it. Cheeseman (2006) proposes analysing patron-client relationships along two dimensions to gauge how power is distributed within them. The first dimension concerns the degree to which they are personalized, that is, what proportion of patronage is channelled through individuals. 'More diffused or collective forms of patronage need not create direct personalized ties of subordination and dependence' (Whitfield & Mustapha 2009, 220). The second dimension concerns how competitive patron-client relationships are, that is, the extent to which the recipients of patronage 'are able to choose between, or periodically change, the source of patronage. This is of great importance because it determines how responsive patrons are likely to be to local need and demands' (Cheeseman 2006, 33).

How do the *almajirai* fit into Cheeseman's matrix? Their relationships to their patrons are highly personalized and usually involve only one *almajiri* per household, ruling out collective forms of bargaining. Also, the *almajirai* are competing for employer-patrons rather than the other way around, which means the latter are under little 'competitive pressure'. Given the oversupply of potential clients ready to fill their posts, the *almajirai* are in a weak bargaining position. Their age may set them apart from potential competitors as domestic service is foreclosed to those to whom adult gender norms apply fully. Also, their identity as religious scholars may distinguish them from other potential young clients as people can gain religious standing by supporting *almajirai*. Yet, this identity has come under attack, and in a society where over 40 per cent of the population are under the age of 15 years (British Council and Harvard School 2010, 13), youth alone hardly works as a 'unique selling point'. Moreover, we should not forget that in a gerontocratic society, age compounds the effect of other axes of inequality, to the effect that young *almajirai* enjoy very little social status. In sum, the terms of the *almajirai*'s incorporation into clientelistic systems are mostly adverse.

Their weak bargaining position notwithstanding, entering patron-client relationships was the primary route through which the *almajirai* envisaged achieving their goals. Some of the *almajirai* I got to know well had developed close bonds with households in the neighbourhood of their school. Salisu (*c.* 10 years), a bright young *almajiri* in Albasu, for instance, could mostly be found at Hauwa's house during his free time. Hauwa was newly married to a man who spent most of his week in Kano City to pursue a master's degree. As the only wife and without children, Hauwa was fairly lonely in her compound, and visibly rejoiced in Salisu's company and in the information he delivered to her about the outside world. Balado's (*c.* 17 years) relationship to Fatima (middle-aged) provides another illustration of how close a bond some *almajirai* develop with their employers. When I came to the school of Balado and the other boys whom I had been teaching at the Child Almajiri Empowerment and Support Initiative (CAESI) for the first time, the second stop (after the obligatory visit to their *malam*'s house) on our visiting tour of the neighbourhood was the house of Balado's *uwar □aki*, his long-term employer. I was surprised to find out that it was her telephone number he had put on the attendance sheet passed around during our training sessions (Balado did not own a phone himself at that time). Even though Balado had stopped working for her as he grew older, he still visited her regularly, and considered her a source of support he could rely on if need be.[13]

If these two examples constituted a 'gold standard' of sorts for *almajirai*'s relationships with employers, most *almajirai* found themselves in less positive arrangements. Most struggled for status and recognition, and

---

[13] Such 'transgressions' of seclusion norms are a sign of *zumuntaka* (closeness), and are common in Hausa society. That young men continue relationships with women who have known them since they were children (e.g. long-term employers or their *malam*'s wives) is not considered to entail any sexual threats. I saw married men in their thirties enter their former *malam*'s house to greet his wife. Of course, such contacts require the (implicit or explicit) consent of the male household head.

found themselves wresting from their employers whatever tangible assistance they received. Employers, on the other hand, sought consciously or otherwise to keep their material obligations to a minimum and to ensure that boundaries and differences were to some extent maintained. The contest over relative status and material entitlements was fought out in a wide range of 'battle fields'. Sleeping arrangements belong at the top of the list of status markers in Hausaland. Sleeping is considered the privilege of the powerful (Last 2000). The *almajirai* usually start their first lesson after the first morning prayer and are kept busy until after the evening prayer. Employers may allow 'their' *almajiri* to sleep in their *soro* (entrance hall), where they can sleep undisturbed only after all household members have returned home. This might nevertheless be a step up from having to crowd into their *malam's soro* or sleep in the open. Bourdillon describes very similar conditions for many child domestic workers who are often 'expected to sleep in the living area of a house: there they cannot retire before the last of the household members, and they must be the first to rise. Their sleep may be broken, as well' (2009, 4). For the *almajirai* too, it is impossible to lie in after other people get up.

Some *almajirai* were entrusted with a key to their employer-patrons' compound when these went out, and they seemed to rejoice at the trust put in them. Several of the *almajirai* could watch television in their employers' houses. Conversely, many *almajirai* struggle to find places to wash and ease themselves. At Sabuwar ☐ofa, there is an ablution space in the mosque, but owing to high demand many students have to rely on rubbish dumps to relieve themselves and on public baths for personal hygiene. Bodies play an important role for constructing hierarchies both as productive bodies (whose labour can be appropriated) and as subjected bodies. Through body postures adopted towards each other, hierarchies are enacted. Servants, Shah writes about Nepal,

> are conditioned to adopt docile and diffident body postures ... When a [servant] is perceived as not doing the bidding or not being as servile as desired, a telling bodily reprimand is issued: 'You have accumulated much fat in your buttocks since you came into our house, why should you obey us now?' (2000, 103)

Aminu, the protagonist of our film, crouches or bends whenever he talks to his (dismissive) employer. When complaining that he had become increasingly insubordinate, she invokes the fact that he had put on weight and developed a healthy skin colour in comparison to when she first employed him. How Aminu should position himself vis-à-vis his employer(s) was never explicitly discussed, but all participants seemed to agree implicitly on what were 'appropriate' postures (those a son would have assumed vis-à-vis his father). While his employer's reprimand surely parodies upper-class behaviour to some extent, this representation enjoyed the approval of the *almajirai* involved.

Meals were the most common form of remuneration. But even the food given was sometimes perceived as second-class. One boy for instance commented about the people for whom he worked, and who paid him with food, that he was never given meat, though he was the one being sent to buy it, so knew exactly what was on the menu. Denigrating treatment was so widespread that one of the urban *malamai* I got to know well told his *almajirai* they should look for other forms of livelihood (*sana'a*), and not look for employment in the houses of the well-to-do. One youth explained that he decided to sell soft drinks rather than continue working as household help because employers would make the *almajirai* do things at their convenience, even if they had class or other obligations. The *almajirai* felt that numerous households think of them as free labour rather than as people, and shun any longer-term responsibility for their wellbeing. During our script discussions for example, one youth lamented that once an *almajiri* falls ill, many employers 'dump' (*ajiye*) him at his *malam*'s place, and are not heard from again: 'often people care about your *healthy* self only, and not about you *yourself*'.[14] An interview with the head of the paediatrics section at Murtala Muhammad Hospital, Kano's largest public hospital, confirmed this: Not their employers, but fellow students or their *malam*'s wives would accompany *almajirai* to hospital in the rare cases that they came at all. In most cases, they would first seek the (cheaper) services of traditional healers, or self-medicate with drugs bought over the counter from a pharmacist, and go to hospital only when already very ill.[15]

Why do the *almajirai*'s domestic work relationships cause so much discontent? Part of the reason, I think, can be found in the different expectations of the *almajirai* and their employers. While the former seek to establish long-term patron-client relationships, and feel let down or betrayed when their patrons 'default' on their presumed obligations, the latter assume more ambiguous positions. Employers benefit for example from vague arrangements regarding working hours and pay, which are possible within more personalized arrangements. At the same time, limiting their commitment to cash-for-service exchanges allows them to eschew longer-term obligations. For some households, this may be a necessity given their own constrained resources; others may conceive of the *almajirai* simply as beyond the scope of their responsibilities. Also, with changing definitions of what it means to be educated, fewer people think it worthwhile to support and sustain the *almajiri* system. Finally, we need to bear in mind that the *almajirai* are in a weak bargaining

[14] Script-writing, 22 July 2011.
[15] Dr Binta Jibr Wudil, 5 April 2011.

position: competition for patrons is fierce and the supply of potential clients abundant.

I have shown so far that the *almajirai* have formative experiences through working in urban neighbourhoods. They learn that many people, including their employers, consider them to be of low status and will not assume longer-term responsibility for their wellbeing. Also, they come to understand that their employers are not planning to put an end to the *almajirai*'s exclusion from certain possessions and privileges. This becomes apparent especially in comparison with their employers' children. While in a gerontocratic society children are used to being treated as low status compared to adults, being treated as low status/less entitled in comparison to other children is a different matter altogether. In 1959 Smith wrote that status differences amongst children are mainly determined by their relative ages: 'Although the nobleman's child should ... rank above commoners, these differences of parental status are often overlooked by adults as well as by children' (1959, 244).[16] However, the *almajirai*'s experiences suggest that this may be changing. Jacquemin queries how young maids in Côte d'Ivoire can ever feel 'like a daughter' to their employers when every day they see their 'boss's children well dressed, going to school, playing, studying, watching television and handing out orders' (2004, 393). Given that the *almajirai* face very similar conditions it is doubtful whether they can feel like true 'sons of the house'. The next section engages with this.

Relationships with employers' children

Bourdillon writes that '[i]n many cases, other children in the household look down on child employees and contribute to the abuse' (2009, 4). Abuse and derision from their employers' children and other children in the neighbourhood was a pressing concern for the *almajirai*. The following draft scenes for the film, where the protagonist they invented suffers various forms of abuse, exemplify this:

- [An *almajiri*] begs from a house, and some boy [from the neighbourhood] ridicules him, and hits him. Then [the neighbourhood boy's] older brother comes out. He doesn't enquire what is happening, he just starts beating [the *almajiri*]. The *almajiri* starts crying, he is exhausted and walks off.
- The children of the neighbourhood often call an *almajiri* to come running but then you'll see there's nothing to be given to him, it's just abuse.

[16] On the other hand, M.F. Smith describes marked status differences between the children of slaves and the children of free parents (1954, 50–51).

Almajirai are likely to be asked to perform tasks that the children of their employers do not do. Khalid writes about urban Sokoto in north-western Nigeria that almost everyone, including those opposed to their presence, 'rely on the labour of the almajirai, especially for chores they would not saddle their own offspring's [sic] with' (cited in Amzat 2008, 61–2; see also Barau & Nuhu 2007, 45; Fada 2005, 92–3). But in those instances in which the *almajirai* had secured access to well paid, trouble-free income opportunities, they felt they had to compete with the children from the neighbourhood. During script-writing, it became apparent that the *almajirai* are very aware of the many inequalities at play:

- People should know that, truly, if all *almajirai* were gathered up and returned home, it's their own children who will have to do all the hard work that the *almajirai* are doing now, like laundry and ironing and emptying the dustbin and so on.
- People should treat *almajirai* just as they treat their own children. I say this because some people don't consider *almajirai* to be like their own children.

Some of the experiences described here may be specific to higher status households and middle/upper-class neighbourhoods. Yet, inequality forms part of the *almajirai*'s daily experiences also in other urban environments. Bourdillon writes that '[w]hen children are employed in domestic work, children overall – both rich and poor – are socialized to perceive that some of their peers go to school while others work for their living' (2009, 5). In the northern Nigerian context, educational inequality may actually in various circumstances be what triggers demand for child domestic servants, as *almajirai* are employed to replace children of the household. One boy at Sabuwar □ofa explained to me why the labour of the children in the households employing *almajirai* was not available:

- In some houses, the children are not old enough to work, while sometimes the children have gone to school, and we, that's the time we are free.
- Which school?
- *Boko* [secular] school, they also go to *Islamiyya* [modern Islamic] school.

Growing up in a social environment that viewed secular and *Islamiyya* education in a predominantly positive light had a significant effect on the *almajirai*'s attitudes and aspirations. Many *almajirai* aspire to such education, and find it increasingly difficult to maintain a positive outlook on themselves and their education in this context, a trend I have described elsewhere in more detail (see Hoechner 2011).

Trapping hazards: Urban aspirations

While *almajirai* experience a vast amount of subtle and not-so-subtle exclusion and abuse, what makes their incorporation into the urban neighbourhoods of their schools, including their employment arrangements, so problematic is that they trap them in ambivalent relationships. If they experienced their employer-patrons as merely exploitative, the *almajirai* could potentially distance/disassociate themselves from them, their lifestyles and their values. But as it is, many hold their *mai gida* (head of the household) in high esteem and pin their hopes for future advancement on these very employers and the support they may provide (often rightly so, as there are few alternative avenues for social mobility). How easy is it for *almajirai* to maintain an ethos of frugality and asceticism if they grow emotionally attached to those on the other side of the socio-economic divide? Can they refrain from considering village life backward and boring when they befriend urbane youngsters seemingly connected to the world at large through modern information technologies (black-berries, televisions, laptops, etc.)?

In a religious 'market' where competition for followers is growing, and pressure mounting to distinguish oneself from others who offer spiritual and education services (see Last 1988; Anon. 2012), some urban *malamai* moreover seem to have relinquished ideals of asceticism and frugality. Malam Usman, at whose school I conducted part of my research, catered not only to *almajirai* but also *Islamiyya* students, had several cars, farms and wives, and travelled to Saudi Arabia frequently on *hajj* and on business. He portrayed himself as a cosmopolitan and took pleasure in introducing me to acquaintances of his in London. For the *almajirai*, it becomes difficult to maintain a positive sense of self and of purpose in a context where religious role models/authority figures, such as the *almajirai*'s teachers, embrace modern forms of knowledge for their own offspring, or exempt these from some of the hardships declared 'educative' for *almajirai*. Several *almajirai* I got to know well in urban Kano complained about their *malam*'s reluctance to let them attend *boko* school, while simultaneously he enrolled his own children in it. *Malamai* may act in this way out of a sense of obligation towards their students' parents, who entrusted their children to them for the sake of their Qur'anic studies. Nonetheless, seeing that their religious authority figures did not fear for their own children's spiritual and moral maturation when educating them at home and in *boko* schools is a challenging experience for the *almajirai*.

From the youths I got to know well during my research I gained the impression that *almajirai* may try to distance themselves as far as possible from their rural origins and to project an image of themselves as urbanite and worldly wise.[17] This transpired for instance from the bodily postures they assumed when snapping photographs, from fashion accessories they deployed (such as sunglasses, wrist watches and finger rings), and from making proud and public use of (borrowed or owned) electronic appliances like MP3 players and mobile phones. During the film production process, the participating *almajirai* seized the opportunity to snap each other behind the computer we used for editing, pretending to be busy working – though most of them hardly knew how to type.[18] On one occasion, some students after a quarrel insulted each other as 'villagers' (ɗan/'yan ɗauye). In 1978, Schildkrout wrote that 'Hausa society is still one in which traditions, both cultural and religious, are revered more than, or at least as much as, change. Wisdom is a quality which is felt to come from experience, and older people receive respect, deference and obedience from the young' (2002 [1978], 353). Given the scorn with which many *almajirai* look upon 'village life,' we may need to reconsider this assumption.

Risks and their social context

What are the implications of their experiences for how the *almajirai* engage with society? Do their experiences single them out as particularly vulnerable to problematic behaviour and Islamic radicalization? The hardships involved in growing up as *almajiri* are often presented as sufficient conditions to make the *almajirai* inherently dangerous. Former Minister of Education Dukku, for instance, declares that '[m]ost of these children, because of the harsh realities they found themselves in, end up becoming juvenile delinquents and, subsequently, adult criminals' (Alkali 2009). Saudatu Sani, a federal legislator from Kano State claims about the *almajirai* that '[t]he pathetic life they live ... breeds heartless criminals' (Abubakar 2009). Often such statements lack nuance and demonize the *almajirai* collectively. Also, they blame negative outcomes on the set-up of 'traditional' Qur'anic schools narrowly, omitting from view their wider social and political context. It is crucial to take this context into account if we want to understand where potential frustration with mainstream society and the state may originate. The *almajirai*'s own views on what are risks in their lives point to such factors located in their social environments.

In a mock interview with an imaginary teacher that the *almajirai* drafted during script-writing for our film, they invoked a number of ways through

---

[17] Cf. Ferguson (1999), who made similar observations with rural migrants on the Copperbelt.

[18] Cf. Behrend (2010), who describes how urban migrants in Tanzania represent themselves in photographs they send to their rural relatives.

which an *almajiri* could go astray. In their view, it is a collective responsibility to ensure this does not happen:

> Their employers send them on errands when it's time for school, but they won't tell them to go to school... Some [*almajirai*] become spoilt through the children of the neighbourhood... [They] join the children of the neighbourhood play[ing] football in the street, even if it's time for prayer... Their employers should always remind them to be clean, if their clothes are dirty, they should give them soap, or money to buy soap, and if it's time for school, they should send them to school.

The torrents of abuse the *almajirai* experience in urban areas, while begging, and in their work roles as domestics are sources of concern. One of the youths involved in the film project, for example, held the *almajirai*'s employers responsible for negative outcomes:

> If an *almajiri* works in his employer's house, if he isn't shown any sympathy by the people for whom he works, then he can develop such a bad character.

The youths also said that *'yan daba*, who are members of urban gangs: un- or under-employed young men spending their days 'hanging out' on the street (Dan-Asabe 1991; see also Casey 2007, 2008; Ya'u 2000), would lure *almajirai* to join them by giving small gifts in exchange for errands. Once used to the *'yan daba* the *almajiri* might consent to their delinquent activities. While neither *almajirai* nor *'yan daba* are homogenous groups with predetermined futures, they share similarly drab economic prospects, which need to be addressed if negative outcomes are to be avoided.

Finally, the youths participating in the film project felt that often *almajirai* are unfairly accused of wreaking havoc in their neighbourhoods. People knew that the *almajirai* had nobody to stand up for them, and therefore considered them convenient scapegoats, they argued (see Hoechner 2013). The misdemeanours of other children and youths in the neighbourhood could be laid at the doorstep of Qur'anic schools, they said. Being accused unfairly and lacking the power to refute such accusations is a frustrating experience for the *almajirai*. The government's increasingly hostile and aggressive approach towards the *almajirai* in the context of the *Boko Haram* insurgency is likely to give rise to similarly frustrating experiences. Security forces pursuing *Boko Haram* members are said to have been intercepting and harassing *almajirai* travelling in intercity shared taxis. *Boko Haram*'s justification for attacks on primary schools in Borno State was alleged raids of Qur'anic schools by security forces.

Given the hostility with which they are frequently met, the *almajirai* would have every reason to resent mainstream society. Yet, the attitudes of the youths I got to know well during my research were ambivalent at most. From what I could gauge, the *almajirai* found themselves caught up in disempowering circumstances with little room for manoeuvre. They were caught midway between urban, cosmopolitan aspirations, which however were difficult or impossible for them to achieve, and discourses that emphasized religious devotion and asceticism, which however no longer earned them much respect or social standing. In a way the promise of an urban, cosmopolitan lifestyle neutralized the *almajirai* politically. A crucial question is under what conditions they will cease to admire and desire such a lifestyle that will most probably elude them. What 'glues' them to such contradictory desires, I think, is their emotional incorporation into employers' households (some of whom become mentors and patrons), and close relationships with urban peers in the workplace or neighbourhood of their schools. Also, some employers help 'their' *almajirai* achieve social and economic mobility. Knowing of this possibility keeps the *almajirai*'s hopes for a similar opportunity alive. If it was not for these factors, I think doctrines critical of materialism and 'modernity' (as espoused for example by *Boko Haram*) would hold much greater appeal for the *almajirai*.

Policy responses to the Almajiri system

In light of the aforementioned, what would be an appropriate policy response to the *almajiri* system? Many people have called for legislative action against the system and in May 2013, a bill aiming to revise the 2003 'Trafficking in Persons (Prohibition) Act' passed its second reading in the Senate. If the legislative proposal succeeds, the *almajirai* would soon fall under national anti-trafficking legislation. Meanwhile, Senate President David Mark urged northern governors to also issue legislation against the *almajiri* system at the state level. A ban would make sense if *almajiri* enrolment could be reduced to 'wrong decision-making' by 'backward' and neglectful parents. But as I have shown here, the conditions and considerations leading parents to enrol children as *almajirai* are far more complex than that. A ban would make no change to the difficulties rural households face, and weaken the legitimacy and social standing of the *almajirai* in urban areas further. Other policy approaches are less detrimental and have actual potential to improve the *almajirai*'s lives.

Given how keen many *almajirai* – and other poor children and youths – are to acquire quality knowledge not merely of the Qur'an, but also of secular subjects and of other Islamic subjects, the 'Almajiri Model Schools' built by the Federal Government across the northern states are certainly a step in the right direction – provided they are well run in a sustainable way. Integrating religious and secular curricula in one and the same school reduces the logistical challenges arising for children from attendance at various different educational institutions. Yet, given how pervasive educational disadvantage is in northern Nigeria, unless it is scaled up the initiative risks being little more than a drop in the ocean. The DFID-funded Education Sector Support Programme in Nigeria (ESSPIN) has found a pragmatic and cost-effective way of imparting secular education to *almajirai*. So-called 'Tsangaya Cluster Schools', community-run 'pop-up' schools that rely on the infrastructure of existing schools (*boko* or *Islamiyya*), and tailor their timetables to the schedules of the participating Qur'anic schools, teach *almajirai* basic literacy and numeracy. The system does not however provide a long-term alternative to urgently needed improvements in education provision by the state (ESSPIN, n.d.). Several civil society organizations have called for community-driven support for the *almajirai*. The Kano-based *Almajiri Foundation*, for instance, suggests that each household should adopt one *almajiri* and take care of his personal, financial and educational needs. Such initiatives are no substitute for concerted state action. But given how crucial the people in the neighbourhoods of their schools and their employers are to the *almajirai* – as potential sources of both support and abuse – these households are well-placed to make a difference to the *almajirai*'s lives. While this does not appear in any of the NGOs' action plans yet, a public code of conduct, developed with both *almajirai* and their employers, and publicized through the media, establishing good practice in terms of care and payment of household helps, could sensitize the population to the *almajirai*'s concerns.

Conclusion

This chapter set out to dispel several myths about the *almajirai*. I have argued that they are not the clearly circumscribed demographic as which they are often portrayed. Many young people switch back and forth between different educational options and many rural youths share the *almajirai*'s predicament of lacking skills to achieve sustainable livelihoods. I have also pointed out that the *almajiri* system cannot be explained merely in terms of parental neglect and 'backwardness'. Multiple economic, social and religious factors play together to sustain demand for the system. Finally, I have shown that it does not suffice to examine 'traditional' Qur'anic schools in the strict sense only to understand what experiences *almajirai* have and what risks they are exposed to. In the course of their schooling, most *almajirai* travel through a wide array of geographical and social settings. They experience rural as well as urban life; they spend time in spartan schools as well as affluent employers' homes. Much of what the *almajirai* learn, think and aspire to is shaped by the environment and circumstances in which they find themselves. We should be concerned about the abuse and denigration the *almajirai* experience when begging or working as household helps. Accusations experienced as unfair are a further source of frustration.

The households of their urban employers play a particularly important role in the *almajirai*'s lives as they are places where they meet, and sometimes befriend, people who have significantly more than them, both in terms of material resources and opportunities (e.g. to acquire knowledge). While some *almajirai* have very positive experiences, many feel their employers look down on them and treat them as underdogs. What frustrates and upsets the *almajirai* are the many inequalities they encounter. These inequalities, and the efforts of the better-off to maintain and to justify them, make living as *almajirai* a very disempowering experience. Putting a ban on the *almajiri* system will not reduce inequalities. Reducing inequalities requires a collective effort – so does alleviating the plight of the *almajirai*.

Bibliography

234NEXT, 2011. 'Rehabilitating our almajiris'. Editorial. *234NEXT*, June 22. http://234next.com/csp/cms/sites/Next/Opinion/5716077-146/story.csp. Accessed 22 July 2012.

Abubakar, A., 2009. Nigeria struggles to curb rise in child beggars. *The Telegraph*, 18 November. www.telegraph.co.uk/expat/expatnews/6596232/Nigeria-struggles-to-curb-rise-in-child-beggars.html. Accessed 25 September 2013.

Adams, K.M., and S. Dickey, 2000. *Home and Hegemony: Domestic Service and Identity Politics in South and Southeast Asia*. Ann Arbor MI: University of Michigan Press.

Adamu, A.U., n.d.. *The Almajirai Sector Study: Concepts and Focus of Target Groups*. Kano: Association for Educational Development Options.

Aigbokhan, B.E., 2008. 'Growth, Inequality and Poverty in Nigeria'. *ACGS/MPAMS Discussion Paper* 3. Addis Ababa: African Centre for Gender and Development for the United Nations Economic Commission for Africa. www.uneca.org/sites/default/files/publications/growthinequalitypoverty.pdf. Accessed 5 October 2013.

Alkali, A., 2009. '10 million kids beg in the North – Minister'. *Leadership*, 22 November.

Aluaigba, M.T., 2009. 'Circumventing or superimposing poverty on the African Child? The Almajiri Syndrome in Northern Nigeria'. *Childhood in Africa*, 1 (1), 1–37.

Amzat, J., 2008. Lumpen Childhood in Nigeria: A Case of the Almajirai in Northern Nigeria. *Hemispheres*, 23, 55–66.

Anon., 2012. The Popular Discourses of Salafi Radicalism and Salafi Counter-Radicalism in Nigeria: A Case Study of Boko Haram. *Journal of Religion in Africa*, 42 (2), 118–44.

Awofeso, N., J. Ritchie, and P. Degeling, 2003. The Almajiri Heritage and the Threat of Non-State Terrorism in Northern Nigeria: Lessons from Central Asia and Pakistan. *Studies in Conflict & Terrorism*, 26 (4), 311–25.

Baba, N.M., 2011. 'Islamic Schools, the Ulama, and the State in the Educational Development of Northern Nigeria'. *Bulletin de L'APAD*, 33.

Bambale, A., 2007. 'Almajiranchi and the Problem of Begging in Kano State: The Role of Shekarau Administration (2003–2007)'. *7th BEN Africa Annual Conference*. www. benafrica.org/downloads/bambale_begging_in_kano.pdf. Accessed 19 January 2010.

Barau, A.S. and H.J. Nuhu, 2007. *Profile of Women and Children Development Initiatives of the Shekarau Administration*. Kano: Research & Documentation Directorate.

Bashir, F.A., 1994. 'Street Children: The Case of Kaduna Metropolis'. In ANPPCAN Child Rights Monitoring Center (ed.), *Child Abuse and Neglect: A Resource Book*. Kaduna: ANPPCAN.

Behrend, H., 2010. '"Feeling Global": The Likoni Ferry Photographers of Mombasa, Kenya'. *African Arts*, 33 (3), 70–77.

Bourdillon, M., 2009. 'Children as Domestic Employees: Problems and Promises'. *Journal of Children and Poverty*, 15 (1), 1–18.

Brigaglia, A., 2008. '"We Ain't Coming to Take People Away": A Sufi Praise-song and the Representation of Police Forces in Northern Nigeria'. *Annual Review of Islam in Africa*, 10, 50–57.

British Council & Harvard School of Public Health, 2010. 'Nigeria: The Next Generation Report'. *PGDA Working Paper* 62. Program on the Global Demography of Aging. http://www.hsph.harvard.edu/pgda/WorkingPapers/2010/PGDA_WP_62. pdf. Accessed 5 October 2013.

Casey, C., 2007. '"Policing" through Violence: Fear, Vigilantism, and the Politics of Islam in Northern Nigeria'. In David Pratten & Atreyee Sen (eds.), *Global Vigilantes*. London: Hurst, 93–124.

Casey, C., 2008. '"Marginal Muslims": Politics and the Perceptual Bounds of Islamic Authenticity in Northern Nigeria'. *Africa Today*, 54 (3), 67–92.

Chabal, P. & J.-P. Daloz, 1999. *Africa works: Disorder as Political Instrument*. Oxford: James Currey.

Cheeseman, N., 2006. 'The Rise and Fall of Civil-Authoritarianism in Africa: Patronage, Participation, and Political Parties in Kenya and Zambia'. D.Phil. thesis, Department of Politics and International Relations, University of Oxford.

Dan-Asabe, A.U., 1991. 'Yandaba: The "terrorists" of Kano Metropolitan?' In Murray Last (ed.), *Kano Studies*, special issue: *Youth & Health in Kano Today*. Kano: Bayero University, 85–111.

Dickey, S., 2000. 'Permeable Homes: Domestic Service, Household Space, and the Vulnerability of Class Boundaries in Urban India'. *American Ethnologist*, 27 (2), 462–89.

ESSPIN and DfID, n.d.. *ESSPIN Experiences. Integrating the old with the new: Islamic education responds to the demands of modern society*. Education Sector Support Programme in Nigeria. www.camb-ed.com/Portals/0/Documents/ESSPIN-Experiences-Integrating-the-old-with-the-new.pdf. Accessed 3 October 2013.

Fada, A.A., 2005. 'Factors Perpetuating the Almajiri System of Education in Northern Nigeria: A Case Study of Zaria and Environs, Kaduna State'. MSc thesis, Department of Sociology, Ahmadu Bello University, Zaria.

Federal Ministry of Health, 2011. 'Saving Newborn Lives in Nigeria: Newborn Health in the Context of the Integrated Maternal, Newborn and Child Health Strategy'. Revised 2nd edition. Abuja: Ministry of Health.

Ferguson, J., 1999. *Expectations of Modernity: Myths and Meanings of Urban Life on the Zambian Copperbelt*. Berkeley CA: University of California Press.

Hansen, K.T., 2000. 'Ambiguous Hegemonies: Identity Politics and Domestic Service'. In Kathleen M. Adams and Sara Dickey (eds), *Home and Hegemony: Domestic Service and Identity Politics in South and Southeast Asia*. Ann Arbor MI: University of Michigan Press, 283–92.

Hassan, T.A., 2013. 'Mark asks northern govs to ban almajiri system'. *Daily Trust*, 23 May.

Hickey, S. and A. du Toit, 2007. 'Adverse Incorporation, Social Exclusion and Chronic Poverty'. *CPRC Working Paper* 81. Manchester: Chronic Poverty Research Centre. www.chronicpoverty.org/uploads/publication_files/WP81_Hickey_duToit.pdf. Accessed 5 October 2013.

Hiskett, M., 1987. 'The Maitatsine Riots in Kano, 1980: An Assessment'. *Journal of Religion in Africa*, 17 (3), 209–23.

Hoechner, H., 2011. 'Striving for Knowledge and Dignity: How Qur'anic Students in Kano, Nigeria, Learn to Live with Rejection and Educational Disadvantage'. *European Journal of Development Research*, 23 (5), 712–28.

Hoechner, H., 2013. 'Traditional Qur'anic students (almajirai) in Nigeria: Fair game for unfair accusations?' In M.-A. Pérouse de Montclos (ed.), *Boko Haram: Islamism, Politics, Security and the State in Nigeria*. Leiden: African Studies Centre, 63–84.

Jacquemin, M.Y., 2004. 'Children's Domestic Work in Abidjan', Côte d'Ivoire. *Childhood*, 11 (3), 383–97.

Jeffrey, C., 2011. 'Youth and Development'. *The European Journal of Development Research*, 23 (5), 792–96.

Johnson, D., 2011. 'An Assessment of the Professional Working Knowledge of Teachers in Nigeria: Implications for Teacher Development, Policy and Implementation'. Report KN 304. Kano: Education Sector Support Programme in Nigeria.

Kane, O., 2003. *Muslim Modernity in Postcolonial Nigeria: A Study of the Society for the Removal of Innovation and Reinstatement of Tradition*. Boston MA: Brill.

Katz, C., 2004. *Growing up Global: Economic Restructuring and Children's Everyday Lives*. Minneapolis MN: University of Minnesota Press.

Klocker, N., 2011. 'Negotiating Change: Working with Children and their Employers to Transform Child Domestic Work in Iringa, Tanzania'. *Children's Geographies*, 9 (2), 205–20.

Kulutempa, 2011 'Almajiris: Nigeria's Ticking Time Bomb'. *Nairaland Forum*, 23 April. www.nairaland.com/nigeria/topic-653197.0.html. Accessed 14 January 2012.

Kumolu, C., 2012. 'Almajiri Education: Modern Gang up against Ancient Tradition?' *Vanguard*, 26 April.

Last, M., 1988. 'Charisma and Medicine in Northern Nigeria'. In D. Cruise O'Brien and C. Coulon (eds), *Charisma and Brotherhood in African Islam*. Harlow: Longman, 116–31).

Last, M., 2000. 'Children and the Experience of Violence: Contrasting Cultures of Punishment in Northern Nigeria'. *Africa: Journal of the International African Institute*, 70 (3), 359–93.

Last, M., 2009. 'Nation-Breaking & Not-Belonging in Nigeria: Withdrawal, Resistance, Riot?' Conference paper, 3rd European Conference on African Studies, from 4–7 June 2009 in Leipzig, Germany. www.uni-leipzig.de/~ecas2009/index.php?option=com_docman&task=cat_view&gid=57&Itemid=24. Accessed 25 September 2013.

Lawal, I., 2011. 'Could Almajirai be easily lured into joining Boko Haram?' *Elombah News*. http://elombah.com/index.php/36-omoba/pointblank/7234-could-almajirai-be-easily-lured-into-joining-boko-haram--v15-7234. Accessed 27 September 2012.

Lees, L., T. Slater and E.K. Wyly, 2008. *Gentrification*. London: Routledge.

Loimeier, R., 1997. 'Islamic Reform and Political Change: the Example of Abubakar Gumi and the 'yan Izala Movement in Nigeria'. In D. Westerlund & E.E. Rosander (eds), *African Islam and Islam in Africa: Encounters Between Sufis and Islamists*. Athens OH: Ohio University Press, 286–307.

Lubeck, P.M., 1985. 'Islamic Protest under Semi-industrial Capitalism: 'Yan Tatsine Explained'. *Africa: Journal of the International African Institute*, 55 (4), 369–89.

Morgan, S.L., I.Z. Mohammed and S. Abdullahi, 2010. 'Patron-Client Relationships and Low Education among Youth in Kano, Nigeria'. *African Studies Review*, 53 (1), 79–103.

Mortimore, M., 1998. *Roots in the African Dust: Sustaining the Sub-Saharan Drylands*. Cambridge: Cambridge University Press.

Mustapha, Abdul Raufu, and Kate Meagher, 1992. 'Stress, Adaptation, and Resilience in Rural Kano'. *Capitalism, Nature, Socialism*, 5 (2), 107–17.

Mustapha, Abdul Raufu and Lindsay Whitfield, 2009. 'African Democratisation: The

Journey So Far'. In Abdul Raufu Mustapha & Lindsay Whitfield (eds), *Turning Points in African Democracy*. Oxford: James Currey, 1–12.

NAN (News Agency of Nigeria), 2013. 'Another 1,000 divorcees, widows up for wedding in Kano'. *Premium Times*, 23 May. http://premiumtimesng.com/regional/135915-another-1-000-divorcees-widows-up-for-wedding-in-kano.html#/jobs. Accessed 4 October 2013.

National Population Commission, 2011. *Nigeria Demographic and Health Survey (DHS) EdData 2010*. Abuja: National Population Commission.

Office of the Special Adviser, 2005. 'Census of Islamiyya, Qur'anic/Tsangaya and Ilmi Schools in Kano State, 2003'. Kano: Research and Documentation Unit, Office of the Special Adviser on Education and Information Technology, Ministry of Education.

Robson, E., 2004. 'Children at Work in Rural Northern Nigeria: Patterns of Age, Space and Gender'. *Journal of Rural Studies*, 20 (2), 193–210.

Salihi, A., 2013. 'Ending the Age-Long Street Begging in Kano'. *Leadership*, 26 May.

Schildkrout, E., 2002 [1978]. 'Age and Gender in Hausa Society: Socio-economic Roles of Children in Urban Kano'. *Childhood*, 9 (3), 342–68.

Shah, S., 2000. 'Service or servitude? The domestication of household labor in Nepal'. In Kathleen M. Adams and Sara Dickey (eds), *Home and Hegemony: Domestic Service and Identity Politics in South and Southeast Asia*. Ann Arbor MI: University of Michigan Press, 87–117.

Smith, M.F., 1954. *Baba of Karo: A Woman of the Muslim Hausa*. London: Faber and Faber.

Smith, M.G., 1954. 'Introduction'. In M. F. Smith (1954).

Smith, M.G., 1957. 'Cooperation in Hausa society'. *Information*, 11, 1–20. www.cifas.us/sites/cifas.drupalgardens.com/files/1957b_CooperationHausaSociety_J.pdf. Accessed 3 October 2013.

Smith, M.G., 1959. 'The Hausa System of Social Status'. *Africa: Journal of the International African Institute*, 29 (3), 239–52.

Soyinka, W., 2012. 'The Butchers of Nigeria'. *Newsweek Magazine*, 16 January, 1–5.

Sule-Kano, A., 2008. 'Poverty and the Traditional Qur'anic School System in Northern Nigeria: The Politics of the Almajiri-Phenomenon'. Paper from Conference on Nigerian Youth and National Development, Centre for Democratic Research and Training, Mambayya House, Bayero University, Kano, from 5–6 August 2008.

Tomasevski, K., 2005. 'Not Education for All, Only for Those Who Can Pay: The World Bank's Model for Financing Primary Education'. *Law, Social Justice & Global Development*, 9 (1), 1–19.

UBEC (Universal Basic Education Commission), 2010. 'National Framework for the Development and Integration of Almajiri Education into UBE Programme'. Abuja: Universal Basic Education Commission, 1–26.

Umar, M., 2003. 'Profiles of New Islamic Schools in Northern Nigeria'. *The Maghreb Review*, 28 (2–3), 146–69.

Usman, L., 2008. 'Assessing the Universal Basic Education Primary and Koranic Schools' Synergy for Almajiri Street Boys in Nigeria'. *International Journal of Educational Management*, 22 (1), 62–73. Wacquant, L., 1999. 'Urban Marginality in the Coming Millennium'. *Urban Studies*, 36 (10), 1639–47.

Wasiuzzaman, S. and K. Wells, 2010. 'Assembling Webs of Support: Child Domestic Workers in India'. *Children & Society*, 24 (4), 282–92.

Whitfield, Lindsay and Abdul Raufu Mustapha, 2009. 'Conclusion: The Politics of African States in the Era of Democratisation'. In Abdul Raufu Mustapha & Lindsay Whitfield (eds), *Turning Points in African Democracy*. Oxford: James Currey, 202–27.

Winters, C.A., 1987. 'Koranic Education and Militant Islam in Nigeria'. *International Review of Education*, 33 (2), 171–85.

Ya'u, Y.Z., 2000. 'The Youth, Economic Crisis and Identity Transformation: The Case of the Yandaba in Kano'. In A. Jega (ed.), *Identity Transformation and Identity Politics under Structural Adjustment in Nigeria*. Uppsala: Nordiska Afrikainstitutet, and Kano: The Centre for Research and Documentation, 161–80.

5

'Marginal Muslims':
Ethnic identity & the *Umma*
in Kano

YAHAYA HASHIM & JUDITH-ANN WALKER

Introduction

Contemporary studies of ethno-religious conflicts in Africa have been particularly interested in protracted social conflicts. Such conflicts have been defined as hostile and violent interactions between identity groups over a long time, based on deep-seated ethnic, racial and religious hatred, structural cleavages between the conflicting groups, and the political oppression of some groups along with the denial of their fundamental needs (Fisher 1993). The focus on identity groups has come to shape the discourse of faith in Africa as a competition between the two big monotheistic religions – Islam and Christianity. The 2010 Pew study on the growth of both religions in Sub-Saharan Africa should be viewed against this background. A similar bifurcated understanding of religious conflict has largely characterized the academic landscape of Nigeria. However, side by side with these conflicts *between* the two great religions are meso-level conflicts taking place *within* each faith. It is therefore important not to concentrate only on inter-faith conflicts, but also to examine the intra-faith dynamics of religious conflict. This study of Muslim minorities falls within this exploration of intra-faith conflicts as it focuses on the numerically significant but often overlooked communities of non-Hausa Muslims in Kano. At the core of our enquiry is the question of the impact of ethnicity on Muslim self-perception.

Through the examination of the experiences of non-Hausa Muslims in the largely Muslim Hausa-Fulani city of Kano, we can observe the consequences of ethnic cleavage for the Muslim *umma* of Kano. The story of the non-Hausa Muslims in Kano is one with parallels throughout urban spaces in northern Nigeria. The contribution of this chapter will therefore be to make more nuanced the usual dichotomous – Muslim against Christian – representations of religious conflict in the north. This will enhance our understanding of minority Muslim communities and their role in the religious conflicts that have plagued northern cities like Kano. The acceptance of diversity of Islamic practice and of differences of understanding is critical to the development of greater tolerance. Indeed the foundation of religious fundamentalism is the rejection of internal diversity within Islam and the attempt to consolidate a 'true' and 'pure' line, ritual or theology. As we demonstrate in this chapter, the refusal to tolerate difference within the Muslim community is not only sectarian, it is also ethnic.

Muslim minorities in Kano

The term 'Muslim minority' is often used to refer to minority Muslim populations within a predominantly Christian or non-Muslim population (for example, in the USA, Western Europe, China, Russia, Thailand, Philippines) (see Kettani 1986, and the numerous publications of the *Journal of the Institute of Muslim Minority Affairs*). These are the Muslims, Faraz Omar refers to when he says 'three hundred million Muslims – one-fifth of the Ummah's population – live as minorities today' (Omar 2011). However, the Muslim minorities of Kano do not fall into this category, since they are part of the majority Muslim population of the city. This chapter defines the term Muslim minority in Kano State to mean Muslims of non-Hausa-Fulani ethnic group. They could be non-Hausa speaking or have no cultural similarities with Hausa Muslims. The key variables at play here, apart from the shared Islamic identity, are the complicating notions of linguistic and cultural affinity to the dominant Muslim Hausa society. Language and culture influence notions of belonging – or lack of it – despite the presumed commonality of being fellow Muslims. Thus, the *umma* is fragmented not just on sectarian lines, but also along the lines of ethnic cleavage. The Muslims of non-Hausa ethnicities, especially those not sharing cultural and linguistic affinities to the dominant Hausa culture, constitute the 'marginal' or minority Muslims.[1] These are mainly Muslims from southern Nigerian ethnici-ties, but they also include Muslims from some parts of the north. More specifically, the chapter focuses on Yoruba, Igbo, Igbira, Igala, Auchi/ Edo Muslims and such others who do not share a strong cultural affinity with the predominant Hausa Muslims. They are Muslim minorities in

---

[1] Some non-Hausa Muslims of northern ethnic groups are not included in the category of Muslim minorities because of the ease with which they assimilate into the dominant Hausa culture. These include the Babur Muslims of southern Borno, Nupe Muslims and even the Kanuri. Being a Muslim 'minority' here is thus a reflection of the cultural distance from Hausa-Fulani culture.

terms of their ethnic identity and many may also be minorities even within their ethnicities because among their kin in Kano, Christians are in the majority. In other words, they are structurally a double minority, albeit one with some important characteristics. While they share religious identity with the dominant Hausa Muslim society, they nevertheless share ethnic identities with the largely Christian southern ethnicities of the 'settler's quarters' of Sabon Gari (New Town). Caught between the two major protagonists of the repeated ethno-religious crises of Kano – the Muslim Hausa-Fulani indigenes on the one hand and the mainly Christian southern ethnicities in Sabon Gari on the other – these marginal Muslims can either constitute a target of attack for both camps, or a bridge of potential peace. Our study sets out to explore their experiences of the repeated conflicts of Kano and what this tells us about the impact of ethnic diversity on the *umma*.

Our study is therefore of Muslim minorities within a Muslim majority context. It is similar to the study, published by the organization '*Faith Matters*', of different categories of Muslim minorities in the United Kingdom – that is, the native British Muslim converts, distinct from the immigrant Muslim populations (Brice 2010). Since 1963, the national census in Nigeria has discontinued data collection on the ethnic and religious affiliations of the population. Thus there is no accurate way of knowing the exact degrees of diversity within Nigerian cities or states. There is the understanding, however, that large cities such as Lagos and Kano are more cosmopolitan and diverse than smaller towns and rural settlements. Hausa ethnic identity is intimately tied to being Muslim; the non-Muslim ethnic Hausas are identified by another label – *Maguzawa*. In pre-colonial times assimilation into Kano society was relatively easy for the Muslim minorities, especially those coming from a Sahelian cultural background. These minorities were known to be dominant in some neigh-bourhoods in the old city of Kano such as Ayagi and Tudun Nufawa. The Yoruba migration to Kano, which is dated to the seventeenth century, has followed this pattern (Abba 1999; Olaniyi 2004). With the estab-lishment of colonial rule, there was an influx of other Christian Africans and Nigerians, some of whom were employed in the colonial adminis-tration. A 'New Town' or *Sabon Gari*, was created for this category of native migrants. This started the segregation of Nigerians into separate areas apart from each other and the hardening of cultural boundaries in Kano. Recent unverified estimates put the volume of Igbo investments in Kano at N10 trillion (Udegbe 2013). The claims may be exaggerated, but what is certain is that ethnic Igbos are possibly the largest non-Hausa migrant population in Kano, but the Igbo Muslims in Kano are much smaller in numbers, compared to the other Muslim ethnic minorities in the city. The large number of Igbo Christians explains the perception of the Igbos as the significant 'other' within Kano, with Sabon Gari as their main locus.

Despite being strongly identified with the Christian Igbo, Sabon Gari has always contained a substantial population of marginal Muslims. Muslims, both marginal and indigenous, were about 54 per cent of the Sabon Gari population of 5,910 in 1939 (Abba 1999). Ahamed Bako, citing the 'Reports of the Native Reservations: Kano Township (1939)' showed that there were 3,194 Muslims in Sabon Gari in that period; out of which 120 and 74 were recorded as members of the predominantly Yoruba Muslim communities of Ansar Ud-deen society and Ahmadiyya respectively (cited in Abba 1999). Similarly, the four largest ethnic groups inhabiting Sabon Gari in 1937 were the Hausas with a population of 1,903, the Yoruba with a population of 1,547, the Igbos with a population of 1,529 and the Nupe with a population of 825. However, over the years, the population mix has changed. The recent demographic composition of Sabon Gari is suggested in a survey of 138 residents conducted by David Ehrhardt (2008) *Perceptions Survey Metropolitan Kano*. In that survey, there was an Igbo majority of 53.6 per cent, followed by the Yoruba at 18.8 per cent. The Hausa representation within the survey was only 7.2 per cent. The survey by Ehrhardt also suggests that Muslims constituted a minority of 12.9 per cent within the Sabon Gari population, with different denominations of Christians constituting 81.3 per cent of the population.

Ethno-religious conflicts in Kano

Kano is the pre-eminent industrial and commercial city in northern Nigeria and it had been the southern hub for the trans-Saharan trade route for centuries. Its cosmopolitan nature has made Kano a diverse melting pot or, as the locals say, a '*Tumbin Giwa*' (the belly of an elephant with the capacity to hold multiple entities). Though Kano is a centre of Islamic scholarship in Sahelian West Africa, since the beginning of the twentieth century, it has had an influx of non-Muslims who live and do business in the city. The same pattern of inward-migration is true for Muslims from other parts of Nigeria and the world. These migrants have lived for the most part side by side and in harmony with the predominantly Hausa Muslim majority population. However, triggered by diverse factors (Deegan 2011), violent ethno-religious conflicts have repeatedly erupted in the city with devastating consequences. Kano's notoriety in communal conflict and riots was established before independence when in May 1953, 21 southern Nigerians and 15 northerners were killed in communal conflicts precipitated by political developments within a Nigeria in the process of negotiating the terms of its decolonization. The political disturbances following the *coup d'état* of January 1966 ignited another series of ethno-religious unrests in Kano, culminating in the targeting of Igbo Christians in the run up to the civil war in 1967. After the civil war in 1970, ethno-religious violence continued in Kano, leading one writer to pose the question whether Kano is 'a blood-letting city?' (Abdu n.d.) The bloody *Maitatsine* crisis of 1980 was a major post-civil war religious crisis in Kano but it was not an inter-religious crisis, being mainly a violent attack on security forces and the dominant Muslim population by a renegade Muslim sect. Throughout the first half of the 1980s the *Maitatsine* crisis engulfed northern Nigeria, leading to a death toll of over 9,000 (Lubeck 1985; Hiskett 1987; Isichei 1987; Akaeze 2009; Ugochukwu 2009).

However, in 1982 a Christian-Muslim crisis erupted in Fagge Local Government Area, over the renovation and expansion of an old Hausa-language Anglican Church originally built in the 1930s, and next to which a huge mosque was built in the 1960s. The visiting Archbishop of Canterbury was to lay the foundation stone of the new church. Since 1982, ethno-religious conflicts have been on the rise in Kano following the religious polarization in the country and what Yusuf Bala Usman characterized as the 'manipulation of religion' for political ends (Usman 1987). Even when the immediate trigger for violent conflict was elsewhere, the repercussions were often felt in the volatile cauldron of Kano. The transportation to Kano for burial of the bodies of Muslim casualties in ethno-religious violence elsewhere in the country frequently ignited violence in Kano itself. For instance, the Kafanchan Muslim-Christian conflict of March 1987 (Ibrahim 1989) rapidly spilled over to Kaduna, Zaria, Katsina and Kano. The repatriation of Muslim corpses from Yelwan Shendam in Plateau State in 2004 sparked off a similar bout of rioting in Kano.

Another violent Christian-Muslim conflict erupted in Kano in 1991 over the proposed 'crusade' of the German evangelist Reinhardt Bonnke. According to some Muslims, holding Bonnke's 'crusade' in Kano was provocative, given that an Islamic rally for Shaikh Deedat, a prominent Muslim preacher from South Africa, was disallowed by the government shortly before the 'crusade' was given permission to take place. The resulting feeling of unfair treatment at the hands of the authorities led to a rampage by Muslim youths. Other crises include the beheading of the Igbo Christian, Gideon Akaluka, in December 1994, allegedly for the desecration of the Qur'an, and the violence of June 1995 following a fight between two men – one Christian Igbo and the other Hausa Muslim – in the Sabon Gari Market. There was also the attack on the Yorubas in July 1999, allegedly as retaliation for the Sagamu communal conflict in Ogun State earlier that year, in which Hausas were killed. Indeed, following the return to civil rule in 1999 there was a sharp increase in communal conflicts across Nigeria. In Kano, international events such as the USA-led 'war on terror' sparked local inter-religious violence. The October 2001 protest over the American attack on Afghanistan sparked religious riots in Kano, as did the outcome of the 2011 Presidential elections in Nigeria. Between 1966 and 2014, there have been 12 instances of widespread religious violence in Kano.[2] While these conflicts have been understood as Muslim–Christian riots, the experiences of the non-Hausa Muslims, caught as they are between the two main protagonists in the rioting, suggest that the situation might be more complicated than that.

Muslim minority associations in Kano

The literature on bridge building in conflict studies identifies actors, processes and structures as key variables for peace and conflict mitigation. The literature identifies NGOs and women, in particular, as key actors in bridge building for peace. They are deemed to be able to work within culturally acceptable parameters and at the grass-roots level. Kaufman (2000, 3) observes the central role of peace builders:

> What peace builders do is bring together people from opposing sides of a conflict to replace the myths about the other side with better information, and replace the hostility and fear with enough understanding to make a compromise peace look attractive. Such efforts among grass-roots leaders can build a political constituency for the diplomatic peace process so leaders can persuade their people to ratify a compromise settlement, then keep it on track during the implementation stage.

Kaufman uses the concept of 'Track II' diplomacy (through informal, non-state structures) to explain how such actors can catalyse 'informal talks between unofficial representatives of both sides … generating creative ideas for mutually acceptable conflict resolution formulas'. Kaufman discusses processes for peace building in terms of social platforms where contact, transaction and interactions take place. During such forums the 'enemy' becomes humanized, his concerns become known and, hopefully, understood. The link between process and structure revolves around community level actors having access to official 'Track I' structures, formally responsible for conflict resolution. For Track II actors to be able to make the peace process work, however, they must have a seat at the table convened by the state and such structures must be capable

---

[2] Ethno-religious violence broke out in Kano in 1953, 1966, 1967, 1982, 1987, 1991, 1994, 1995, 1999, 2004 and 2011, while *intra*-Muslim violence broke out on a small scale in 1978 and on a large scale in 1980 and since the Boko Haram insurgency from 2009.

of receiving their inputs and translating them into action. Thus actors, processes and structures are linked in the peace-building process. Scholars emphasize the role of the state in peace-building processes through setting up and ensuring that the work of conflict resolution structures leads to meaningful reconciliation.

In the case of Nigeria, discussions of peace building have tended to explore the capacity and willingness of the state to initiate meaningful conflict resolution strategies (Jinadu 2007, Osaghae 2007). Agbede (2007, 3) argues that

> the most important ingredient for a peaceful society is the existence of government that believes in conflict resolution. Ideally, this is what every democratic government should aspire towards. A conflict resolving government has been described as a government ... of reconciliation that facilitates the healing of past divisions.

While citing Section 14 of the Nigerian Constitution that 'the security and welfare of the people shall be a primary purpose of government' Kwaja notes the inability of the Nigerian state to be effective at meaningful conflict resolution. Against this background he argues for re-building state capacity to manage ethnic and religious conflict in Nigeria. In addition to the role of the state the literature on peace building in Nigeria also focuses on the role of associations, and women in the peace process. Given their liminal position between the two contending forces in the ethno-religious violence of Kano, can the marginal Muslims play such a bridging role?

To answer this question, this study focused on associations registered locally with the Kano State Government under the Youth Club Edict No. 17 of 1976. Groups registered at the Federal level or operating outside the 1976 law are not considered in this study. At the time of the research in 2011–12, the Kano State Ministry of Information and Youth had a total of 3,000 organizations registered with its Voluntary Organization Unit. The records of the Ministry indicate that roughly 20 per cent of all organizations registered are no longer in existence. From the total number of active associations, 101 Muslim associations were identified, 23 of which were identified as groups belonging to Muslim minorities. The study used in-depth interviews for individuals and group interviews for executives of the Muslim minorities associations. Of the 23 associations identified only 17 associations could be traced by the research team: 6 groups could not be found at their given addresses. Of the 17 associations surveyed, 16 have a male leader and could be described as male dominated; 2 groups have no female members and 1 group is not only female led, it has no male members. Of all the 16 male interviews conducted only 3 were interviews with the Chief Executive Officers of the association; 13 were

Table 5.1 Study sample of Muslim minorities associations in Kano

Number of interviews conducted	Male dominated associations with no female sections N=2		Associations with female sections N=14		Associations with no male representation N=1	
	Male	Female	Male	Female	Male	Female
	2	–	14	6	–	1
Total number of interviews conducted	23					

group interviews with 4 to 6 senior executive members of the association. Additionally, 15 interviews were conducted with female leaders of associations with a women's wing; all of these were conducted as group interviews.

Of the 17 associations surveyed, 4 associations were branches of groups founded in southern Nigeria which later spread throughout the West African region. These groups included Nurudeen, Ansarudeen, Nawarudeen and Nasrul-Lahi-Fatih Society (NASFAT). For example, Nawarudeen Society of Nigeria was founded in November 1939 in Abeokuta and has branches in Ghana, Sierra Leone and 3 other West African countries. Three other associations were branches of organizations founded outside of Kano, having branches in other states. These are the Anwarul Islam Movement, Akhbarudeen Society of Nigeria and the Federation of Muslim Women Associations of Nigeria (FOMWAN) Sabon Gari branch.[3] All 7 groups were also registered with the Corporate Affairs Commission in Abuja. The remaining 10 groups were founded locally in Kano. One of these groups, the Islamic Aiders Marshals was also active in Edo State in southern Nigeria, but is only registered in Kano State. Of the 10 local groups, two were veritable home-town ethnic associations and two were umbrella associations (the Joint Association of Muslim Youth (JAMYO) and the Council of Muslim Community (CMC)), 5 were Yoruba associations and one was the Igbo Muslim Association. The name Joint Association of Muslim Youth is somewhat of an anomaly as age was not a precondition for membership. Indeed, the Ithad Ansarul Faedati Tijaniyya and 13 other associations in Kano were members of the Joint Association.

The Muslim minority associations in Kano view themselves as representing a numerically significant community. Data on the membership

---

[3] Though at the national level FOMWAN provides a platform for joint action by Muslim women across ethnic lines, at the Kano level there is an ethnic segmentation in the organization, with western-educated indigenous Hausa-Fulani women having a distinct branch from the Yoruba-dominated Sabon Gari branch.

strength of the organizations is based on the self-reporting of the executive members interviewed. The study triangulated this information by conducting a second round of interviews with female members, by asking respondents to differentiate between active and non-active members, by asking questions about total dues collected and dues per member and by consulting the annual reports and other printed materials of the groups which give information on membership numbers. Most groups claimed membership strengths of between 5,000 to 1,000 members but report active members to be between 52 and 105. NASFAT however, differs from this pattern claiming to have 10,000 active members with 6,500 being female and 3,500 being male. Of the 17 groups, 14 have male, female and youth members. Only two groups, the umbrella group, the Council of Muslim Community (CMC) and the Igbo Muslim Association had neither female nor youth wings. In the 14 groups with female members, the ratio of male to female members was generally about 3:1. Only in three associations did female members outnumber males – NASFAT (65 per cent), Ansaruddeen (60 per cent) and Nurudeen (56 per cent).

Of the 17 groups, 11 were dominated by ethnic Yoruba Muslims. However, this is not the complete picture as the diversity of membership within Yoruba associations and mosques must also be taken into consideration. Igbos, Igala, Igbira, Idoma and even the indigenous Hausa-Fulani were identified by respondents as non-Yoruba ethnic groups who were also members of these largely Yoruba associations. Of the 11 groups with majority Yoruba members, only 1, the CMC, did not have a mosque and of the other 10 Yoruba groups with mosques, male Hausa-Fulani who were traders, urban market garden farmers and workers around the Sabon Gari area constituted the majority amongst regular worshippers and congregants. Their dominance in the Nurudeen Friday mosque led to agitation and a strong request for the translation of sermons from Yoruba into Hausa. There is a sense therefore in which these largely Yoruba Muslim associations constitute a prayer bridge across ethnic boundaries. But can this intermediary role at the level of ritual practices be translated into a positive conflict management role? Diversity in state of origin was also evident amongst the Yoruba-Muslim-dominated associations. For example, in the case of Nurudeen, Yoruba members came from Kwara, Oyo, Ogun, Osun, Ondo and Ekiti States, and the current Chairman is from the non-Yoruba Edo State. Another example is the Akhbarudeen whose Imam is from Niger State, while the Chairman is from Ondo State and the grand patron from Oyo State. The Igbo Muslim Association did not have a mosque in Kano.

The Muslim minority associations have a membership of diverse occupational and class positions, consistent with the demography of Sabon Gari. However, in many cases, founders, leaders and executive members of the associations were often the most educated. For example, the Igbo Muslims Association was headed by a barrister while most of its members were traders and artisans. The associations are organized as formal groups with regular meetings and scheduled social and religious programmes, especially on Sundays. The choice of Sundays for association activities reflects the important position in the associations of Western-educated functionaries of various public and private bureaucracies who tend to have a relatively 'modernist' orientation which distinguishes them from the more traditional outlook of the indigenous Hausa Muslims. The groups have a strong emphasis on record keeping almost to the point of reification. Election of officials is determined by organizations' constitutions and their structure generally reflects specialization of functions. Most associations are headed by a Chairman who is supported by 5 to 6 executive members consisting of Deputy Chairman, Treasurer, Assistant Treasurer and Secretary. As many associations also run mosques, the Imam is also an influential though unelected member of the executive. In addition to the central executive, most associations have women's and youth wings with their own hierarchy of elected officials. The women's wing is separate, with activities specifically targeted at women. Respondents explain this by saying 'you know Islam does not allow us to mingle together and the women play a better role in educating our children' (interview with the Ansarul Islam Society of Nigeria). Despite the attention to the norm of separate spheres for men and women, the emphasis on women's active roles distinguishes these Muslim minority associations from their Muslim Hausa hosts.

In many of the associations, new structures have evolved in response to social and economic needs. For example in NASFAT there is a marriage committee which resolves marital conflict and arranges marriages between unmarried men and women of the association. There is also a scholarship committee and an economic livelihood committee which provides sewing machines, motorcycles and computers to members. Committees are formally organized with appointed heads and established procedures for making awards. Election of officials varies according to the terms of office specified in the associations' constitutions. The range of variation is from 1 to 3 years. While most organizations do not have a dispute resolution procedure, they generally aim to solve problems internally through dialogue without recourse to the courts or public authority. Within these associations, however, there have been inter-association conflicts occasioned by what is perceived to be the Kano State Government's preference for working with only one particular society to the neglect of other groups. According to one interviewee, 'Government used to think they are touching every non-indigenous Muslim when they contacted … They did not know they are only one out of many Islamic societies in Kano'.

Three sources of funding for the associations were identified by respondents. They included member's dues, levies and contributions; donations from the Kano State Government and local philanthropists; contributions from national and African regional parent bodies and contributions from Islamic bodies overseas. In addition to these regular sources of funding are ad hoc donations from Federal Government agencies as well as State governments in the south-west after violent conflicts. Associations which were involved in *Hajj* operations reported receiving funding and official cooperation.

Of the 17 associations surveyed, 14 gave religious propagation and religious teachings as the primary reasons for the establishment of their organization. The two umbrella associations and the Islamic Aiders Marshals did not give religious teachings as their main purpose. Youth and women were especially mentioned as the intended beneficiaries of religious programmes of the associations. Respondents explained that the *raison d'être* of many of the associations was to provide Islamic morals and teachings especially for the youth who they perceived to be at risk of deviance. Women were also singled out for moral education and religious teachings in the 14 associations. In all 14 cases the motive for forming the associations was directly related to the internal needs and dynamics of the community. While some associations did carry out propagation for purposes of conversion within their ethnic communities and amongst the non-Muslim Hausa, the *Maguzawa*, their main focus was servicing the needs of their members. For the groups undertaking conversion, the Igbo Muslim Association was perhaps the most interesting as its main focus was the propagation of Islam in Igboland rather than in Kano itself. Members of the association explained that they were all second- or third-generation Muslims whose main concern was to attract new converts to Islam in their largely Christian south-eastern homeland.

Social and economic services such as health clinics, micro-credit schemes and referrals for employment were identified as a second cluster of reasons for the formation of the 14 associations. For example, the Ansaruddeen Society provides a mini clinic for members and gave out 'empowerment' loans to members, while the Islamic Aiders Marshals provide first aid and health support to their members and other Muslim groups. Many groups also confirmed that they tapped into informal networks to secure employment within state agencies or to obtain privileges such as the allocation of market stalls. In the case of the Igbo Muslim Association, this group reported that members made contributions to 'uplift their brothers who wanted to start business but had no capital'. When providing social services however, the associations often move beyond targeting only their members to supporting all the needy in hospitals, prisons, remand homes and orphanages.

Peaceful co-existence between the various religious and ethnic groups in Kano was mentioned as a third reason for the establishment of the associations. This was stated as the primary reason for their existence by the 2 federated associations. With regard to peaceful co-existence the associations explained that they organized regular lectures to 'tell people to be law abiding according to the dictates of the Islamic religion'. The advancement of peace, security of life and property and the adequate representation of the community to authoritative institutions were the primary reasons listed for the formation of the two federated groups, the CMC and the JAMYO. The JAMYO comprises 14 associations representing communities from Kogi, Benue, Edo and 5 states from the south-west. The group conducts workshops on Islam and democratic governance, and represents members on cases of conflict with public authorities. The CMC, an association of 10 Muslim minority associations was established with a primary mission to further the goal of peace and unity among all Muslims and the propagation of Islam through public lectures and Islamic quiz competitions. Social services to members and needy Muslims were also identified as secondary reasons for the establishment of both JAMYO and CMC. Similar to the 2 federated associations, the Islamic Aiders Marshals is primarily concerned with the maintenance of law and order, keeping the peace and providing security at public functions. Security services provided include first aid, traffic regulation, road safety, fire-fighting and accident prevention.

Muslim minorities & ethno-religious conflicts

Politics and the politicization of religion are the most important risk factor consistently mentioned by all associations interviewed. In the context of repeated cycles of ethno-religious violence in Kano, the Muslim minorities perceive two sources of threats: the first from their co-religionists, the Hausa Muslim community, who identify them as the 'ethnic other'; and the second from their Christian co-ethnics in Sabon Gari who regard them as a Muslim 'fifth column' within their midst. The groups' experience of conflict is related to the location of their mosques and homes. Most Muslim minorities interviewed reported that while their mosques were in Sabon Gari they resided outside of this area in culturally mixed locations such as Naibawa, Hotoro, Katsina Road, Badawa, Sheka, Tsamiyar Boka and Gezawa. This exposed them to double jeopardy in moments of ethno-religious violence. Their mosques in the largely Christian Sabon Gari are potential targets of revenge attacks from their co-ethnics, while their residences in mixed neighbourhoods expose them to potential attacks, not so much from neighbours but from roaming youth gangs.

Muslim minorities' experience of conflict varies according to whether they were at home, on the road between destinations or at the associations' offices or mosques during any particular bout of violence. For the Muslim minorities who were at home during conflicts, the location of residence is a fairly good predictor of experience of conflict. Those living in mixed or Hausa dominated communities, especially outside of the six main urban local governments in Kano explained that they felt safe. They explained that this was particularly so if they were known and accepted within the community. While some Muslim minorities were unlucky to be attacked in-transit others said they were attacked when they intervened to save victims. Muslim minorities residing in Sabon Gari or groups with mosques in this location had stories of woe to tell during religious violence. Officials of the CMC had this to say:

> [W]e the Yoruba Muslims are experiencing two attacks, from indigenes and from Christians from southern Nigeria living in Sabon Gari. So when we are running away from [Muslim Hausa] indigenes and coming to Sabon Gari, we are not safe as well. If you dress like a Hausa man you could be killed. Our mosques are burned by the Igbos [Christians] as revenge.

In a similar vein, an official of the Ansarul Islam Society stated that: 'Each time we have religious conflict we are at the centre, our mosques are always attacked since the beginning of *Maitatsine* crisis'.

Overall, 16 of the 17 associations surveyed reported that they were adversely affected by religious conflicts. The Igbo Muslim Association was the only group to insist that they had no significant negative experience of conflict – despite the fact that the conflicts were often framed as Hausa Muslim indigenes against Igbo Christian settlers. The Igbo Muslims explained that they have no mosques in Kano (that might be burnt in retaliation), while their homes are safe because they live in mixed peri-urban local communities where they are clearly identified as co-Muslims. They added that their shops in Sabon Gari are not attacked as their Igbo kinsmen are not interested in destroying commercial property, most of which is owned by the Igbo. They only faced danger if they are on the road during a crisis. For the 16 groups who were victims of the conflicts their experience is captured in Table 5.2.

It would seem therefore that a high number of the Muslim minorities are negatively affected by religious violence. The Igala Muslim Community reported the highest number of loss of life in recent crises. The CMC's submission to the 2011 Post-Election Violence Panel documents the experience of conflict in the following terms:

Table 5.2 Experiences of violence among Muslim minorities in Kano, 1991–2012

	Experience of Violent Conflict between 1991 and 2012					
Number of associations with experience of violent conflict	Loss of lives amongst respondents' family members	Loss of lives amongst members of the association	Executive members experienced threat to life	Association's property lost	Respondent's personal property lost	Member's personal property lost
N=16	4	10	16	15	13	14

We the Council of Muslim Community of No. 20 Emir Road, Sabon Gari Kano, an umbrella organization of all Yoruba Muslim societies in Kano … humbly forward our complaint to your honorable panel … What we are saying here is that during the period of any crises lasted [*sic*] in Kano, the Yoruba Muslims and other ethnic groups of Nigeria living outside Sabon Gari areas are subject to terrorizing, killings and all sort of inhuman maltreatment. Women, children and aged persons are not exempt. Also in Sabon Gari, an area dominated by Southerners, here is another battle field for the Yoruba Muslims. We are faced with transfer of anger from other ethnic groups of the south which always resulted to attacks on Yoruba Muslims and our Mosques destroyed and burnt down. (CMC July 2011, 1–2)

A Muslim minority belonging to Ithad Ansrul Faedati Tijania testified about his experience of conflict:

I found myself to be a victim as I was coming back from Naibawa through Ring Road on my motorcycle. A group [of rampaging Muslim Hausa youth] stopped me and asked me to recite some Suras [chapters] from the Qur'an, which I did … only one of them argued that I should be allowed to go, the others still were not satisfied and wanted to kill me … in the process, they injured my hand. I know it is only God that saved me that day, they could have killed me.

Muslim minorities who intervened in an attempt to save the lives of Christians were particularly at risk and it was reported that these were the four cases in which association members lost their lives. We sought to understand how the ethnic minorities understood the differences between themselves and their Hausa Muslim hosts. Ethnic bigotry was the recurring explanation advanced by most association members for the persistent attack on them by the Hausa Muslims. As evidence of the ethnic bias of the violence, some Muslim minorities pointed out that Hausa Christians and the *Maguzawa* were never attacked by the Muslim Hausa, while the Muslim Yoruba were constantly being targeted. A female representative of an association explained that 'they categorize all of us together with Igbo [Christians], even we that are Muslim, they don't even take us as a Muslim ... no matter how we pray or recite in front of them, we are nothing'. The representative of the Council of Muslim Community (CMC) put it this way:

> [W]e as Muslims are not spared from attacks ... but if you go to villages outside Kano there are Maguzawa and some Hausa who are converted to Christianity. They did not fight them so it's tribal. I am telling you that if you are not Hausa/Fulani Muslim, even if you recite the Qur'an from Fatiha to Nas, you are not guaranteed not to be killed.

Interestingly, the Muslim minorities attributed the ethnic roots of religious violence in Kano to the low level of Islamic education amongst the Hausa community. In effect, the Muslim minorities are challenging the claims of some of their Hausa Muslim hosts of being 'proper' and 'better' Muslims. Linked to the ethnic factor were other explanations for religious violence suggested by our respondents. These included religious intolerance, youth unemployment, poor child rearing practices of the Hausa community – especially the ubiquity of *almajirai* from traditional Qur'anic schools within the city, the politicization of religion in the new democratic era, and the preponderance of illegal aliens from Niger, Chad and Mali. Global factors such as the invasion of Afghanistan and national ones, such as the cycles of ethno-religious violence in Jos were also identified as remote causes for violence.

Muslim minorities: from bridge builders to para-military protectors

The potential for the Muslim minorities in Kano to serve as bridge builders between their Hausa co-religionists and their southern co-ethnics can be considered in terms of:

1 the role of the associations in contributing to a culture of understanding through grass-roots interactive platforms and processes;
2 the role of Muslim minorities women as a distinct category of actors who also contribute to building a culture of inter-communal under-standing;
3 the ability of Muslim minority actors to participate in and influence official conflict resolution and peace-building structures.

The first and second indicators of bridge building potential operate at the informal level (Track II) while the third indicator operates at the formal level (Track I).

The Muslim minorities in Kano have developed relationships with both Hausa Muslims and southern Christians. Interviews revealed that despite their differences with the Hausa Muslim community there was rich and reciprocal interaction around social ceremonies such as naming of babies and religious ceremonies such as *Maulid* (birthday of the Prophet or of leading Sufi saints). For the male members of Muslim minority associations with mosques in Sabon Gari, their interaction with Hausa male Muslims also revolved around praying together in congregations in the Muslim minority mosques. Indeed, the study found that in most Muslim minority mosques in Sabon Gari the predominant worshippers are male Hausas to the extent that strong demands have been made for the translation of sermons into Hausa. For Muslim minorities conflict prevention was an area of special importance for engagement with Christians. This was particularly so for associations of Muslim minorities with mosques in the Christian-dominated Sabon Gari. For groups such as the Ansarul Islam Society located at No. 25 Freetown Street in Sabon Gari, regular meetings are held with the Christian Igbo community to explain the ways of Islam. Moreover, as one respondent of the Society explained:

> We ask them, do we attack you? We are all non-indigene. We even allow them to be using our borehole to fetch water in the mosque, so that is when some of them realized that these people are our brothers ... That is why in the last riot our mosque was saved.

In addition to interacting with Christians around conflict prevention, 12 of the 17 interviewees representing Muslim minorities associations reported that in their private capacities they also interacted with their ethnic associations which often contained both Muslims and Christians. This was particularly so for the Igala and Igbira associations which appeared to serve dual functions as ethnic and Islamic associations. Muslim minorities active in home-town associations reported that their contribution toward understanding and tolerance towards the Christians of their ethnic group was enhanced by the fact that 'our people are used to Christians and Muslims being together, we understand each other'. Exceptions to this trend must be noted however as 5 Muslim minority groups were explicit in their rejection of membership of home-town associations. The representative of one such group explained 'there is nothing like town union for us, it's religion that binds us together', while the representative of another stated:

> I belong to Isaako [ethnic group] but since I entered Kano I had not been attending the Isaako town union meeting because of the position I am holding in this [Muslim] organization, I told them that whoever is calling meeting it must be on Islamic basis. I don't do ethnic meetings.

Bridge building activities of the women's wings of Muslim minority associations revolved around social welfare initiatives for the indigent and poor of the society in general. Such activities included donations to hospitals, orphanages, remand homes and prisons. During the holy month of Ramadan and on *Maulid* days the women's wings provide food and in some cases clothing for Hausa Muslim neighbours and *almajirai*. Interviews with women's wings of associations reveal that they also contribute to peace through encouraging prayer within the association and by discouraging their youth from any retaliatory actions in violent situations. After conflicts the women's wings swing into action providing medical support and raising funds for injured members in hospitals or at home. Social assistance is also provided to the family of the injured members and in some cases general assistance is provided to community members in the wider ethnic community. Members of the women's wing are also active in reaching out to Hausa Muslim women's associations and to the wives of prominent politicians to brief them about the extent of losses within their community after violent conflicts and to mobilize support for rehabilitation.

Even as Islamic values and institutions were being integrated into the structures of the modern state after 1999, the ethnic minority Muslims were conspicuously absent from such structures, despite their roles in informal Track II processes of peace building. Respondents interviewed, however, noted that they did have informal representation in the *Hisbah* Board when it was first introduced as a voluntary body without pay during the first Kwankwaso administration. At that time, the Kwankwaso government solicited for volunteers for the newly formed *Hisbah* from non-Hausa Muslims by appealing to the CMC. Later, the Muslim minority associations described a situation of intensive but unsuccessful lobbying to secure jobs with the *Hisbah* during the Shekarau administration. Respondents reported that lobbying bore little fruit as all they got from the *Hisbah* were calendars and security services for their Sunday *Assalatu* prayers and gatherings. With regard to the Council of 'Ulama, a nongovernmental body embedded within state religious agencies and affiliated to the Emirate Council, the Muslim minority associations claimed partial involvement based on their Imams' participation in some of the religious activities of this group.

Regarding the representation of Muslim minorities on official post-conflict reconciliation bodies, it is important to note that the post-conflict structures were often constituted as ad hoc committees with terms of reference covering fact finding and reconciliation. No respondent interviewed was ever invited to participate in any of the six or seven post-conflict committees set up over the years in Kano to look into cases of communal violence. Respondents, however, reported that unsolicited memoranda were submitted to the committees and in one case, a memorandum was solicited from a Muslim minority organization. Respondents report that their memoranda were often not even acknowledged, and none of their suggested corrective actions was ever considered. They seldom received compensation for losses incurred during instances of religious violence and committee findings were not shared with them. The failure of official post-conflict structures to address Muslim minority grievances has resulted in letters of protest addressed to the Emir of Kano, seeking his intervention.

The failure to incorporate Muslim minorities into the formal post-conflict reconciliation structures of the state has led to a situation where the associations initiate parallel reconciliation structures and activities at the informal level. Interviews reveal that after almost every conflict since 1991, Muslim minorities convene meetings with the Christian Association of Nigeria, town unions and associations of businessmen in Sabon Gari to discuss the conflict and devise strategies to avoid its reoccurrence.

Against the background of lack of official recognition and support described above, most groups of Muslim minorities have increasingly retreated into the role of para-military protectors of their own narrow community when religious violence takes place. They are responding as aggrieved parties, rather than as a resource for peace building. They give more attention to ensuring the security of their mosques, preserving the life and properties of their members and of extracting compensation from the state when they have come under attack. In doing so, the groups seem to be drawing more deeply from informal ethnic community networks, including within the police and military, to help protect their mosques and property. Side by side with this trend is the increasing involvement of the youth wings of the Muslim minorities association in para-military self-defence activities. Over the years the Muslim minority groups have developed a high capacity for documenting the negative effects of the conflicts on their communities. They are adept at taking photographic evidence and listing properties lost in violent conflicts. If individual members experience loss of life, the groups are also adept at identifying such members and documenting the circumstances. Where members become displaced many associations keep a list of such people. The Muslim minorities associations have also developed capacity to identify the specific state authorities to whom their grievances and demands for compensation should be directed. Unfortunately, the efficiency of the post-conflict activism of the Muslim minority associations contrasts sharply with the lackadaisical approach of formal state institutions.

Conclusion

The study of Muslim minorities in Kano reveals the challenges of ethnic diversity within the Muslim *umma*. Our findings suggest that the failure to accept diversity is closely associated with the doctrinal intolerance that drives the repeated cycle of crises in Kano. Evidence points to a failure in the dominant Hausa Muslim community to accept the Muslim minorities as Muslims of equal status to themselves, preferring instead to define them as parts of ethnic communities with whom they are in a state of ongoing conflict. Intolerance towards Muslim minorities becomes part of a wider cycle of 'othering' which feeds ethno-religious crisis. As this situation spirals out of control and conflicts become more frequent, Muslim minorities are unable to seize opportunities for bridge building and conflict mitigation. Try as they may, circumstance delimit their peace-building role and render them *de facto* parties in a conflict where they must increasingly protect their interest and increasingly take sides.

Failure of state structures to award compensation and to even acknowledge letters from Muslim minority associations on the one hand, while distributing millions of Naira, buses and land to a few individual clients within the Muslim minorities on the other, perpetuates the notion that political interests rather than justice is being served. The irony of this situation cannot be missed by the informed observer, given that the Governor of Kano State between 2003 and 2011 was himself of Muslim minority origin – albeit from a group assimilated into the dominant Hausa-Fulani culture. Narrow political partisanship, the psychology of political leaders and the widespread 'othering' of people from different ethnic backgrounds are the explanations for the failure to recognize Muslim minorities in Kano as a distinct group and tap into their potential for peace building.

Bibliography

Abba, Muhammad Jamilu, 1999, 'Kano City and Fagge: A Historical Perspective', Kano: Triumph Publishing.
Abdu, Hussaini, n.d. (c. 2002), 'Ethnic and Religious Crisis in Northern Nigeria: Issues in Informal Repression', unpublished paper, Kaduna: Nigeria Defence Academy.
Abdulkadir, S.M., 2011, Islam in the Non-Muslim Areas of Northern Nigeria, c1600–1960. *Ilorin Journal of Religious Studies*, 1 (1).
Agbede, I.O., 2007, 'Dynamics of Ethno-Religious Conflicts in Nigeria', African Centre for Contemporary Studies.

Akaeze, Anthony, 2009, 'From Maitatsine to Boko Haram', *NewsWatch Magazine*, Lagos, 28 October.

Barzilai, Gad, 2003, Communities and Law: Politics and Cultures of Legal Identities, Ann Arbor MI: University of Michigan Press

Brice, Kevin M.A., 2010, 'A Minority within a Minority: A Report on Converts to Islam in the United Kingdom' Faith Matters. Online at www.faith-matters.org, accessed 20 January 2012.

Casey, C., 2008, '"Marginal Muslims": Politics and the Perceptual Bounds of Islamic Authenticity in Northern Nigeria', *Africa Today*, 54 (3), Special Issue: 'Muslim West Africa in the Age of Neoliberalism', 67–92.

Crenshaw, Kimberle, 1991, 'Mapping the Margins: Intersectionality, Identity Politics, and Violence against Women of Color', *Stanford Law Review*, 43 (6), 1241–99. Online at www.jstor.org/stable/1229039, accessed: 18 August 2008.

Deegan, H., 2011, 'Religious Conflict in Kano: What are the Fundamental Issues?' *Commonwealth & Comparative Politics*, 49 (1), 80–97.

Economic Confidential, 2012, 'Igbo Businessmen Refuse to Relocate from the North', reported in *People's Daily*, 4 (74), 15 February 2012, Abuja.

Egwu, S.G., 2001, 'Ethnic and Religious Violence in Nigeria', Abuja: African Centre for Democratic Governance (ARIGOV).

Ehrhardt, David, 2008, *Perceptions Survey Metropolitan Kano*, mimeo, NRN, Queen Elizabeth House, Oxford.

Feagin, J.R., 1984, Racial and Ethnic Relations, Englewood Cliffs NJ: Prentice-Hall.

Fisher, R.J., 1993, 'The Potential for Peace-building, Forging a Bridge from Peace-keeping to Peacemaking', *Peace & Change*, 18 (3), 247–66.

Henrard, K., 2000, *Devising an Adequate System of Minority Protection: Individual Human Rights, Minority Rights and the Right to Self-Determination*, Leiden: Martinus Nijhoff.

Hegre, H., 2001, 'Towards a Democratic Civil Peace? Democracy, Political Change and Civil War, 1816–1992', *American Political Science Review*, 95 (1), 33–48.

Hiskett, M., 1987, 'The Maitatsine Riots in Kano: An Assessment', *Journal of Religion in Africa*, 17 (3), 209–23.

Ibrahim, J., 1989, 'The Politics of Religion in Nigeria: The Parameters of the 1987 Crisis in Kaduna State', Review of African Political Economy (ROAPE), 16 (45/46), 65–82.

Ibrahim, J., 1999, 'Ethno-Religious Mobilization and Sapping of Democracy in Nigeria', in J. Hyslop (ed.), *African Democracy in the Era of Globalization*, Johannesburg: Wits University Press.

Ibrahim, J., 2000, 'The Transformation of Ethno-Religious Identities in Nigeria', in A. Jega (ed.), *Identity Transformation and Identity Politics under Structural Adjustment in Nigeria*, Stockholm: Elanders Gotab.

Isichei, E., 1987, 'The Maitatsine Risings in Nigeria 1980–1985: The Revolt of the Disinherited', *Journal of Religion in Africa*, 17 (3), 194–208.

Jinadu, A.L., 2007, 'Explaining & Managing Ethnic Conflicts in Africa: Towards a Cultural Theory of Democracy', Claude Ake Memorial Paper Series (CAMP) 1, Uppsala: The Nordic Africa Institute.

Kaufman, S., 2000, Peace-Building and Conflict Resoultion in Nagorno-Karabakh, PONARS Policy Memo 164, Lexington KY: University of Kentucky.

Kettani, Ali M., 1986, *Muslim Minorities in the World Today*, London: Mansell.

Kwaja, C.M.A., 2009,Strategies for [Re]Building State Capacity to Manage Ethnic and Religious Conflict in Nigeria, *Journal of Pan African Studies*, 3 (3), 105–15.

Lubeck, Paul M., 1985, 'Islamic Protest under Semi-Industrial Capitalism: 'Yan Tatsine Explained', in John D.Y. Peel and Charles C. Stewart (eds), *Popular Islam South of the Sahara*, Manchester: Manchester University Press, 369–90.

Mustapha, Abdul Raufu, 2003, Ethnic Minority Groups in Nigeria: Current Situation and Major Problems. UN Commission on Human Rights, Sub-Commission on Promotion and Protection of Human Rights, Working Group on Minorities. Ninth Session, 12–16 May.

Oladimeji, O.A., 2009, 'Evil Forces and Shirk Among the Yoruba Muslims in Nigeria with Special Reference to Ilorin City', M.Phil. thesis, University of Birmingham, eTheses Repository.

Olaniyi, Rasheed, 2004, 'Yoruba Commercial Diaspora and Settlement Patterns in Pre-Colonial Kano', in T. Falola and S.J. Salm (eds), *Nigerian Cities*, Trenton NJ, Africa World Press, 79–99.

Omar, F., 2011, 'What are we doing for Muslim Minorities?' *Saudi Life*. Online at www.saudilife.net/sportlight/115-muslim-world, accessed on 11 April 2011.

Osaghae, E., 2007, 'Federalism and the Management of Ethnicity in Nigeria: The 1999 Constitution in Focus', in C. Bassey and O. Oshita (eds), *Conflict Resolution, Identity Crisis, and Development in Africa*, Lagos: Malthouse Press.

Oseni, Z.I., 1986, 'Modern Arabic and Islamic Studies in Bendel State of Nigeria', *Journal of the Institute of Muslim Minority Affairs*, 8 (1).

Ostien, Philip, 2012, 'Percentages by Religion of the 1952 and 1963 Populations of Nigeria's Present 36 States' NRN Background Paper 1, Oxford: Nigeria Research Network Oxford Department of International Development.

Paden, J, 2008, *Faith and Politics in Nigeria: Nigeria as a Pivotal State in the Muslim World*, Washington DC, United States Institute for Peace.

Pew Forum on Religion & Public Life, 2010, 'Tolerance and Tension: Islam and Christianity in Sub-Saharan Africa', Washington DC: PEW Research Center.

Rotberg, I.R., 2004, 'The Failure and Collapse of Nation-States: Breakdown, Prevention, and Repair', in I.R. Rotberg (ed.), *When States Fail: Causes and Consequences*, Princeton NJ, Princeton University Press.

Takaya, B.J., 1992, 'Religion, Politics and Peace: Resolving the Nigerian Dilemma', in J.K. Olupona (ed.), *Religion and Peace in a Multi-Faith Nigeria*, Ile-Ife: Obafemi Awolowo University Press.

Uchendu, E., 2010, Being Igbo and Muslim: 'The Igbo of South-Eastern Nigeria and Conversions to Islam, 1930s to Recent Times', *Journal of African History*, 51 (1), 63–87.

Udegbe, Clement, 2013, 'The Igbos have more at stake in Nigeria', *Vanguard*, www.vanguardngr.com, 26 July 2013.

Ugochukwu, Francoise, 2009, 'Nigerian Video-Films on History: Love in Vendetta and the 1987 Kano Riots, in *African Film: Looking Back and Looking Forward*, 26–30 Jan 2009, Ife Film Festival.

Usman, Y.B., 1987, *The Manipulation of Religion in Nigeria, 1977–1987*. Kaduna: Vanguard Printers and Publishers.

Wink, W., 1997, *Healing a Nation's Wounds: Reconciliation on the Road to Democracy*, Uppsala: Sweden, Life and Peace Institute.

Yuval-Davis, Nira, 2006, 'Intersectionality and Feminist Politics', *European Journal of Women's Studies*, 13 (3), 193–209.

Documents
Annual Reports, Constitutions and Correspondences of the 17 Associations of Muslim Minorities.Government of Kano State, Youth Club Edict No 17 of 1976.

6

Understanding *Boko Haram*

ABDUL RAUFU MUSTAPHA

Introduction

By 2003, the cycle of violence that we now identify with *Boko Haram* had started in the north-east. Between that year and 2014, the group metamorphosed from a group of angry Islamist young men wielding sticks on the streets of Maiduguri to an entrenched insurgency capable of deploying Armoured Personnel Carriers (APCs) and Somalia-type mounted machine guns or 'technicals', and engaged in ruthless bombing campaigns across numerous Nigerian cities. It is a testament to the poor management of the situation by political and military authorities at all levels of the Nigerian federation that this transformation from a rag-tag mob in 2003 to a so-called Caliphate in 2014 was able to take place unchecked. Given the level of misinformation, biased and fanciful reporting and politically motivated reporting on *Boko Haram*, in this chapter I draw together as much of the publicly available evidence on the group as is available. This then forms the basis of my analysis of the group and its campaign of violence. The history of the establishment and transformation of *Boko Haram* has been recounted in some detail in A. Mohammed (2010), Salkida (2013a, 2013b), Higazi (2013a, 2013b) and Pérouse de Montclos (2014). Their narratives do not always fully agree with each other, but the general thrust of their accounts is fairly consistent.

On the other hand, many international narratives are beclouded by Western policy concerns about the threat of Islamist terrorism. Worse still, as Pérouse de Montclos (2014b, 2, 7) rightly points out, most writings on *Boko Haram* are pure speculation from analysts with little familiarity with the local terrain. At best, the resulting analysis amounts to only 'some evidence and a lot of confusion'. Nowhere is such speculative confusion more apparent than in the analysis of the CNN journalists, Lah and

Johnston (2014) who argue that *Boko Haram* is engaged in kidnapping and piracy off the Gulf of Guinea, or in the sensationalist accounts of Jacob Zenn (2014a, 2014b) who embellishes events with an excessively Western security mind-set.[1] These cobwebs of confusion, along with the difficulty of researching such a violent group, make it difficult to easily gather the necessary evidence for our analysis.

Early history

In the course of the Salafi conflict with the Sufis (see Chapter 3), Salafi scholars like Shaikh Ja'afar Mahmud Adam of Kano broke away from *Izala* and formed their own independent organizations. One such was Shaikh Ja'afar's *Ahl al-sunna*. Mohammed Yusuf was the leader of the youth wing of *Ahl al-sunna*. Between 1998 and 2003, Yusuf used the support of Shaikh Ja'afar to build up a following, not just at the Indimi Mosque in Maiduguri where Shaikh Ja'afar preached during every month of Ramadan, but also across the borders in Chad, Cameroon and Niger Republic, where the religious influence of the Salafis was also felt (see Masquelier 1996; 2009). As he became increasingly radicalized, Mohammed Yusuf developed doctrines which put him at odds with Shaikh Ja'afar and subsequently led to his being banned from preaching at the Indimi Mosque. At the same time, however, he was becoming a very popular magnet for various disaffected youth, in search of an Islamic solution to the problems of life. Mohammed Yusuf formed the *Yusufiyya* movement which later transformed into *Jama'atu Ahlul Sunna li Da'awati wal Jihad* (People Committed to the Propagation of the Prophet's Teachings and Jihad) (*Boko Haram*). According to K. Mohammed (2014) the group underwent three overlapping phases in its evolution.

The first, 'Kanama', phase (2003–2004) started when a group of about 200 young men, including many followers of Mohammed Yusuf decided to disengage from the secular state and established a revolutionary Islamic community in the rural setting of Kanama in Yobe State on the Nigeria-Niger border. This utopian/insurrectionary phase was led by Muhammad Ali, a Nigerian radicalized in Saudi Arabia and who was believed to have fought alongside the *mujahideen* in Afghanistan. The group referred to themselves as the 'Nigerian Taliban', or the *Ahl al-sunna*

---

[1] For example, after arguing that, '[d]espite Shekau's efforts to reach out to al-Qaeda with the praise for "soldiers of God in the Islamic State of Mali" when al-Qaeda in the Islamic Maghreb (AQIM) controlled territory in northern Mali in 2012, no other al-Qaeda affiliate has recognized Shekau or Boko Haram as one of their own', Zenn still went on to title a recent paper 'Nigerian al-Qaedaism' (Zenn 2014a). In another sensationalist and frivolous essay (Zenn 2014b), Zenn even contradicts himself by asserting that 'Boko Haram operates as al-Qaeda's representative in Nigeria'!

wa'l-jama'a (Followers of the Prophet's Teaching). Between December 2003 and October 2004, the group launched a series of deadly attacks on police stations, government buildings and prisons in Kanama, Damaturu, Gwoza, Bama and the Mandara Mountains along the Nigeria-Cameroon border. Clashes with the Nigerian military ensued, leading to heavy loss of lives on both sides and the flushing out of the group from their rural redoubts. Mohammed Yusuf, blamed by the state for the insurrection, fled to Saudi Arabia and the surviving members of the sect returned to Maiduguri to re-group.

The second phase, the *daawa* (radical proselytization) phase (2005–2009), started after Mohammed Yusuf returned from his self-imposed exile in Saudi Arabia in 2005. A rapprochement between him and the state had been brokered by the Borno State deputy Governor, Adamu Shettima Dibal and Shaikh Ja'afar, during the 2005 pilgrimage in Saudi Arabia. According to Shaikh Ja'afar, Mohammed Yusuf claimed not to have been party to the Kanama uprising[2] and swore never to espouse violent jihadi ideology (Mohammed 2014, 13). This promise notwithstanding, the phase was marked by doctrinal extremism, recruitment, indoctrination and the radicalization of its members. Buoyed by resources from political patrons and sales of audio cassettes containing his fiery sermons, Mohammed Yusuf built a base for his sect on land given to him by his father-in-law in Maiduguri. At the heart of this base was the *Markaz* Ibn Taymiyya[3] and its annexes of mosque, schools, clinics and similar ancillary facilities for sect members. The full elaboration of Mohammed Yusuf's doctrines at this time (see Chapter 3) was coupled with strident criticism of the corruption and bad governance under Governor Ali Modu Sheriff of Borno State (2003–2011). The sect had fallen out with the Governor, after collaborating with him in the 2003 elections. Yusuf also criticized the conspicuous consumption and opulence of the wider Western-educated elite in the midst of the abject poverty of the bulk of the population (Mohammed 2014). On account of his incendiary sermons, Yusuf was arrested on numerous occasions and taken to Abuja, but on each occasion, he returned unscathed to Maiduguri, further fuelling his reputation amongst his followers as a 'Robin Hood' figure – one no doubt wearing a turban – capable of standing up to the high and mighty in the name of Islam and in defence of their interests.

The third phase of armed insurrection was from June 2009. In that month, following disagreements with some sect members on a motor-

---

[2] According to K. Mohammed (2014, 12) his role 'was talent spotting, recruitment, and indoctrination of members', while Mohammed Ali provided the actual leadership.

[3] 'The markaz is the place of "sociability" and appears as a place of continuous education. With a library and a weekly sermon every Thursday, this place attracts merchants, young people and other categories of people. The markaz is a place for building social networks. It can be compared with the Zāwiya in the Sufi context' (Ben Amara 2011, 38).

cycle procession without wearing the protective helmet required by law, clashes broke out with the police in Maiduguri. Fourteen sect members were shot and wounded in the ensuing fracas. Thereafter, Mohammed Yusuf swore revenge against the state. In July 2009, the sect launched its retaliation against the police in Borno, Bauchi, Yobe, Gombe, Kano and Katsina States. According to a Borno State Government official inquiry, 800 people were killed in the ensuing violence in Borno, including 40 Christians and 22 policemen killed by the sect. Some more casualties were recorded in other states. The *Markaz* Ibn Taymiyya was razed to the ground by the army, while the sect was said to have burnt 25 churches. In total, 200 houses including police stations were destroyed in Maiduguri. Hundreds of *Boko Haram* members are arrested,[4] including Mohammed Yusuf who was handed over to the police for interrogation by the army. However, he was summarily executed on 30 July. Alhaji Buji Foi, the former Commissioner of Religious Affairs and a financier of *Boko Haram*, and Alhaji Baba Fugu Mohammed, the 72-year-old father-in-law of Mohammed Yusuf, were also arrested and summarily executed (see Ola 2009).[5] Governor Modu Sheriff dismissed the public outcry over Mohammed Yusuf's extra-judicial execution, referring to him as a 'lunatic':

> You know, I can't understand this kind of law, or even this type of emotions. Why should a man kill over 700 people and when he dies, you want to make him a hero of sorts? Why should people be sympathetic to a hardened criminal who died, or begin to question how he died? I'm baffled by that type of reasoning, because it goes counter to common sense. (Governor Modu Sheriff in Bello, 2009)

Boko Haram went underground, re-organized and resurfaced in 2010 under the leadership of Abubakar Shekau.[6] This rebirth was announced

[4] 190 Boko Haram suspects were subsequently arraigned before the Maiduguri High Court for alleged illegal assembly, arson, breach of peace, culpable homicide and the torching of police stations. They were specifically charged with killing 22 police officers, setting 25 churches ablaze, burning down the Maiduguri Prison and releasing all the inmates, as well as setting public buildings on fire. See Njadvara (2009a).

[5] The Maiduguri High Court subsequently indicted President Umaru Musa Yar' Adua, Borno State Governor, Ali Sheriff, and Inspector General of Police (IGP), Ogbonna Onovo, for the extra-judicial killing of Alhaji Baba Fugu and ordered them to pay compensation of N100 million to the family. The case against some policemen who allegedly executed Mohammed Yusuf is still before the courts (October 2014) in Abuja.

[6] Under Shekau, the sect has become more ruthless, violent and destructive, with the slaughtering and beheading of their victims as one of their gruesome trademarks. In one of his many video postings on YouTube, Shekau declared that: 'I enjoy killing anyone that God commands me to kill the way I enjoy killing chickens and rams' (see *Vanguard* 2014a). Some have even raised concern over his state of mind, based on his YouTube appearances. In one such an appearance, 'he often interjected his message with cynic leers, song and even dancing' (Haruna 2014b). It would seem that the internet has shifted Islamist propaganda from texts to visual iconography – video clips in which flags, chants and Kalashnikovs are common motifs.

through the raid on Bauchi prison in September 2010, during which five prison staff were killed and 721 prisoners, including over 100 *Boko Haram* members, were set free. The group also made clear its sectarian intentions in a poster released throughout Maiduguri in which it announced: 'Any Muslim that goes against the establishment of Sharia [law] will be attacked and killed.' Vengeful animosity towards Governor Modu Sheriff is a defining characteristic of the resurgent sect.

Boko Haram *after 2010*

Since 2009 *Boko Haram* has used targeted assassinations, drive-by shootings, suicide bombings, improvised explosive devices (IEDs) and vehicle-borne IEDs to spread death and destruction across northern Nigeria. The targets have been individuals with whom they disagree on doctrinal or political grounds, schools, churches, mosques belonging to their perceived opponents, the police, the military, traditional authorities, political leaders, symbolic targets like the Police Headquarters in Abuja, bombed in June 2011 and the UN building in Abuja, bombed in August 2011. According to the Shehu of Borno, Alhaji Abubakar El-Kanemi, by 2014, 14 out of the 59 district heads in his kingdom have been killed by *Boko Haram* (Utebor & Uka 2014). In occasional forays outside its north-east heartland, *Boko Haram* launched attacks on St Theresa's Catholic Church on 25 December 2011 in Madalla, near Abuja, killing 43 church-goers. Coordinated attacks were also launched on Kano in January 2012, targeting police formations, the State Security Services, and prisons with a death toll of about 186 people. Suicide bombers also attacked *ThisDay* newspaper offices in Abuja and Kaduna in April 2012 (Eboh and Mohammed 2012).

In June 2011 the Nigerian Government established a Joint Task Force (JTF) called 'Operation Restore Order' in Borno State, made up of personnel drawn from the Nigerian Armed Forces, the Nigeria Police Force, the Department of State Services (DSS), the Nigerian Immigration Service and the Defence Intelligence Agencies. Its mandate was to 'restore law and order' to north-eastern Nigeria. This militarization of policing mirrors what has been happening in other parts of Nigeria since the return to democratic rule ushered in a wave of civil unrest across the country. The special-purpose security organs – Joint Task Forces (JTF) or Special Task Forces (STF) – are now responsible for everyday policing in 28 out of Nigeria's 36 states (Emewu 2013). The Government also revamped the Multi-National Joint Task Force (MNJTF), set up in 1998 by the governments of Niger, Chad and Nigeria to patrol restive areas of their common borders. Cameroon subsequently joined the MNJTF (Obada 2013). The

JTF and the MNJTF have been accused of widespread atrocities and even crimes against humanity by Borno Elders as well as many domestic and international human rights organizations (see Amnesty International 2012, 2014, and Human Rights Watch 2012). The White Paper on the Report of the Presidential Committee on the Security Challenges in the North-East Zone also noted some of the 'allegations of high-handedness against the JTF, bordering on rape, destruction of property belonging to sect members, extra-judicial killings and harassment and intimidation of Maiduguri residents' (Federal Government of Nigeria 2012).

In January 2012, President Goodluck Jonathan declared a state of emergency in 16 Local Government Areas (LGAs) across four states.[7] This basically gave the President and his agents the additional powers that may be necessary to maintain public order. Yet, the spate of violence continued unabated. In 10 out of the 27 LGAs of Borno State, Government activities were paralysed as Council chairmen, their councillors and other top officials abandoned their duty posts in affected areas and relocated to Maiduguri, the state capital (Alli 2013).[8] *Boko Haram* was even reported to have hoisted its jihadist flag in some of these rural locales. Another state of emergency was declared in May 2013 and extended in November 2013, covering the whole of Borno, Yobe and Adamawa States. Also, in May 2013, local youths in Maiduguri, caught between *Boko Haram* on the one hand and the security forces on the other, formed a vigilante group known as the 'Civilian Joint Task Force' (CJTF), with the objective of rooting out *Boko Haram* members from their midst. Over a period of months, it succeeded in chasing *Boko Haram* members out of Maiduguri and the sect moved its base of operations into the surrounding countryside.

In August 2013, the 7th Infantry Division of the army was created with an initial complement of 8,000 troops to take over from the JTF in prosecuting the war against *Boko Haram*. However, these various security measures adopted by the state have hardly made a dent in the level of worsening violence. What they have achieved is to force a change of tactics on *Boko Haram*. Along with targeted assassinations, *Boko Haram*'s repertoire of violence expanded to include the burning of schools and telecommunications base stations, the kidnapping of locals and foreigners for ransom, sometimes in neighbouring countries and the wholesale sacking of villages perceived as hostile to its ambitions. The group roams the Borno hinterland, extorting money and provisions from the population and in many cases forcibly recruiting young men to join its ranks, or inducing them with money or the prospects of youthful excitement to join the sect

[7] These are Maiduguri Metropolitan, Gamboru Ngala, Banki, Bama, Biu and Jere LGAs in Borno State; Jos North, Jos South, Barkin Ladi and Riyom in Plateau State; Damaturu, Geidam, Potiskum, Buniyadi Gujba and Gashua Bade in Yobe state; Suleja in Niger State.

[8] The ten LGAs are Marte, Magumeri, Mobbar, Gubio, Guzamala, Abadamin, Kukawa, Kaga, Nganzai and Monguno.

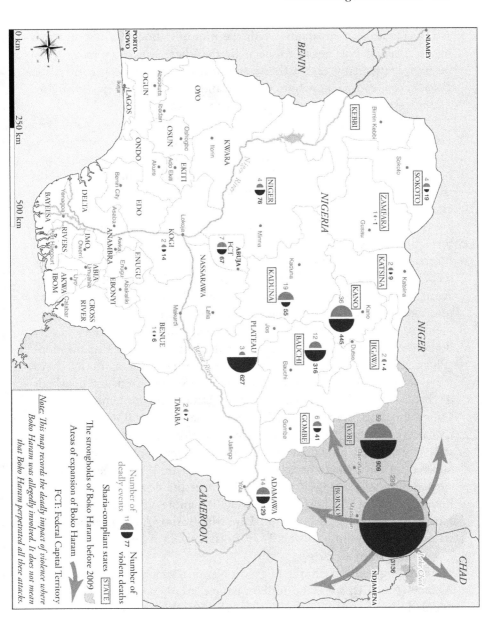

Map 6.1
Sharia-compliant states
and the Boko Haram
crisis in Nigeria
(courtesy of Institut Français
de Géopolitique, 2013; Nigeria
Watch data June 2006 –
October 2013)

as informants or combatants. With the multiplication of different types of violence, analysts began to speculate that there were now many 'Boko Harams', with many criminal and political elements hiding behind the Boko Haram label to perpetrate violence and mayhem. The extent of Boko Haram-related violence by 2013 is shown in Map 6.1.

Dislodged from their incipient fiefdoms in northern Borno State, Boko Haram has moved into the more peripheral parts of Borno, especially to the Sambisa forest in southern Borno, and over the borders into neighbouring countries. Villages in the Gwoza Hills in the Mandara Mountains that straddle north-east Nigeria and Cameroon have been particularly affected (Higazi 2013b). Since late 2010, but especially from 2013, there are increasing signs that Boko Haram has been undergoing a major transformation in its capacity, tactics and ideology. The crisis in Mali from March 2012 is thought to have created avenues for some members of the sect to be trained by other Islamist groups in the West African sub-region. Arms from post-Gaddafi Libya are also thought to be making their way into Boko Haram hands through these same channels. These developments suggest expanding links between what had hitherto been a largely domestic Nigerian sect and international Islamist terrorist organizations (Pham 2012).[9] By mid-2014, the war with Boko Haram is reported to have led to over 12,000 deaths, more than 8,000 persons injured, and hundreds of thousands displaced (Jonathan 2014). Data from the United Nations Office for the Coordination of Humanitarian Affairs (OCHA) suggest that no fewer than six million residents of Borno, Adamawa and Yobe states – half of the total population in the three states – have been directly affected by Boko Haram attacks. Since the start of 2014, Boko Haram has carried out daily killings, bombings, lootings and destruction of schools, homes, markets and hospitals in over 40 remote villages in the three North-Eastern states. At least 38 LGAs in Borno, Adamawa and Yobe states were badly hit – all the 27 in Borno, six in Adamawa and five in Yobe (Oketola et al. 2014).

According to data from the Nigerian National Emergency Management Agency (NEMA), some 3.2 million people, nearly a third of the overall population in the three states, are affected by the crisis, most of them women, children and older people. It added that between January and March 2014, more than 1,000 people have been killed and 249,446 displaced in the three states, with one in five of the total population not living in their own homes (AFP 2014). Data from Maplecroft Terrorism and Security Dashboard (MTSD) suggests that Nigeria has the world's highest casualty rate from terrorism with an average of 24 deaths per attack out of 146 recorded

[9] The five main Islamists groups in Mali are Ansar Dine, Movement for Unity and Jihad in West Africa (Mujao), al-Qaeda in the Islamic Maghreb (AQIM), the Signed-in-Blood Battalion and the Islamic Movement for Azawad (IMA) (BBC 2013).

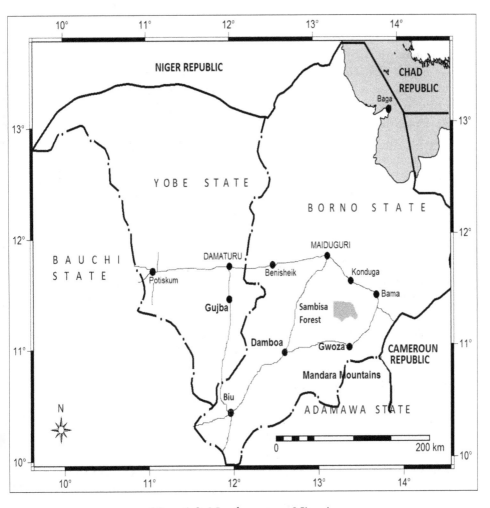

Map 6.2 North-eastern Nigeria
(courtesy of A.K. Monguno and M. Gambo, University of Maiduguri)

between January and June 2014. The global average is two deaths per attack. Nigeria recorded 3,477 deaths in those attacks, representing a doubling of the 1,735 deaths recorded in the same period in 2013 (Abdallah 2014).[10] Regardless of the exact numbers of the people affected, all are agreed on the exceptionally high death rates, and the devastation of health facilities, schools, markets, farms and even infrastructure like bridges. The areas in southern Borno around the Sambisa forest and the Mandara Mountains, as well as the borderlands between Nigeria, Cameroon and Chad have been

[10] According to Human Rights Watch, in the first six months of 2014, *Boko Haram* killed at least 2,053 civilians in an estimated 95 attacks; 1,446 people died in Borno, 151 in Adamawa state and 143 in Yobe. In 14 bomb blasts in crowded public facilities across many cities, 432 people were reportedly killed (Somorin 2014).

particularly affected in the escalating conflicts of 2014 (Haruna 2014a). The town of Chibok, from where over 200 school girls were abducted by *Boko Haram* in April 2014, is in this zone.

In 2014 *Boko Haram* also made efforts to extend its insurgency westwards to Balmo forest which stretches from Bauchi State into Jigawa State, with links to the fringes of Sambisa forest (Ibeh 2014). There is, however, no let-up in its main theatre of operations in southern Borno, with 18 attacks launched over a two-week period in June–July 2014 (Umar & Odemwingie 2014). In one such attack, 60 cows were seized from villagers in Mandaragirau village of Biu LGA (Idris 2014a). From a sect of a few angry young men in Maiduguri in 2003, *Boko Haram* increasingly took on the form of a destructive and unfathomable guerrilla movement, similar to the Ugandan Lord's Resistance Army, that has turned pillaging, forcible recruitment of young people and violence in the countryside into a long-term way of life in its own right, devoid of any discernible political or ideological objectives. Increasingly, women are being recruited into the organization, not just as informants, cashiers or those responsible for domestic chores such as cooking and fetching firewood and water, but as suicide bombers and active combatants (Idris 2014b). Bombing campaigns have been launched across many northern urban centres, and there are growing signs that *Boko Haram* is trying to penetrate into southern cities like Lagos, Port Harcourt and Owerri.[11]

Perspectives on Boko Haram *violence*

The very metamorphosis of *Boko Haram* suggests that its dynamics cannot be fully captured just by examining the sectarian conflicts that have plagued the Muslim communities of Nigeria for so long. According to Chouin (2014, ix):

> For a movement such as *Boko Haram* to mutate from a sectarian group splitting away from the *Izala* movement to a full-grown rebellion threatening the integrity of the most powerful state in West Africa, you need more than religious fanatics, violent Salafist ideology, and intolerance. The ingredients that fuel the fire spreading across north-eastern Nigeria are yet to be fully described.

The situation is further compounded by domestic Nigerian narratives on *Boko Haram* which tend to be coloured by the fractious ethnic and religious politics of the country. In this context, conspiracy theories that are passion-

---

[11] *Boko Haram* claims to have carried out two suicide bomb explosions, one by a female, at a Lagos fuel depot in June 2014 (*Punch* 2014b).

ately held but little substantiated, have proliferated, given the levels of anxiety and fear that the atrocities of *Boko Haram* have generated.[12]

CONSPIRACY THEORIES

While some are more fanciful than others, they are all to be taken seriously to the extent that they shape the perceptions of significant proportions of the population. These conspiracy theories also tend to reflect the ethnic, religious and regional divisions within Nigerian society and thereby feed into an extant fractious political process. Though they are passionately held and articulated within public discourses, there is often very little supporting evidence put forward to support the claim of the alleged conspiracies. We can discount conspiracy theories that claim that the United States of America created *Boko Haram* to break up Nigeria because some American institutions twice 'predicted' that Nigeria will break up as a country in 2015 or 2030, and that *Boko Haram* is therefore a wish-ful-filling project sponsored to achieve this end.[13] We can then concentrate on conspiracy theories of a domestic nature, which can be divided into three categories, depending on the focus of the alleged conspiracy: religious, political and military.

The religious conspiracy theories reflect the Muslim-Christian cleavage within Nigerian society. For some Muslims, like the former President of the National Council of Muslim Youths (NACOMYO), Alhaji Ishaq Kunle Sanni, *Boko Haram* is not about Islam, but is 'a conspiracy hatched to tarnish the image of Islam and tag Muslims as violent and rebel-lious people' (Aliyu 2014). Details of who is behind this conspiracy are often vague, sometimes pointing to either domestic or global forces. It would seem that some Muslims cannot come to terms with the atroc-ities being committed in the name of their religion, and would rather look for other forces to blame. However, most religious conspiracies

---

[12] As Hiskett (1987, 222, fn. 1) noted, such conspiracy theories are not new in Nigeria. In the aftermath of the *Maitatsine* crises in the 1980s, the 'Nigerian press favoured conspiracy theories involving the Libyans, Iranians, et al. [One] even carried a report alleging the involvement of the Israeli security organisation, Mossad.'

[13] The second 'prediction' that Nigeria would break up was by the Washington-based National Intelligence Council (NIC) which, in its *Global Trends* report of December 2012, predicted that 15 countries in Africa, Asia and the Middle East will become 'failed states' by 2030, due to their 'potential for conflict and environmental ills'. Nigeria is one of the 15. The views of some Nigerians is reflected by Shilgba (n.d.): 'There is a role that the United States of America (USA) has been playing in the past few years that convinces me that the utmost collapse of Nigeria is a strange desire of that country. A prediction by the USA that Nigeria would break up in 2015 is definitely not news. What seems to be news now is the present effort by the USA under the Obama government to make that prophecy to come to pass.' Even as late as 11 April 2014, US Ambassador James Entwistle was having to issue denials on behalf of his government ('U.S. denies predicting Nigeria's break-up in 2015', www.theguardianmobile.com/readNewsItem1. php?nid=24871, 11 April 2014).

regarding *Boko Haram* are promoted by some leaders of the Christian community. According to the President of the Christian Association of Nigeria, Pastor Ayo Oritsejafor, the 'menace of *Boko Haram* is primarily a religious issue. They believe they have a mandate from Allah to Islamise Nigeria' (Olokor et al. 2013). He also stated that 'the hidden agenda of *Boko Haram* is to have an Islamic state in Nigeria as we now hear and see in Iraq and Syria. I think the insurgents are gradually advocating for a Jihad in Nigeria' (Duru 2014). In a similar vein, the President of Church of Christ in Nations (COCIN), Rev. Dachollom Datiri, described *Boko Haram* as 'a child of Islamic fundamentalism nurtured over the years by radical Muslim youth groups, trained and indoctrinated both locally and internationally by extremists to hate and kill Christians' (Adinoyi 2014). With no supporting evidence to back them up, these conspiracy theories only point to the high level of religious polarization and mistrust between Nigerian Christian and Muslim communities.

In a similar manner, the conspiracy theories of a political nature also highlight the political cleavages within Nigerian society. The immediate context for these theories is the Presidency of Goodluck Jonathan, a Christian from a southern minority ethnic group. Two elements of the elite pact that undergirded the return to democratic politics in 1999 are the distribution of the key offices of the state and the ruling People's Democratic Party (PDP) to different ethno-regional constituencies in the country under a zoning formula, and the rotation of the office of President between north and south. President Olusegun Obasanjo, a southern Yoruba Christian, was President from 1999 to 2007, having served the constitutionally prescribed two terms of four years. The ruling party then put forward a Muslim, Hausa-Fulani candidate, Umaru Musa Yar' Adua, for President. By the zoning and rotational arrangements of the ruling party, Yar' Adua, representing the north, was expected to serve for two terms, 2007 to 2015. Unfortunately, Yar' Adua died in office in 2010, leading to the assumption of office by Vice President Goodluck Jonathan as Acting President. This development upturned the zoning and rotational arrangements of the ruling party and struck at the heart of the elite pack holding the various ethno-regional factions together. After just two years in office of a northern candidate, power was effectively returning to the south. Acrimonious efforts by some northern political interests to stop Goodluck Jonathan from contesting the 2011 Presidential elections on the platform of the ruling party failed, leading to a deep sense of alienation and disgruntlement in many northern political circles.

As *Boko Haram* atrocities intensified after 2009, many conspiracy theorists were quick to link it to the ethno-regional manoeuvring surrounding Goodluck Jonathan's ascendance to the Presidency in 2010. According to the Middle Belt Dialogue (MBD), an umbrella body of professionals and politicians in the Middle Belt region, *Boko Haram* is 'the military wing of the northern political elite who seek to use Islam to dominate and control Nigeria … After all, *Boko Haram* is acting out the script the leaders wrote for it' (Shiklam 2013). The view that *Boko Haram* is a tool deliberately crafted to blackmail and undermine the authority of President Goodluck Jonathan is widespread amongst some Christian and southern Nigerians (Kayode-Adedeji 2011). For example, the South South Peoples Assembly (SSPA), an assemblage of the very senior citizens from the south–south geo-political zone, expressed the view that it

> does not believe that the Boko Haram of today is the offshoot of the one crushed by the Yar' Adua administration. Rather, we are convinced that the name has become a metaphor for a more sophisticated struggle for political power. We dare say that it is a tool in the hands of those who threatened to make this country ungovernable … for the Jonathan presidency … Boko Haram cannot be pursuing a religious agenda … On the contrary, we are convinced that the group's agenda, which clearly is that of its urbane sponsors, is to make the presidency of Goodluck Jonathan unworkable. (Ebiri 2011)

Similar views have also been expressed by the Southern Nigeria Peoples Assembly (SNPA), a group of statesmen and prominent leaders from the three geo-political zones of the southern part of the country:

> Let it be known that the people of Southern Nigeria shall not allow themselves to be ruled by any government that is a product of insurgency or blackmail if the sponsors of insurgency in this country think they can brow-beat and pummel the government of President Goodluck Jonathan to abdicate the authority and mandate freely given to him by Nigerians to rule this country. (Umoru 2014)

It is this strong suspicion that *Boko Haram* is the handiwork of his political detractors that has influenced the deleterious way the Jonathan administration has addressed the insurgency. For example, when the Chibok girls were abducted from their hostels on the night of 14 April 2014, the Government refused to engage with the problem for over two weeks. Thereafter, the Leader of the Women's Wing of the ruling PDP publicly cast doubt on the idea that any girls were missing, asking for the 'names and pictures of the 234 schoolgirls abducted by *Boko Haram* members two weeks ago … There are many questions to be asked and many more to be answered' (Okocha & Olugbode 2014). A leading supporter of President Jonathan and leader of the Niger Delta Peoples Volunteer Force, Alhaji Asari Dokubo even went as far as to describe the abduction of the

students as a 'scam' perpetrated by some top northern opposition politicians who 'knew the whereabouts of the girls' (Onoyume, 2014). These
insinuations, often without proof, are buttressed by the pronouncements
of the ruling party itself, which has frequently accused members of the
opposition All Progressive's Congress (APC) of being linked to the insurgency. The PDP claims that the opposition is 'behind the insurgency' and
that 'the manifesto of the party [is] … a product of Janjaweed ideology'.
Furthermore, it claims that its 'verifiable evidence' of the guilt of the APC
is the fact that the 'body language of some APC leaders had given it away
as the face behind the mask of insurgency' (Okocha & Ezigbo 2014)!

The evidentiary basis for these claims by the ruling party is rather thin.
Former President Obasanjo has dismissed the idea that the abduction
of the Chibok girls was orchestrated by President Jonathan's political
enemies. He added: 'If the presidency is obsessed with one thing and
one thing only [President Jonathan's electoral prospects in 2015] and any
other thing of concern to Nigeria is secondary then … It will be unfor-
tunate' (Okojie 2014). It is also noteworthy that despite repeated insinuations that some bigwig northern politicians are behind *Boko Haram*, only
two high-profile people from the north have been charged in court in
connection with *Boko Haram*. One, Senator Ali Ndume, is a Senator from
Borno on the ticket of the President's party. In August 2014, that case is
still in court. The second is the former Governor of the Central Bank of
Nigeria and current Emir of Kano, Mallam Sanusi Lamido Sanusi. The
judge in the Sanusi case, Justice Ibrahim Buba of the Federal High Court,
Lagos, observed that the various government agencies seeking to establish
before his court that Mallam Sanusi was aiding and abetting terrorism
were presenting conflicting statements in their arguments. He observed
that the government agencies were 'not on the same page' and had only
begun to sing discordant tunes as an afterthought, showing that they had
'acted in bad faith'. He added that the 'court believes the way Mr. Sanusi
was treated by the respondents deserves condemnation and exemplary
damages' and went on to order the Government to issue an apology to
Mallam Sanusi and pay him damages of N50 million (Ezeamalu 2014).
It is also noteworthy that President Jonathan's Special Assistant on New
Media, Reno Omokri, was uncovered as hiding behind the pseudonym
of 'Wendell Simlin' to write and distribute an article attempting to link
Mallam Sanusi to *Boko Haram* and Alhaji Umaru Abdul-Mutallab, father
of Umar Farouk Abdul-Mutallab, the Nigerian operative of Al-Qaeda
in the Arabian Peninsula who tried to blow up a plane over Detroit on
Christmas day in 2009 (*Premium Times* 2014).

As Adio (2014) notes, the mind-set of the Jonathan administration
which sees *Boko Haram* essentially as a tool for seeking political advantage
by its opponents illuminates 'why the war against terror has been prose-

cuted in such a half-hearted and ineffectual way'. He points out that this mind-set is built on two frames of reference, first that

> the elders and other members of the communities where Boko Haram operates not only know the terrorists but are also complicit. This has not been said publicly, but the immediate frame of reference for the president and his inner caucus is the Niger Delta militancy where the political leaders and the militants worked for the same goal, and possibly had open lines of communication … However, a superficial comparison of the modes of operation of the two terrorist groups shows that while one was projecting a group's interest and rarely attacked its own people, the major casualties of the other have largely been members of its immediate communities … The other and the more dangerous frame is that this administration believes that Boko Haram is the creation of those who had promised to make the country ungovernable for the president.

Adio argues that as a result of this mind-set, the Government is burdened with a persecution complex and siege mentality that has crippled its capacity for clear thinking and effective action.

However, the political conspiracy theories on *Boko Haram* are not limited to the supporters of the ruling PDP and President Jonathan. For example, in a speech read at the US Institute of Peace in Washington in 2014, opposition politician and Governor of Adamawa State, Vice Admiral Murtala H. Nyako[14], argued forcefully that the 'security situation we are … facing in Northern Nigeria today could be sponsored, financed and supported by evil minded and over-ambitious leaders of Government and the society for political gains' (Nyako 2014). Arguing that 'there is simply no person(s) in the North-Eastern zone rich enough to foot the financial and logistic bills on Boko Haram activities', he adds that it

> is now clear to all and sundry that there is an unhindered coordination between the activities of Boko Haram cells and some strategic commanders sitting in some high offices in our national Defence system. How else could there be such timely actions regarding the immediate withdrawal of the Military near vital positions such as schools and colleges with the immediate arrival of Boko Haram squad of murderers. Not only are these withdrawals of the Military and the attacks of Boko Haram timely, it is noticed that such attacks would last for hours without counter response by the Military even if they are located at a hearing distance … The people in the North have

---

[14] Governor Nyako was impeached in July 2014, allegedly at the behest of President Jonathan and the PDP. A number of other opposition governors are also facing similar threats.

also begun to suspect that the Objective of all this is to create enough mayhem for an excuse to deny them their democratic right of Vote by cancelling the forthcoming General Elections in the region and also reduce the Voting power of the people there now and in the future through mass killings of its populace especially its youths.

Though Nyako does not name 'the evil-few in Abuja' to whom he is referring, it is clear to most observers that he has President Jonathan in his sights. On his part, the Sultan of Sokoto and President-General of the Nigerian Supreme Council for Islamic Affairs (NSCIA), Alhaji Mohammed Sa'ad Abubakar III, has equally linked the nation's current security challenges to the 2015 elections. Speaking to newsmen in his palace, the Sultan – a former military officer – suggested that the insecurity challenges facing the north were 'all about people trying to put themselves at vantage point to gain extra mileage ahead of others, lamenting, however, that the blood of innocent people was being shed' (Abuh et al. 2014). However, it is unclear who the Sultan had in mind. In a similar vein, the pre-eminent Tijaniyya cleric, Shaikh Dahiru Bauchi who survived two suicide bombing attacks in July 2014 asserts that: 'Government officials are behind *Boko Haram*, there is no doubt about it and that is why it refuses to end the insurgency. I have no doubt that there is a strong hidden agenda in the whole thing' (*The Sun* 2014).

The final set of conspiracy theories pertain to the state's military response to the insurgency. Governor Nyako's insinuation of complicity between *Boko Haram* and the military high command under the auspices of the 'evil-few in Abuja' has already been mentioned. Similar allegations have come from private and public entities, mostly from the north. For example, when *Boko Haram* attacked the town of Gamboru Ngala, killing three hundred people and burning down most of the town, a man purporting to be a Nigerian soldier was reported by the BBC Hausa Service as claiming that apart from the foot soldiers of *Boko Haram*, helicopters 'were seen hovering in the air while the attacks were ongoing, but no assistance was rendered to the people' (Krishi 2014). Worst still, the soldier claimed that though the Nigerian troops were close to the town, 'their commander instructed them not to repel the insurgents'.

Echoing the same sentiments, the umbrella organization for northern political and economic elites, the Arewa Consultative Forum (ACF) has come out to voice its disquiet about the role of the military in the north-east. Its National Executive asserted that it 'is strongly believed that without the support and cooperation from within the military and security circles, the insurgents would not have been succeeding so easily in their dastardly acts' (Isenyo 2014). In another position paper, the ACF argued that there is certainly more than meets the eye about the military operations in the north-east: 'Or else how come a convoy of thirty to sixty vehicles full of arsenal-men and material, travel five to ten kilometers, conduct an operation, killing people and destroying property and return to base unchallenged?' (ACF 2014). Another observer, the immediate past Governor of Abia State in the south-east, and a former resident of Maiduguri, Dr Orji Uzor Kalu has argued that 'Boko Haram are too illiterate for their sophisticated attacks', and he suggests that there might be 'a linkage between security agencies and the spate of bombings in the country' (Aziken 2013).

Finally, the Borno-Yobe People's Forum, a high-level community group in both states has raised suspicious questions about the conduct of the military in both states:

Who authorized the withdrawal of security personnel from the Federal Government College, Buni Yadi hours before the attack that claimed the lives of 59 innocent children? ... Why were security reports from the communities on impending attacks ignored or not promptly responded to? ... How were the insurgents able to attack the Maiduguri Air-force Base and de-mobilize as well as burn planes and other military installations despite the existing state of emergency and curfew in the town? ... Are the authorities unaware of helicopters dropping arms and ammunition, food and medical supplies to areas well-known to be strong holds of the insurgents? ... How could 20 to 30 Toyota Hilux vehicles move in a convoy freely with a subsisting curfew and still go undetected? ... How did a little band of rag-tag misguided youths metamorphose into a well kitted, well-armed killing machine moving freely in convoy of vehicles and supported by helicopters.[15]

The Forum called on the Government to 'un-mask the sponsors of terror and bring them to justice'.

The conspiracy theories were taken to a higher plane in August 2014, when Dr Stephen Davis, an Australian hostage negotiator involved, at various times, in negotiations with insurgents in the Niger Delta and *Boko Haram* at the behest of different Nigerian governments made a string of public allegations concerning those he regarded as the key supporters of *Boko Haram* in Nigeria. Davis, 63 years old, holds a Ph.D. in political geography from the University of Melbourne in Australia. A former Canon Emeritus at Coventry Cathedral, in the United Kingdom, he had been involved in peace negotiations in Nigeria since 2004 when President Olusegun Obasanjo invited him to intervene in the Niger Delta crisis.[16]

---

[15] Borno-Yobe People's Forum, 2014, 'World Press Conference on the Crises in the North East', Held on 31 March 2014 at Barcelona Hotel, Abuja.

[16] Justin Welby, a former oil company executive in the Niger Delta and current Archbishop of Canterbury is a probable connecting link between Davis and the initial foray into the Niger Delta militancy. In his interviews, Davis claims that his closeness to a major Niger Delta militant

In 2007 President Umaru Musa Yar'Adua appointed him a presidential envoy to help in ending the militancy in the Niger Delta, while in 2011 President Jonathan involved him in negotiations with *Boko Haram* leaders, some of whom he had met since 2007. When the Chibok girls were abducted on 14 April 2014, Davis turned up in Nigeria at the end of the month to help negotiate their release (*Sahara Reporters* 2014d; *TheCable* 2014). To facilitate the release of the girls, he claims that the: 'president gave me a military jet and a military convoy and ambulance from the local hospital' (Egene & Somorin 2014). There is therefore every reason to take seriously his allegations which he said were 'informed by discussions he had with several *Boko Haram* field commanders over a long period of time' (*Sahara Reporters* 2014d). The *Sahara Reporters* even published a picture he took with some hooded men purported to be *Boko Haram* commanders.

According to Davis, his *Boko Haram* sources told him that four individuals, two of whom he named, are their main backers:

> former Governor Modu Sherriff [sic] of Borno State and a former Chief of Army staff, General Azubuike Ihejirika (ret.), were among the top sponsors of the Islamist insurgents … an unnamed senior official of the Central Bank of Nigeria as well as a man based in Cairo, Egypt whom he claimed operates as Boko Haram's bagman. He said both men, in addition to Mr. Sheriff and former General Ihejirika, were major players in the funding and continued existence of the deadly Islamist sect. (*Sahara Reporters* 2014d)

In addition to these four, Davis also mentioned 'a senior official of CBN [Central Bank of Nigeria], who recently left the bank' and is reported to have been 'very close to Sodiq [sic] Aminu Ogwuche, the mastermind of the Nyanya bombings who also schooled in Sudan'. Ogwuche's wife is said to have 'visited this official in his office at the headquarters in Abuja before the bombings. They were very close' (*TheCable* 2014). He also suggested that the *Boko Haram* finance man in the CBN 'used to report to his superior, the official who recently left the bank'. Finally, Davis also alleged that 'there is a politician who was supplying operational vehicles for the suicide bombers. He gave them Hilux vans. He is a prominent politician' (*TheCable* 2014). Significantly, asked whether Malam Nasir El-Rufai and former military ruler, Muhammadu Buhari, both being prominent Muslim northern opposition politicians frequently mentioned as *Boko Haram* supporters in some conspiracy theories, had a hand in funding or sponsoring *Boko Haram*, Dr Davis 'said their names have not been mentioned to him by any Boko Haram connections' (*Sahara Reporters* 2014d).

(cont.) leader, Asari Dokubo, who also happens to be a Muslim, introduced him to the *Boko Haram* leaders at the formative stage of the sect.

Some motives for this bewildering cast of alleged *Boko Haram* supporters can be gleaned from Davis' three interviews. Former Governor Modu Sheriff's motive is ostensibly political. According to Davis:

> He used them for his elections. They worked for him. However, in 2007, the leader of the group, Muhammed Yusuf, collected money from Sheriff in return for support. Yusuf's mentor, Ja'afar Mahmud Adam, exposed and criticised him for collecting money from Sheriff, and Yusuf ordered his killing in April 2007. But eventually, Yusuf and Sheriff fell out. However, it is acknowledged that Sheriff was and is a major financier of the group. He pays for young men to go for lesser hajj. From there they are recruited into the group. (*TheCable* 2014)

As for the former Chief of Army Staff, Lt-Gen. Azubuike Ihejirika, who is a Christian Igbo from the south-east, Davis suggests that the motive is the corruption which is often alleged to pervade the military budget in Nigeria: 'You have senior military officers who are benefiting from the insurgency because of the security budget. It pays them to keep the insurgency going so that they can continue to make money' (*TheCable* 2014). The motive for the unnamed politicians is suggested to be political office, while that of the two unnamed CBN officials seem to be ideological. It is difficult to ascertain the alleged motives of the supplier in Cairo; being a Kanuri from Borno, it might also be ideological, though a purely financial motive cannot be ruled out.

Davis implicitly exonerated President Jonathan: 'If the president goes after these guys, they will say it is political. That is part of the problem. Everybody will say the president is going after his political opponents, especially as there is a general election next year' (*TheCable* 2014). However, some critics have been quick to interpret his allegations as further proof that the President is complicit. According to the opposition politician, Malam El-Rufai, all those mentioned by Davis are either from the President's party or are his appointees:

> I think the ruling party and the presidency feel that sustaining the insurgency is going to be helpful to them in 2015 elections. As long as the country is getting divided along religious and ethnic lines, Mr. Jonathan thinks that will help him in 2015, which is why desperate efforts are being made by the ruling party to link the APC [the main opposition party] to the insurgency, to be a Muslim party, to be linked to the Muslim brotherhood and all that. (Egene & Somorin 2014)

For their part, both Ihejirika and Sheriff have dismissed the allegations against them as false (Soriwei 2014). Ihejirika's brother officers have also leapt to his defence, with one charging that some 'unscrupulous citizens of this country are using the advantages that they enjoy under democracy to malign the military with innuendos and statements without facts. All the things that Mr. Davis said for instance, there was nothing in it and no facts to buttress anything' (Omonobi 2014). Given the weightiness of the allegations, the Government has had to respond through the secret service organization, the Department of State Services (DSS) which sought to undermine Davis' credibility by describing him as 'a self-styled and self-appointed negotiator', while the allegations against Ihejirika were dismissed out of hand because 'it couldn't be true' and it 'would be wicked of anyone to link him with the sect'. The DSS statement said Modu Sheriff had been investigated on these allegations twice in the past (apparently without finding him liable to any charges) and that further investigations were ongoing. The details of the allegations regarding one of the CBN officials were dismissed as untrue (Ochayi 2014).

These conspiracy theories, taken together, speak to the climate of distrust that currently pervades Nigerian society. While not explaining the phenomenon of *Boko Haram* in any satisfactory evidence-based way, they nevertheless point to serious internal divisions within the society and similar factors inhibiting an effective, collective response to the scourge of terrorism within Nigerian society. Important as they are as the context for the public reactions to the insurgency, these conspiracy theories cannot give a satisfactory explanation of the phenomenon of *Boko Haram*, given their obvious lack of any concrete supporting evidence.

Boko Haram: *A multi-dimensional evidence-based approach*

As the surfeit of conspiracy theories suggest, *Boko Haram* is a difficult and complex phenomenon. Part of the problem is the constant evolution of the sect and its frequent reincarnation in different, even contradictory, guises. Another reason is the tendency to look at it purely from one point of view, be that poverty and marginalization, religious extremism, or ethno-regional power politics. I suggest that that is akin to approaching the problem in the same way the four blind men sought to understand the elephant. It is by putting all the pieces of the mosaics together, that we begin to get a fairly accurate description of the beast. I therefore base my analysis on five inter-related factors which I consider to be of the outmost importance in the understanding of *Boko Haram* violence: 1) religious doctrines, 2) poverty and inequality – vertical and horizontal, 3) the political context of post-1999 electoral competition, 4) the personal agency of the youth directly involved in *Boko Haram*, and 5) the geographical and international context of the insurgency.

RELIGIOUS DOCTRINES

The doctrinal branching away of different groups from the Salafist *Izala* main stem, ultimately leading, in the case of Mohammed Yusuf, to *Boko Haram*, has been discussed in Chapter 3. What this section seeks to highlight is the relative power of doctrinal forces in shaping what *Boko Haram* has been doing since its emergence. Two quasi-religious ideas have dominated *Boko Haram* thought since its transformation into an insurgent movement in 2009: death and vengeance.

According to Governor Kashim Shettima of Borno State,

> For me, there are two major factors that drive the Boko Haram sect, which are spiritual belief and economic desires. Those with spiritual beliefs are led into believing that when they kill, they obtain rewards from Allah and the rewards translate into houses in paradise. When they are killed, they automatically die as martyrs and go to paradise straight away. In other words, death is the beginning of their pleasure. Then, whoever they target to kill is an infidel and will go to hell. They mostly target security personnel, government officials and politicians. They also target residents who they assume support government and security agencies or do not share their ideology of being opposed to western education ... One dangerous thing about their ideology is their belief that when they attack a gathering or a community, any righteous person in the sight of God, who dies as a result of their attack, will go to paradise, which means they would have assisted the person to go to paradise in good time by their actions, and any infidel killed by their attack will go to hell, which to them is what he or she deserves and no regret for his death. This is the spiritual aspect that drives the sect, to the best of my understanding. (Abbah & Idris 2014)

This belief system is hinged on the assumption that the sect is doing 'God's work'.[17] According to a *Boko Haram* spokesperson, what they 'are doing is divine worship' (Abubakar 2010). When the suspected *Boko Haram* member, Mustapha Umar, did not die in his suicide mission to bomb a plaza housing the offices of some newspapers in Kaduna in April 2012, he was reported to have wept bitterly over his failure to die during the mission. He reportedly told police he 'was unhappy because not dying with victims of the attack had denied him the opportunity to make heaven' (Chiedozie 2013).

This suggests that the motivation for extremist behaviour may not lie in immediate economic deprivation or religious indoctrination, but from a

---

[17] A Boko Haram member who accidentally set off his bomb in Bauchi and had his legs blown up said as he lay dying: 'We are doing God's work'.

perverse 'rational' pursuit of 'an afterlife consumption motive' or the search for assurance and security in a changing world. But these religious ideals only gain force when they are 'seen to help address the everyday realities of life' (Bano 2012, 8–9). In north-eastern Nigeria, the realities of everyday life are characterized by poverty, inequality and a deep sense of 'the state of lawlessness and injustice' (Salkida 2013b) that has de-legitimated the modern secular state and made Sharia law attractive to a large section of the population. According to a survey conducted by Gallup:

> The majority of residents in the Northeast region said in 2010 that Sharia must be one of the sources of legislation – making them among the most likely in Nigeria to say so. However, no resident in the Northeast region said Sharia must be the only source of law, while 36% said it should not be a source at all. (Rheault & Tortora 2012)[18]

It is this state of alienation from the secular state that explains the emergence of 'God's warriors' (Salkida 2013b) dedicated to cleansing society through Sharia, as a divine antidote to corrupt governance and injustice, and jihad as a legitimate method, embracing death in the process. The power of this doctrinal commitment to 'God's work' explains why individuals, who are not themselves poor, are nevertheless drawn to Boko Haram. For example, Nigeria's first suicide bomber and *Boko Haram* member, a certain Mohammed Manga, 'was a 35-year-old married man with five children who … left N4 million in his will' (Salkida 2011). Though he cannot be regarded as wealthy, he can hardly be counted among the poor by Nigerian standards. This quest for 'an afterlife consumption motive' also explains why some 'children of notable public figures, including a nephew of the then serving Governor of Yobe State, a son of the secretary to Borno State Government, and five children of a local wealthy contractor' (Mohammed 2014), along with Alhaji Buji Foi (an ex-commissioner in Borno State), Kadiru Atiku (a former university lecturer) and Bunu Wakil (a very rich Borno-based contractor) (Onuoha 2014) all joined *Boko Haram* at its inception. It also explains why many university students were alleged to have burned their certificates and joined the sect (*Vanguard* 2014b).

If doing 'God's work' and getting the 'reward' of dying in the process is the first doctrinal motor of *Boko Haram*, ironically, the second is the quest for vengeance once any of them is killed or harmed. At the reincarnation of the sect in 2010, its signature act was to launch an attack on Bauchi prison on 7 September 2010 to free more than 100 members detained after

---

[18] Results are based on face-to-face interviews with 1,000 adults, aged 15 and older, conducted in April 2010 and in August 2011 in Nigeria. For results based on the total sample of national adults, one can say with 95% confidence that the maximum margin of sampling error is ±3.9 percentage points.

the 2009 crisis. During the attack, it also distributed pamphlets signed by its new leader, Abubakar Shekau, threatening vengeance. The pamphlet warned that 'we will not forget the way our members were killed in Dutsen Tanshi Police Station and Yankari Park. Whoever had a hand in the killing of our members from the state governor down to district and ward heads, we have not forgotten and you will see what it will look like in the future' (Garba 2010). This theme of vengeance, fuelled by a sense of victimhood at the hands of unjust powers, runs deep in *Boko Haram* thinking and is connected to the Islamic concept of *al-Qisas* or 'retaliation'. The concept stands for equality in punishment; justice in an 'eye for an eye' fashion. An example of this is if a person is murdered, a member of the family has the right to demand the execution of the murderer or carry out the execution on his own. In the Qur'an, *al-Qisas* is linked to 'life': 'And there is [a saving of] life for you in al-Qisaas, O men of understanding, that you may become righteous' (2: 179). *Al-Qisas* is also one of the four pillars in Islamic criminal jurisprudence: *Hadd* (violation of the right of God), *Ta'zir* (violation of the right of an individual), *al-Qisas* (a violation of the right of God through the violation of the right of the individual – so it is a hybrid) and finally, *siyasah* (violation of the right of the state).[19]

These doctrinal drivers of *Boko Haram* since 2009 explain the ready recourse to suicide bombing, the reckless killing of people that has become the hallmark of the sect, and even the frequent resort to the ritualistic slaughter of their victims as if in some manner these were some sacrifices to Allah.

POVERTY AND INEQUALITY

There is much controversy about the contribution of poverty to the phenomenon of *Boko Haram* violence. Contributing to the debate, the Nobel laureate Wole Soyinka is of the opinion that *Boko Haram* violence is the 'physical actualisation' of a malignant fanaticism within northern Islam that has indoctrinated Muslim youth with intolerance and a sense of impunity, best captured by the slogan: 'Killing is Believing'. This fanaticism breeds 'the will to dominate, to control, to enforce conformity' through the promotion of the ideals of theocratic rule in a supposedly secular democratic state. He decries the attempt to explain *Boko Haram* violence solely in terms of economic factors, arguing against 'propositions that the root cause of any social eruption, wherever it involves the … under-privileged, will be found solely in social inequality' (Soyinka 2009). Though Soyinka is careful not to dismiss economic factors completely, the main problem with his perspective is that it creates a false picture

[19] I am grateful to Sherine El-Taraboulsi for this exposition.

of a homogeneous bloc of Muslims, and glosses over the many internal cleavages within the Muslim community. Also denying the importance of economic factors, President Jonathan asserted in an interview that 'Boko Haram is not as a result of misrule; definitely not … And sometimes people feel like it is a result of poverty; definitely not. Boko Haram is a local terror group' (Ekott 2013). Weighing in in support of the President, the ruling PDP added that poverty was not a recent phenomenon in the country 'and therefore cannot form the basis of the sudden wave of criminal attacks on innocent victims', most of whom are themselves poor (Umoru 2013). The President of the Christian Association of Nigeria asserts authoritatively: 'Boko Haram is propelled by a religious ideology, it is not poverty. Anyone who tells you it is poverty is not telling you the truth. It is not poverty' (Onafuye 2014).

On the other side of the poverty argument, on a visit to Nigeria, President Bill Clinton suggested that though the language of *Boko Haram* is rooted in the language of religious difference, 'the truth is the poverty rate in the north is three times of what it is in Lagos' and lack of economic opportunity in the north is an issue (Ekott 2013). Arguing along the same lines, the former Governor of the Central Bank of Nigeria, Mallam Sanusi Lamido Sanusi, suggested that the absence of job opportunities and the poor quality of life of the majority of the people in the north were fundamentally linked to terrorism and insecurity (Onuba & Adesomoju 2013). After *Boko Haram* launched coordinated attacks on Kano in January 2012 killing 185 people, the State Government set up a committee to investigate the event. The committee, headed by elder statesman Magaji Danbatta, returned the verdict that poor governance, poverty and unregulated migration were at the root of the crisis in Kano (*Vanguard* 2012).

Some of the confusion surrounding the relationship between Islamic radicalization and poverty is obviously driven by the political interests of those involved in the analysis. The tendency of those in positions of some responsibility to shift attention away from the possible 'root causes' of terrorism is not unique to Nigeria. As Schmid (2013, 2) notes on the positions of various governments at the United Nations General Assembly concerning the 9/11 terrorist attacks on the United States, the representatives of Western countries 'generally avoided engaging in a discussion of root causes, emphasising instead the criminal and inexcusable character of the 9/11 attacks'. The confusion about the impact of poverty on radicalization is further exacerbated by the fact that most of the literature on Islamic radicalization is based on alienated young Muslims in Western or Arab countries who are generally not personally poor (Schmid 2013, 25).

However, Schmid also notes that the notion that radicalization is not connected to poverty 'is a myth or at best a half-truth' (2013, 25). Whilst agreeing that the disenfranchised are generally too poor and too concerned with mere survival to start rebellions, he nevertheless notes that 'some of them might join terrorist groups, attracted by the prospect of money, having a gun or simply because they have nothing to lose'. For such poor people, sectarian radicalization comes 'after joining a group and partaking in various illegal activities' (Schmid 2013, 25). Finally, in the context of northern Nigeria, poverty is an important factor in radicalization not just because radical groups offer a possible economic prospect for deprived unemployed *individual* youth, but also because relative poverty fuels a sense of *group* resentment in the context of high levels of ethnic and regional inequalities and competition which have characterized Nigerian society from the 1950s.

The evidence from the political economy of the north-east geo-political zone suggests that poverty is an important factor in the rise and sustenance of *Boko Haram*. It is not the only factor, as I have already suggested, but it is an important one. Just as important as actual poverty, is the factor of vertical (class based) and horizontal (regional and ethnic) inequalities. Between them, poverty *and* inequalities have been important factors in the trajectory of religious extremism in the north-east.

Since the return to civil rule in 1999, the Nigerian economy has grown at a fast rate. Over the last decade, the annual growth rate has been in the region of 7 per cent. Nigeria has even been promoted into the ranks of the expected next wave of emerging markets' success stories: MINT – Mexico, Indonesia, Nigeria and Turkey (Meagher 2014). The country remains one of the top three destinations for Foreign Direct Investment in Africa, getting a net inflow of about US$6 billion in 2013. In the context of this ostensible success story, a middle class, 'confident about economic growth and … highly optimistic about their personal prosperity' (Chima 2014), has emerged in the country. Writing about this middle class, following a survey, Standard Chartered Bank notes that 'Ghanaians and Nigerians demonstrate the highest appetite for luxury clothing – demand to buy designer clothing, accessories and/or footwear is expected to more than double in the next five years (compared to the previous five years). The study concluded that this middle class 'expect their wealth to grow and have clear aspirations to build a better life for themselves and their families' (quoted in Chima 2014). Unfortunately, as the evidence suggests, this optimistic picture of economic expansion and rising consumption is not shared by most Nigerians, especially those in the north-east. Data from the Oxford Poverty and Human Development Initiative (OPHI), using the most sophisticated measurements for poverty,[20] gives us a picture of

---

[20] OPHI's Multidimensional Poverty Index (MPI) measures three dimensions of poverty – education, health and standard of living – based on ten indicators: years of schooling, school attendance, child mortality, nutrition, access to electricity, sanitation, water, floor type, cooking fuel and assets. This is based on the Demographic and Health Survey (DHS) data set for 2013.

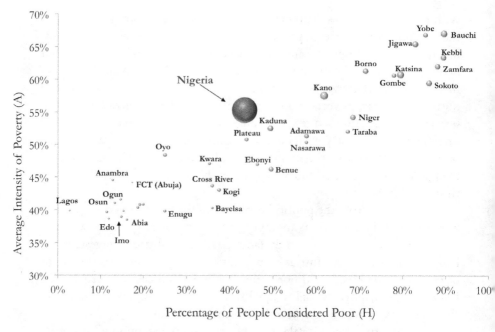

Figure 6.1 Distribution and intensity of poverty in Nigeria
(courtesy: Oxford Poverty and Human Development Initiative)

where the north-east sits within this rosy Nigerian picture of economic growth.

As Figure 6.1 shows, the growth in the Nigerian economy has not trickled to the northern states which remain largely poor. Two things are worthy of note in Figure 6.1: first, virtually all the northern states, with the exception of Kwara and Kogi, have a percentage of people living in poverty that is much higher than the national average, while the opposite is the case for all southern states; second, the *intensity* of poverty – in how many of OPHI's ten indicators of poverty are the people poor (the more the indicators, the higher the cumulative intensity) – is also higher in the northern states. Therefore, poverty in the northern states not only involves more people, it is also more severe. By contrast, the economy of southern states, especially the south-west, seems to be benefitting from deregulation and increased incorporation into the global economy. This is especially notable in the emerging sectors of the economy such as banking, telecommunications, food processing, entertainment industries and manufacturing.[21] Meanwhile, the economy of most northern states, dependent as they are on small-scale agriculture and formal sector state employment, has shrunk since the 1980s with the introduction of structural adjustment and

---

[21] Manufacturing capacity utilization rose from 46.3 per cent in the first half of 2013 to 52.7 per cent in the second half (Ventures-Africa.com 2014).

the withdrawal of the state from many sectors of the economy. The impact of economic policy, high population growth, recurrent drought and a lack of investment in small-scale farming – along with overall poor governance systems – has undermined the agricultural economy and destabilized the statist employment market. At the same time, the north's urban economy has been gutted by structural-adjustment-induced de-industrialization: the textile industry based in Kaduna and Kano has gone down from about 175 textile and garment firms in the mid-1990s to fewer than 25 in 2010, with a loss of over 110,000 jobs (Meagher 2014).

The evidence from OPHI is supported by data from the Nigerian Bureau of Statistics whose *Poverty Profile 2012* shows that the north-east zone is the poorest part of the country with 75% of the population being relatively poor, 71.5% being absolutely poor and 51.5% hardly able to feed itself. The states of Yobe (58%), Borno (56%), Katsina (50%) and Bauchi (49%) have the highest poverty indices in Nigeria. All except Katsina are in the north-east. The north-east is also said to have the highest levels of unemployment in Nigeria: Yobe, 39%; Bauchi, 30%; Gombe, 29%; Borno, 27%. The same figures for Lagos are 8% and nationally, 21% (El-Rufai 2012). OPHI data suggests that poverty is highest in the north-east with a Multidimensional Poverty Index (MPI) of 0.56 compared to the south-west with the lowest MPI of 0.12. Not only is poverty an essentially northern phenomenon, there is also the fact that the regional distribution of poverty (Map 6.3) perfectly replicates the distribution of *Boko Haram* violence (Map 6.1). While this is suggestive of a Weberian 'elective affinity' between poverty and *Boko Haram* violence, it is not a proof of causation.

Not only are the northern zones and states suffering from horizontal inequalities relative to the southern zones and states, as Figure 6.2 and Map 6.3 show, they are also more unequal *internally*, pointing to high levels of vertical or class inequalities.

Muslim northern societies are generally more hierarchical than most other parts of Nigeria because of the heritage of pre-colonial aristocracies, colonial Indirect Rule policies and the relatively limited spread of Western education in the region. However, as Figure 6.2 shows, even amongst the poor or non-elites, the northern states tend to have far higher levels of inequalities, compared to the national average.

Data from the National Bureau of Statistics suggest that young people in the north, especially in rural communities, are particularly hard-hit by this combination of poverty and inequality. While youth unemployment nation-wide is said to be very high at 54 per cent[22], the

---

[22] 'According to available data from National Bureau of Statistics (NBS), unemployment rate was highest for young people aged 15–24 years at 34.2 per cent, about 3 times the global unemployment rate for youth, estimated at about 12 per cent and the sub-Saharan Africa average rate of about 12 per cent' (NBS 2013, 11–12).

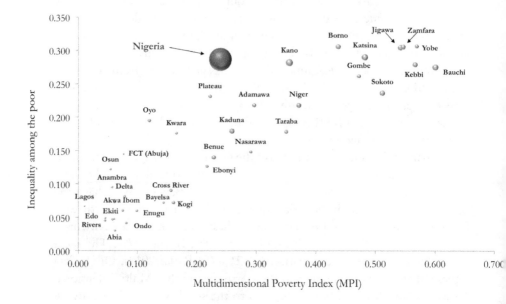

Figure 6.2 Inequalities in Nigeria
(courtesy: Oxford Poverty and Human Development Initiative)

migratory pattern of the youths suggests that more of them are moving from rural to urban areas, and from the north to the south, in search of better opportunities:

> [T]he predominant type of movement among Nigerian youths is inter-state migration (49.9 per cent) … rural-urban (21.4 per cent); inter-local governments (16.2 per cent) and urban-rural (9.1 per cent) … movements across geopolitical zones had more youths (1.6 per cent) migrating North-South than South-North (0.7 per cent), West-East (0.7 per cent) and East-West (0.4 per cent). (NBS 2013, 53)

As might be expected, the levels of poverty and inequalities that have characterized the north have been sources of concern for many people in the region. In surveys of Nigeria in 2010 and 2011, Gallup found that 'the lack of improvement in their standard of living is a concern for North-erners, especially those in the Northeast' (Rheault & Tortora 2012).[23] Gallup also found out that while more than 6 in 10 Nigerians said they

---

[23] See footnote 18.

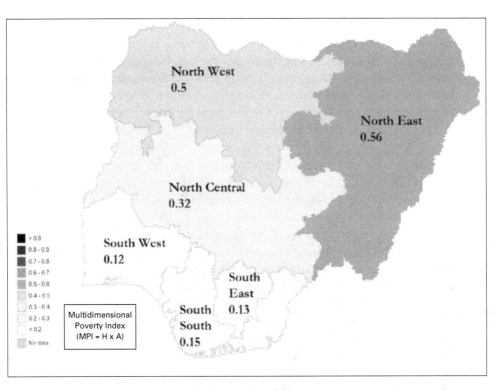

Map 6.3 Nigeria – Zonal distribution of poverty
(courtesy of Oxford Poverty and Human Development Initiative)

approve of their country's leadership, this approval rating was lowest in the North-east region with 4 in 10 approving the leadership. The survey also noted that 'this relatively low level of approval is statistically on par with levels in the other two northern regions …the only statistical difference is between the Northeast and the three southern regions' (Rheault & Tortora 2012).

There is overwhelming global evidence that the patterns of poverty, inequalities and concerns highlighted above have a high potential to lead to political instability. Using data from 71 countries for the period between 1960 and 1985, Alesina & Perotti (1996, 1203–05) demonstrate that income inequality fuels social discontent which in turn exacerbates political instability, defined as 'more or less violent phenomena of political unrest'. They argue that their evidence suggests that 'more unequal societies are more politically unstable'. Their conclusion is supported by Nafziger & Auvinen (1997, 69) who argue that inequality is dangerous because it 'contributes to regional, ethnic, and class discrepancies that engender crises', and by Meier & Rauch (2000) who argue that societies with higher income inequalities are more likely to experience political instability.

A study in Nigeria (NSRP 2014) also supports this link between poverty, inequality and violent conflict. It argues that unemployment and lack of economic opportunities are significant factors in aggravating conflict, especially amongst young people who may be drawn into violence as both perpetrators and victims. It suggests that available evidence shows that lack of alternative sources of livelihood and 'unemployment increases individuals' vulnerability to being mobilised both by rebel movements and urban gangs ... The destructive, long-term psycho-social effects of such inequality in economic opportunities, has also been documented' (NSRP 2014, 6). The report notes that while poverty, inequality and unemployment do not in themselves cause violence, they act as enabling factors, especially in contexts where youth feel that power structures exclude or marginalize them from economic and other resources necessary to achieve financial security, features of adulthood and social recognition. In such situations, 'violence can offer opportunities to gain control' (NSRP 2014, 6). Finally, the report notes that in Nigeria there is 'evidence of a close correlation between youth unemployment and rising armed violence' and that Nigeria is now the most violent country in Africa that is not at war, with estimates of an average of 3,000 conflict-related deaths each year between 2006 and 2011.

Boko Haram violence must therefore be understood, not just in the context of its extremist doctrinal positions, but also in the more immediate context of poverty, inequality and alienation. Indeed, the doctrines take on their 'rationality' from this wider socio-economic context. The importance of this socio-economic context for understanding *Boko Haram* has in fact been pointed out by many analysts with first-hand experience of the sect. For example, Governor Kashim Shettima of Borno State has argued that

> over a period of thirty years the ruling establishment abandoned the common people ... Nobody bothered about their education and health, and nobody cared how they made their living ... This was the ready-made situation that the late leader of Boko Haram Islamic sect, Mohammed Yusuf, capitalised on. He started organising the youth, procuring motorcycles for them for their transport business, helping them set up small businesses, assisting them to get married at little cost and generally creating ... 'an alternative society'. (Nnanna 2012)

Governor Shettima noted in another interview that the *Boko Haram* leader was able to give these alienated youth 'personal dignity and self-worth' (Abdallah 2012). It is also this context of poverty which explains why youth who are not particularly attracted by religious ideology would nevertheless join *Boko Haram* for the material benefits they can get from the sect. In a BBC interview in Diffa town in neighbouring Niger

Republic, youths who had been recruited by *Boko Haram* explained to the reporter that 'Boko Haram Islamist militants from Nigeria regularly come across the border, looking for recruits. We can't contact them, they come to us … We have no jobs; some of us are still at high school but we need money. Violence has become a form of work for us.'[24] In Nigeria itself, some youth are recruited into the sect based on similar material incentives, with payments of around N5,000 (US$32) to burn down schools or spy on troops movements for the sect (Abbah & Idris 2014).

POLITICAL CONTEXT

Doctrinal differences and economic inequality, on their own, do not automatically translate into violent conflict. They have to be actively mobilized (Tarling & Gomez 2008, 8–9) since the world is full of many instances of injustice and cultural/religious difference, yet we have only relatively few cases of conflict. It is through a trigger event and the active linking, by political or cultural entrepreneurs, of such grievances to an identifiable enemy who is held responsible for them that grievance and difference are converted into conflict. Three trends of a structural and contingent nature were crucial to that process of political mobilization leading to *Boko Haram*. The first is the collapse of the surveillance and control functions of local state institutions, including those of traditional authorities, making it practically possible for the unhindered mobilization of disaffected youth. This collapse, coupled with rapid urbanization, population growth, poverty and inequality and the problem of youths, have created very difficult political challenges in many northern Nigerian cities.

In the 1940s and 1950s, the Native Authority (NA) administration and its NA police kept a tight, some would say authoritarian, grip on community level activities. Through its open and secretive channels, the local administration knew about every major development within its domain, including the movement of persons and what they said or did. Unwanted guests were frequently 'deported' at the Emir's orders or flung into the NA prison. Since 1967, there has been a gradual and systematic reform and dissolution of the NA architecture. The Emirs lost control of the police, courts and prisons, and representation on the various councils responsible for local government were opened up to new constituencies either through appointment or through elections. The local government reforms of 1976 sought to systematize these changes across the country, and created the basis for the current local government administration system.

---

[24] The BBC documentary is entitled 'Niger hit by Nigeria's Boko Haram fallout', and summarized in *Vanguard* (2014c).

As a result of all these changes, traditional authorities are now a pale shadow of their former status[25] and local governments, with their poor staffing and funding situation, and constantly changing political leadership, have lost the capacity to monitor their constituencies and prevent potentially undesirable developments from taking root. In the words of one keen observer, with this 'virtual collapse of governance structure at community level … it [is] impossible to keep track of activities in local communities' and cities like Kano and Maiduguri have 'unfortunately been reduced to an urban jungle'.[26] In this urban jungle, many disaffected and alienated youths have thrived and sometimes got out of control of law enforcement agencies. Some belonged to semi-criminal youth gangs like the *'yan daba*, and others to religious sects like the *Yusufiyya*. The poor quality of urban governance made possible the sprouting and unhindered growth of *Boko Haram*.

The second enabling political factor is the nature of the sub-national elite political competition. The return to civilian democratic politics in Nigeria in 1999 happened through political parties that are essentially an agglomeration of many local patron-client networks often with a local 'godfather' dictating events. While the national party structures are composed of the coming together of these local 'heavyweights', fierce battles for control of the political turf have often taken place at the local level, especially in contexts where competing patronage networks jockey for control. In these highly personalized local contests for political supremacy, the contending factions have often recruited unemployed youths who 'see political thuggery as the only available option for their livelihood' (Akpeji & Gombe 2014). These youths, formed into gangs like the 'Kalare' in Gombe and 'ECOMOG' in Maiduguri, have become a prominent violent feature in intra-elite competition in many states of the Nigerian federation.

In Maiduguri in 2003, one such contingent battle for local political supremacy broke out amongst the elite for the control of the State Government. On 9 January 1999, Governor Mala Kachalla – ironically nicknamed 'capital of peace', given what was to unfold in subsequent years – was elected Governor of Borno State on the platform of the All Nigeria Peoples Party (ANPP). Seeking re-election for the second term in 2003, he faced stiff opposition from a Senator from within the same party, Senator Ali Modu Sheriff. After losing the political battle within the ANPP, Governor Kachalla, decamped to the Alliance for Democracy (AD). The 2003 gubernatorial election was fought between Governor

---

[25] A senior Emir was reported to have told a visiting dignitary: 'In days past, we got things done. Then things changed such that we were consulted before things were done. Now, people don't bother consulting us at all before things are done.'

[26] Magaji Danbatta, cited in *Vanguard* (2012).

Kachalla (AD), Senator Ali Modu Sheriff (ANPP) and Alhaji Kashim Ibrahim Imam (PDP), and was described as 'a battle of dramatic, even bitter, twists' (Bego 2003) and Senator Ali Modu Sheriff was declared winner of the elections. It is very difficult in Nigerian politics to overcome the enormous powers of incumbency and deny a sitting governor the party's nomination and then defeat him in the actual poll. To achieve this feat, Senator Modu Sheriff was alleged to have deployed two effective tactics: appeal to religion and the recruitment of political thugs (Reinert & Garçon 2014).

Senator Ali Modu Sheriff was alleged to have run on the platform of criticizing the flawed implementation of Sharia in the state by Governor Kachallah, and promised a stricter and more vigorous enforcement of Sharia law. Through this tactic, Modu Sheriff is said to have gotten the support of Mohammed Yusuf and the *Yusufiyya* sect.[27] On his election as Governor, Ali Modu Sheriff chose a close associate of Mohammed Yusuf, Alhaji Buji Foi, as the Commissioner for Religious Affairs. Abubakar Adam Kambar, another Yusuf ally, was released from jail, where he had been held for armed robbery (Pérouse de Montclos 2014a, 148). Mohammed Yusuf was also allowed to further develop the facilities at the *Markaz*. Senator Modu Sheriff's second tactic was to recruit unemployed youth as political thugs. Some of these were armed and, through the campaign for the 2003 elections, ideologically driven youth in the *Yusufiyya* sect and the more criminally inclined youths in gangs like the 'ECOMOG' in Maiduguri began to make common cause and link up together.

When Mohammed Yusuf became disaffected with the pace of reinvigoration of Sharia implementation by the Modu Sheriff administration, he fell out with the Governor, and Alhaji Buji Foi withdrew from the Government. The breach between Modu Sheriff and Mohammed Yusuf became increasingly bitter, as Mohammed Yusuf became more bellicose in his sermons. In 2005, Governor Sheriff was sufficiently alarmed as to set up a multi-agency JTF called Operation Flush. Escalating friction between the *Yusufiyya* sect and Operation Flush in 2009 finally led to violent conflict and the transformation of the sect into an insurgency (Agbakwuru 2014).

The final political factor of note in the explanation of *Boko Haram* is the adverse incorporation of unemployed youths into patron–client political networks at all levels of the Nigerian federation. This pattern of unfavourable incorporation into the political sphere has often increased, rather than lessened, the sense of alienation felt by many of the youths. As pointed out in the study by NSRP (2014), the response

---

[27] Onuoha (2014, 166) claims that 'Ali Modu Sheriff promised the group strict implementation of Shari'ah, 50 million naira reward, 50 motorcycles and the office of the Commissioner for Religious Affairs in exchange for their support'.

to youth unemployment and lack of livelihood opportunities has been the unfolding of a plethora of 'youth empowerment' schemes by different levels of government. Primary amongst these schemes are the Subsidy Reinvestment and Empowerment Programme (SURE-P), the Youth Enterprise with Innovation in Nigeria Programme (YouWIN!), and the Youth Employment and Social Support Operation (YESSO). Others include the Youth Employment in Agriculture Programme, the Agricultural Transformation Action Plan, the National Enterprise Development Programme, the University Entrepreneurship Development Programme, as well as the Integrated Youth Development Initiative. The report notes, however, that notwithstanding 'the number of such schemes and the resources that have been poured into them ... both youth unemployment and levels of insecurity continue to grow in Nigeria' (NSRP 2014, 8).

What is apparent is that due to the adverse incorporation of the youths through these schemes, programmes that were supposed to mitigate violence through the creation of employment and income generation opportunities for the youth were actually having the perverse effect of generating a higher sense of exclusion and frustration. This is because the opportunities created through these programmes were widely 'perceived to be unjustly distributed, largely ineffective or otherwise beyond reach' (NSRP 2014, 8) of the average youth. 79 per cent of youth surveyed in eight conflict-prone states in Nigeria 'agreed that only youth close to politicians are selected'. Through the dynamics of adverse incorporation, even programmes meant to ameliorate the exclusion and alienation of youths were having the opposite effects. Without trust in the normal processes of governance, these youths have become available for recruitment into other forms of mobilization, including religious extremist groups. A nation-wide poll in 2014 'revealed that almost 4 in 10 (38 per cent) of Nigerians were willing to accept a gift from a political party or aspirant if offered'. Significantly, the poll also discovered that 'the willingness to accept a gift decreased with a progression in age since respondents aged between 18–21 years (65 per cent) were most willing to accept a gift, and is also most likely to be influenced by a gift (43 per cent) in their voting decisions' (Iroegbu 2014).

Boko Haram must be understood in the context of poor urban governance, elite manipulation of the political system and the adverse incorporation of youths into that system. Between them, these three political factors provide the motivations and opportunities for such a group to thrive. There is therefore some merit in the assertion by Pérouse de Montclos (2014, 149) that more 'than poverty, bad governance in Borno helped Mohammed Yusuf to become popular'.

PERSONAL AGENCY

When seeking to understand *Boko Haram*, the tendency is to look to economic, doctrinal and governance issues only. One issue that is frequently under-studied is the personal agency of the individuals who choose to join the insurgency. As Schmid (2013, 22–8) notes, there are many pathways to Islamic radicalization. While some join because of doctrinal conviction, others join 'for thrills and status, some for love, some for connection and comradeship'. We often assume, wrongly, that doctrinal or economic motivations fully account for the decision to participate in groups like *Boko Haram*. In reality there are as many motivations for joining an insurgency as there are individuals, and we must never lose sight of this heterogeneity of motivation. For some, doctrinal motivation is primary. One example of this is Aminu Sidiq Ogwuche, the alleged 2014 Nyanya bombing mastermind, who wrote on his Facebook page: 'Those who strive in the path of Allah love death like the kuffar love life … Let them know, we are always ready to meet our lord anytime he wills' (*Punch* 2014a). If Ogwuche is motivated by the prospects of martyrdom, others have more pecuniary motivations, and 'insecurity can also present local opportunities for illicit profit, such as through smuggling, bank robberies, cattle theft, armed robbery or kidnapping. This may be an incentive for some young men to join Boko Haram' (Higazi 2013a, 25). Others, like the young man who 'was said to have been paid the sum of two thousand Naira (N2,000), to burn down [a] few houses at Mandara Girau village', (Marama 2014) may see it as a one-off chance of making some money, while some others still may join for what we may even consider to be idiosyncratic reasons. For example, one captured *Boko Haram* member told his BBC interviewers: 'It was the mood of Mohammed Yusuf's teaching – the energy that helped me to join him' (Musa 2009b). Finally, some have been forcibly conscripted (Olanrewaju 2014).

Joining a group like *Boko Haram* is not necessarily the result of deeply held motivations, but may be dictated by situational and contingent factors of a more mundane nature within a localized context. For example, during the Ivorian crisis, one youth joined the militia because transport money to leave the district was too expensive. Being unable to flee the conflict zone, the youth in question did the next best thing – he joined the militia controlling the area (Guichaoua 2012, 4). Similarly, it is instructive that a large-scale survey of former left-wing guerrillas and right-wing paramilitaries who fought each other in Colombia showed that 'those who joined insurgent groups do not appear to be significantly more aggrieved than those who joined counter-insurgent groups' (Guichaoua 2012, 8). The survey also found that recruits 'tend to come from places where armed groups were actively present, where members of these groups had a strong influence on local life and where violence was relatively high' (Guichaoua 2012, 8).

In short, individuals join groups like *Boko Haram* for a variety of conscious or unconscious, tactical or strategic, and doctrinal or contingent reasons and we must not seek to homogenize these motivations around the concept of 'extremism' for the ease of our own representation of the group. Studies have found that even among religious terrorists theological knowledge is frequently thin and generally skewed with the leaders (doctrinal entrepreneurs) having better understanding than the follow-ership for whom the need to take revenge and other situational factors may be more important. It is after such followers join the group that doctrinal justification of their actions may become important (Schmid 2013, 28). From 2013 *Boko Haram* began to recruit/conscript youths from a wide zone in rural Borno and neighbouring areas in Niger Republic, Chad and Cameroon, and the original core of the sect has been diluted with recruits of potentially different motivations.

Second, the reasons an individual may join such a group may be different from the reasons why they stay on as members (Guichaoua 2012, 4). Just as the group metamorphoses and transforms over time, so do the individuals who compose it. Some violent groups become even more radicalized with time, and adopt more cruel methods against their opponents. A similar transformation is possible for some individuals, though in some other cases, such a transformation in the group may force the individual to re-evaluate their continued membership.

Third, even the very act of taking part in the violence can (re)shape an individual's perspective since 'armed organizations should be recognized as places where new behavioural norms are produced through the inter-action of their members' (Guichaoua 2012, 10). Finally, we should also bear in mind that the motivation for the leaders may be different from those of the rank and file, who may or may not share in the vision of the leadership. This factor, along with the contingent and situational nature of individual enlistment, points to the possible fragility and reversibility of allegiances. To police the group boundaries and prevent defection, groups like *Boko Haram* have designed enforcement mechanisms. Under the leadership of Abubakar Shekau since 2009, dissenting members are frequently beheaded.

In seeking to understand the sort of collective violence *Boko Haram* epitomizes, we must look at the structural social factors which frame the group, the doctrinal ideological ideals it upholds, as well as the trajectory and internal dynamics of the group. However, we must also seek to under-stand the role of the individual insurgent – their motivations and personal agency – because group and individual motivations and attributes are not always identical.

GEOGRAPHICAL AND INTERNATIONAL CONTEXTS

All the domestic factors discussed so far make possible a process of radicalization which ultimately led to the phenomenon of *Boko Haram*. However, this gradual radicalization takes place within a specific geographical and international context which is especially propitious to terrorist activities. Thus, the international context is the final factor that contributes to a better understanding of *Boko Haram* violence. Here, three factors are of utmost importance. These are, first, the 'internationalist' vision of the sect leadership, guided by the Islamic concept of the *Umma*; second, the violent history of the Lake Chad region which is contiguous to most of the north-east zone; and last, recent regional developments like the fall of Gaddafi in Libya and the Tuareg crisis in Mali.

Regarding the vision of the sect, a *Boko Haram* spokesman once said that 'Islam doesn't recognise international boundaries; we will carry out our operations anywhere in the world if we can have the chance' (Abubakar 2010). This 'internationalist' perspective informs the constant positive mention of global Islamist terrorist groups and personalities in *Boko Haram* propaganda. It is further expressed in the readiness of *Boko Haram* to seek sanctuary, resources and recruits from Niger Republic, Chad and Cameroon. In fact, its military operations are predicated on its ability to move freely across these international boundaries. The Niger Republic Region of Diffa is not only contiguous to Borno State, there is the added fact of an indigenous ethnic Kanuri population to be found there, making it easier to mesh into the local population. *Boko Haram* has therefore been active in Diffa, which it uses as a rear base and as a recruiting ground. Occasionally, it even carries out robberies in Diffa to raise resources (Sule 2014).

While Diffa is more of a rear base, Chad is used by *Boko Haram* for recruiting fighters and obtaining military supplies. Marielle Debos (2013) situates Chad in the context of the long history of violent conflict in the Lake Chad region. She notes that postcolonial Chad has a long history of 'living by the gun', and violence has become entrenched in everyday life. Since the 1970s, violence has become endemic in the political and economic life of the country and political power is exercised, not in spite of disorder, but through disorder itself. Along with the prevalence of real or threatened violence is the institutionalization of impunity which breeds fear in the civilian population and demobilizes its capacity to face up to the various armed factions operating in the country. Since 2010, Debos notes, Chad has been increasingly regarded as a 'stable' country by the international community. But that surface stability is because overt violence has sometimes been replaced by the threat of violence. Within this matrix, the state no longer claims the monopoly of violence. The proximity of Chad to Borno State means that *Boko Haram* can tap into this 'bad neighbourhood' effect. Indeed, Chadian security reports suggest that 'Boko Haram has received sophisticated weapons from the Middle East and the Maghreb through Sudan and Chad to Nigeria and Cameroon' (*The Nation* 2014).

Of all the neighbouring countries, however, Cameroon is the most strategic in *Boko Haram* operations. Illustrative of this is the situation in the town of Amchide, in the far north of Cameroon near the Nigerian town of Banki in Borno State, where local police sources claim – rightly or wrongly – that *Boko Haram* supporters account for 90 per cent of the population. 'Amchide is Boko Haram's local fiefdom', said Lieutenant-Colonel Thierry Foumane, the regional commander of Cameroon's Rapid Intervention Battalion (BIR), an elite army unit recently deployed to the remote area (*PMNews* 2014). The population is so mixed up across an ill-defined boundary that it is often difficult to differentiate the nationals of either country: 'Look at this house. The living room is in Cameroon, but the other rooms are in Nigeria' the Lieutenant pointed out to visiting journalists. Within this confused context, *Boko Haram* has deployed various tactics to secure or extract support and recruits from the local population: 'They have offered money to youths to rally them to their cause, and they have coerced the more fearful ones into joining them', said the local police chief who also noted that beatings and blackmail have also been used, concluding that 'anything goes in Amchide'. *Boko Haram* infiltrators have also been accused of running a protection racket through which they 'forced others to finance their activities' (*PMNews* 2014). It was only after the international outcry against the abduction of the Chibok school girls in April 2014 that Cameroon began to take concerted steps against *Boko Haram* in northern Cameroon. Prior to that, many felt that Cameroon ignored the sect, so long as it restricted its military operations to Nigerian territory. *Boko Haram* opened a Cameroonian front effective from mid-2014.

The fact that Borno State is contiguous to these three countries is therefore an important factor to be taken into account in understanding the escalation of *Boko Haram* violence since 2009. Just as important are developments in the regional international situation, especially the chaotic fall of Gaddafi in Libya in 2011 and the knock-on effect of the coup in Mali in 2012.[28] Some have cautioned against the tendency to regard *Boko Haram* as part of a wider global network of Islamist terrorism, stressing instead its domestic provenance (Pérouse de Montclos 2014). While this

---

[28] The abuse, for 'regime-change' purposes, of the UN Security Council Resolution 1973 authorizing the Anglo-French-led intervention in Libya led to a chaotic dismantling of the Gaddafi regime and the dispersal of considerable weaponry into the Sahelian countries of West Africa.

is a correct reading of the evidence, there are also indicators that the sect has been straining to establish wider terrorist connections in order to strengthen its tactical capabilities and burnish its symbolic credentials. Asked if *Boko Haram* has any links with Algeria's al-Qaeda (AQIM), the Nigerian journalist with the closest connections to the sect said: 'Yes, they are in touch and in some kind of partnership and collaboration, and I think that relationship is growing' (Salkida 2013b). This obser-vation is consistent with the accounts of another Nigerian journalist who conducted interviews in northern Mali, shortly after the Islamist forces were driven out of the area in January 2013. He reports on an interview with someone who acted as a cook for over 200 Nigerians – presumably *Boko Haram* members – training with the Islamists:

> They then met with specialists, the cook said. He described an arms specialist from Pakistan, who he said taught Boko Haram and Ansar Dine members how to break apart and reassemble assault rifles, over and over again. There was a computer specialist who appeared, to the cook, to be mostly occupied making fliers extolling the fundamentalist cause. A heavy arms specialist who the cook said was from Afghanistan told militants how to breathe steadily when firing a shoulder-mounted rocket. (Pindiga 2013)

Further corroboration of this external link comes from the testimony of Shaikh Albani of Zaria, a Salafist opponent of *Boko Haram* who was assas-sinated by the sect in Zaria in February 2014. According to Shaikh Albani, 'Most of the [Mohammed] Yusuf's boys were trained in Algeria. And they were taken there through the assistance of a Kano-based businessman on the pretext that they were going to study fiqhu'[29] (Omipidan 2009). Finally, there are also strong speculations from multiple sources that the Chadian-born Mamman Nur, formerly number three in *Boko Haram*'s leadership behind Mohammed Yusuf and Abubakar Shekau, and the alleged mastermind of the *Boko Haram* bombing of the UN building in Abuja in August 2011, fled to Somalia after the government crackdown on the *Yusufiyya* sect in 2009. He was alleged to have trained in *al Shabaab* camps before returning to Nigeria in 2011 (Pham 2012).

The staircase to mayhem

The various factors outlined above – the importance of doctrines, the structural context of poverty and inequality, the political context, the

---

[29] *Fiqh*, rendered as *fiqhu* in Hausa, is the study, interpretation and development of Sharia law – Qur'an and Sunna – by Islamic jurists.

186 Understanding Boko Haram

importance of personal agency, and the international geo-political situation – are seemingly unrelated processes that, nevertheless have collectively resulted in the phenomenon of *Boko Haram*. How the diverse factors come together in a vortex of religious violence can best be captured in the staircase model of radicalization developed by Fathali M. Assaf Moghaddam (see Schmid 2013, 24). The model uses the metaphor of a narrowing staircase leading step-by-step to the top of a building which has a ground floor and five higher floors, each representing a phase in the radicalization process with the topmost floor representing participation in acts of terrorism:

> The ground floor, inhabited by more than one billion Muslims worldwide, stands for a cognitive analysis of the structural circum-stances in which the individual Muslim finds him- or herself. Here, the individual asks him- or herself questions like 'am I being treated fairly?' The individual begins to interpret an ascribed causality to what he or she deems to be unjust. According to Moghaddam, most people find themselves on this 'foundational level'. Some individuals who are very dissatisfied move up to the first floor in search for a change in their situation. On the first floor, one finds individuals who are actively seeking to remedy those circumstances they perceive to be unjust. Some of them might find that paths to individual upward social mobility are blocked, that their voices of protest are silenced and that there is no access to participation ... They tend to move up to the second floor, where these individuals are directed toward external targets for displacement of aggression. He or she begins to place blame for injustice on out-groups ... Some are radicalised in mosques and other meeting places of Muslims and move to the third floor on the staircase to terrorism. This phase involves a moral disengagement from society and a moral engagement within the nascent terrorist organ-isation. Within this phase, values are constructed which rationalise the use of violence by the terrorists while simultaneously decrying the moral authority of the incumbent regime. A smaller group moves up the narrowing staircase to the fourth floor, where the legitimacy of terrorist organisations is accepted more strongly. Here the attitude is: 'you are either with us or against us'. They begin to be incorporated into the organisational and value structures of terrorist organisations. Some are recruited to take the last steps on the staircase and commit acts of terrorism when reaching the top fifth floor. (Schmid 2013, 24)

Boko Haram insurgency is often presented in a number of erroneous ways that fail to take account of its historical and socio-political complexity. Some see it as a mere franchise extension of global jihadi forces into a religiously troubled part of Africa, while others see it as the manifestation of local theocratic intolerance and the urge to dominate dating from the early decolonization period of the 1950s in Nigeria. Yet some others see it as the instrumentalization of religious difference by disgruntled northern regional elites since 2010, intent on destabilizing a southern Christian presidency. That public policy has so far failed to come to grips with the insurgency is a reflection of this confusion caused by this multiple (mis) perception.

What I have tried to show in this chapter is that *intra*-Muslim doctrinal disputes dating back to the jihad of 1804, but especially since the 1940s, and the increasingly intolerant, disruptive and violent way they have been pursued are critical to the understanding of the emergence of *Boko Haram*. By the 1970s, with the rise of Salafist and Shi'a doctrinal tendencies, we see the intensification of a sectarianism that was previously limited in its scope and intolerance. Doctrinal fragmentation coincided not just with height-ening sectarianism, but also with the increasing prominence of Islamic symbols within the wider society. Placed against the background of a corrupt military centralized state from the mid-1960s, increasing author-itarian and manipulative politics from 1999, inequality and economic crises, these tendencies led to a radicalization and mobilization of Muslim identities from the 1970s. For example, when the *Jamat al-Tajdeed al-Islami* (JTI) was formed in 1994 from the Shi'a-inclined Islamic Movement of Nigeria (IMN) (see Chapter 3), it derived its doctrines and positions, not just from the Qur' an and the Sunna, but also from Ḥasan al-Bannā (1906–1948), the founder of the Muslim Brotherhood in Egypt. The tone of the new organization, captured in its slogan 'Allah is our target, the Prophet is our example, the Qur'ān is our canon, jihād is our way, and dying for the cause of God is our noble wish' (Ben Amara 2011, 139), suggested a level of radicalization and politicization that would have been unusual in the 1950s.

It is this twin process of doctrinal fragmentation and radicalization *within* the Muslim community that provided the initial propulsion towards social disorder. The coincidence of this process with wider social, economic, political and military dystopias of Nigerian society could best be seen as enabling or aggravating conditions. Such was the long road to the *Boko Haram* insurgency, the politicized ahistorical understanding of which has made an appropriate response to be beyond the Nigerian state. The longer the violent insurgency has lasted, the further away we move from its original doctrinal motivations, and the more its violence becomes routinized in everyday life, especially in the north-east. For the youth directly involved either forcibly or by choice, violence becomes a way of life, albeit a short and violent one, that might nevertheless be more attractive to them than their previous marginalized humdrum existence.

A Caliphate without a Caliph?

In August 2014, Abubakar Shekau, described as 'the mercurial leader' of *Boko Haram*, declared a Caliphate in parts of the north-east, but without naming a Caliph![30] He asserted: 'We are in an Islamic Caliphate. We have nothing to do with Nigeria. We don't believe in this name' (*Sahara Reporters* 2014b). Though this bold gesture may be regarded as a cruel joke mimicking the more sinister Islamic Caliphate previously declared by ISIS in Iraq and Syria, it nevertheless reflected a major strategic shift in the north-east from approximately May 2014. From that month, disturbing reports began emerging regarding the circumstances of the troops of the 7th Division of the Nigerian Army, which was specifically created to address the insurgency in the north-east.

On 14 May, soldiers at the Giwa Barracks in Maiduguri were reported to have fired in the general direction of their General Officer Commanding (GOC) in a protest over inadequate weapons and the resulting high rate of casualties they were suffering. Whilst disciplinary actions against these troops were ongoing, demonstrations erupted on 9 and 11 August, led this time by wives of soldiers claiming that their husbands were being sent out as cannon fodder without adequate equipment. These demonstrations also aimed at thwarting further deployments. Again on 19 August, another group of soldiers from the Maimalari Barracks in Maiduguri were alleged to have refused orders to deploy to fight *Boko Haram* on the grounds of poor equipment. While denouncing some of the specific claims in these reports as lies, the military authorities asserted that the 'overwhelming majority of the Nigerian soldiers remains as brave and disciplined as ever. They will certainly not join any renegade, coward, deserter or those trying to incite mutiny in the military to betray the nation at a time like this' (Idris, Adibe et al. 2014; Idris 2014c). However, the fact that disciplinary actions were being taken within the military, and that open demonstrations by the military wives took place, suggest that there were at least some problems within the military institution. Similarly, the statement by the Chief of Defence Staff, Air Marshal Alex Badeh, at a Senate hearing in September 2014 that 'for the country to win the war against terrorism, there was the need for diplomatic lobbying for foreign assistance in areas of equipment' is indicative of a problem with military

---

[30] This is unprecedented in standard Islamic practice. In 1804 when Shaikh 'Uthman dan Fodio declared a similar jihad, he advanced reasons why the local entity created out of the effort could not be part of a wider pan-Islamic Caliphate, hence the Sokoto Caliphate. Was *Boko Haram* intending to join the Caliphate already declared by ISIS? Or was the 'mercurial' Shekau conscious of the likely public opprobrium that would greet his claim to such an office?

supplies (Ujah et al. 2014). As the military situation became increasingly uncertain, some soldiers were even reported to be sending their families away from the barracks (Idris 2014d).

The disquiet within the military also coincided with a period of expanded insurgent attacks with relatively little resistance from the military. As one observer described it, 'when Boko Haram members leave their camps they travel without interference to a town, they destroy six villages on their way to a particular town, and no-one touches them … For goodness sake, it is arid area, you can see a convey six miles away and these guys travel with 20, 40 or 60 vehicles with armed personnel' (Egene & Somorin 2014). Independent security analysts are beginning to suggest that the insurgency has moved into a new phase in which for 'the first time in its history, Boko Haram is seizing and holding onto territory outside of its hideouts in Sambisa and the Mandara Mountains' (NSN 2014). Over a five-day period, 1–5 September, the insurgents were reported to have seized five towns, including major local administrative centres in Borno and Adamawa States (Soriwei et al. 2014). In the face of what seems like the implosion of military capability and morale, fears began to be expressed that 'Nigeria is losing control of large parts of the north-east region' (NSN 2014).

Towns and villages either seized by the insurgents or contested with the army multiplied in rapid succession. These included Gamboru Ngala, Dikwa, Gwoza, Marte, Bama, Damboa, Banki, Kerawa, Ashigashiya, Ngoshe, Pulka, Liman Kara and Goniri in Borno State, Madagali and Gulak in Adamawa State, and Bara and Buni Yadi in Yobe State (NSN 2014; Soriwei et al. 2014). In Liman Kara, for instance, the sect seized a high-profile police training academy, looted the armoury and even forced some of the captured policemen to join *Boko Haram* as instructors, with one local church observer reporting: 'The guys are multiplying in number, weaponry and geographical expansion' (Idowu 2014). *Boko Haram*, which one informed observer estimated to have the strength of about 5,000 (*Sahara Reporters* 2014c) while another less believable account put its strength at 50,000 (Elebeke 2014), was reported to be in control of 16 towns and villages in which it has hoisted its jihadist flag (Musa 2014).

The insurgency is reported to have secured two major clusters of territory to the north-east and east of Borno State, along with some territory in northern Adamawa State and southern Yobe State (NSN 2014). Anxiety has mounted that Maiduguri, the Borno capital, was being encircled and might itself be attacked. The NSN report stated that since July 2014 the *Boko Haram* insurgency has entered a dangerous new phase in which the sect, through direct confrontation in open and sustained battle and using armoured vehicles, tanks and heavy weapons, is beginning to operate like a conventional army. 'This marks a major change from how the insurgency operated before July, when it focused on carrying out short-lived hit-and-run assaults and attacking undefended communities' (NSN 2014). It is also different from how the insurgency operates elsewhere in Nigeria where the sect continues to behave more like a terrorist organization, carrying out a small number of attacks for psychological effect.

The Chairman of the Senate Committee on Defence, Senator George Sekibo has, however, contested these claims of the loss of territory, suggesting that 'the insurgents were strong in about one or two towns and not more' (Ameh et al. 2014). In a similar vein, when in late August 2014 about 480 Nigerian soldiers abandoned their posts in Gamboru Ngala and fled to Cameroon during a gunfight with *Boko Haram*, the Defence Headquarters described their action as mere 'tactical manoeuvres'. Meanwhile, another legislator and a retired general, Senator Ahmed Saleh said 'what we are seeing is a complete deterioration of the situation' (Ujah et al. 2014). To say the least, these conflicting narratives have only helped to spread unease and suspicion regarding the true situation in the military within the general public. Even the international community is beginning to express open concern with the US Assistant Secretary of State for African Affairs, Linda Thomas-Greenfield claiming, in the heart of Abuja itself, that the 'reputation of Nigeria's military is at stake. But more importantly, Nigeria's and its children's future is in jeopardy' (Ujah et al. 2014; Ameh et al. 2014). She added that 'we are past time for denial and pride'.

Conclusion

It has been argued that any terrorist group that has lasted for more than eight years after its initial formation would likely exist for another 20 or more years before it can be dismantled as it would have become embedded for a generation and the likelihood of dismantling it would be that much more difficult (*Sahara Reporters* 2014d). With the military increasingly relying on airstrikes to limited effects, ordinary citizens in the north-east are resorting to self-help to protect their communities. The youth vigilantes, the 'Civilian JTF' (CJTF) who rose in May 2013 and successfully cleansed Maiduguri of *Boko Haram* are now arming themselves with Dane guns, daggers, cutlasses, swords, knives, and bows and arrows in anticipation of more fighting. They have been joined by retired servicemen and local hunters. According to a CJTF leader and local hunter: 'We know we don't have the AK-47 and other weapons that Boko Haram fighters have, but we have the heart, we also have dane guns, talismans and charms. And

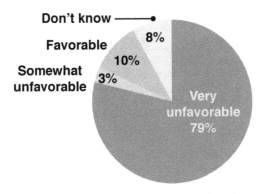

Figure 6.3 Nigerian views of Boko Haram
(courtesy of the Pew Research Center; 'Increasing concerns about extremism in
Middle East', Spring 2014 Global Attitudes survey Q15q)

most importantly, we have God on our side' (Idris, Ibrahim & Sawab
2014). Needless to say, this desperate move might not be enough in the
face of an increasingly sophisticated and ruthless enemy. What is not in
doubt, however, is the sense of abandonment felt by the citizens of the
north-east and the increasing sense of alarm and unease felt by the rest of
the country.

A 2014 Survey by the Pew Foundation suggests that Nigerians do not
embrace *Boko Haram*'s extremist doctrine or its rhetoric of hate. As Figure
6.3 shows, 82% of Nigerians have an unfavourable view of *Boko Haram*,
including 79% who have a *very* unfavourable view. It is noteworthy
that these negative opinions are shared by Muslims (80%) and Christians (83%) alike. From the survey data, only 10% of Nigerians have a
favourable view of the group in 2014 – roughly about the same level
as in 2013 (PewResearch 2014). Meanwhile, Nigerians of all religious
persuasions live in fear in the shadows of *Boko Haram* violence. With the
increased campaign of indiscriminate bombings, scorched earth assaults
on border villages, and the declaration of a so-called Caliphate, many
are beginning to view *Boko Haram* as an existential threat. According to
a 2014 poll by Gallup, nearly all Nigerians (95%) say the group presents
a 'major threat' to their country's future, while 3% say a 'minor threat'
(Loschky 2014). What remains to be seen is whether the state is capable
of rising above the level of ethno-regional suspicion, prejudices and
self-serving politicking in order to generate the needed appropriate
response.

Bibliography

Abbah, Theophilus and Hamza Idris, 2014, 'What Boko Haram fighters told me about sect', *Sunday Trust*, 4 May, http://dailytrust.com.ng, interview with Governor Kashim Shettima of Borno State, accessed on 4 May 2014.

Abdallah, Nurudeen, 2012, 'Shettima: How to end Boko Haram menace', *Daily Trust*, 19 February, http://dailytrust.com.ng, accessed on 20 February 2012.

Abdallah, Nurudeen, 2014, 'Nigeria beats Iraq, Somalia in terror casualties – Report', *Daily Trust*, 25 July, http://dailytrust.com.ng, accessed on 25 July 2014.

Abubakar, A., 2010, 'Nigerian Islamist sect threatens to widen attacks', *AFP*, 29 March, accessed on 29 March 2010.

Abuh, Adamu, Isa Abdulsalami Ahovi, Njadvara Musa, Hendrix Oliomogbe, Kanayo Umeh, and Eric Meya, 2014, 'We're closer to rescuing Chibok girls, says govt', *Guardian*, 7 July, www.ngrguardiannews.com, accessed on 7 July 2014.

ACF, 2014, 'There is more to insurgency attacks than meets the eye', *Daily Trust*, 10 March, http://dailytrust.com.ng, accessed on 10 March 2014.

Adinoyi, Seriki, 2014, 'Boko Haram is a child of Islam, Says Cleric' *ThisDay Live*, 16 May, www.thisdaylive.com, accessed on 16 May 2014.

Adio, Waziri, 2014, 'Fighting terror from faulty premises', *ThisDay Live*, 10 March, www.thisdaylive.com, accessed on 10 March 2014.*AFP*, 2014, '1,000 killed in Boko Haram conflict this year – NEMA', *Vanguard*, 26 March, www.vanguardngr.com, accessed on 26 March 2014.

Agbakwuru, Johnbosco, 2014, 'My Boko Haram story, by Senator Khalifa', *Vanguard*, 16 March, www.vanguardngr.com, accessed on 16 March 2014.

Akpeji, Charles and Ali Garba Gombe, 2014, 'Two feared killed by political thugs in Gombe' *Guardian*, 20 August, www.ngrguardiannews.com, accessed on 20 August 2014.

Alabi, S.A., forthcoming, 'One Encounter; Three Streams: Ulama Responses to Western Education in Colonial Ilorin', *Africa*.

Alesina, Alberto and Roberto Perotti, 1996, 'Income distribution, political instability, and investment', *European Economic Review*, 40 (1996), 1203–28.

Aliyu, Abdullateef, 2014, 'Boko Haram insurgency hatched to tarnish Islam', *Daily Trust*, 10 July, http://dailytrust.com.ng, accessed on 10 July 2014.

Alli, Yusuf, 2013, 'Tension as Boko Haram grounds 10 LGs in Borno', *The Nation*, 19 April, http://thenationonlineng.net, accessed on 20 April 2013.

Ameh, John and Ramon Oladimeji, 2014, 'Corruption stalls Nigeria's war against B'Haram –US', *Punch*, 23 May, www.punchng.com, accessed on 23 May 2014.

Ameh, John, Adelani Adepegba, Kayode Idowu and Allwell Okpi, 2014, 'Maiduguri youths march against Boko Haram', *Punch*, 5 September, www.punchng.com, accessed on 5 September 2014.

Amnesty International, 2012, 'Nigeria: Trapped in The cycle of violence', www. amnesty.org/en/library/asset/AFR44/043/2012/en/04ab8b67-8969-4c86-bdea-0f82059dff28/afr440432012en.pdf, accessed on 12 January 2013.

Amnesty International, 2014, 'Nigeria: More Than 1,500 Killed in Armed Conflict in North-Eastern Nigeria in Early 2014', www.amnesty.nl/sites/default/files/public/nigeria__more_than_1500_killed_in_armed_conflict.pdf, accessed on 10 June 2014.

Andrews, Jaiyeola, 2014, 'FG needs to do more in the north, says Misau', *ThisDay Live*, 29 June, www.thisdaylive.com, accessed on 29 Jun 2014.

Aziken, Emmanuel, 2013, 'Boko Haram are too illiterate for their sophisticated attacks –Kalu', 5 April, *Vanguard*, www.vanguardngr.com, accessed on 5 April, 2013.

Bano, Masooda, 2012, *The Rational Believer: Choices and Decisions in the Madrasas of Pakistan*, Ithaca NY and London: Cornell University Press.

BBC, 2013, 'Mali crisis: key players', BBC, 12 March, www.bbc.co.uk/news/world-africa-17582909, accessed on 12 March 2013.

Bego, Abdullahi, 2003, 'Borno: why Governor Mala Kachalla lost to Modu Ali Sherrif', 26 April, *Weekly Trust*, http://dailytrust.com.ng, accessed on 26 April 2003.

Bello, Emma, 2009, 'Boko Haram crisis: crisis was not religious – Gov Modu Sheriff', *Leadership*, 8 August, http://leadership.ng, accessed on 8 August 2009.

Ben Amara, Ramzi, 2011, 'The Izala Movement in Nigeria: Its Split, Relationship to Sufis and Perception of Sharī'a Re-Implementation', D.Phil. dissertation at Bayreuth International Graduate School of African Studies, BIGSAS, Universitat Bayreuth, Germany.

Best, S.G. and Carole Rakodi, 2011, 'Violent Conflict and its Aftermath in Jos and Kano, Nigeria: What is the Role of Religion?' Working Paper 69, Religions and Development Research Programme, University of Birmingham, UK.

Casey, C., 2008, '"Marginal Muslims": Politics and the Perceptual Bounds of Islamic Authenticity in Northern Nigeria', *Africa Today*, 54 (3), 67–92.

Chiedozie, Ihuoma, 2013, 'ThisDay bomber cried for missing heaven – witness', *Punch*, 15 May, www.punchng.com, accessed on 15 May 2013.

Chima, Obinna, 2014, 'Middle class, key driver of economic growth', *ThisDay Live*, 24 June, www.thisdaylive.com, accessed on 24 June 2014.

Chouin, Gérard, 2014, 'Foreword', in Marc-Antoine Pérouse de Montclos (ed.), *Boko Haram: Islamism, Politics, Security and the State in Nigeria*, West African Politics and Society Series, Vol. 2, Leiden and Ibadan: African Studies Centre and Institut Français de Recherche en Afrique.

Debos, Marielle, 2013, *Le Métier des Armes au Tchad*, Paris: Karthala.

Duru, Peter, 2014, 'Oritsejafor accuses Boko Haram of plot to Islamise Nigeria', *Vanguard*, 10 July, www.vanguardngr.com, accessed on 10 July 2014.

Ebiri, Kelvin, 2011, 'Boko Haram, tool to destabilize govt, says SSPA', *Guardian*, 27 August, www.ngrguardiannews.com, accessed on 29 August 2011.

Eboh, C. and G. Mohammed, 2012, 'Suicide car bombs hit Nigerian newspaper offices', Reuters, 26 April, www.reuters.com/article/2012/04/26/us-nigeria-bomb-idUS-BRE83P0NR20120426, accessed 6 October 2014.

Egene Goddy and Zacheaus Somorin, 2014, 'Australian Negotiator Names Ihejirika, Sheriff as Sponsors of Boko Haram', *ThisDay Live*, 29 August, www.thisdaylive.com, accessed on 29 August 2014.

Ekott, Ini, 2013, 'Bill Clinton counters Jonathan, insists poverty behind Boko Haram, Ansaru insurgency', *Premium Times*, 27 February, www.premiumtimesng.com, accessed on 27 February 2013.

Elebeke, Emmanuel, 2014, 'Boko Haram has 50,000 members in its camp – BBOG', *Vanguard*, 28 August, www.vanguardngr.com, accessed on 28 August 2014.

El-Rufai, Nasir, 2012, 'Bauchi's hopeless budget', *ThisDay Live*, 13 April, www.thisdaylive.com, accessed on 13th April 2012.

Emewu, Ikenna, 2013, 'Insecurity stretches military operations in 28 states – NSA', *The Sun*, 5 July, http://sunnewsonline.com/new, accessed on 5 July 2013.

Ezeamalu, Ben, 2014, 'Update: Court dismisses terrorism allegations against Sanusi, orders Nigerian govt to apologize, pay N50M damages', *Premium Times*, 30 April, www.premiumtimesng.com, accessed on 30 April 2014.

Federal Government of Nigeria, 2012, *White Paper on the Report of the Presidential Committee on Security Challenges in the North-East Zone*, May.

Garba, Ali, 2010, 'Boko Haram: how attackers outwitted security agencies' *Guardian*, 10 September, www.ngrguardiannews.com, accessed on 11 September 2010.

Guichaoua, Y., 2012, 'Introduction: Individual Drivers of Collective Violence and the Dynamics of Armed Groups', in Yvan Guichaoua (ed.), *Understanding Collective Political Violence*, Basingstoke: Palgrave Macmillan.

Haruna, Kareem, 2014a, 'Gwoza suffers humanitarian crisis as insurgents displace over 1000 villagers', *Leadership*, 8 June, http://leadership.ng, accessed on 8 June 2014.

Haruna, Kareem, 2014b, 'Bring back my men, I'll release your schoolgirls, Shekau tells FG', *Leadership*, http://leadership.ng, accessed on 14 July 2014.

Higazi, A., 2013a, 'Les origines et la transformation de l'insurrection de Boko Haram dans le nord du Nigeria', *Politique Africaine*, 130, 137–64.

Higazi, A., 2013b, 'Insurgency and Counter-Insurgency in North-East Nigeria', CERI publication, Sciences Po, Paris, 4 July.

Hiskett, M., 1987, 'The Maitatsine Riots in Kano, 1980: An Assessment', *Journal of Religion in Africa*, 17 (3), 209–23.

Human Rights Watch, 2012, 'Spiraling Violence: Boko Haram Attacks and Security Force Abuses in Nigeria', New York: Human Rights Watch, www.hrw.org/sites/default/files/reports/nigeria1012webwcover_0.pdf, accessed on 30 December 2012.

Ibeh, Nnenna, 2014, 'Nigerian soldiers kill 44 insurgents, reclaim dangerous forest – DHQ', *Premium Times*, 7 July, www.premiumtimesng.com, accessed on 7 July 2014.

Ibrahim, J., 1989, 'The politics of religion in Nigeria: the parameters of the 1987 crisis in Kaduna State', *Review of African Political Economy*, 16 (45–46), 65–83.

Idowu, Kayode, 2014, 'Boko Haram turns Police college to training camp – Survivor', *Punch*, 30 August, www.punchng.com, accessed on 30 August 2014.

Idris, Hamza, 2014a, 'Gunmen attack police station, seize 60 cows', *Daily Trust*, 1 July, http://dailytrust.com.ng, accessed on 1 July 2014.

Idris, Hamza, 2014b, 'Behold the women of Boko Haram', *Weekly Trust*, 12 July, http://dailytrust.com.ng, accessed on 12 July 2014.

Idris, Hamza, 2014c, 'Boko Haram: When soldiers' wives "fight" for husbands in Borno' *Weekly Trust*, 16 August, http://dailytrust.com.ng/, accessed on 16 August 2014.

Idris, Hamza, 2014d, 'Soldiers evacuating families out of barracks in Maiduguri', *Daily Trust*, 5 September, http://dailytrust.com.ng, accessed on 5 September 2014.

Idris, Hamza, Tony Adibe, Ibrahim Kabiru, and Ronald Mutum, 2014, 'Boko Haram crisis: Soldiers revolt over inadequate weapons', *Daily Trust*, 20 August, http://dailytrust.com.ng, accessed on 20 August 2014.

Idris, Hamza, Yahaya Ibrahim and Ibrahim Sawab, 2014, 'Boko Haram: why Borno residents are arming themselves', *Weekly Trust*, 6 September, http://dailytrust.com.ng, accessed on 6 September 2014.

Iroegbu, Senator, 2014, '2015: Polls Show Political Aspirants, Parties, Traditional Media as Factors Influencing Voters', *ThisDay Live*, 28 June, www.thisdaylive.com, accessed on 28 June 2014.

Isenyo, Godwin, 2014, 'Military aiding, abetting Boko Haram – ACF, *Punch*, 2 May, www.punchng.com, accessed on 2 May 2014.

Jonathan, Goodluck Ebele, 2014, 'Address By President Goodluck Ebele Jonathan, GCFR President Federal Republic of Nigeria at the Regional Summit on Security in Nigeria, Paris, France – 17 May 2014', in *Premium Times*, www.premiumtimesng.com, 'Boko Haram has killed over 12,000 Nigerians, plans to take over country, Jonathan says', accessed on 17 May 2014.

Kane, Ousmane, 2003, *Muslim Modernity in Postcolonial Nigeria: A Study of the Society for the Removal of Innovation and Reinstatement of Tradition*, Leiden: Brill.

Kayode-Adedeji, Dimeji, 2011, 'Boko Haram established to discredit the Jonathan administration', *234Next*, www.234Next.com, accessed on 14 September 2011.

Krishi, Musa Abdullahi, 2014, 'We were barred from repelling Gamboru attack – Soldier', *Daily Trust*, 22 May, http://dailytrust.com.ng, accessed on 22 May 2014.

Lah, Kyung and Kathleen Johnston, 2014, 'Kidnapped ship's captain told ransoms may be funneled to Boko Haram', *CNN Investigations*, 25 June, http://edition.cnn.com/2014/06/24/world/africa/nigeria-kidnapped-captain/index.html, accessed on June 25 2014.

Loschky, Jay, 2014, 'Nearly all Nigerians see Boko Haram as a major threat: majority do not think the government is doing enough to fight terrorism', July 9, *Gallup World*, www.gallup.com/poll/172241/nearly-nigerians-boko-haram-major-threat.aspx, accessed on July 9 2014.

Marama, Ndahi, 2014, 'Boko Haram: Boy confesses to razing houses in Borno village for N2,000', 29 May, *Vanguard*, www.vanguardngr.com, accessed on 29 May 2014.

Masquelier, Adeline M., 1996, 'Identity, Alterity and Ambiguity in a Nigerien Community: Competing Definitions of "True" Islam', in Richard Werbner and Terence Ranger (eds), *Postcolonial Identities in Africa*, London: Zed Books.

Masquelier, Adeline, 2009, *Women and Islamic Revival in a West African Town*, Bloomington IN: Indiana University Press.

Meagher, K., 2014, 'MINTs and mayhem: a tale of two Nigerias', *Premium Times*, 20 May, www.premiumtimesng.com, accessed on 20 May 2014.

Meier, G., and J. Rauch, 2000, *Leading Issues in Economic Development*, Oxford: Oxford University Press.

Mohammed, A.S., 1983, 'A Social Interpretation of the Satiru Revolt of c. 1894–1906 in Sokoto Province', M.A. Thesis, Department of Sociology, Ahmadu Bello University, Zaria.

Mohammed, Abdulkareem, 2010, *The Paradox of Boko Haram*, Kano: Moving Image.

Mohammed, Kyari, 2014, 'The Message and Methods of Boko Haram', in Marc-Antoine Pérouse de Montclos (ed.), *Boko Haram: Islamism, Politics, Security and the State in Nigeria*, West African Politics and Society Series, Vol. 2, Leiden and Ibadan: African Studies Centre and Institut Français de Recherche en Afrique.

Musa, Njadvara, 2009a, '190 Boko Haram members arraigned in Maiduguri', *Guardian*, 5 October, www.ngrguardiannews.com, accessed on 5 October 2009.

Musa, Njadvara, 2009b, 'We trained in Afghanistan as bomb specialist, say sect members', *Guardian*, 3 September, www.ngrguardiannews.com, accessed on September 3 2009.

Musa, Njadvara, 2014, 'Boko Haram captures another Borno town in fresh attacks', *Guardian*, 29 August, www.ngrguardiannews.com, accessed on 29 August 2014

Nafziger, E., and J. Auvinen, 1997, 'War, Hunger and Displacement: An Econometric Investigation into the Sources of Humanitarian Emergencies', United Nations University, World Institute for Development Economic Research, *Working Paper* 142.

NBS (Nigerian National Bureau of Statistics), 2013, '2012 National Baseline Youth Survey', Abuja: NBS.

Nnanna, Ochereome, 2012, 'An encounter with Gov Shettima of Borno', *Vanguard*, 27 February, www.vanguardngr.com, accessed on 27 February 2012.

NSN (Nigeria Security Network), 2014, 'Special Report: North-East Nigeria on the Brink', https://nigeriasecuritynetwork.files.wordpress.com/2014/09/ne-on-the-brink-special-report.pdf, accessed on 5th Sept. 2014.

NSRP (Nigeria Stability and Reconciliation Programme), 2014, 'Winners or Losers? Assessing the Contribution of Youth Employment and Empowerment Programmes to Reducing Conflict Risks in Nigeria', Abuja: NSRP.

Nyako, Vice Admiral Murtala H., 2014, 'Governor of Adamawa State's contribution at the 3-Day Symposium on Current Economic, Social and Security Challenges Facing Northern Nigeria', Washington DC, organized by US Institute of Peace. 17–19 March.

Obada, Hon. Erelu Olusola, Minister of State for Defence, Nigeria, 2013, 'Nigeria's Defence Priorities: Domestic Stability for Regional Security', Chatham House, London, 18 July.

Ochayi, Chris, 2014, 'Davis, Australian negotiator is self-appointed – DSS', *Vanguard*, 6 September, www.vanguardngr.com, accessed on 6 September 2014.

Oketola, Dayo, Fisayo Falodi, Kayode Idowu, Ademola Olonilua, Eric Dumo, and Jesusegun Alagbe, 2014, 'Boko Haram victims hit six million – UN', *Punch*, 28 June, www.punchng.com, accessed on 28 June 2014.

Okocha, Chuks and Michael Olugbode, 2014, 'PDP asks Principal to publish names, pictures of abducted students', *ThisDay Live*, 1 May, www.thisdaylive.com, accessed on 1 May 2014.

Okocha, Chuks and Onyebuchi Ezigbo, 2014, 'In a daring move, PDP Says Buhari, El-Rufai "know more about B'Haram"', *ThisDay Live*, 23 March, www.thisdaylive.com, accessed on 23 March 2014.

Okojie, George, 2014, 'Insurgency: Obasanjo rules out political undertone', *Leadership*, 1 June, http://leadership.ng, accessed on 1 June 2014.

Ola, Timothy, 2009, 'Jungle justice: family narrates how police killed 72-year-old father-in-law to Boko Haram sect leader', *The Sun*, 10 August, http://sunnewsonline.com, accessed on 10 August 2014.

Olanrewaju, Timothy, 2014, 'Suicide bomber opens up', *The Sun*, 5 May, http://sunnewsonline.com, accessed on 6 May 2014.

Olokor, Friday, John Alechenu, Sunday Aborisade, Olalekan Adetayo and David Attah, 2013, 'Boko Haram bent on Islamising Nigeria – CAN', *Punch*, 12 April, www.punchng.com, accessed on 12 April 2013.

Omipidan, Ismail, 2009, 'Boko Haram: How Yusuf imported arms into the country', *The Sun*, 10 October, http://sunnewsonline.com/new, accessed on 10 October 2009.

Omonobi, Kingsley, 2014 'Boko Haram: Jonathan declares full-scale war, deploys warplanes', *Vanguard*, 6 September, www.vanguardngr.com, accessed on 6 September 2014.

Onafuye, Abiodun, 2014, 'Jonathan can't end Boko Haram – Pastor Oritsejafor', *PMNews*, 24 July, www.pmnewsnigeria.com, accessed on 24 July 2014.

Onoyume, Jimitota, 2014, 'Chibok kidnap a scam, says Asari Dokubo', *Vanguard*, 19 May,www.vanguardngr.com, accessed on 19 May 2014.

Onuba, Ifeanyi and Ade Adesomoju, 2013, 'Unemployment, poverty responsible for terrorism in North – Sanusi', *Punch*, 16 January, www.punchng.com, accessed on 16 January 2013.

Onuoha, Freedom, 2014, 'Boko Haram and the Evolving Salafi Jihadist Threat in Nigeria', in Marc-Antoine Pérouse de Montclos (ed.), *Boko Haram: Islamism, Politics, Security and the State in Nigeria*, West African Politics and Society Series, Vol. 2, Leiden and Ibadan: African Studies Centre and Institut Français de Recherche en Afrique.

Pérouse de Montclos, Marc-Antoine, 2014a, 'Boko Haram and Politics: From Insurgency to Terrorism', in Marc-Antoine Pérouse de Montclos (ed.), *Boko Haram: Islamism, Politics, Security and the State in Nigeria*, West African Politics and Society Series, Vol. 2, Leiden and Ibadan: African Studies Centre and Institut Français de Recherche en Afrique.

Pérouse de Montclos, Marc-Antoine, 2014b, 'Introduction and Overview', in Marc-Antoine Pérouse de Montclos (ed.), *Boko Haram: Islamism, Politics, Security and the State in Nigeria*, West African Politics and Society Series, Vol. 2, Leiden and Ibadan: African Studies Centre and Institut Français de Recherche en Afrique.

PewResearch Global Attitudes Project, 2014, 'Concerns about Islamic Extremism on the Rise in Middle East: Negative Opinions of al Qaeda, Hamas and Hezbollah Widespread', www.pewglobal.org/2014/07/01/concerns-about-islamic-extremism-on-the-rise-in-middle-east, accessed on 1 July 2014.

Pham, J. Peter, 2012, 'Boko Haram's Evolving Threat', *Africa Security Brief* 20, Africa Center for Strategic Studies, April, http://africacenter.org/wp-content/uploads/2012/04/AfricaBriefFinal_20.pdf, accessed on 30 April 2012.

Pindiga, Habeeb I., 2013, 'Boko Haram training camps found in Mali – 'Over 200 Nigerians trained for 10 months in Timbuktu', *Daily Trust*, 6 February, http://dailytrust.com.ng, accessed on 6 February 2013.

PMNews, 'Cameroon battles Boko Haram in remote border city', *PMNews*, 24 June, www.pmnewsnigeria.com, accessed on 24 June 2014.

Premium Times, 2014, 'Editorial: Mr. President, sack Reno Omokri now!' *Premium Times*, 28 February, www.premiumtimesng.com, accessed on 28 February 2014.

Punch, 2010, 'Boko Haram posters flood Borno', *Punch*, 23 October, www.punchng.com, accessed on 23 October 2010.

Punch, 2014a 'Allah's enemies should be maimed, killed – Ogwuche, Nyanya bomb mastermind', *Punch*, 17 May, www.punchng.com, accessed on 17 May 2014.

Punch, 2014b, 'Boko Haram claims responsibility for Lagos blast', *Punch*, 13 July, www.punchng.com, accessed 13 July 2014.

Reinert, Manuel and Lou Garçon, 2014, 'Boko Haram: A chronology', in Marc-Antoine Pérouse de Montclos (ed.), *Boko Haram: Islamism, Politics, Security and the State in Nigeria*, West African Politics and Society Series, Vol. 2, Leiden and Ibadan: African Studies Centre and Institut Français de Recherche en Afrique.

Rheault, Magali and Bob Tortora, 2012, 'Northern Nigerians' views not in line with Boko Haram's', Gallup World, 20 February, www.gallup.com/poll/152780/northern-nigerians-views-not-line-boko-haram.aspx, accessed 12 September 2012.

Sahara Reporters, 2014a, 'Army general opens up, says there is shortage of funds to fight Boko Haram', *Sahara Reporters*, 22 May, http://saharareporters.com, accessed on 22 May 2014.

Sahara Reporters, 2014b, 'In new gruesome video, Boko Haram declares caliphate, shows scenes of fleeing soldiers, civilian massacres', 24 August, http://saharareporters.com, accessed on 24 August 2014.

Sahara Reporters, 2014c, 'Australian negotiator insists Modu Sheriff, Ihejirika sponsor Boko Haram, exonerates Buhari, El-Rufai', *Sahara Reporters*, http://saharareporters.com, accessed on 31 August 2014.

Sahara Reporters, 2014d, 'Australian Negotiator Insists Modu Sheriff, Ihejirika Sponsor Boko Haram, Exonerates Buhari, El-Rufai', *Sahara Reporters*, 31 August, http://saharareporters.com, accessed on 31 August 2014.

Salkida, Ahmad, 2011, 'The story of Nigeria's first suicide bomber', *BluePrint Magazine*, *Sahara Reporters*, 27 June, http://saharareporters.com, accessed on 27 June 2011.

Salkida, Ahmad, 2013a, 'Genesis and consequences of Boko Haram crisis', *Kano Online*, http://kanoonline.com, accessed on 30 April 2013.

Salkida, Ahmad, 2013b, 'How to end Boko Haram crisis', reprinted in *Nairaland Forum*, 17 May 2013, www.nairaland.com/1294203/time-pay-attention-ahmad-salkida , accessed on 3 October 2014.

Schmid, Alex P., 2013, 'Radicalisation, De-Radicalisation, Counter-Radicalisation: A Conceptual Discussion and Literature Review', *ICCT Research Paper*, March, The Hague: International Centre for Counter-Terrorism.

Shiklam, John, 2013, 'Boko Haram, military wing of northern politicians, says group', *ThisDay Live*, 20 May, www.thisdaylive.com, accessed on 20 May 2013.

Shilgba, Leonard Karshima, n.d., 'When Nigeria shall be no more: painting scenarios', *Gamji*, www.gamji.com/article9000/NEWS9040.htm, accessed 1 May 2014.

Somorin, Zacheaus, 2014, 'HRW: Boko Haram kills 2,053 civilians in 6 months' *ThisDay Live*, 15 July, www.thisdaylive.com, accessed on 15 July 2014.

Soriwei, Fidelis, 2014, 'B'Haram allegation against me baseless – Ihejirika', *Punch*, 6 September, www.punchng.com, accessed on 6 September 2014.

Soriwei, Fidelis, Okechukwu Nnodim, Leke Baiyewu and Umar Muhammed, 2014, 'Boko Haram seizes five Nigerian towns in five days', *Punch*, 6 September, www.punchng.com, accessed on 7 September 2014.

Soyinka, Wole, 2009, 'The precursors of *Boko Haram*', *Guardian*, www.ngrguardiannews.com, accessed on 24 September 2009

Sule, Kabiru, 2014, 'Niger arrests 14 Boko Haram suspects', *Daily Trust*, 8 May, http://dailytrust.com.ng, accessed on 8 May 2014.

Tarling, N., and T. Gomez, 2008, 'Introduction', in N. Tarling and T. Gomez (eds), *The State, Development and Identity in Multi-Ethnic Societies: Ethnicity, Equality and the Nation*, London: Routledge.

The Nation, 2014, 'Cameroun, Chad to battle Boko Haram', *The Nation*, 22 May, http://thenationonlineng.net, accessed on 22 May 2014.

The Sun, 2014, 'Boko Haram: day devil descended on Kaduna', *The Sun*, 27 July, http://sunnewsonline.com, accessed on 27 July 2014.

TheCable, 2014, 'Exclusive: Boko Haram "funded through CBN"', *TheCable*, 31 August, www.thecable.ng, accessed on 31 August 2014.

Ujah, Emma, Kingsley Omonobi, Johnbosco Agbakwuru and Joseph Erunke, 2014, 'Capture of Borno towns: reputation of Nigeria's military at stake – US', *Vanguard*, 5

September, www.vanguardngr.com, accessed on 5 September 2014.

Umar, Abdullahi and Edegbe Odemwingie, 2014, 'Boko Haram responsible for 18 attacks in two weeks – UN', *Leadership*, 9 July, http://leadership.ng, accessed on 9 July 2014.

Umar, M.S., 2006, *Islam and Colonialism: Intellectual Responses of Muslims of Northern Nigeria to British Colonial Rule*, Leiden: Brill.

Umoru, Henry, 2013, 'Poverty, misrule, not responsible for Boko Haram – PDP', *Vanguard*, 26 January, www.vanguardngr.com, accessed on 26 January 2013.

Umoru, Henry, 2014, 'We'll not accept govt of insurgency, blackmail – Southern peoples' assembly', *Vanguard*, 8 May, www.vanguardngr.com, accessed on 8 May 2014.

Utebor, Simon and Stephen Uka, 2014, 'B'Haram has killed 14 district heads – Shehu of Borno', *Punch*, 23 June, www.punchng.com, accessed on 23 June 2014.

Vanguard, 2012, 'Poverty fueling unrest in Kano, says report', *Vanguard*, 15 February, www.vanguardngr.com, accessed on 15 February 2012.

Vanguard, 2014a, 'Shekau made Boko Haram more ruthless', *Vanguard*, 8 May, www.vanguardngr.com, accessed on 8 May 2014.

Vanguard, 2014b 'Boko Haram members burn their university certificates – Shehu Sani', interview, *Vanguard*, 14 May, www.vanguardngr.com, accessed on 14 May 2014.

Vanguard, 2014c 'Boko Haram pays N500,000 to Niger recruits – Gang members', *Vanguard*, 24 April, www.vanguardngr.com, accessed 24 April 2014.

Ventures Africa, 2014, 'Manufacturing Now Biggest Driver of Nigeria's Growth', *Ventures Africa*, 20 July, www.ventures-africa.com/2014/07/manufacturing-now-biggest-driver-of-nigerias-growth, accessed on 24 July 2014.

Yusuf, S., 1999, 'Nigeria's Membership in the OIC: Implications of Print Media Coverage for Peace and National Unity', *Journal of Muslim Minority Affairs*, 19 (2), 235–47.

Zenn, Jacob, 2014a, 'Nigerian al-Qaedaism', Washington DC: The Hudson Institute, www.hudson.org/research/10172-nigerian-al-qaedaism-, accessed on 11 March 2014.

Zenn, Jacob, 2014b, 'Exposing and Defeating Boko Haram: Why the West Must Unite to Help Nigeria Defeat Terrorism', The Bow Group, www.bowgroup.org/sites/bowgroup.uat.pleasetest.co.uk/files/Jacob%20Zenn%20Bow%20Group%20Report%20for%2022.7.14.pdf, accessed on 22 July 2014.

7

Conclusion
Religious sectarianism, poor governance
& conflict

ABDUL RAUFU MUSTAPHA

Introduction

In this concluding chapter, I seek first to draw attention to the violent conflicts that have often characterized doctrinal disputes between Islamic groups in northern Nigeria over the past decades. This historical context sheds further light on the phenomenon of *Boko Haram*. Second, I argue that this long-run process of religious sectarianism has been made worse by poor governance processes.

Sufism has been central to Islam in Sub-Saharan Africa since the fifteenth century (Kane 2003, 59). Over the centuries, many reform movements emerged within this Islamic milieu to reinterpret the earlier messages. Such reformist impulses were important reflectors or initiators of processes of social change, such as the jihad of 1804. But even these reformist movements remained within the fold of Sufi doctrine. It was not until the 1970s that we begin to see a serious challenge to the hegemony of Sufism with the emergence of Salafist and Shi'a groups in northern Nigeria. The rise of these new groups has led to the fragmentation of sacred authority (Kane 2003, 103) and the emergence of new ways of being Muslim. Today, the Muslim *umma* in northern Nigeria can be said to be fragmented along doctrinal, ethnic, and class lines. Unfortunately, these divisions have also fuelled conflict, some violent, within the Muslim community. A central objective of this book has been to make sense of these conflicts.

Indeed, it might be said that since the 1940s, the northern Nigerian Muslim community has experienced four overlapping patterns of violent conflict. The first pattern, from the late 1940s, but especially from the 1970s, is driven by doctrinal differences within Islam. The second pattern, seen largely from the 1950s, had an ethnic and regional logic at its core, but with strong religious undertones. The third pattern, discernible from 1980, was characterized by millenarian uprisings against the state and society by sects composed of marginalized and disgruntled Muslims, while the fourth, starting in 2009, is characterized by the emergence of Islamist insurgencies by groups like *Boko Haram* (*Jama'atu Ahlul Sunna li Da'awati wal Jihad*) and *Ansaru* (*Jama'atu Ansarul Muslimina fi Biladis Sudan*) (Vanguards for the Aid of Muslims in Black Africa). Each of these patterns was also based on the politicization of religious difference, but some more so than others.

While the first pattern represented the politicization of religion in the context of the historical tensions between aristocrats and commoners within Hausa-Fulani society, the second pattern represented the politicization of religion in the context of ethnic and regional competition within the Nigerian federation. The last two patterns reflected doctrinal and class differences within northern Nigerian Muslim societies. However, in the popular press in Nigeria, there is often a tendency to merge all these four patterns of violence into one seamless alleged Muslim 'Jihadist conspiracy' against non-Muslims, when in fact they are better understood as distinct but related phenomena with roots within the Muslim communities. Furthermore, if we broaden our definition of disorder to include pacifist disruptions of the social order, we should take due note of non-violent disruptions caused by sects such as the *Darul Islam* who withdraw from society in the hope of realizing a puritanical utopia in their secluded enclaves. The periodic forcible disbanding of these utopian enclaves by the security forces shows how threatening they sometimes appear to the state.

Prior to the 1940s, the process of doctrinal fragmentation was largely confined to a narrow circle of religious and political elites. However, from the 1940s, with the arrival on the scene in northern Nigeria of the Tijaniyya sub-sect (Tijaniyya-Ibrahimiyya) and modern party politics, the doctrinal struggles took on a mass character drawing in wider sections of society (Loimeier 1997, 71). Since the 1940s, Islamic sects have tended to enhance their distinctiveness and cohesion by re-orienting their members into exclusive identities through the use of distinctive religious rituals, symbols, hierarchies, social practices, and even para-military uniforms and epaulettes. Each sect also tended to lay claim to being the right path. As might be expected, the zero-sum nature of the competing doctrinal claims often created the basis for violent conflict between the sects. In some instances, this violence is targeted at specified rival sects; in other cases, the violence is directed at the state or at segments of the wider society such as Christians or members of non-northern ethnicities. The prevalence and nature of religious violence in northern Nigeria today cannot be properly understood outside of this history.

Religious violence: From sufism to Boko Haram

From the 1940s in Sokoto Province, a violent confrontation developed between the two Sufi orders, the Qadiriyya and the Tijaniyya (Tijaniyya –Ibrahimiyya). The emergence of Tijaniyya was interpreted as a challenge to the authority of the Sultan as doctrinal differences (see Chapter 3) were overlain with the political antagonism between the traditional aristocracy represented in the ruling Northern People's Congress (NPC), on the one hand, and members of the commoner class of farmers, traders and artisans, many of whom were members of the populist opposition, the Northern Elements Progressive Union (NEPU), on the other.[1] In some major provinces of northern Nigeria such as Kano, Adamawa and Zaria, the Tijaniyya sect had important support within the local aristocracy. In another important Islamic centre, Ilorin, the Qadiriyya clerical estab-lishment was more concerned about protecting Islam against challenges posed by Christian, Western education (see Alabi forthcoming). Most of the violence between the Qadiriyya and the Tijaniyya was therefore concentrated in Sokoto. That the Sultan took offence at the Tijaniyya infiltration of his domain in the 1940s was hardly surprising, after some Tijaniyya members described him as 'a block on the way to the redemption of the Muslims'. A leading Tijani even penned an abusive poem, beseeching God 'to destroy the chief of Sokoto … to ruin his house, to overthrow his rule, to put him to shame'[2] (Loimeier 1997, 74). Such intemperate and intolerant vitriol has often characterized doctrinal disputes within the wider Muslim community.

In response, in 1949 the Sultan ordered the demolition of all Tijaniyya mosques in Sokoto territory. However, the running battle between the Qadiriyya and the Tijaniyya persisted right through the 1950s and 1960s. In 1955, 40 members of the Tijaniyya were arrested in Argungu and sentenced to a month in jail for 'obstructing the road' when the Emir of Argungu was passing by. A few months later, another 30 members of the sect were rounded up by the Native Authority police. In 1956 four persons were killed in anti-Tijaniyya riots in the Districts of Isa and Zurmi (Mohammed 2010, 8). In 1965, another riot broke out in Argungu, osten-sibly over the vaccination of cattle, but the pattern of attacks suggested a

---

[1] In 1906 the local Sokoto aristocracy and the colonial British forces faced a major challenge in the Satiru Revolt, led by Mahdists (see Mohammed 1983; Umar 2006). This revolt was ruthlessly crushed by the combined forces of the British and the Sultan. It has been suggested that the remnants of the Satiru community thereafter embraced Tijaniyya (personal communication, Prof. Mukhtar Bunza). In Sokoto therefore, conversion to Tijaniyya was seen as potentially dangerous.

[2] By referring to the Sultan as 'chief of Sokoto', the poet was challenging the religious creden-tials of the Sultan as the Amir al Mumineen (Head of all Muslims).

selective assault on Tijaniyya members. From 1952 to 1982, members of Qadiriyya and Tijaniyya in Kaura Namoda would not pray together in the Central mosque; it took the coming to town in 1980 of the Salafist *Izala* – *Jama'atu Izalatil Bid'a wa iqamat al-Sunnah*, (Society for the Eradication of Innovation and the Reinstatement of Tradition) to force them back together in a common congregation from 1982 (Loimeier 1997, 239).

From the early 1980s, this new conflict between both Sufi orders and the *Izala* Salafists was even more disruptive of the social order than the earlier one between the Qadiriyya and Tijaniyya. It also spread across the whole of northern Nigeria. The substance of *Izala*'s doctrinal challenge to the Sufi orders is covered in the contribution by Mustapha and Bunza in Chapter 3. What need emphasizing at this point are the *manner* in which *Izala* and the Sufi orders conducted this dispute, and the *consequences* for the social order. It was also significant that Shaikh Abubakar Gumi, the inspiration for the creation of *Izala*, was very concerned about the political fragmentation of the old Northern Region, caused by the death of Premier Ahmadu Bello and the balkanization of the region into smaller states, and the resulting erosion of the powers of Muslim politicians within the Nigerian federation.[3]

At the doctrinal level, *Izala* sought to destroy centuries-old systems of Sufi thought and networks of scholars. In their place, the group sought to erect new doctrines, ethics and world-view, with serious ramifications for individual behaviour, the family and society as a whole. This 'revolution' in the way society was understood to function was also characterized by the group's 'unwillingness to compromise' (Loimeier 1997, 259) and the use of aggressive and militant methods. In reply, the Sufi orders also deployed their considerable arsenal of intemperate and intolerant language. Both groups frequently resorted to violence against their opponents.

The *language* used on both sides of the *Izala*-Sufi dispute was itself an incitement to violence. According to the spiritual leader of *Izala*, Shaikh Abubakar Gumi, a Muslim who sins repeatedly and openly in words and deeds, and declares such actions to be consistent with the *Sunna* of the Prophet is in reality an unbeliever (Loimeier 1997, 189). By this logic, Shaikh Gumi was deploying the instrument of *takfir* against his Sufi opponents. Shaikh Gumi also argued that anyone who recited a major Tijani litany, the *salat al-fatih*, was a *kafir* whom it was legitimate for any Muslim to kill or get divorced from (Loimeier 1997, 209). Shaikh Gumi's disciples followed in the same intemperate spirit with one of them, Tahir Maigari, arguing that Tijaniyya was a completely different religion from

---

[3] For instance, in the run-up to the 1982/83 presidential elections, Shaikh Gumi appealed to all Muslims to ensure that their wives were registered to vote so that the voice of Muslims was not diminished. He added 'Siyasa tafi muhimmanci da salla' (Politics is more important than prayers), Loimeier (1997, 17).

Islam and its founder was an immoral character, while another disciple, Al-Kathini, argued that Tijani meetings frequently ended in orgies and incestuous practices (Kane 2003, 129–30).

The language used by members of the Sufi orders against their *Izala* opponents was not any less provocative. The leading Qadiriyya Shaikh, Nasiru Kabara, condemned Shaikh Gumi as a 'dirty and wicked he-goat' who had no knowledge of the language of the Sufis, and erroneously attacked the founder of Qadiriyya, Abd al-Qadir al-Jilani and, worse still, 'attacked the Prophet'. According to Shaikh Kabara, such a person can only be a *kafir*. He derogatorily referred to Shaikh Gumi as a 'Wahhabi' – implying he was a Saudi stooge – who would 'fight against God and seduce people to devilry'. On his part, a leading Tijaniyya scholar, Muhammad Sani Kafanga, dismissed Shaikh Gumi's views as *kalam jahil* – ignorant chatter (Loimeier 1997, 197, 199, 278). The language of doctrinal disputation is deliberately antagonistic, and calculated to destroy the opponent's social image. Masquelier (1996) writes of the use of idioms of the 'animalized other' to describe one's opponents.

This use of intolerant language on both sides created a climate which justified the use of violence against one's doctrinal opponents. Particularly between 1978 and 1980, northern Nigeria was swept by a wave of violent clashes between *Izala* and Sufi supporters. Rural areas were just as badly affected as urban areas. Violence tended to erupt around two key issues: the control of mosques and the right to preach peacefully in public. In places where they felt they had sufficient support, the *Izala* forcibly took control of the mosque, disrupting the rituals of the Sufis and forcing them out of the mosques. For example, in the Muslim neighbourhood of Badarawa in Kaduna metropolis, of the forty-odd mosques belonging to different Sufi groups in the 1970s, only seven are still controlled by the Sufis in 2014.[4]

In some instances, as in Jos, *Izala* attempts to seize control of the Central Mosque failed because of concerted Sufi opposition.[5] In others, as in Zuru in 1988, the clash over the mosque led to 3 deaths, 100 wounded, and 50 houses and many cars burnt (Loimeier 1997, 314). Where the *Izala* failed to take over an existing mosque, they constructed their own, thereby splitting the congregation along doctrinal lines.[6] With regard to public preaching, provocative preaching by *Izala* often led to violence, as in the riot that engulfed Kano in 1982, sparked by *Izala* preaching at the Bayero University mosque. In places where they were not welcomed to preach, the *Izala*

---

[4] Fieldwork census of Badarawa mosques in 2014.
[5] Personal communication, Prof. Muhammad Sani Umar.
[6] A Sufi opponent of the *Izala* pointed out to me that while Sufis tended to build their mosques within the midst of their Muslim congregations, the *Izala* tended to locate their mosques by the main roads and highways of towns and villages, and not necessarily within their congregation. This gave *Izala* mosques higher visibility, and frequently put them at odds with other road users, especially during Friday prayers.

frequently went about armed with knives. They even disrupted Sufi rituals, such as the Tijani *wazifa* (repeated recitation of litanies, often in praise of Allah, the Prophet and the Sufi saints), by seizing the *izar* (piece of white cloth placed at the centre of the *wazifa*). Many Tijani modified their ritual practices by ceasing to spread out the *izar* (Loimeier 1997, 178, 215).

However, the *Izala* were also victims of violence at the hands of Sufi members. In Kaura Namoda in the 1980s, Sufi members gathered in front of the homes of prominent *Izala* members and sang mocking songs. *Izala* proselytization cassettes were seized and destroyed, and teaching at their new Islamiyya school was disrupted (Loimeier 1997, 238). Throughout the 1980s, attempts by *Izala* members to preach openly in Kano City 'were ruthlessly suppressed' by their Sufi opponents. Indeed, the *Izala* members were forced out of the City and relocated to more receptive 'foreigner' neighbourhoods of Fagge and Brigade. Similarly, all efforts by the *Izala* to build a mosque in Kano City before 1991 failed, because their opponents forcibly pulled down the structures before completion (Kane, 2003, 88, 90). The Sufi members also formed new associations to counter the *Izala*, the two most prominent ones being *Fityan al-Islam* and *Jundullahi*. The latter was particularly notorious because of its violent aggressiveness towards *Izala* members, and its open declaration of 'total war' against them (Loimeier 1997, 281). Following the *Maitatsine* millenarian riots in Kano in 1980, many Sufi members seized advantage of the mayhem to lynch *Izala* sympathizers who had nothing to do with *Maitatsine*. In the melee, the Imam of the *Izala* mosque in Fagge was seized by Sufi thugs: 'To save his life, he publicly rejected the reformist ideology and provided the thugs with a list of all committed *Izala* members' (Kane 2003, 88–9). These *Izala* members had to flee their homes to save their lives. Finally, in September 1984, an attempt was made to assassinate the *Izala* leader, Shaikh Gumi, during a trip to Kano.

Though *Izala* set out with a doctrine to abolish *bid'a* (bad innovations) and unite the Muslim *umma*, their activities led to the opposite effect of polarizing the community to an unprecedented level. Mosque congregations were split in two, numerous marriages were dissolved, and sons disowned their parents and vice versa. Both *Izala* and the Sufis considered the other as non-Muslims; many even considered it a virtuous act to harm members of the opposing group. These sectarian clashes affected all spheres of the community's life, from the mosque, to the market, the family and even politics.[7] They also set the tone for subsequent high levels of sectarian intolerance.

[7] In the non-party Local Government elections of 12 December 1987, while Shaikh Gumi advised Muslims to 'vote only for a good Muslim [meaning *Izala* member] not for a Christian', Shaikh Dahiru Bauchi of the Tijaniyya countered by arguing that 'if in one place there are three candidates, one Muslim, one Christian and one *Izala* [by implication he did not regard *Izala* as Muslims], then one can make one's choice among all three of them but one should not vote for the candidate of the *Izala* [by implication, Christians are to be preferred over the *Izala*]' (Loimeier 1997, 306).

In late 1980, the situation in northern Nigeria was further convulsed by the violent activities of the *Maitatsine* millenarian sect (see Mustapha and Bunza in this volume for the sect's doctrines). This sect set itself at war against the rest of the *umma* and the state, and ignited violent conflict in Kano in December 1980, leading to over 4,000 deaths (Clarke & Linden 1984, 119). Though the sect's leader was subsequently killed and its members dispersed, the sect mutated and re-emerged over the years in other northern cities like Maiduguri, Kaduna, Gombe, Funtua and Yola and its sporadic violence lasted from 1980 to 1993 (Loimeier 1997, 220). This sect represented the revolt of the poor and the ethnic outsiders against modernity and Islamic intellectualism which left them religiously and materially excluded (Hiskett 1980, 220). Thousands of lives were lost over the decade of millenarian violence that the group unleashed across northern Nigeria.

If the *Izala*-Sufi violence characterized the 1970s, and the *Maitatsine* riots characterized the 1980s, the 1990s were marked by the frustrations of radical Muslim youth, many of them current or former members of the Muslim Students Society from the institutions of higher education that had proliferated in northern Nigeria from the 1970s. As Loimeier (1997, 300, 302) noted, the emergence of economic crisis from the early 1980s, coupled with the political authoritarianism of successive military regimes created 'a sufficient reason to create revolutionaries, and Islam has never ceased to provide the ideological basis'. The political vacuum, created by corrupt and authoritarian politics that failed to respond to popular needs, created a fertile ground for Islamic movements. Many of these Muslim radicals demanded a state based on Islamist precepts. As pointed out in Mustapha and Bunza (Chapter 3), one of such student revolutionaries was Shaikh Ibrahim El-Zakzaky, the founder and leader of the Shi'a sect in northern Nigeria. In the 1990s, the violence of the Shi'a was directed, not at other Muslims as in the case of the *Izala* and the Sufi, or at the wider society as in the case of *Maitatsine*'s rabble, but specifically against the Nigerian state, which the group saw as illegitimate and a tool of American imperialism. Some Christians accused of 'blasphemy' were also attacked by the sect, though Christians as a group were not necessarily defined as 'targets'.

In March and April 1991, riots broke out in Katsina, instigated by an Islamic group led by one Mallam Yakubu Yahaya, a protégé of Shaikh El-Zakzaky. The group was allegedly protesting the appearance of a cartoon in a national newspaper, the *Daily Times*, which they regarded as blasphemous in its depiction of the Prophet. Even after the group had seized and burnt all the copies of the offending publication, the rioting continued. Attempts by the state security forces to restrain the group soon led to attacks on government institutions. When the Military Governor of the state, Col. John Madaki, threatened to summarily execute Mallam Yakubu Yahaya for disturbing public peace, the latter retorted that he was ready for martyrdom. The intransigence of Yakubu Yahaya was supported by Shaikh El-Zakzaky, who publicly called for the assassination of Col. Madaki for tolerating 'blasphemy against the Prophet' (Loimeier 1997, 300–302). In this manner, religious extremism and state high-handedness fed off each other.

The Shi'a were also alleged to be involved in the beheading of the Igbo Christian, Gideon Akaluka in Kano in1994, allegedly for desecrating the Qur'an. Similarly, in 1996, the Shi'a in Kafanchan kidnapped a Christian preacher they accused of blasphemy, setting off retaliatory attacks on Muslims by Christians (Mu'azzam & Ibrahim 2000). Shaikh El-Zakzaky was frequently imprisoned by the state. Though the vitriol of the group against the Nigerian state and America has persisted, in recent times Nigerian Shi'ites have not dabbled in any violent acts[8], and have maintained cordial relations with other religious groups, including Christians.

Since the 1980s, religious violence in northern Nigeria has also tended to overlap with ethno-regional conflict. Despite the Islamization campaigns of Regional Premier Sir Ahmadu Bello between 1964 and 1966, relations between Muslims and Christians, and between the ethnic Hausa-Fulani on the one hand, and other ethnic nationalities like the Igbo, Yoruba and northern Christian ethnic minorities, on the other, did not deteriorate to levels of violent conflict. The only exceptions were in 1953, during an acute crisis in the constitutional negotiations leading to decolonization; and in 1966–67, in the period of the two contentious 1966 coups and the lead-up to the civil war in 1967. Indeed, Clarke and Linden (1984, 128–9) argue that the period between 1962 and 1974 was 'one of relatively intense dialogue between Christians and Muslims'. The Nigerian Civil War between 1967 and 1970 changed this scenario of peaceful dialogue into one of religious confrontation, given some narratives on the war as being between a Christian Biafra and a Muslim-dominated Nigeria. Despite this setback, a Muslim-Christian Dialogue took place in Ibadan in 1974 (the first Dialogue took place in Kano in 1962). However, it was the Muslim demand for a Federal Sharia Court of Appeal during the constitutional negotiations of 1976–78, thought by some to be motivated as much by elite political expediency as by religious fervour, that led to the breakdown in Muslim-Christian relations. Dialogue was replaced by 'a growing rivalry and competitiveness, and little practical joint endeavour'

[8] On Friday 25 July 2014, the sect organized its annual Al-Quds procession in Zaria. A conflict arose over the right of way between the procession and a military convoy. This allegedly led to the shooting and killing of 35 members of the sect by soldiers. The dead included three sons of Shaikh El-Zakzaky, two of whom were allegedly arrested alive but subsequently killed in detention. While the army claimed that it was first shot at, there is no report of any casualty amongst the soldiers or the seizing of any weapons from the sect (see: Tukur 2014a; Premium Times 2014a).

(Clarke & Linden 1984, 137). This climate of mutual suspicion and antagonism deteriorated even further with the crisis over Nigeria's membership of the Organization of Islamic Countries (OIC) in 1986 (Yusuf 1999) and the Kafanchan Muslim-Christian riots in 1987 (Ibrahim 1989).

Since the 1980s, religious revivalism by both Muslims and Christians, growing competition between the two, shrinking state resources, growing poverty and inequality, and increased international influences have all contributed to the salience and increased frequency of ethno-religious violence (Best & Rakodi 2011, 1). As Hashim and Walker point out in Chapter 5, between 1982 and 2011 ten such ethno-religious riots took place in Kano and other northern Nigerian cities, involving considerable loss of lives and properties. In the process, the dynamic of a hitherto Muslim versus Muslim sectarian violence from the 1940s began to take on the additional guise of Muslim versus Christian, and Hausa-Fulani versus southern ethnicities violence.[9] According to a former Director General, Military Intelligence, Brigadier-General Ibrahim Alhaji Sabo (rtd), 'when intra-religious squabbles took inter-religious dimensions and later ethno-religious dimensions, it complicates the insecurity in the north' (Salihi 2013). With the eliding of religious and ethnic identities, the mood of religious intolerance and the occasional use of violent methods which had characterized doctrinal disputes within the Muslim communities began to be displayed at the wider national level. In this sense, the logic of intra-Muslim disputes began to shape Muslim-Christian relations as the *inter*-religious violence between Muslims and Christians became more pronounced in the face of the political instrumentalization of religion by both sides.

In 1982, when the old Anglican church built in the Fagge neighbourhood of Kano in the 1930s was to be renovated, Muslim students rioted and destroyed the church on the grounds that it was standing next to a mosque built in the 1960s. In 1991, riots also took place against the visit to Kano of the German evangelist, Reinhard Bonnke. The rioters claimed that since government had earlier allegedly prevented the South African Muslim preacher, Ahmed Deedat, from coming to Nigeria to preach, there were no grounds for allowing a Christian preacher to undertake a similar mission. Between 1994 and 1996, three episodes of ethno-religious violence occurred in Kano, culminating in 1999 in attacks on Yoruba Muslims by *'yan daba* as 'retribution' for the Yoruba attacks on Muslim Hausa in Sagamu, a town in the south-western Ogun State (Casey 2008, 84). As Hashim and Walker show in this volume, since then, Yoruba Muslims in Kano have been victims of periodic violence at the hands of their co-religionists, the indigenous Hausa-Fulani Muslims.

---

[9] This is the subject of the companion volume to this one: Mustapha & Ehrhardt (eds), forthcoming 2015, *Creed & Grievance: Muslims, Christians & Society in Northern Nigeria*, James Currey.

It is instructive, however, that the attacks are attributed to *'yan daba*, described by a leading northern newspaper as a 'reserve army of unemployed youths ... that can metamorphose into a tribal army' (Casey 2008, 84). Casey argues that, as a result of economic hardship caused by structural adjustment programmes from the 1980s, new sectors of Nigerian society were falling into poverty (2008, 75). She suggests that the ranks of the *'yan daba*, gangs of urban unemployed youth living on the margins of social respectability and even the law, expanded exponentially from about 14 per Kano City ward in 1991 to between 50 and 200 per ward in 2000. She also notes that these youth gangs were increasingly imbued with 'cynicism and hostility' towards authority figures. The combination of religion and the *'yan daba* in the explanation for communal violence suggests that economic hardship was overlapping with religious intolerance and political instrumentalization to influence the pattern of communal violence. Identities rooted in religion were increasingly overlaid with identities rooted in place of origin, at the same time as violent crime, rooted in poverty and economic deprivation merged with communal violence, rooted in religion and politics (Best & Rakodi 2011, 62).

From 1998, the ethno-religious crisis in Jos and Plateau State raged intermittently, as have the more recent conflicts in southern Kaduna State. The latest rioting in Jos was in 2008, while the killings in southern Kaduna State are ongoing in 2014. In 2000 another wave of ethno-religious riots took place across northern Nigeria in the wake of the declaration of 'full Sharia' in 12 northern states while, in 2004, the killing of Muslims in Yelwan Shendam in southern Plateau State sparked off retaliatory rioting in other northern cities. In 2002 and 2006, protests over the Miss World beauty contest and the Danish cartoons, respectively, also led to ethno-religious rioting. Finally, the Presidential election of 2011 was greeted with rioting along ethno-religious lines in many northern cities. As Best and Rakodi (2011, 6) note, 'the frequency with which violence occurs has increased ... and ... it is increasingly likely to take the form of clashes between Christians and Muslims'.

Since the 1940s, the sectarian dynamic within the Muslim communities has interacted with wider social processes to generate a measure of social disorder. This process was driven by party politics mixing up with the Qadiriyya-Tijaniyya dispute from the 1940s, the doctrinal intolerance of *Izala* and its efforts to consolidate a Muslim hold on the state from the 1970s, the politicization of Muslim-Christian relations by both sides from the 1980s, and the underlying frustration and desperation of the poor and marginalized, faced with economic crises, structural adjustment policies and the lack of an effective political platform for articulating their concerns, except through increasingly intolerant forms of Islamic expression from the 1980s. This was the wider historical context for the emergence of *Boko Haram*.

Poor governance & Boko Haram

The lack of an effective political platform for articulating the grievances of ordinary citizens points to a wider failure of governance within Nigeria. The state has found it difficult to regulate dysfunctional aspects of religious life – from the promotion of hate speech to opportunistic charlatanism – because of weak capacity and the penetration of state institutions by religious forces. On the other hand, important groups within the religious community find it expedient to seek influence and allies within the political sphere. This mutual penetration of politics and religion amplifies and reinforces centrifugal ethno-regional forces in their competition over the state and contributes to the general weakening of the regulatory capacity of the state. This historical weakness has deteriorated further since the *Boko Haram* challenge from 2009.

Regarding *Boko Haram* violence, the security response from the state has been flabby, despite the declaration of a state of emergency in the north-east since 2013 and the heavy presence of the military. This has led to the occupation of swathes of Nigerian territory and the declaration of a so-called Caliphate in which the sect 'cut-off fingers, flog offenders and marry off spinsters' (Olanrewaju & Molomo 2014). This failure to effectively defend the territory of the country has drawn the ire of apprehensive citizens. In a nation-wide poll by the Pew Foundation in 2014, 72 per cent of the Nigerian public expressed concern about Islamic extremism; both Muslims (76 per cent) and Christians (69 per cent) expressed high levels of concern (PewResearch 2014). Similarly, given the lackadaisical way the abduction of the 200 girls from the Chibok school in April 2014 was handled, international actors have also begun to question the abilities of the Nigerian Government to handle the challenges posed by *Boko Haram*. According to Hillary Clinton, the 'government of Nigeria has been … somewhat derelict in its responsibility for protecting boys and girls, men and women' (Falayi 2014a). That poor governance of the security challenge has eroded the confidence of Nigerians in important institutions of the state is shown in Figure 7.1, based on nation-wide polling by Gallup. While 78 per cent expressed confidence in the military in 2011, this figure has gone down to 57 per cent by 2014. Over the same period, confidence in the leadership of the country has gone down from 65 per cent to 27 per cent, while the same figures for the local police are 49 per cent to 33 per cent (Loschky 2014).

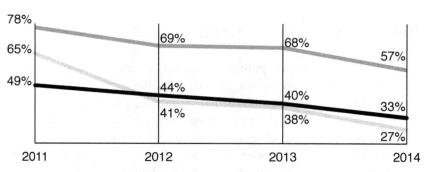

In the city or area where you live, do you have confidence in the local police force, or not?
In Nigeria, do you have confidence in each of the following, or not? How about the military?
Do you approve or disapprove of the job performance of the leadership of the country?

Figure 7.1 Leadership approval and confidence in security
services decline among Nigerians, 9 July 2014
(copyright © 2014 Gallup, Inc. All rights reserved. The content is used with permission;
however, Gallup retains all rights of republication)

Reversing these negative trends in public confidence in major national institutions is central to successfully dealing with *Boko Haram*. Three key areas need serious attention: (1) the inadequate military-political management of the insurgency; (2) a need for a more purposive approach to poverty and livelihood issues in the north; and (3) – something that is not receiving sufficient attention in the public discourse – the need for a counter-doctrine from within the Muslim communities.

INADEQUATE MILITARY-POLITICAL RESPONSE

The rapid expansion of the territory seized by *Boko Haram* was only stopped in mid-September 2014 with the repeated defeat of *Boko Haram* fighters in five battles for control of Konduga, a strategic town in the sect's drive to capture Maiduguri, the state capital (Soriwei & Adesomoju 2014). Though Konduga is indicative of a new resolve to fight within the armed forces, the military has so far failed to expel the insurgents from the vast territories they have occupied in three states. The governance challenges facing the military are many, including corruption, cowardice, indiscipline and the lack of coordination within different wings of the armed forces.

Between 2010 and 2014, a total of US $14 billion (GBP £8.7 billion, N2.27 trillion) was allocated for defence, security and the police in the Nigerian budget (Tukur 2014a). However, it is widely believed that corruption in the security sector is leading to massive leakages of these resources. For example, testifying before the US House Foreign Affairs Committee, the United States Under Secretary of State for Civilian Security, Democracy and Human Rights, Sarah Sewall, expressed the view that despite Nigeria's $5.8 billion (£3.6 billion) security budget for 2014, 'corruption prevents supplies as basic as bullets and transport vehicles from reaching the front lines of the struggle against Boko Haram' (Ameh & Oladimeji 2014). Even Nigerian Army Generals have openly admitted that they have problems getting funding approvals for military operations (*Sahara Reporters* 2014). Despite four years of fighting *Boko Haram*, it was only in 2014 that the training of Special Forces started in earnest (Agande 2014). The chronic situation of poor equipment and low morale has led to a widespread insubordination and near-revolt within the army.

The Chief of Army Staff, Lt-Gen. Kenneth Minimah confirmed that 'acts of cowardice, indiscipline and desertion from duty within the rank and file of the Nigerian military constitutes the greatest danger in the ongoing fight against terrorism and insurgency in the country' (Iroegbu 2014). In particular, he drew attention to the mutinies in the 7th Division which was specifically established to confront *Boko Haram*. Some officers and men from the Division were arraigned before a court martial for 'negligence of duty, cowardice, failure to perform military duty and leakage of information to the enemy' (Soriwei 2014). On 16 September 2014, a court martial in Abuja sentenced 12 soldiers of the 7th Division to death by firing squad for mutiny. It also convicted the soldiers of criminal conspiracy and attempt to commit murder, for which they were sentenced to life imprisonment. Another 13 soldiers are to be court marshalled for cowardice for failing 'to advance when an order was given to them to do so' (Soriwei & Idowu 2014).

So bad is the situation within the military that a senior American official, US Air Force Chief of staff, Gen. Mark Welsh III, testifying before the US Senate Foreign Relations Committee, said: 'We're now looking at a military force that is, quite frankly, becoming afraid to even engage' (Falayi 2014b). At the same hearing, another senior American official, the Specialist at African Affairs Congressional Research Service, Lauren Blanchard, argued that 'gross violations [of human rights] committed by the Nigerian forces, the Nigerian government's resistance to adopting a more comprehensive approach to Boko Haram, and the continued lack of political will' were making it difficult for the US to adequately assist Nigeria in tackling the menace of *Boko Haram*. She added that Nigerian troops were 'slow to adapt with new strategies, new doctrines and new tactics' (Akinloye 2014).

In the meantime, Nigeria's various intelligence units continue to operate in silos, refusing to share information that could advance the counter-insurgency drive. For example, when Aminu Ogwuche, the alleged mastermind of the 14 April 2014 bomb blast in Nyanya, Abuja, was brought before the courts for trial in September 2014, there was an unseemly public squabble between the police and the Department of State Services over which institution had the right to prosecute him. While the two agencies fought each other, the presiding judge noted that the 'necessary documents that should accompany the charges ... were not before the court' (Ughegbe 2014).

As part of its wider strategy of dealing with the insurgency, the army has declared that it is considering the 'Sri Lankan method', a move condemned by Human Rights Watch as capable of leading to human rights abuses on a grand scale, as happened in Sri Lanka, where 40,000 Tamil non-combatants were allegedly massacred by government troops in the dying days of the Tamil Tigers insurgency (Stroehlein 2014). This is a serious concern, given the repeated accusations of human rights abuses by all the sides in the conflict in the north-east (Amnesty International 2012a, 2014; Human Rights Watch 2012). In April 2014, the independent official body responsible for human rights monitoring in Nigeria, the Nigerian Human Rights Commission (NHRC), indicted the Nigerian Army, the Directorate of State Security and the Attorney General of the Federation of culpability in the unlawful killing of eight youngsters in September 2013 in the Apo District of Abuja for allegedly being armed members of *Boko Haram* with 'no credible evidence' to back up the allegations (Ibeh & Ugonna 2014). In mid-2014 Amnesty International released a video which further reinforced these accusations:

> The footage obtained by Amnesty International includes a gruesome incident that took place near Maiduguri, the Borno state capital, on 14 March 2014. It shows what appear to be members of the Nigerian military and CJTF [Civilian Joint Task Force pro-government militia] using a blade to slit the throats of a series of detainees, before dumping them into an open mass grave. The video shows 16 young men and boys seated in a line. One by one, they are called forward and told to lie down in front of the pit. Five of them are killed in this way; the fate of the remaining detainees is not shown on video, but eyewitness accounts confirmed that nine of them had their throats cut while the others were shot to death. (Amnesty International 2014b)

These serious lapses in the governance systems within the military will need to be seriously addressed if *Boko Haram* is to be successfully dismantled. Since the battles for Konduga in September 2014, the military seems to have initiated a process of reform and re-armament. How far this seeming rejuvenation of the military will go remains to be seen.

The poor governance of the military institution is matched by an equally poor governance of the political sphere. Instead of providing a leadership to unite all Nigerians against the insurgency, most political leaders – from the President downwards – are more interested in scoring cheap political points by pinning the blame for the insurgency on their opponents. The resulting lack of purposeful political will and leadership in the conflict with *Boko Haram* has been noted by many. In an oblique criticism of his political masters, the Chief of Defence Staff, Air Marshal Alex Badeh, whilst testifying before a Senate committee in September 2014, noted that 'right now, the element of national power we are using is the military. Other elements of national power are not being engaged sufficiently' (Ujah et al. 2014). As the prevalence of conspiracy theories on *Boko Haram* suggests (see Chapter 6), the orientation of many politicians towards the insurgency is coloured by the extant cleavages in Nigerian ethno-regional politics.[10]

Beyond this wider political elite failure, however, there have also been political failures that can be put squarely at the foot of the Goodluck Jonathan administration which has failed to develop a clear and consistent strategy for dealing with the insurgency. As one American observer, former United States Assistant Secretary of State, Mr James Rubin put it during a visit to Nigeria, either 'the government or another one makes a decision to confront the situation. One day it is amnesty, another day it is military operation. Then you talk about assistance from outside' (Onoyume & Eboh 2014). Having a President living in virtual denial of what is happening in the north-east, and seeing the hands of his political opponents behind every incident, has not made for coherent policy-making. The wide vacillations in government policy create a climate of confusion and lack of credibility, thus failing to mobilize the citizenry behind the Government: one day the Government wants to dialogue with *Boko Haram* and the next it declares its intention to militarily crush it; on some occasions *Boko Haram* is declared a domestic Nigerian problem, while on other occasions, it is defined as part of a global terrorist threat[11]; sometimes amnesty is promised to the insurgents by one government official, only for the offer to be denied by another official.

---

[10] A cleavage 'denotes an institutionalized political conflict that is anchored in a society's structure' (Erdmann 2004, 70).

[11] In May 2014, the Chief of Defence Staff, Air Chief Marshal Alex Badeh announced that 'the nation is at war with the international terror organisation, Al-Qaeda, ... and not Boko Haram' (Ogunwale 2014). When President Jonathan referred to *Boko Haram* as the 'al Qaeda of West Africa' in the same month at an international conference in Paris, the US Under Secretary of State for Political Affairs, Wendy Sherman retorted that the US did not see *Boko Haram* as an al-Qaeda affiliate: 'Boko Haram is its own terrorist group ... In this day and age, there is probably no terror group that does not have some links somehow, even if tenuous, to some other organisation. But for the most part, we treat Boko Haram as its own terror organisation' (Famutimi 2014b).

According to the influential Borno Elders Forum, President Goodluck Jonathan lacks the political will to confront Boko Haram: 'We have reached a point ... where we have to accept that the government has failed in its responsibility of protecting us, not because it is not capable, but because it lacks the political will to do so' (Mudashir 2014). The group further asserted that 'the state of emergency declared in Borno, Yobe and Adamawa states has made no positive impact because the soldiers fighting insurgency are not well equipped and catered for' (Baiyewu 2014a). They note regretfully that 'the insurgency had increased under the emergency'. In a similar vein, former military and democratic president, Olusegun Obasanjo, questioned the reaction of President Goodluck Jonathan when over 200 Chibok girls were abducted from their school on 14 April 2014:

'The president did not believe that those girls were abducted for almost 18 days. If the president got the information within 12 hours of the act and he reacted immediately, I believe those girls would have been rescued within 24 hours, maximum 48 hours.' Mr. Obasanjo said that rather than spring into action after receiving briefings about the abduction, 'the president had doubts.' He said the president's initial action was to ask: 'Is this true, or is it a ploy by people who don't want me to be president again?' (*Premium Times* 2014b)

Instead of concentrating on the challenges of dealing with *Boko Haram*, many feel that President Jonathan is more engrossed with his campaign for re-election in 2015, using the Transformation Ambassadors of Nigeria (TAN) which 'obviously well-oiled from an abundance of unexplained resources' (Olorunfemi 2014), has been running a massive campaign across Nigeria since January 2014. Even when the President asked Nigerians to avoid public meetings because of Ebola Virus Disease (EVD), TAN was still allowed to hold a mass rally in Port Harcourt, where cases of EVD had been reported. Worse still, even 'technocratic' Ministers like Dr Ngozi Okonjo-Iweala attended the Port Harcourt rally. Instead of providing the necessary leadership, President Jonathan frequently implores Nigerians 'to pray for the security forces as they battle the insurgency' (Omonobi et al. 2014).

Faced with a government and an army that will not or cannot protect their property or lives, some Nigerians in the north-east are creating vigilante groups to do so themselves. In Maiduguri, the emergence of the youth vigilante, the 'Civilian JTF' provided the local intelligence needed by the military to weed out *Boko Haram* elements from the city. In the outlying villages, however, the role of the vigilante groups included providing their own physical defence in the face of repeated *Boko Haram* attacks. Three closely linked vigilante groups in the north-east are said to have taken root over the past year, with more than 11,000 members between them: 'At first, they were equipped with sticks, machetes and table legs. Now, they are scaling up, procuring locally made barrel-loaded shotguns cobbled together from car parts and scrap wood' (Baiyewu 2014b).

A MORE CONCERTED APPROACH TO POVERTY AND LIVELIHOODS ISSUES

After vacillating between various approaches to tackling the *Boko Haram* insurgency, the Goodluck Jonathan administration slowly came round to the necessity of a multi-pronged approach. After repeated prompting from the US which accused the administration of 'failing to address the "grievances among northern populations" which it listed as high unemployment and dearth of basic services' (Famutimi 2014a), the administration came round to the view that a development 'track' needs to be added to its military track in response to the insurgency. President Jonathan announced a three-point strategy focused on: (a) security through improved intelligence gathering and military capability; (b) seeking political solution through working with local governments and communities; and (c) an economic strategy through various empowerment and job creation programmes. All these strands are brought together under the Presidential Initiative in the North East (PINE) (Wakili 2014a). A Presidential Committee on the Reconstruction of North East has also been set up to promote emergency assistance stabilization projects covering education, health, infrastructure, agriculture (*Premium Times* 2014c). The Government also announced a N15.8 billion ($97.6 million, £60.35 million) National Emergency Relief Programme largely focused on the rehabilitation of the north-east. The programme seeks to involve the federal, state and local governments, the private sector and international partners, in the provision of relief to victims of the insurgency, repair of infrastructure and implementation of the Safe Schools Initiative adopted in the wake of the abduction of the Chibok girls (*Vanguard* 2014).

Laudable as these policy pronouncements seem, they have left many observers unconvinced about the Government's determination and seriousness in implementing them. Even the non-partisan *Guardian* newspaper, not given to attacking the administration, was forced to ask a number of searching questions regarding the Government's plans: has the plan been drawn up or just hastily announced? When? Who prepared it? What are its contents? Were there consultations and input from stakeholders? Is the plan predicated on the subsisting situation in the area, or in anticipation of the restoration of peace? (*Guardian* 2014). The paper concluded by calling on the Finance Minister, Dr Ngozi Okonjo-Iweala, who announced the Government's plans, to reassure the public that her statement was well considered and backed by facts, otherwise, she would be seen as a mere political jobber seeking to deceive … Let it not be that she is raising false hopes for the region; or that her statement was simply geared towards the 2015 general elections. (*Guardian* 2014)

While the Federal Government's special plans for the north-east remain fuzzy at best, there has been little positive change within the mainline budgetary process in the overall allocation to peasant agriculture, the mainstay of the economy of the north-east. Federal Government budgetary allocation to agriculture from 2007 to 2011 was an annual average of 3.5 per cent of the national budget, falling to 1.7 per cent, 1.3 per cent and 1.4 per cent in 2012, 2013 and 2014 respectively (Ayansina 2013; Iroegbu & Chimezie 2014). The agricultural policy has also been criticized as being too focused on the development of commercial agriculture, while ignoring peasant farmers who constitute the bulk of the farming population. Indeed, according to Oxfam, fewer than 2 per cent of Nigerian farmers have so far benefited from the Growth Enhancement Support Programme (GES) of the government, meant to support peasant farmers (Falaju 2014).

In the meantime, there have been some promises of investments from the state governments in the north-east, the World Bank and the private sector. The six states in the north-east have agreed to increase the proportion of their budgets devoted to agriculture from an annual average of 4 per cent to 10 per cent; from an average annual allocation of N24 billion to over N60 billion (Alkassim & Saleh 2014). On its part, the World Bank has approved a $495.3 million (£306.3 million) International Development Association credit to improve farmers' access to irrigation and drainage services in the north of Nigeria (Amaefule 2014). At the level of the private sector, much of the initiative has come from the Dangote Group.[12] According to the Group: 'We are investing in sugar production in the North-East, Adamawa in particular where there is Boko Haram. The only way to solve Boko Haram is to create jobs' (Wakili 2014b). The Group pledged to invest $2.3 billion (£1.4 billion) in sugar-cane and rice production in the northern parts of the country by 2017. It also announced that it would require about 250,000 hectares of land for sugar-cane production and 130,000 hectares for rice farming (*ThisDay* 2014). Alhaji Dangote also promised to look for 'the best way to help and mobilize our people to at least get a daily income' (*The Sun* 2014). He hoped to achieve this objective through

[12] The group is mainly owned and led by Alhaji Aliko Dangote, a business tycoon from Kano who is reported by Forbes magazine to be the richest African, and one of the richest men in the world.

helping peasant farmers gain access to credit in order to boost agricultural production.

The 'development track' of the Federal Government's response to the security challenge in the north-east remains a work-in-progress at best, or a half-thought-through political gimmick, depending on who you talk to in Nigeria. There is also little change in the operations of the core ministries to suggest that agricultural and infrastructural development would be accelerated in the north-east. Federal officials in Nigeria are yet to show the level of zeal and enthusiasm for agricultural and infrastructural development in the north-east which is discernible even amongst US officials (Okocha et al. 2014; Carson 2014). Some developmental investments might occur through the intervention of the private sector in agricultural transformation. But the promotion of commercial agriculture through the alienation of peasant and communal lands holds the risk of further fanning the disenchantment of some rural communities (see Mustapha 2011 for the example of Zimbabwean capitalist farmers in Kwara State). There are already indications that the communities in Numan in the Benue Valley in Adamawa State are beginning to resist the activities of the Dangote Group in the Savanna Sugar plantation recently taken over by the Group through the privatization of state assets.

NEED FOR A COUNTER-DOCTRINE

Ahmad Salkida has done more than most to monitor and report on the rise and progress of *Boko Haram*. One important observation he has made is that 'since this is a problem of doctrine then it must be tackled through a coherent, profound counter-doctrine' (Salkida 2013). Similarly, the influential Catholic Archbishop of Abuja, Cardinal John Onaiyekan has expressed the view that while it is commendable for Muslim leaders in Nigeria to condemn the doctrines and activities of *Boko Haram*, it is vital to go beyond mere condemnation and engage in 'an in-house dialogue within the Nigerian Muslim community'. He adds that 'such a dialogue would make it possible to courageously and sincerely deal with currents and movements that create the kind of religious climate and atmosphere in which Boko Haram and similar groups emerge and thrive' (Onaiyekan 2014).

While Nigerian Muslim leaders are increasingly overcoming their fear of being attacked and publicly condemning *Boko Haram*'s atrocities, the key task of addressing the bigotry, intolerance and incendiary language which has for long characterized doctrinal disputes within the Muslim *umma* has yet to be squarely addressed. The *takfiri* tendency through which some Muslims label others as non-Muslims on account of doctrinal and ritual differences runs counter to the spirit of a religion which, from the very start, has known and tolerated differences – including different legal codes and different prayer rituals. Al-Maghili's dictum that '[n]one of the people of the *qiblah* may be adjudged an unbeliever on account of sin' (Hodgkin 1976, 112) should be a guiding principle in this matter. It is also pertinent to draw attention to the continuing relevance of the 'Kufr Agreement' reached between warring Muslim sects at the height of the Sufi-Salafi conflicts in northern Nigeria in the late 1970s. According to that Agreement brokered by the government and with all Muslim groups, including 'neutral Muslims' in attendance, all the Muslim groups agreed to renounce any mutual accusations of *kufr* (*takfir*). The Agreement went on to assert that: 'Any Muslim who calls another Muslim an unbeliever is a *kafir* himself' (Loimeier, 1997, 282).

The refusal of some Muslims to pray behind somebody who is not of their sect, or even greet such a person, or attend their funeral is contrary to the traditions of *al-Salaf al-Ṣāliḥ* 'since many *ulama* accept differences and criticism' (Ben Amara 2011, 275). Tolerance of difference and conducting one's dissent in a way that respects the religious values of others remain to be established as guiding principles within the Muslim communities. Those Muslims who insist on forcing their views and ways on others are not only violating the basic constitutional guarantee of freedom of conscience and worship which secures the rights of all, more importantly, they are creating the conditions for *fitna* (secession, upheaval) which threatens the ability of most people to practise their faith in peace. This plea for *intra*-Muslim tolerance must necessarily be extended to *inter*-religious relations in a country wracked by religious intolerance from all sides.

Credibility and legitimacy are core ingredients of a counter-radical narrative (Schmid 2013) so it is vital that learned and knowledgeable actors within the Muslim communities speak up.[13] A step in this direction was taken in April 2012, when a high-level coalition of many concerned Muslim organizations in Nigeria met to deliberate on the topic of 'Muslims and Democracy'. Amongst its resolutions, the conference re-affirmed its commitment to 'the history of pluralistic, multicultural and tolerant Muslim societies' which have been part of the historical legacies of Islam. The conference also noted that guided by the values of justice, fairness and good governance, Muslims should continue to demand efficient and effective service delivery, social justice, improvement in the standard of living, as well as protection and advancement of people's rights and freedoms. Finally, the conference noted the 'need to engage construc-tively with members of other faiths to tackle common problems'. The conference committed itself to the pursuit of the ideals of the 'Madina Model State [in early Islam] that was religiously pluralistic and multi-ethnic'[14] (Bilkisu 2012). The ideological work needed to sustain the

---

[13] A good example of such a counter-narrative is the detailed rebuttal of the doctrines of the Islamic State by 124 Muslim leaders from across the world. See *Premium Times*, 2014d.

[14] On the pluralistic nature of the Madina state, see Al-Umari 1995 and Abdulsalam 2006.

vision of these Muslim organizations remains unrealized even within the *umma*. However, if anything positive can be said to have resulted from the long history of doctrinal intolerance culminating in the tragedy of *Boko Haram*, it is that many Muslims in northern Nigeria are now coming to the realization that this ideological work in support of the values of tolerance and mutual respect cannot start a moment too soon if the society is to survive and prosper.

Bibliography

Abdulsalam, M., 2006, 'The Tolerance of the Prophet towards Other Religions: Part 1 of 2 – To Each Their Own Religion', www.islamreligion.com/articles/207/viewall/#_ftn10613, accessed on 13 August 2014.

Agande, Ben, 2014, 'Terrorism: 400 Nigerian security personnel leave for Russia', *Vanguard*, 26 September, www.vanguardngr.com, accessed on 26 September 2014.

Akinloye, Bayo, 2014, 'Nigerian military uncooperative, slow to learn – US hearing', *Punch*, 13 July, www.punchng.com, accessed on 13 July 2014.

Alabi, S. A., forthcoming, 'One Encounter; Three Streams: Ulama Responses to Western Education in Colonial Ilorin', *Africa*.

Alkassim, Balarabe and Adamu Saleh, 2014, 'North-east govs to raise agric vote to 10%', *Daily Trust*, http://dailytrust.com.ng, accessed on 6 December 2013.

Al-Umari, Akram Diya, 1995, *Madinan Society at the Time of the Prophet*, Riyad: International Islamic Publishing House.

Amaefule Everest, 2014, 'World Bank okays $495.3m for northern farmers', *Punch*, 23 June, www.punchng.com, accessed on 23 June 2014.

Ameh, John and Ramon Oladimeji, 2014, 'Corruption stalls Nigeria's war against B'Haram – US', *Punch*, 23 May, www.punchng.com, accessed on 23 May, 2014. Amnesty International, 2012, 'Nigeria: Trapped in the Cycle of Violence', www.amnesty.org/en/library/asset/AFR44/043/2012/en/04ab8b67-8969-4c86-bdea-0f82059dff28/afr440432012en.pdf, accessed 15 December 2012.

Amnesty International, 2014a, 'Nigeria: More Than 1,500 Killed in Armed Conflict in North-Eastern Nigeria in Early 2014', www.amnesty.nl/sites/default/files/public/nigeria_more_than_1500_killed_in_armed_conflict.pdf, accessed on 4 April 2014.

Amnesty International, 2014b, 'Nigeria: gruesome footage implicates military in war crimes', www.amnesty.org/en/news/nigeria-gruesome-footage-implicates-military-war-crimes-2014-08-05, accessed on 5 August 2014.

Ayansina, Caleb, 2013, 'Nigeria investment in agriculture alarming – ActionAid', *Vanguard*, 13 December, www.vanguardngr.com, accessed on 13 December 2013.

Baiyewu, Leke, 2014a, 'Boko Haram: Borno elders decry soldiers' poor welfare', *Punch*, 25 May, www.punchng.com, accessed on 25 May 2014.

Baiyewu, Leke, 2014b, 'Vigilante groups buy arms to fight Boko Haram', *Punch*, 29 June, www.punchng.com, accessed on 29 June 2014.

Ben Amara, Ramzi, 2011, 'The Izala Movement in Nigeria: Its Split, Relationship to Sufis and Perception of Sharī'a Re-Implementation', D.Phil. dissertation, Bayreuth International Graduate School of African Studies, BIGSAS, Universitat Bayreuth, Germany.

Best, S.G. and Carole Rakodi, 2011, 'Violent Conflict and its Aftermath in Jos and Kano, Nigeria: What is the Role of Religion?' Working Paper 69, Religions and Development Research Programme, University of Birmingham, UK.

Bilkisu, Hajiya, 2012, 'Nigerian Muslims and Democracy II', *Daily Trust*, http://dailytrust.com.ng, accessed on 26 April 2012.

Carson, Johnnie, 2014, 'Nigeria: worsening security demands new strategy', *Premium Times*, 7 June, www.premiumtimesng.com, accessed on 7 June 2014.

Casey, C., 2008, '"Marginal Muslims": Politics and the Perceptual Bounds of Islamic Authenticity in Northern Nigeria', *Africa Today*, 54 (3), 67–92.

Clarke, Ian and Peter Linden, 1984, *Islam in Modern Nigeria: A Study of a Muslim Community in a Post-Independence State (1960–80)*, Mainz: Gruenewald.

Erdmann, G., 2004, 'Party Research: Western European Bias and the "African Labyrinth"', *Democratization*, 11, 3, 63–87.

Falaju, Joke, 2014, 'Oxfam scores Nigeria low on farm input distribution scheme', *Guardian*, 28 May, www.ngrguardiannews.com, accessed on 28 May 2014.

Falayi, Kunle, 2014a, 'Nigerian govt irresponsible in protecting youths – Hillary Clinton', *Punch*, 10 May, www.punchng.com, accessed on 10 May 2014.

Falayi, Kunle, 2014b, 'Nigerian soldiers reluctant to fight – US General', *Punch*, 17 May. www.punchng.com, accessed on 17 May 2014.

Famutimi, Temitayo, 2014a, 'FG not supporting northern govs' development efforts – US', *Punch*, 2 May, www.punchng.com, accessed on 2 May 2014.

Famutimi, Temitayo, 2014b, 'Boko Haram not al-Qaeda affiliate – US', *Punch*, 20 May, http://www.punchng.com, accessed on 20 May 2014.

Guardian Editorial, 2014, 'Special plan for the northeast', *Guardian*, 8 May, www.ngrguardiannews.com, accessed on 8 May 2014.

Hiskett, M., 1980, 'The "Community of Grace" and its opponents, the "Rejecters": A Debate about Theology and Mysticism in Muslim West Africa with Special Reference to its Hausa Expression', *African Language Studies*, 17, 99–140.

Hodgkin, T., 1976, 'The Radical Tradition in Muslim West Africa', in Little, D.P. (ed.), *Essays on Islamic Civilization: Presented to Niyazi Berkes*, Leiden: Brill.

Human Rights Watch, 2012, 'Spiraling Violence: Boko Haram Attacks and Security Force Abuses in Nigeria', www.hrw.org/sites/default/files/reports/nigeria1012web-wcover_0.pdf, accessed 20 November 2012.

Ibeh, Nnenna and Chinenye Ugonna, 2014, 'Apo 8: Nigerian Rights Commission indicts Army, SSS, for unlawful killing', *Guardian*, 7 April, www.ngrguardiannews.com, accessed on 7 April 2014.

Ibrahim, J., 1989, 'The Politics of Religion in Nigeria: The Parameters of the 1987 Crisis in Kaduna State', *Review of African Political Economy*, 16 (45–46), 65–83.

Iroegbu, Senator, 2014, Some Soldiers Run Away From Battlefield, Laments Chief of Army Staff, *ThisDay Live*, 18 July, www.thisdaylive.com, accessed on 18 July 2014.

Iroegbu, Senator & Grace Chimezie, 2014, 'ActionAid Faults 2014 Proposed Agricultural Budgetary Allocation', 21 February, *ThisDay Live*, www.thisdaylive.com, accessed on 21 February 2014.

Kane, Ousmane, 2003, *Muslim Modernity in Postcolonial Nigeria: A Study of the Society for the Removal of Innovation and Reinstatement of Tradition*, Leiden: Brill.

Loimeier, R, 1997, *Islamic Reform and Political Change in Northern Nigeria*, Evanston IL, Northwestern University Press.

Loschky, Jay, 2014, 'Nearly all Nigerians see Boko Haram as a major threat: Majority do not think the government is doing enough to fight terrorism', *Gallup World*, 9 July, www.gallup.com/poll/172241/nearly-nigerians-boko-haram-major-threat.aspx, accessed on 9 July 2014.

Masquelier, Adeline M., 1996, 'Identity, alterity and ambiguity in a Nigerien community: Competing definitions of "true" Islam', in: Richard Werbner and Terence Ranger (eds), *Postcolonial identities in Africa*, London: Zed Books.

Mohammed, Abdulkareem, 2010, *The Paradox of Boko Haram*, Kano: Moving Image.

Mohammed, A.S., 1983, 'A Social Interpretation of the Satiru Revolt of c. 1894–1906 in Sokoto Province', M.A. Thesis, Department of Sociology, Ahmadu Bello University, Zaria.

Mu'azzam, Ibrahim and Jibrin Ibrahim, 2000, 'Religious Identity in the Context of Structural Adjustment in Nigeria', in A. Jega (ed.), *Identity Transformation and Identity*

Politics Under Structural Adjustment in Nigeria, Uppsala: Nordiska Afrikainstitutet.

Mudashir, Ismail, 2014, 'Jonathan lacks political will to confront Boko Haram – Borno elders', *Daily Trust*, http://dailytrust.com.ng, accessed on 11 March 2014.

Mustapha, Abdul Raufu, 2011, 'Zimbabwean Farmers in Nigeria: Exceptional Farmers or Spectacular Support?' *African Affairs*, 110 (441), 535–61.

Ogunwale, Gbade, 2014, 'We are fighting Al-Qaeda, not Boko Haram, says CDS', *The Nation*, 29 May, http://thenationonlineng.net, accessed on 29 May 2014.

Okocha, Chuks, Chineme Okafor and Kasim Sumaina, 2014, 'Investors plan North's economic resurgence', *ThisDay Live*, 11 May, www.thisdaylive.com, accessed on 11 May 2014.

Olanrewaju, Timothy and David Molomo, 2014, 'B'Haram: 30 killed in camp shoot-out', *The Sun*, 26 September, http://sunnewsonline.com, accessed on 26 September 2014.

Olorunfemi, Simbo, 2014, 'What manner of democracy is this?' *The Nation*, 5 September, http://thenationonlineng.net, accessed on 7 September 2014.

Omonobi, Kingsley, Umar Yusuf, Caleb Ayansina, 2014, 'Boko Haram: Tension heightens in Adamawa', *Vanguard*, 8 September, www.vanguardngr.com, accessed on 8 September 2014.

Onaiyekan, John Cardinal, 2014, Sultan, Nigeria Muslims and Boko Haram, *Leadership*, 30 May, http://leadership.ng, accessed on 30 May 2014.

Onoyume, Jimitota & Michael Eboh, 2014, 'Take a stand against Boko Haram, Ex-US Asst Secretary of State tells FG', *Vanguard*, 2 July, www.vanguardngr.com, accessed on 2 July 2014.

PewResearch Global Attitudes Project, 2014, 'Concerns about Islamic Extremism on the Rise in Middle East: Negative Opinions of al Qaeda, Hamas and Hezbollah Widespread', www.pewglobal.org/2014/07/01/concerns-about-islamic-extremism-on-the-rise-in-middle-east, accessed on 1 July, 2014.

Premium Times, 2014a, 'Zaria Procession Killings: Army opens probe, but says soldiers were fired upon', *Premium Times*, 27 July, www.premiumtimesng.com, accessed on 27 July 2014.

Premium Times, 2014b, 'Jonathan lived in denial, acted slowly to #BringBackOurGirls – Obasanjo', *Premium Times*, 31 May, www.premiumtimesng.com, accessed on 31 May 2014.

Premium Times, 2014c, 'Boko Haram: Nigerian Government set to rebuild conflict-torn north east', *Premium Times*, 1 August, www.premiumtimesng.com, accessed on 1 August 2014.

Premium Times, 2014d, 'Refuting the ISIS misanthropic ideology, By 124 Islamic Scholars', *Premium Times*, 26 September, www.premiumtimesng.com, accessed on 26 September 2014.

Sahara Reporters, 2014, Army General opens up, says there is shortage of funds to fight Boko Haram, *Sahara Reporters*, http://saharareporters.com, accessed on 22 May 2014

Salihi, Abubakar, 2013, 'FG responsible for underdevelopment of the north – Buhari', *Leadership*, http://leadership.ng, accessed on 25 January 2013.

Salkida, Ahmad, 2013, How to end Boko Haram crisis reprinted in *Nairaland Forum*, 17 May 2014, www.nairaland.com/1294203/time-pay-attention-ahmad-salkida, accessed on 3 October 2014.

Schmid, Alex P., 2013, 'Radicalisation, De-Radicalisation, Counter-Radicalisation: A Conceptual Discussion and Literature Review', *ICCT Research Paper*, The Hague: International Centre for Counter-Terrorism.

Soriwei, Fidelis, 2014, 'Boko Haram: Army court-martials officers for cowardice, others', *Punch*, 7 June, www.punchng.com, accessed on 7 June 2014.

Soriwei, Fidelis and Ade Adesomoju, 2014, 'Military kills Abubakar Shekau "again"', *Punch*, 25 September, www.punchng.com, accessed on 25 September 2014.

Soriwei, Fidelis and Kayode Idowu, 2014, '13 soldiers to face trial for cowardice', *Punch*, 26 September, www.punchng.com, accessed on 26 September 2014.

Stroehlein, Andrew, 2014, 'Dispatches: 40,000 Reasons Why Sri Lanka Is No Model for Nigeria', Human Rights Watch, www.hrw.org/news/2014/06/16/dispatches-40000-reasons-why-sri-lanka-no-model-nigeria, accessed on 16 June 2014.

The Sun, 2014, 'Dangote to partner with North East in agricultural investments', *The Sun*, 2 June, http://sunnewsonline.com, accessed on 2 June 2014.

ThisDay, 2014, 'Dangote Group Pledges to Invest $2.3bn in Northern Nigeria,' *ThisDay Live*, 11 May, www.thisdaylive.com, accessed on 11 May 2014.

Tukur, Sani, 2014a, 'Zakzaky Speaks: My sons were taken alive, then summarily executed by soldiers', *Premium Times*, 26 July, www.premiumtimesng.com, accessed on 26 July 2014.

Tukur, Sani, 2014b, 'APC calls for new thinking, not just new money, to tackle Boko Haram', *Premium Times*, 22 July, www.premiumtimesng.com, accessed on 22 July 2014.

Ughegbe, Lemmy, 2014, 'Police, SSS clash over prosecution of Nyanya bomb blast mastermind', *Guardian*, 26 September, www.ngrguardiannews.com, accessed on 26 September 2014.

Ujah, Emma, Kingsley Omonobi, Johnbosco Agbakwuru and Joseph Erunke, 2014, 'Capture of Borno towns: Reputation of Nigeria's military at stake – US', *Vanguard*, 5 September, www.vanguardngr.com, accessed on 5 September 2014.

Umar, M. S., 2006, *Islam and Colonialism: Intellectual Responses of Muslims of Northern Nigeria to British Colonial Rule*, Leiden: Brill.

Vanguard Editorial, 2014, 'Rehabilitation, new route to North East', *Vanguard*, 20 June, www.vanguardngr.com, accessed on 20 June 2014.

Wakili, Isiaka, 2014a, 'Terror war: no to collateral damage – Jonathan', *Daily Trust*, 9 July, http://dailytrust.com.ng, accessed on 9 July 2014.

Wakili, Isiaka, 2014b, 'Dangote: Job creation, only way-out of Boko Haram', *Daily Trust*, 8 May, http://dailytrust.com.ng, accessed on 8 May 2014.

Yusuf, S., 1999, 'Nigeria's membership in the OIC: Implications of print media coverage for peace and national unity', *Journal of Muslim Minority Affairs*, 19 (2), 211–21.

Index

CPSIA information can be obtained
at www.ICGtesting.com
Printed in the USA
LVHW080905130422
716030LV00010B/332